GLOBAL STRATEGY

Global Strategy: Competing in the Connected Economy details how firms enter, compete, and grow in foreign markets. Jain moves away from the traditional focus on developed countries and their multinational enterprises, instead focusing on emerging economies and their interaction with developed nations.

As the current global business environment is increasingly shaped—and connected—by faster technological developments, geopolitical forces, emerging economies, and new multinationals from those economies, this highly charged dynamic provides rich opportunity to revisit mainstream paradigms in globalization, innovation, and global strategy. The book rises to the challenge, exploring new competitive phenomena, new business models, and new strategies. Rich illustrations, real-world examples, and case data provide readers with the insight necessary to connect, compete, and grow in a globalized business.

This bold book succinctly covers strategy models and implementation for a range of global players, providing students of strategy and international business with a rich understanding of the contemporary business environment.

Vinod Jain received his Ph.D. in Strategy and International Business from the University of Maryland, Smith School of Business in 1994 and taught there from 2005 to 2012. At Maryland, he also founded and served as director of the Center for International Business Education and Research. Since leaving the University of Maryland, he has been a visiting professor in China, Denmark, and India. Early in his career, he worked for many years with multinational enterprises, including Macmillan Publishers, Molins, and Coca-Cola. Vinod is a member of several scholarly and professional associations and serves on the Maryland/Washington D.C. District Export Council.

Advance Praise for
Global Strategy: Competing in the Connected Economy

"An excellent, comprehensive and balanced combination of the theoretical and practical aspects of global strategy, which will appeal to both the academic savants and operational practitioners, clarifying abstruse issues for the former and practical guidelines for the latter."
— Lemuel Lasher, former President of global solutions and services and Chief Innovation Officer at Computer Sciences Corporation

"*Global Strategy in the Connected Economy* does a masterly job in simplifying the complexity of today's globalized environment. Vinod Jain captures the essence of the digital transformation lucidly. This will be a refresher to practitioners as well as students of global business. While learning from rich facts Vinod Jain expertly weaves into the narrative, it prompts one to think as well."
— Janamitra Devan, Former Vice-President at the World Bank and International Financial Corporation, and former Global Director of Operations of McKinsey's Strategy Practice

"Along with the book's reliance on diverse experiences throughout, it is strong on dynamics and implementation. It should motivate managers to reflect on the potential applicability of each distinct example to their own organizations. The book's conciseness and division into 10 chapters makes it highly appropriate for executive courses."
— John D. Daniels, Samuel N. Friedland Chair Professor Emeritus, Management, University of Miami, and former President, Academy of International Business and Dean of AIB Fellows

"In this state-of-the-art book, Vinod Jain provides managers and business students with a road-map for navigating today's hyper-connected, hyper-innovative, and hyper-competitive global economy. Drawing on the latest research, he presents practical frameworks managers can use to enter, compete, and grow in foreign markets as well as manage their global operations. Jain's use of many fascinating examples from around the world makes his points come alive. I strongly recommend the book to executives looking to get them up to speed quickly on the essentials of global strategy in the contemporary world."
— Ravi Ramamurti, D'Amore-McKim School of Business Distinguished Professor of International Business & Strategy, and Director, Center for Emerging Markets, Northeastern University

"Vinod Jain's book couldn't be more timely in its exploration of the modern, connected or platform economy and its call for a refresh of traditional strategic thinking. As network effects penetrate more and more sectors of society, market entry, product and capability building strategies have to adjust, and new approaches and frameworks are needed. Most importantly, the book takes a global view and points us to important phenomena, such as frugal, multipolar and reverse innovation across developed and developing economies. As such, Vinod's book is at once a primer and a welcome thought-provocation for those wanting to explore the future of strategy more deeply."

—Olaf J. Groth, Global Professor and Discipline Lead, Strategy, Innovation and Economics, Hult International Business School, and Founding Director, Hult-Ashridge Center for Disruptive Innovation

"I highly recommend reading this book, which is an excellent overview of global strategy, to managers and students of global strategy alike. This book provides an insightful, fresh, and up-to-date look at key issues affecting global strategy which benefits from the author's diverse international background. The interesting mini case studies which the book includes are one of its key strengths, making it easy to understand and fun to read."

—Carl Fey, Professor of International Business, Aalto University School of Business, Finland, and former Dean, Nottingham University Business School China

GLOBAL STRATEGY

Competing in the Connected Economy

Vinod K. Jain

Routledge
Taylor & Francis Group

NEW YORK AND LONDON

First published 2017
by Routledge
711 Third Avenue, New York, NY 10017

and by Routledge
2 Park Square, Milton Park, Abingdon, Oxon OX14 4RN

Routledge is an imprint of the Taylor & Francis Group, an informa business

© 2017 Taylor & Francis

The right of Vinod Jain to be identified as author of this
work has been asserted by him in accordance with
sections 77 and 78 of the Copyright, Designs
and Patents Act 1988.

Library of Congress Cataloging in Publication Data
A catalog record for this book has been requested

ISBN: 978-1-138-84420-9 (hbk)
ISBN: 978-1-138-84424-7 (pbk)
ISBN: 978-1-315-73054-7 (ebk)

Typeset in Times New Roman
by codeMantra

To Kamlesh, Sumita, and Anupama

CONTENTS

CONTENTS

x

FIGURES

TABLES

PREFACE

This book is about the business transformation that began in the 1990s and will likely continue through at least the next one or two decades as well as how multinational enterprises do business and should prepare themselves to meet the challenges and leverage the opportunities presented by the connected economy. The connected economy is today's global economy. It consists of markets, firms, consumers, governments, and other actors that are more connected to each other than at any time in previous decades. As in the past, such connections are facilitated by the twin forces of globalization and technology but now at an unprecedented and increasing speed of change.

While I had been teaching undergraduate and graduate courses in strategy and international business since the early 1990s, it was only in 2003 that I taught an MBA course on global strategy at the Robert H. Smith School of Business, University of Maryland, for the first time. Since then, I have taught the global strategy course as well as a somewhat related course on strategy for emerging markets at Smith School and elsewhere numerous times. Before my academic career, I worked in middle and senior executive positions with major U.S. and British multinationals for many years. I have continued a deep involvement with the business and nonprofit worlds through research, consulting, speaking assignments, leading trade delegations, participation in trade and professional associations, and board positions. So, it was about time that I sat down and wrote a book on global strategy.

While much of the book derives its underpinnings from theory, its focus is more on the real world than on theory, especially on how business is conducted in the evolving global business environment. The reader will find dozens of examples and case studies from throughout the connected economy, examples of both mid-sized and large MNEs in advanced and emerging economies. My preference has been to use company examples from more recent time periods than from decades earlier. The book contains the latest research conducted by major consulting firms, such as PwC and McKinsey & Company, as well as research published in practitioner journals such as the *Harvard Business Review*.

The book is aimed primarily at the executives of multinational enterprises (including those of the aspiring MNEs) as well as students in MBA and Executive

MBA programs, though senior undergraduate business students will also find it valuable. Readers with a basic understanding of strategy and global business, through study or professional experience, will benefit the most from the book.

Implementing global strategy is always challenging because the MNE has to contend not only with multiple geographies, fast-changing technologies, and an unforgiving competitive landscape, but also with the diverse social, economic, and political contexts in which it operates. Strategy books devote considerable attention to strategy-formulation frameworks but often give short shrift to implementation issues. Strategies fail not because they were not designed well, but because they were not executed well. The last part of the book, therefore, contains four chapters on strategy implementation, including organizational architecture and control systems, global learning and capability building, innovation, and, finally, how to leverage opportunities in the connected economy.

I have learned, and continue to learn, a great deal from the work of other scholars, executives, and professional as well as scholarly books – too numerous to mention. While much of the content and perspectives included in the book are a product of the last one/two decades, what I learned during my doctoral studies at the Smith School, University of Maryland, in the early 1990s provided the foundation that set me on a learning journey. I would like to specially acknowledge the education and support I received from my professors there, including Anil Gupta, Ken Smith, and the late Lee Preston. And, I have learned much from my students in MBA/EMBA programs as well as from the participants in my executive seminars in many countries.

I would also like to acknowledge several individuals, both academics and senior executives, who read early chapters of the book and provided me with much valuable advice and suggestions. These included Subash Bijlani, John Daniels, Lem Lasher, Ravi Ramamurti, Mark Rice, and Suresh Shenoy. My editor at Routledge, Sharon Golan, and her staff were a source of continuing support during the more than a year it took me to work on the manuscript. Finally, my wife, Kamlesh, also a former business school professor, has been a source of great support and advice throughout this journey.

Vinod K. Jain
Ashburn, Virginia
2016

ABOUT THE AUTHOR

 Vinod Jain is a Washington D.C.-based strategy consultant and Research Fellow at the Hult-Ashridge Center for Disruptive Innovation. He served as Professor of Global Economics and Strategy at the Hult International Business School, Shanghai, China, during 2013–2015 and as Visiting Associate Professor of International Business and Strategy at Nottingham University Business School, China, during 2012–2013. Before going to Nottingham China, he served for seven years on the faculty of the Robert H. Smith School of Business, University of Maryland, where he also founded and served as Director of the Center for International Business Education and Research. A Fulbright Scholar and true cosmopolitan, Vinod has lived and worked in India, the United States, Western Europe, Eastern Europe, China, and the Middle East.

Vinod has taught strategy and international business for almost 20 years and has twice held Fulbright positions – at the Polish-American Management Center, University of Lodz, Poland, and the Indian Institute of Management, Bangalore. He is a recipient of the prestigious Krowe Excellence in Teaching Award at Smith School, University of Maryland, and has been honored by the Governors of both Ohio and Maryland for his services to their states.

Before returning to academia in 1989, Vinod worked in industry for many years and held middle and senior executive positions with multinational enterprises, including Macmillan Publishers (Vice President), Molins (Manager Coordination), and Coca-Cola (Marketing Research Executive). He has conducted over 100 executive and scholarly seminars worldwide and has been active on a number of boards and professional and trade associations.

Vinod has a Ph.D. in Strategic Management and International Business from the University of Maryland, M.S. in Management from UCLA, and B.S. (Hons.)

and M.S. in Statistics from the Indian Statistical Institute. He is a member of
the Academy of Management, the Academy of International Business, Mensa,
a charter member of TiE-DC and serves on the Maryland/Washington D.C.
District Export Council. Vinod is the former President and CEO of the
Washington D.C.-based India-US World Affairs Institute, a nonprofit educational and research organization he founded in 2006.

Part I

THE CONTEXT OF GLOBAL BUSINESS

1

INTRODUCTION

The Connected Economy

It's all so simple, Anjin-san. Just change your concept of the world.
—James Clavell, *Shōgun*, 1975

Baltimore was once a quintessential manufacturing city with an economic base spanning steel processing, shipping, auto manufacturing, transportation, and other industries. Over the last several decades, however, the Maryland city, like many other industrial cities and towns in the United States, has been experiencing deindustrialization and declining population. Today, while manufacturing remains an important part of Baltimore, the city is increasingly a hub for higher education, healthcare, and many other high-technology enterprises, including high-tech manufacturing enterprises. This, along with immigrant-friendly policies, has allowed the city to begin seeing some population growth as well.[1]

According to a Brookings Institution study, almost a quarter of Baltimore jobs are in the STEM (science, technology, engineering, and math) fields.[2] In fact, Greater Baltimore is among the top six percent of all U.S. metropolitan areas in terms of the percentage of jobs requiring STEM skills. According to another Brookings Institution study, the Baltimore metropolitan area has "a robust network of colleges and universities, several world-class hospital systems, close proximity to the nation's capital, and, importantly, sophisticated firms, skilled talent and formidable research capacity."[3]

The American Can Company building in Baltimore's historic Canton neighborhood is a classic example of how the old smokestack brownfields became home to established companies and high-tech startups. The American Can Company had operated at this site since 1895, when the first factory building was constructed by the Norton Tin Can and Plate Company. By 1900, the company was the largest can manufacturer in the United States. Construction of other buildings and structures and expansion of the site continued through the early 1960s. In the late 1980s, however, when the American Can Company merged with the National Can Company, the Baltimore factory shut down; the property became a brownfield. In the 1990s, after the cleanup of the environmental contamination at the site, it was reborn as a mixed-use retail and office complex (Figure 1.1).

Figure 1.1 The Can Company, Baltimore

In 1998, DAP Products, Inc., the largest manufacturer of sealants and adhesives in the world, made the former Can Company complex its world headquarters. The Emerging Technology Center (ETC), a nonprofit tech incubator that works with almost a hundred tech startups at different stages in their evolution, is among other high-tech tenants of the complex. In late 2013, ETC moved its operations to, perhaps unsurprisingly, a former, huge brownfield owned by the Crown Cork & Seal Co., which had abandoned the site in 1959. The Crown Cork & Seal complex in Baltimore, once the largest bottle cap factory in the world, today houses cabinet makers, a craft brewer, an eclectic mix of musicians, artists, studios, and now the ETC, along with its several dozen resident companies.

This story of converting former abandoned industrial sites into new uses is being repeated in hundreds of cities across the United States and around the world. Cities and towns once home to manufacturing industries, the "old economy," are increasingly transitioning to what may be referred to as a "new economy." This highlights two important trends in the U.S. (and other developed countries[4]). First, the old economy survives and even thrives in America, though it is now also focused on high-tech products and services—the U.S. is the world's second largest manufacturing nation. Second, the "old" and the "new" economies continue to co-exist and co-evolve—one at a snail's pace and the other at warp speed. This is the context of business today, which is defining how we live, work, and do business. The context in which business operates in different countries must be taken into account when firms craft their strategies for international markets.

"New Economy"

"New economies" emerge following major technological innovations, which typically redefine the rules of the game and how people live and work. The term "new economy" has been in use as a metaphor for transformational change in

4

societies for a long time, but it acquired almost a new meaning in the dot-com era of the late 1990s and early 2000s when the digital economy was the new economy. The world has seen many new economies since the first Industrial Revolution of the late 18th century, which ushered in disruptive change in most industries of the time and led to rising prosperity in Britain. These changes then spread to Europe, North America, and eventually to the rest of the world.

Venture capitalist and economist William Janeway has charted the evolution of new economies over the last 250 years.[5] In Britain, a period of extensive canal building began in the 1760s to improve the transportation of coal to the north-west of the country. Canals, combined with turnpikes and related infrastructure in the early 1770s, formed the backbone of the first Industrial Revolution. As the Industrial Revolution progressed, and the tempo of industrial activity picked up in Britain, more efficient transportation for people and freight was needed, which led to developments in railway technologies. During the 1830s and 1840s, Britain experienced what came to be known as the two "Railway Manias" that led to huge investments in railways, despite the economic depression of the late 1830s, and high financial rewards for investors. The canal-turnpike-railroad transportation networks enabled the new economy of the latter 19th century in Britain.

In the United States, canals and turnpikes were being constructed in a big way in the early 1800s, leading to the use of steam power for river transportation. The railroad boom in the U.S. began in the late 1840s, culminating with the construction of over 30,000 miles of railroad tracks by the early 1860s. The 1880s saw a second wave of American railroad construction, with an additional 75,000 miles of track. According to business historian Alfred Chandler, the growth of railroads (and, concurrently, of steamships and telegraph) enabled a transportation and communication revolution in the United States. For instance, the Post Office benefited greatly from "faster, cheaper, and more certain" communications and even dropped postage rates in 1851 from 5 cents for 300 miles to 3 cents for 3,000 miles.[6]

In addition to the direct macroeconomic effects of the transportation and communication networks, they also made mass production and mass marketing in America possible in the decades that followed. More specifically, the networks encouraged the rise of wholesalers and middlemen, the movement of people from East to West, the development of new management and organization practices such as the multi-divisional structure and accounting practices, and the emergence of nationally branded goods. With the second great wave of American railway construction, "a new economy in the country had definitely arrived."[7]

Innovations in technology, and especially in transportation and communication networks, have typically been behind the emergence of new economies. These have ranged from canals, turnpikes, and railroads in the 1700s and 1800s, to the information superhighway in the 1990s, and to the social networks of the last decade. Networks create network externalities ("network effects"), which essentially means that the value of a network (to its owners and users) rises exponentially as the number of users increases. Thus, technology and networks

5

have been the key building blocks of new economies ever since the first Industrial Revolution.

The end point of a new economy typically merges with the beginning of another new economy, though both continue to co-exist and co-evolve. And, so it was with the dawn of the second Industrial Revolution in the early 20th century with Henry Ford's moving assembly line that launched the era of mass production and continuing rise of prosperity in America. This transformational change in manufacturing technologies and processes indeed changed how people lived and worked in the decades that followed.

In May 1983, *Time* magazine carried a cover story on "The New Economy" with the subheading, "Technology has set off a scramble for jobs, profits and global markets."[8] It highlighted the transformational change that was occurring in the business and economic environment of the time—a shift from heavy industry to a technology and service-based economy. Even in manufacturing, according to the cover story, growth was coming from "high-tech fields such as semiconductors and computers." Some 25,346 businesses had gone bankrupt during 1982, but 566,942 new companies had been launched the same year. According to Pierre du Pont IV, the Governor of Delaware at the time, "[T]he transformation of our jobs, the movement of our people, the improvements in our skills over the first 80 years of this century have been stunning. But it is entirely likely that those changes will be matched and exceeded during the final 20 years of this century."

The final two decades of the 20th century did indeed prove the Governor right. Since the 1980s, the term "new economy" has found increasing usage in both professional and scholarly publications. The term became really popular in the dot-com era of the 1990s. Some of the monikers given to the economy of that era were: the digital economy, the information economy, the e-conomy, or simply the new economy. This new economy, like the earlier ones, was born out of technological innovations (the Internet), had its own players (e.g., the dot-coms), playing fields (e.g., the World Wide Web), rules of the game (e.g., "information rules"), and business models (e.g., clicks-and-bricks).

The Connected Economy

Today, the world has both the old economy and the digital economy, as well as a "new" new economy that has emerged in the last 5 to 10 years. This "new" new economy has been called by various names, such as the second Machine Age,[9] the third Industrial Revolution,[10] and the age of smart machines.[11] For sake of simplicity, we will refer to today's economy as the "connected economy," for reasons that will soon become clear. This term comprises the old economy, the digital economy, and the age of the smart machines.

The connected economy is today's global economy. It consists of markets, firms, consumers, governments, and other actors that are more connected to each other than at any time in previous decades. As in the past, such connections are facilitated by the twin forces of globalization and technology, but now at an unprecedented and increasing rate of change.

Economics Nobel Laureate Michael Spence has explored the growing convergence between developed and developing countries.[12] About 60 percent of the world's population, starting with China, India, and some other developing countries, is on track to achieve the living standards of the richest 15 percent of the world's population in the coming decades. The developing world started on a century of growth, development, and convergence with the developed world and, according to Spence, is currently midway through this process. By the end of this development process, in another 30 to 40 years, China and India would have traded places with the United States and Europe in terms of their share of the world gross domestic product (GDP) and some other measures.

Such convergence between nations has been enabled and enhanced by multilateral institutions, governments, multinational enterprises, technology, global value chains, outsourcing and offshoring, and global competition. On top of that, there are growing connections between humans and machines and between machines and machines, via the Internet—through the use of analytics, algorithms, cloud and mobile technologies, sensors, and social networks.

The connected economy enables the sharing of resources and capabilities in ways that could not have been imagined even 5 or 10 years ago. This "sharing economy"[13] encourages peer-to-peer rentals and collaborative consumption, partly because technology has reduced transaction costs, similar to what eBay did for peer-to-peer online shopping. There are online services that allow people (and companies) to rent out their underutilized assets, such as cars, rooms, clothing, and even lab space for research and development. Companies such as Uber (a "taxi" service provided by owners of private cars) and Airbnb (renting out spare rooms) are already multi-billion-dollar businesses.

Some key features of the connected economy are:

- Global—encompassing both developed and developing nations.
- Goods—range from physical goods to digital goods and smart machines, i.e., goods with digital characteristics (hardware, software, and sensors) embedded into them and connected to the Internet.
- Services—range from simple location-bound services to services that can be performed anywhere and everywhere, not necessarily close to the customer.
- Connectivity—provided by multilateral institutions, governments, multinational corporations, competition, and digital technologies and networks.
- Speed—business and economic phenomena operate in real time, 24/7, and at increasing speeds.

The connected economy is characterized by three interconnected phenomena that, taken together, form its backbone: globalization, technology, and competition. Each represents trends that began centuries ago but are today orders of magnitude greater than what they were even 10 years ago.[14]

Globalization: From Divergence to Interdependence to Convergence

Globalization is today's big reality and a "defining issue" for the 21st century.[15] It is driven by technology, communication, and transportation networks, the arrival of several developing countries on the global stage, multinational enterprises from both developed and developing countries, the actions of governments and multilateral institutions such as the International Monetary Fund and the World Trade Organization, geopolitics, and even the actions of non-governmental organizations.[16] Most of these actors have been in business for decades, but their impact today is much greater than it used to be in earlier eras.

The Industrial Revolutions created extraordinary economic growth but also huge *divergence* in living standards between industrialized countries and the rest of the world—the haves and the have-nots. Over time, however, the world has been experiencing greater interactions between countries with the rise of cross-border trade, investment, and technology flows and through the efforts of multilateral institutions. *Interdependence* between nations has been the hallmark of growing globalization over recent decades. Such interdependence is not just between developed nations (North-North), but also between developed and developing nations (North-South), as well as between developing nations (South-South).

While the Industrial Revolutions and the digital economy continue to bestow great benefits upon advanced countries, many developing countries that had previously been left out of the bounty have also lately been experiencing dramatic increases in growth and prosperity. In China, for instance, hundreds of millions of people have been lifted out of poverty. A similar decline in poverty can be seen in India and some other developing countries, though not to the same extent. Now, as industrialized countries are beginning to experience lower growth rates, and developing countries higher growth rates, there is a growing *convergence* between developed and developing countries on several dimensions.[17] Let us take just two examples of how some developing countries are beginning to have the characteristics of developed countries and even surpassing them on certain dimensions, such as GDP and the number of Fortune Global 500 companies.

Ranked number 6 in the list of the world's Top 10 Economies, China's GDP in 2000 was only $1.193 trillion (at current prices)—compared to $10.285 trillion for the United States—less than 12 percent of the U.S. GDP. Who could have imagined that in just 15 years, China's economy would be second only to the U.S. economy in terms of GDP at current prices and actually larger than that of the U.S. economy in terms of GDP at purchasing power parity, or PPP (Table 1.1). The other BRIC countries, India, Russia, and Brazil, also achieved higher ranks in terms of GDP at PPP over the last 15-year period. The Top 10 list now includes Indonesia, but excludes Italy! The world's economic center of gravity has definitely moved away from industrialized economies toward emerging economies.

Table 1.2 shows the number of Fortune Global 500 (FG500) companies headquartered in the G7, BRIC, and what used to be known as the "newly industrialized

Table 1.1 World's Top 10 Economies Ranked by GDP at Current Prices, 2000 and 2015

Rank (2000 GDP at Current Prices)	Country	2000 GDP		Rank (2015 GDP at Current Prices)	Country	2015 GDP	
		At Current Prices ($ Trillion)	At PPP ($ Trillion)			At Current Prices ($ Trillion)	At PPP ($ Trillion)
1	U.S.A.	10.285	10.285	1	U.S.A.	17,968	17,968
2	Japan	4.731	3.237	2	China	11,385	19,510
3	Germany	1.892	2.341	3	Japan	4,116	4,842
4	U.K.	1.497	1.467	4	Germany	3,371	3,842
5	France	1.372	1.678	5	U.K.	2,865	2,660
6	China	1.193	3.608	6	France	2,423	2,647
7	Italy	1.107	1.565	7	India	2,183	8,077
8	Brazil	0.645	1.524	8	Brazil	1,800	3,208
9	India	0.477	2.148	9	Russia	1,236	3,474
10	Russia	0.260	1.531	10	Indonesia	873	2,839

Source: IMF World Economic Outlook Database, 2000 and 2015.

Table 1.2 Number of Fortune Global 500 Companies in the G7, BRICs, and NICs, 2005, 2010, and 2015

Category	Country	2005	2010	2015
G7	United States	175	141	128
	United Kingdom	33	29	29
	Germany	34	36	28
	France	40	40	31
	Japan	81	71	54
	Canada	14	11	11
	Italy	10	11	9
NICs	South Korea	11	11	17
	Taiwan	1	7	8
	Singapore	1	2	2
BRICs	China	18	47	98
	India	5	8	7
	Brazil	4	8	7
	Russia	3	6	5

Source: Fortune magazine, various issues.

countries" (NICs) for 2005, 2010, and 2015. Each of the G7 countries shown in the table experienced a decline in the number of FG500 companies headquartered there over the 10-year period, with the U.S. and Japan experiencing the largest declines. The 2015 list had almost 50 fewer U.S.-headquartered FG500 companies than there were in 2005.[18] The biggest increase was achieved by China, with an increase of 80 companies from 2005 to 2015; the 98 FG500 companies in China in 2015 included 76 state-owned enterprises (SOEs). In 2015, China had more FG500 companies than the U.K., Germany, and France combined.

Beijing, the Chinese capital, has 52 FG500 companies headquartered there, more than any other city in the world and more than most other countries. The 2015 list included 40 FG500 companies in Tokyo, 19 each in London and Paris, 17 in New York City, and 13 in Seoul. The BRIC nations now account for 117 FG500 companies, compared to just 30 10 years ago. Clearly, the world's economic center of gravity is moving from the developed toward the developing world and generally from West to East.[19] There is of course a lot more to globalization, and we will explore in Chapters 2 and 3.

Technology: Technology on Steroids

Technology is the second big reality in today's world and, in fact, provides the glue for the connected economy. Technology and globalization have gone hand in hand for centuries, each impacting and being impacted by the other. As we noted earlier, technology has been behind the evolution of new economies ever since the first Industrial Revolution. Over the last several decades, technology has been advancing at an increasing rate of change in multiple fields—information technology, manufacturing and automation, life sciences, genetic engineering, renewable energy, materials, automotive, services, processes, and more.

Information technology (IT) has seen the greatest advances during the last two–three decades. There are many more advancements yet to come, some of which cannot even be visualized at this time. This is partly because information technologies are "general purpose" technologies that can be used in multiple industries in multiple ways. Janeway believes that we are at a midpoint of the digital revolution… "this is an economic landscape whose investment opportunities will not be exhausted for decades."[20] And, according to Erik Brynjolfsson's and Andrew McAfee's 2014 book, *The Second Machine Age*, today's IT is quantitatively and qualitatively different from its earlier heyday in that it is digital, exponential, and recombinant.[21] Digital technologies are behind most of the innovations we see today in practically all fields of human endeavor, and their progress has been exponential as suggested by Moore's Law and Metcalfe's Law of network effects. Moore's Law states that, for a given price, computing power doubles every 18 to 24 months, and according to Metcalfe's Law, the value of a network equals the square of the number of its users; hence, the exponential characteristic of the IT revolution. Finally, borrowing the term recombinant from genetics research, Brynjolfsson and McAfee observe that digital innovation is recombinant in the sense that each innovation "becomes a building block of future innovations."[22] Innovations from multiple sources get connected and enhanced through networks and open innovation to create entirely new products and services that may or may not bear much semblance to the products/services from which they evolved.

Digitization and globalization have disintegrated value chains, and specialist firms have emerged to take up specific parts of the formerly vertically integrated value chains. This has enabled outsourcing and offshoring, not just of back office IT processes, but also of research and development, engineering services, education, healthcare, and most manufacturing.

In terms of size, speed, and directional flow, the global shift in relative wealth and economic power now under way—roughly from West to East—is without precedent in modern history.
—*Global Trends 2025: A Transformed World.* Washington, DC: National Intelligence Council, November 2008

Digital (and information) products have at least four properties that distinguish them from physical products. The cost of developing a new digital product can run into millions or even billions of dollars. The marginal cost of producing additional copies of the same product, however, is zero or almost zero. Consider Microsoft Office Professional 2013, which probably cost Microsoft a billion dollars or more to develop, test, and make user friendly over its many incarnations. Microsoft Office Professional 2013 can be downloaded for $399.99 from Microsoftstore.com; however, selling an additional copy of the software costs Microsoft practically nothing.[23] Second, the same physical product can be used by only one person at a time. A digital product, however, can be owned and used by hundreds or even millions of people at the same time. Third, a digital product, like information, cannot be used up, though it can become obsolete. Finally, because digital products exhibit network effects, their value rises exponentially as more and more people use the product.[24]

Computers and IT form the backbone of an increasing number of new products and services that simply did not exist 5 to 10 years ago. In manufacturing, 3D printing technologies have taken the world by storm. One can now literally *print* not only complex pieces of jewelry at home, but also a hand gun using a 3D printer and design software downloaded from the Internet. The 2015 Detroit and Washington, DC, auto shows presented a working model of a car that had been produced on a 3D printer. Other developments include self-driving cars, drones for delivering packages to customers, robots for delivering food on tables at a restaurant, and personalized medicine based on a person's genes—all courtesy of computers and IT. Many such products, e.g., cars that can parallel-park themselves, are quite commonplace by now (2015). According to Gartner, an IT research and advisory firm, autonomous (self-driving) vehicles such as driverless cars, drones, and warehouse robots will likely disrupt one-third of industries in the developed world by 2020—by reshaping transportation, logistics, distribution, and supply chain management.[25] Then, developing countries will begin adopting and improving such technologies through frugal innovation.

These are smart machines—products that are both physical and virtual, i.e., physical products with digital technologies (hardware, software, and sensors) embedded into them and connected to the Internet. Smart machines are able to perform a variety of physical and intellectual tasks, including tasks that require cognitive skills, such as cars that can parallel-park themselves and the Internet-connected Barbie doll ("Hello Barbie") that listens to children and uses artificial intelligence to respond. Another good example is the Nest thermostat. It's a self-programming, self-learning, Wi-Fi-enabled thermostat (and smoke detector) that learns what temperature the home owners/residents like and can program itself to provide the most efficient energy usage. It can be controlled using a smart phone or tablet because it is connected to the Internet through Wi-Fi.

Another example is the old, trusted Crock-Pot®, the slow cooker originally patented in 1940. It became very popular in the United States in the 1970s when it was marketed to working women who could put food in the pot in the morning before going to work and return home in the evening to a cooked meal. Now, however, the Crock-Pot slow cooker is also available with an embedded WeMo® smartphone app. The cooking settings (temperature, times, etc.) can be adjusted to suit one's schedule during the day from anywhere with a smart phone or tablet. Gartner estimates that by the end of 2015 there are almost 5 billion "connected things" (smart machines), a number which will likely go up to 25 billion by 2020.

Competition: A Changing Paradigm

What pulls together the other forces in the connected economy is competition—competition for markets, technology, investment, talent, and other resources. Economic competition typically refers to competition for markets, i.e., rivalry between two or more sellers for sales, market share, and profits. How firms go about trying to secure the business of prospective customers changes with the emergence of new economies. Also, there has been a fundamental change in how firms compete in the connected economy, which is the crux of this book.

Harvard Business School professor Michael Porter popularized the concepts of industry analysis, competitive strategy, competitive advantage, and competitive advantage of nations, among other core strategy ideas.[26] His theories developed at the height of the old economy (the 1970s and 1980s) are still relevant today, especially for old economy companies and industries, i.e., industries in the connected economy that tend to be relatively stable and mature. Using Porter's five forces model for a digital economy industry would be a stretch, though some of his other theories are still applicable for digital economy firms and industries.[27]

As economies become more services oriented[28] and more connected and include digitized goods and services, competition is becoming ever more international in its reach. A company that operates in multiple markets has the opportunity to spread parts of its value chain among countries as it competes for customers, markets, and resources. In markets worldwide, it often repeatedly meets the same global players and has the opportunity to dovetail its competitive stance against specific competitors differently in different markets. At the same time, it must meet the assault on its home market by companies from throughout

12

the world and increasingly by companies from emerging markets. With new players emerging on the global scene, new playing fields, and new rules of the game, competition is now an entirely new ball game.

New Players

These are companies that have joined the ranks of global competitors from emerging markets, as well as many small and medium-sized enterprises (SMEs) new to international competition from both developed and emerging markets.

New Playing Fields

The fall of the Berlin Wall on November 9, 1989, opened up huge new markets—markets that had been behind the Iron Curtain for over 50 years—for companies from all over, though largely from the developed world. The growth of developing economies since the 1990s and 2000s has created a much larger market for companies with international operations or aspirations. These new markets comprise some four billion consumers and millions of businesses—more than the world has experienced at any time in the past. The new consumers include people at all socio-economic levels. The late C.K. Prahalad highlighted the importance of the billions of poor people in developing countries, people at the bottom-of-the-pyramid, who collectively represent huge buying power.[29] Developing countries also have a growing middle class as well as a small but growing class of richer people whose consumption patterns are similar to those in developed countries. Research by Homi Kharas of the Brookings Institution shows that by 2050, over half of the world's total middle class will likely live in India and China (Figure 1.2).[30] Tarun Khanna refers to them as "billions of entrepreneurs."[31] India already has the world's third largest number of billionaires among all countries.

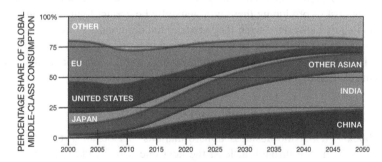

Figure 1.2 The Global Middle-class Wave in Developing Countries

Source: H. Kharas, "The Emerging Middle-Class in Developing Countries," OECD Development Centre Working Paper No. 285, 2010. Reprinted with permission.

Note: Global middle-class consumption will shift heavily toward China, India and other Asian countries (excluding Japan) as the high-income countries see their share decrease.

New Rules of the Game

In the connected economy, firms have many more competitive tools available to them than in any one of the previous economies. This is partly because it consists of the old economy, the digital economy, and the age of the smart machines—each with its own competitive tools. For old economy firms, Michael Porter's generic strategies framework should work well. In other words, companies in old economy industries compete through cost leadership, differentiation, and/or scope. Digital economy firms, for which economies of scale and scope tend to be very significant, are subject to Carl Shapiro and Hal Varian's "information rules."[32] Digital or information goods are goods that can be digitized, i.e., converted into bits (the smallest possible piece of information, represented by a 1 or a 0) and bytes (groups of 8 bits). As was observed earlier, it is very costly to produce the first copy of a digital good, but it is inexpensive to produce it again and again because the marginal cost is zero or nearly zero. What is more, its quality does not deteriorate as more and more copies are produced. Like information, a digital good cannot be used up and does not need to be stocked in an inventory. Millions of exact duplicates of the original product, indistinguishable from its first copy, can be sold and delivered to customers almost instantaneously over the Internet, at zero or near zero cost. With zero or near zero marginal cost, and with significant economies of scale, "[T]he returns in such markets typically follow a distinct pattern—a power law, or Pareto curve, in which a small number of players reap a disproportionate share of the rewards. Network effects, whereby a product becomes more valuable the more users it has, can also generate these kinds of winner-take-all or winner-take-most markets."[33] Examples of such digital products, with one/two winners in the market, the rest being niche players, are not difficult to find. The Microsoft application software is but one.

Smart products ("connected things"), on the other hand, are both physical and digital. Because they are physical, they do not have zero marginal cost. Because they are also digital, i.e., since they have software and sensors embedded in them, the cost of producing them will generally be greater than for their purely physical equivalents. However, they are able to command premium prices. The rules of the game for the age of the smart machines are still evolving and would likely include technology leadership, increasing returns to scale, and first mover advantages, among others.

Organization of the Book

This book is about the business transformations that began in the 1990s and will likely continue through at least the next one/two decades and about how multinational enterprises should prepare themselves to meet the challenges and leverage the opportunities presented by the connected economy. The first part of the book (Chapters 1–3) is designed to set the context for business in the 2010s and beyond. The current chapter (Chapter 1) defines the key characteristics of the connected economy and how it evolved over the last two and a half centuries. Chapters 2 and 3 are about economic globalization, in particular, the globalization of industries and firms and what that means for a connected-economy enterprise, namely, the multinational enterprise (MNE). The second part of the book presents frameworks for answering questions such as why go abroad and how and when to enter foreign markets (Chapter 4), how to compete in foreign markets (Chapter 5), and how to grow in foreign markets (Chapter 6).

Implementing global strategy is always challenging because the MNE has to contend with not only multiple geographies, fast-changing technologies, and an unforgiving competitive landscape, but also the diverse social, economic, and political contexts in which it operates. Strategy books devote considerable attention to strategy-formulation frameworks but often give short shrift to implementation issues. Strategies fail not because they were not designed well, but because they were not executed well. The last part of the book contains four chapters on strategy implementation, including organizational architecture and control systems (Chapter 7), learning and capability building (Chapter 8), innovation (Chapter 9), and, finally, leveraging opportunities in the connected economy (Chapter 10). Most chapters have examples and mini case studies of how companies from different parts of the connected economy attempted to enter, compete, and grow in foreign markets—successfully or unsuccessfully—thus, offering valuable lessons for the multinational enterprise.

Notes

1 According to the latest Census data, the city of Baltimore experienced a nominal 0.2% increase in population between 2010 and 2013, though population increased by 2.2% in Baltimore County during the same period.
2 Jonathan Rockwell, *The Hidden STEM Economy* (Washington, DC: Brookings Institution, June 2013).
3 Jennifer S. Vey, *Building from Strength: Creating Opportunity in Greater Baltimore's Next Economy* (Washington, DC: Brookings Institution, 2012), p. 6.
4 The trend is visible in many emerging economies as well, though perhaps not as pronounced as in the highly developed economies.
5 William H. Janeway, *Doing Capitalism in the Innovation Economy* (Cambridge, UK: Cambridge University Press, 2012).
6 Alfred D. Chandler, "The Organization of Manufacturing and Transportation." In *Economic Change in the Civil War Era*, edited by David T. Gilchrist and W. David Lewis, pp. 137–51 (Greenville, DE: Eleutherian Mills-Hagley Foundation, 1965).
7 Janeway, 2012, p. 197.
8 Charles P. Alexander, "The New Economy," *Time*, May 30, 1983.
9 Erik Brynjolfsson and Andrew McAfee, *The Second Machine Age: Work, Progress, and Prosperity in a Time of Brilliant Technologies* (New York, NY: W.W. Norton & Co., 2014).
10 The Economist, "Manufacturing: The Third Industrial Revolution," *The Economist*, April 21, 2012. See also: Jeremy Rifkin, *The Third Industrial Revolution: How Lateral Power is Transforming Energy, the Economy, and the World* (New York, NY: Palgrave MacMillan, 2011).
11 The Economist, "The Age of Smart Machines," *The Economist*, May 25, 2013.

12 Michael Spence, *The Next Convergence: The Future of Economic Growth in a Multispeed World* (New York: Farrar, Straus and Giroux, 2011).

13 Several recent articles on the sharing economy. See for example: *The Economist*, "The Rise of the Sharing Economy," and "All Eyes on the Sharing Economy," May 9, 2013; Arun Sundararajan, "From Zipcar to the Sharing Economy," *Harvard Business Review*, January 3, 2013.

14 We can of course add many more trends, but the three trends listed here are the underlying phenomena that impact most other current and future trends.

15 Jagdish Bhagwati, *In Defense of Globalization* (New York: Oxford University Press, 2007), p. 3.

16 Globalization is not new. We are here concerned with the latest, emerging trends in globalization. And, there are many types of globalization, including ecological globalization, economic globalization (trade and investment), globalization of terrorism, money laundering, etc. We are concerned mainly with economic globalization in this book.

17 Spence, 2011.

18 In 1995, the U.S. had 151 companies on the FG500 list, which rose to 175 in 2005 but suffered a steady decline over the next decade. This does not indicate decline of American business, but the rise of everyone else and the fact that there can only be 500 companies in the FG500 list. Japan, however, has been losing ground for two decades. The number of FG500 companies headquartered in Japan was 149 in 1995, which dropped to 81 in 2005, 71 in 2010, and 54 in 2015.

19 For a counterargument to the rising power of Asia, see: Minxin Pei, "Think Again: Asia's Rise," *Foreign Policy*, July/August 2009.

20 Janeway, 2012, p. 282.

21 Brynjolfsson and McAfee, 2014.

22 Brynjolfsson and McAfee, 2014, p. 81.

23 See also: Jeremy Rifkin, *The Zero Marginal Cost Society: The Internet of Things, the Collaborative Commons, and the Eclipse of Capitalism* (New York: Palgrave Macmillan Trade, 2014).

24 Carl Shapiro and Hal R. Varian, *Information Rules: A Strategic Guide to the Network Economy* (Boston: Harvard Business Review Press, 1998).

25 Gartner, "Smart Machine Disruption Will Dominate This Decade." October 8, 2014. Retrieved from http://gartnernews.com/smart-machine-disruption-will-dominate-this-decade/.

26 See Michael Porter's classic books: *Competitive Strategy* (New York: The Free Press, 1980); *Competitive Advantage: Creating and Sustaining Superior Performance* (New York: The Free Press, 1985); and *The Competitive Advantage of Nations* (New York: The Free Press, 1990).

27 In fairness to Prof. Porter, he does show the relevance of his theories to the digital economy and to what he calls the third IT revolution. See his March 2001 article, "Strategy and the Internet" and his co-authored November 2014 article, "How Smart, Connected Products are Transforming Competition," both in *Harvard Business Review*.

28 Services account for almost 80 percent of the U.S. economy and about 70–80 percent of the economies of most other developed countries. Even developing countries are increasingly services focused. For instance, the contribution of services to GDP is 57% for India, 60% for Russia, and 69% for Brazil. Source: https://www.google.com/#q=share+of+services+in+gdp.

29 C.K. Prahalad, *The Fortune at the Bottom-of-the-Pyramid: Eradicating Poverty through Profits* (Philadelphia: Wharton School Publishing, 2006).

30 Homi Kharas, *The Emerging Middle Class in Developing Countries* (Washington, DC: The Brookings Institution, 2010).
31 Tarun Khanna, *Billions of Entrepreneurs: How China and India Are Reshaping Their Futures and Yours* (Boston, Harvard Business School Publishing, 2011).
32 Carl Shapiro and Hal R. Varian, *Information Rules: A Strategic Guide to the Network Economy* (Cambridge, MA: Harvard Business School Press, 1998).
33 Erik Brynjolfsson, Andrew McAfee, and Michael Spence, "New World Order: Labor, Capital, and Ideas in the Power Law Economy," *Foreign Affairs*, July/August 2014.

2

GLOBALIZATION
Yesterday–Today–Tomorrow

The extension and use of railroads, steamships, telegraphs, break down nationalities and bring peoples geographically remote into close connection commercially and politically. They make the world one, and capital, like water, tends to a common level.
— David Livingstone, missionary (1813–73),
The Last Journals of David Livingstone

David Livingstone, of "Dr. Livingstone, I presume?" fame, was a Scottish medical practitioner, missionary, and anti-slave crusader who traveled though Africa for almost 30 years until his death in 1873. He was an explorer, the first European to visit certain areas in Africa, who received much fame after the publication of his travelogue—somewhat in the tradition of Marco Polo who traveled to the East in the 13th century. In addition to his scientific research and missionary work, Livingstone was a proponent of trade and commerce, believing that if a country had legitimate trade, it would not need to trade in slavery. Explorers like Marco Polo (13th/14th centuries), Christopher Columbus (15th/16th centuries), Vasco da Gama (15th/16th centuries), and David Livingstone were some of the early torchbearers of globalization.

What is Globalization?

It depends on whom you ask. Views on globalization range from its being the root of all evil to its being a solution for many of the problems the world is facing. Those who take a demagogic view of globalization ascribe many of the problems in the world to globalization, problems such as growing income inequality, environmental decay, child labor, brain drain, loss of national sovereignty, spread of disease, rise of terrorism, and the like. Those taking a favorable view of globalization believe that it has led to better resource utilization, lower prices for goods and services, greater choices for consumers and businesses, economic progress, creation of wealth, greater attention to human

18

rights and environmental concerns, progress toward democracy, and the enrichment of life through sharing of ideas, cultures, and foods. The debate between anti-globalizers and pro-globalizers continues.

Perhaps there's some truth to both positions. However, there are many kinds of globalization, such as cultural, ecological, economic, and political. Even though these types are somewhat interconnected, economic globalization tends to be the most prominent and bears the brunt of criticism. Some people have a tendency to ascribe anything and everything to (economic) globalization, without making a distinction between the different kinds. In this book, we will mostly be concerned with *economic globalization*, which is defined as growing integration and economic interdependence between nations—through "trade, direct foreign investment (by corporations and multinationals), short-term capital flows, international flows of workers and humanity generally, and flows of technology."[1] Economic globalization derives its underpinnings from Adam Smith's *The Wealth of Nations*, published in 1776 during the early years of the first Industrial Revolution, which explored the role of free trade, specialization, division of labor, and markets in raising productivity and prosperity in nations.[2] As discussed in the next section, globalization might have actually preceded Adam Smith by thousands of years.

When Did Globalization Begin?

Thomas Friedman, in his phenomenally successful 2005 book, *The World Is Flat: A Brief History of the 21st Century*, distinguished among three eras of globalization—Globalization 1.0 (1492–1800), Globalization 2.0 (1800–2000), and Globalization 3.0 (2000 onwards).[3] In his view, Globalization 1.0 was driven by countries' search for resources and by imperial conquests, aided by power—military power, horsepower, and steam power. Globalization 2.0 was driven by multinational companies' search for markets and labor, aided by falling costs of transportation and telecommunication—telegraph, telephone, fiber-optic cable, and the Internet. Globalization 3.0 is driven by individuals sharing ideas with each other and accessing markets worldwide without having to relocate, aided by technology—software and the global fiber-optic networks. Globalization 3.0 is what led to a "flattening of the playing field," where anyone and everyone, irrespective of their location, can participate in the global economy, the key idea behind Friedman's "flat world" construct.

Well, if globalization implies growing integration and interdependence between nations, it actually began with the Silk Road and the Spice Routes some 4,000 to 5,000 years ago, perhaps even earlier. Both these trade and cultural routes helped connect the East and the West.[4] The Silk Road was a network of international trade and cultural routes connecting China, India, Persia, and the Mediterranean and intermittently bringing together traders, merchants, monks, pilgrims, thieves, and soldiers from different countries. The Silk Road (shown as a dark line in Figure 2.1) is claimed to have begun around 3200 BC and lasted several millennia.[5] Not just silk and cultural influences, but many other goods, even disease and technologies of the time, traveled along the road. Buddhism was "exported" from India to China, and Islam and Christianity traveled along the Silk Road—early signs of growing integration in the world. In the early 7th century, Christian evangelists even tried to convert Buddhists into Christianity claiming that Christianity was compatible with Buddhism, "it was Buddhism."[6]

Marco Polo traveled the Silk Road with his uncle and father eastwards from their home in Venice in 1271, taking a somewhat different route from the one his uncle and father had taken 10 years earlier. While in China, Marco Polo served in the court of the Great Kublai Khan for 17 years, in various important, high-ranking positions and traveled a great deal on official missions within China and even to Burma and India. Some of the places Marco Polo visited during his travels were not seen by the Europeans until hundreds of years later. The Polos returned to Venice in 1295 with great wealth, including jewels and gold, and singing tales of the wonders and the wealth of the Chinese civilization. Three years after his return to Venice, war broke out between Venice and the rival city of Genoa. Marco joined the army and commanded a galley but was captured and spent a year in a Genoese prison. While in prison, he dictated the story of his travels to a fellow prisoner, a writer, who recorded his tales. The story turned out to be one of the greatest travelogues in history, *The Description of the World* or *The Travels of Marco Polo*, a "bestseller" in Medieval Europe.

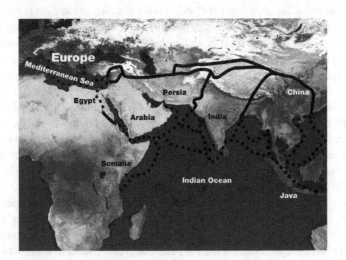

Figure 2.1 The Silk Road and the Spice Routes
Source: Adapted from http://commons.wikimedia.org/wiki/File:Silk_route.jpg.
Note: The Silk Road is shown in dark lines, and the Spice Routes in dotted lines.

However, the book came to be known as *Il Milione* (*The Million Lies*) since no one believed that any country could actually be as rich and as cultured as China. The book had tremendous impact as Europeans began to learn more about the East, and future explorers, including Columbus, read it with interest. Much of what Marco Polo wrote was later verified by travelers in the 18th and 19th centuries. Even Chinese historians found the book of great value as it helped them better understand the China of the 13th century.[7]

The Spice Route(s), the less famous but no less important of the two ancient trade routes, was a contemporary of the Silk Road and was just as instrumental in connecting East and West. The two routes met and extended each other at some places. As shown in Figure 2.1, the spice trade grew more by sea routes (dotted lines) than land routes. Arab traders had been traveling to spice-producing lands (the East Indies) since around 3000 BC, bringing spices and herbs with them to the Middle East. During the earliest evolution of trade, spices such as cinnamon, cardamom, ginger, pepper, and turmeric were important items of trade. Spices are commonplace now but were once considered luxuries similar to jewels and gold. In fact, spices were once the world's biggest industry. At different points in time, the Arabs, Romans, and other Europeans took control of the spice trade. According to a description of the Spice Routes at a UNESCO website:

> The principal and most profitable goods they traded in were spices. ... But precious goods were not the only points of exchange between the traders. Perhaps more important was the exchange of knowledge: knowledge of new peoples and their religions, languages, expertise, artistic and scientific skills. The ports along the Maritime Silk Roads (Spice Routes) acted as melting pots for ideas and information. With every ship that swept out with a cargo of valuables on board, fresh knowledge was carried over the seas to the ship's next port of call.[8]

Some of the "more recent" traders were the various East India Companies of the 17th to 19th centuries from Britain, the Netherlands, France, etc. For example, the British East India Company was chartered in Britain in 1600 to trade with the East Indies, and the Dutch East India Company was chartered in the Netherlands in 1602 with a 21-year monopoly to trade with Asia. Some have referred to them as the first "multinational corporations."[9] Not really—they were indeed chartered to conduct trade, but they also carried with them armies, conquered lands, and subjugated native populations in those lands. The British East India Company became involved in politics and acted as an agent of British imperialism in India from the early 18th to the mid-19th century.[10] The company was also a catalyst for British imperialism in China.[11] The Dutch East India Company was, in fact, given "quasi-government powers, including the ability to wage war, imprison and execute convicts, negotiate treaties, strike its own coins, and establish colonies."[12] Vasco da Gama led two of the four Portuguese armadas (the first and the fourth) destined for India in the 15th and 16th centuries and was the first European to reach India by sea route in 1498; he was declared Governor of India in 1524. He not only opened Asia for the Portuguese to establish their long-lasting empire there, but also opened Asia for global imperialism by other European countries.

During the Age of Discovery, a period of time from the 15th to the 18th centuries, Europeans carried out many global explorations and discovered many ocean routes, such as to the West in 1492 when Christopher Columbus reached the Americas and to the East in 1498 when Vasco da Gama reached India. The conquistadors, professional warriors from Portugal and Spain, conquered the Americas, especially Mexico and Peru in the 16th century, and ruled the region for 300 years. European explorers also set up trading posts in Africa, the Americas, and Asia for tradable goods such as spices, gold, silver, firearms, and slaves.

What Is Behind the Growth of Globalization in Recent Periods?

In more recent periods, i.e., over the last 200 years or so, integration of the world was driven by technology—such as steam power, telegraphy, telephony, radio, television, and the airplane. Some of these developments were explored in the previous chapter. And, still more recently, i.e., over the last 70 years or so, economic integration of the world (globalization) has been driven by at least four forces—multilateral institutions, governments, multinational enterprises, and information and communication technologies.

Multilateral Institutions

Representatives from 44 nations met in Bretton Woods, New Hampshire, in the U.S. from 1944 to 1947 to try and develop international *institutions* that would help create stability in the world's economic, financial, and trading systems and to help rebuild Europe after the devastation caused by the two world wars. They created three multilateral institutions; namely, the International Bank for Reconstruction and Development (IBRD or the World Bank), the International Monetary Fund (IMF), and the General Agreement on Tariffs and Trade (GATT). The idea behind the creation of these institutions was that they would help manage, regulate, and police the global marketplace and also provide financial assistance to countries when needed. They did and continue to do all of that—at least to some extent—and have had a major influence in helping to create an increasingly integrated and interdependent world.

The role of the World Bank was to help facilitate the reconstruction and development of post-war Europe, but, after the U.S. started providing help directly to European countries under the Marshall Plan, it shifted its focus in the 1950s to providing assistance to developing countries on a variety of poverty-reduction and developmental programs. The IMF was established to bring some order to the foreign exchange markets, which had been badly affected during and between the two world wars, and to foster full employment and price stability. The role of GATT was to encourage member countries, through consensus, to open up their markets to imports from other member countries and to reduce barriers to trade. In January 1995, GATT was absorbed into the World Trade Organization (WTO) along with the creation of two new entities, GATS (General Agreement on Trade in Services) and TRIPS (the Agreement on Trade-Related Aspects of Intellectual Property Rights). The WTO, like GATT, has been quite successful in helping to create a level playing field for nations in matters involving trade, as well as helping to resolve trade disputes between nations. All three institutions have mostly stayed true to their original purpose, though evolving with changing needs and marketplace imperatives. Furthermore, as mentioned earlier, they did indeed help create greater integration and interdependence among nations.

Governments

Individual countries have to fulfill their obligations as members of the three multilateral institutions—obligations to which they agreed at the Bretton Woods Conference and at later meetings and rounds of discussions. For instance, countries agreed to reduce their tariff and non-tariff barriers under GATT (WTO) regulations, which they have done successively over GATT's/WTO's 70-year history. Average tariff rates for the import of manufactured products into most developed countries ranged between 18 percent and 44 percent in 1913, between 9 percent and 26 percent in 1950, and are now generally less than 4 percent. In developing countries, tariffs are still high, but much less than they were even a decade or two ago.

Over the years, governments of individual countries have taken many other actions in their own interest, but some of them also helped bring countries together economically, politically, and culturally. For instance, countries within certain regions (though not necessarily in the same region) have formed economic integration agreements, such as the European Union (EU) and the North American Free Trade Agreement (NAFTA). Such agreements are designed to help countries benefit from free trade over and above what they could achieve as WTO members. There are many other such actions taken by country governments to foster their economic interests and allow them to have a greater say in world affairs, which also led to greater integration and interdependence among nations.

Multinational Enterprises

A multinational corporation or a multinational enterprise (MNE) is a firm that has a manufacturing and/or service (physical) presence in two or more countries. The number of MNEs in the world today is estimated at over 65,000, with some 20,000 headquartered in the United States. Unlike a few decades ago, many of today's MNEs come from developing countries. Some MNEs are small

23

and medium sized enterprises (SMEs), and some are even "born globals." The latter category typically includes companies that operate on the Internet, serving customers anywhere and everywhere, e.g., Skype. Over time the born globals may develop a physical presence in one or more countries. This category also includes companies that see the whole world as their market from the very beginning. MNEs, as we shall see in the next chapter, have played a crucial role in globalizing the world.

Information and Communication Technologies

We discussed the role of technologies, including information and communication technologies (ICTs), in the first chapter. The ICTs have indeed made a "smaller world," bringing people, companies, and nations together more than at any time in the past. These four forces are, of course, not the only factors behind recent growth of globalization, but they are the more important ones. Another major factor in globalization in the last few decades has been the development of containers in shipping; there will be more on that in the next chapter. We can highlight the role of NGOs (non-governmental organizations or civil society organizations), which are set up by concerned citizens as not-for-profit entities. An NGO often addresses a specific issue(s) and raises funds to work on it (them), over and above what governments do. Most NGOs typically work within the countries in which they are established, but many have cross-border charters, such as Greenpeace, CARE, and OXFAM. A discussion of NGOs is beyond the scope of this book.

Globalization Today and Tomorrow: Role Reversal?

The end result of all of the above is that the world today is much more integrated and more interdependent than it was even 10 or 15 years ago, and the trend continues. Furthermore, there is a growing convergence between the developed and developing worlds.[13] However, the impacts of globalization extend much beyond that. We now observe trends depicting *role reversal* between developed and developing nations, as well as between the MNEs from these nations, which is redefining the rules of global competition.

Reversal of Attitudes Toward Globalization

With the formation of GATT in 1947, developed countries began promoting the idea of liberalizing trade, investments, and capital flows in the 1950s and 1960s as means of achieving prosperity for both rich and poor countries. The developing countries, however, had been fearful of integration and turned away from utilizing trade and investments as instruments for growth and development. Many of them adopted import-substitution policies in their economies as

24

a means to reduce foreign dependence and to protect domestic industries and jobs. Lack of foreign competition, generally a lack of manufacturing expertise, and the existence of government interventions to the operation of free markets led in most cases to reduced productivity rather than the increased productivity that the import-substitution model was meant to accomplish. Over time, such policies produced high economic and social costs for the countries in the Global South (countries such as India, Brazil, and Argentina) that adopted them. This, coupled with the economic gains made by countries in the Far East that opened up their economies to international opportunities, turned out to be a wake-up call for economists, politicians, and national planners worldwide.[14]

While in the 1950s/1960s developed countries were generally pro-globalization and developing countries anti-globalization, national sentiments seem to have reversed over the past one or two decades. Lately, anti-globalization sentiment has been running high in developed countries, while the emerging and developing countries are beginning to see globalization as a positive force. The 2014 Global Attitudes Survey of 44 countries conducted by the Pew Research Center of the United States found that most countries believe that globalization is good for their country. However, respondents in advanced countries are not so sure that it is good for them personally, i.e., in matters involving jobs and wages. Such sentiments are particularly strong in advanced countries (Table 2.1). Developing countries are the strongest supporters of trade and investment. Some 87 percent of respondents from developing countries say that trade is good for their countries, including 47 percent who say it is very good.[15]

The Pew Research Center conducts the Global Attitudes Survey every year. Table 2.2 shows the views of respondents from selected developed and developing countries about trade and globalization from the 2009 survey. Notice that support for trade and international business ties has generally been declining in developed countries and improving in developing countries.

Table 2.1 Faith and Skepticism about Globalization

Views on Globalization	Advanced Countries (% of)	Emerging Countries (% of)	Developing Countries (% of)
Trade is good	84	78	87
Foreign companies building factories in our countries is good	74	70	85
Trade creates jobs	44	52	66
Foreign companies buying domestic companies is good	31	44	57
Trade decreases prices	28	24	29
Trade raises wages	25	45	55

Source: Adapted from the Spring 2014 Global Attitudes Survey, Pew Research Center.

Reverse Innovation

The *2005 World Investment Report* (*WIR*) documented emerging trends in the globalization of research and development (R&D) by transnational corporations. The publication found that R&D work was growing in complexity and was being increasingly performed in certain developing countries. "Developing Asia is the preferred destination; firms based in the US, for example, carried out 10% of their overseas R&D in such countries in 2002, up from 3% in 1994, and more than half of the world's top R&D spenders are already conducting research and development in China, India or Singapore."[16]

The trend toward offshoring R&D to developing countries has accelerated since the *2005 WIR* was published. According to the Booz & Company's 2008 survey of the world's top 1,000 R&D spenders, "[B]etween 2004 and 2007, multinationals increased their total R&D sites by 6 percent, and of those new sites, 83 percent were in China and India. They also increased R&D staff by 22 percent, and 91 percent of that increase was in China and India."[17] Multinationals began offshoring simple R&D work to developing and middle-income countries in the last 10 to 15 years to arbitrage the cost advantage of such countries for R&D work. Some of this R&D was intended to develop products and processes suitable for host markets. For the past 5 to 10 years, however, MNEs have begun to also arbitrage the talent advantage of developing countries, not just their cost advantage. Bringing some of the products developed for emerging markets back to MNEs' home markets, a phenomenon known as "reverse innovation," is much more recent.[18] Also, some MNEs are now starting to use R&D teams based in emerging markets to take leadership roles

Table 2.2 Support for Key Features of Globalization in Developed vs. Developing Countries, 2002–2009

Country	% Who Say That Trade and Business Ties Are Good for Their Country			
	2002	2007	2008	2009
United States	78	59	53	65
United Kingdom	87	78	77	82
France	88	78	82	83
Germany	91	85	87	85
Japan	72	72	71	73
South Korea	90	86	88	92
Russia	88	82	81	80
China	90	91	87	93
India	88	89	90	96
Mexico	78	77	69	79
Brazil	73	72	80	87

Source: Adapted from The Pew Global Attitudes Project, "Views on Trade and Globalization," 2009.

in the development of products and services for global markets, not just for host markets.[19]

The case we are making very strongly is that there are a lot of opportunities out there. If the UK can get the right mix of policy and incentives to encourage our best scientists to collaborate with these countries [China, India and South Korea], that would be for the greater good of everyone. Britain needs to act now to ready itself for a world where innovation was not dominated by Europe and the US – or face being left behind.
                    —James Wilsdon, Head of Science and Innovation,
                                DEMOS, The Atlas of Ideas (UK), 2007

The Booz & Company's 2014 survey of the world's top 1,000 R&D spenders reveals other interesting trends in developing countries' R&D investments. In 2005, only eight China-based companies were included in the Global Innovation 1,000 list, the list of top 1,000 R&D spenders worldwide. By 2014, the list included 114 Chinese companies among the world's 1,000 biggest R&D spenders. Furthermore, these 114 Chinese companies increased their annual spending in 2014 by 46 percent, compared to 3.4 percent by North American companies and 2.5 percent by European companies. R&D spending by companies from the rest of the world, including companies from India and Brazil, increased by 12.9 percent from 2013 to 2014. These numbers, however, understate the extent of innovation activity in China, India, and Brazil, because they do not include the significant R&D being undertaken by MNEs from developed countries there, the results of some of which have found their way back to the MNEs' home markets as reverse innovation.[20]

Reverse FDI

For too long, international investment between developed and developing countries was a one-way street, with investment flowing from the developed to the developing countries. In the last 10 years or so, we have been seeing a dramatic reversal, whereby developing countries are also making investments in developed countries. China, for instance, was the world's third largest foreign direct investor in 2013 after the United States and Japan, with a total outward FDI of $101 billion.[21] China's overseas investments are increasingly in highly developed countries, though the bulk of their investments are still in the developing countries of Asia, Africa, and Latin America. State-owned enterprises (SOEs) account for a dominant share of Chinese firms' foreign direct investments.

According to Sanford C. Bernstein, a Wall Street research firm, the Chinese are "increasingly aspirational and conspicuous consumers."[22] The same can be said of Chinese corporates. Chinese carmaker Geely acquired Volvo from Ford, and Lenovo acquired IBM's PC division with the right to use the IBM logo for five years. There are many other examples of Chinese firms going after well-known global brands.[23] In the spring of 2013, a group of about 30 executives and professionals of a large Chinese state-owned enterprise in the transportation industry (here referred to as "Chinese SOE") was attending a 3-month training program at the Nottingham University Business School China.[24] During a visioning exercise in the session on strategy, the professor asked the participants to write the kind of headline they would like to see for their company in business newspapers 10 years into the future. One of the student teams wrote, "Chinese SOE acquires GE Transportation." Indeed, the Chinese are aspirational.[25] It is already happening. In January 2016, China's appliance maker, the Haier Group, agreed to acquire the GE home-appliance division for $5.4 billion. GE's previous bid to sell the division to Sweden's Electrolux for $3.3 billion failed due to objections of the antitrust regulators in the U.S. GE had been trying to sell its home-appliance business since 2008 to strengthen its industrial-manufacturing operations, including gas turbines, oilfield equipment, and jet engines.[26]

Chinese companies go to highly developed countries for a variety of reasons, including seeking new markets, global brands, advanced technologies, and global management expertise. With China's "going out" policy, companies often receive significant government support in their efforts to become world leaders in their respective industries. SOEs may especially be driven to be seen as "national champions" in the eyes of their government.[27] Their rationale seems to be that in order to be a world leader in an industry, one must be in the world's major economies.

Companies from India have been making investments abroad for at least two decades, though mostly to other developing countries in past decades (South-South investment). They typically invested through minority joint ventures, a requirement of the Government of India at the time. Since about 2000, however, some two-thirds of Indian MNEs' foreign direct investments have gone up-market—to highly developed countries such as the United States, the United Kingdom, and Germany.[28] Indian companies are now investing abroad through both greenfield and merger- and-acquisition (M&A) routes. Essar Steel of India invested almost $2 billion to set up a greenfield project, an integrated steel plant, in the United States during 2008–2012. In fact, during 2004–2009, some 90 Indian companies invested in 127 greenfield projects in the U.S.[29] In 2006, Tata Steel from India acquired the British-Dutch steelmaker Corus for $7.6 billion. For a complete list of Tata Group's acquisitions worldwide, in both developed and developing countries, see the group's website (www.tata.com).[30] In June 2007, Suzlon Energy of India took controlling stake in Germany's REpower after a five-month takeover battle with the huge, state-owned French nuclear power company, Areva, and later increased its stake in the company to 100 percent. In May 2002, South African Breweries acquired Miller Brewing from Philip Morris Cos., creating the world's second largest beer company. There are dozens of other examples of FDI from developing countries into developed countries.

India Inc.'s investments in developed countries result from several factors, including Indian companies' ability to arbitrage their cost advantages; India's human capital, both technical and managerial; a huge domestic market with cut-throat competition in many industries; well-developed institutions (compared to many other emerging markets), such as capital market and the rule of law; business acumen resulting from deeply embedded entrepreneurial traditions; business sophistication and financial market sophistication;[31] production efficiency; and a long exposure to Western and Japanese multinationals and their management practices. The Government of India's progressive relaxation of foreign exchange controls, which now allow Indian companies to invest up to 300 percent of their adjusted net worth in companies abroad without prior approval, also enabled them to enter into larger deals in developed markets.[32]

When Mexico's cement firm, CEMEX, decided to go global in 1992, it acquired two cement firms in Spain, Valenciana and Sanson, for reasons of cultural and linguistic affinity. However, much of the investment between Spain and Latin America had been a one-way street for decades. In 2013 for the first time, reversing two decades of Spain's acquisition spree into Latin America, Latin American firms spent more acquiring Spanish firms than the other way around. These included the acquisition of a bus company, Avanza, and stakes in two Spanish banks, Banco Popular and Sabadell, by Mexican firms, which were the biggest acquirers of Spanish firms from Latin America in 2013. Banesco from Venezuela acquired Spain's NCG for one billion euro in 2014.[33]

With regard to international joint ventures (JVs), in decades prior to the 2000s, a JV typically meant a company from a developed country taking a majority share, and a company from a developing country taking a minority share, with the two being at different stages of the global value chain for their industry. For example, the developed-country partner in a JV could be a manufacturer and the developing-country partner a distributor. With the emergence of global players from many developing countries, there has also been role reversal in how some JVs are established and the functions they perform. Today, we can see a number of cases where the controlling partner is from a developing country and the minority partner from an advanced country, with the two being at a similar stage of the global value chain in their industry, even being direct competitors.

In September 2014, Movile and iFood from Brazil entered into a 50.02:24.98:25.00 JV with Just Eat of Britain, with Just Eat's share being only 25 percent. According to press reports, Just Eat, Britain's online food-ordering giant, decided to join its competitor in Brazil rather than continue fighting it. The JV, called IF-JE Participações, is operating under Movile's iFood brand.[34] Some other examples of developing-country companies forming majority JVs with companies from advanced countries follow. In September 2013, Haier from China formed a 51:49 JV with the Fagor Group of Spain to establish a refrigerator manufacturing plant in Poland. In 2005, India's automotive maker Mahindra & Mahindra entered into a 51:49 joint venture with America's commercial vehicle leader Navistar to form Mahindra Navistar Automotive Limited. This was followed by another JV between the two global automotive leaders in 2007. The two JVs produce diesel engines and an extensive line of trucks and buses in India. In 2013, Mahindra & Mahindra acquired Navistar's full stake in both joint ventures. In May 2014, Suzlon Energy Ltd. of India entered into a 75:25 JV with Austria's Elin EBG Motoren GmbH to manufacture slip-ring generators for Suzlon's windmills.

Reverse Outsourcing/Offshoring

Multinationals from developed countries have been outsourcing production work to developing countries for decades, with the emergence over time of East Asia as a choice location for the outsourcing of intermediate and final production in most industries. In the 1990s, they also began to outsource (offshore) a variety of corporate services functions to developing and middle-income countries, such as India, China, and countries in Central and Eastern Europe—countries that offered highly skilled workers at low cost. There have been many instances of role reversal between firms from developed countries and those from developing countries, especially in the last 5 to 10 years. Many developing-country firms have gone from being outsourcees in earlier decades to now being outsourcers to developed-country firms—a trend likely to continue and accelerate in the coming decades.

Embraer, the maker of small and midsized jet planes in Brazil, pioneered the use of reverse outsourcing in the 1990s and 2000s. It does the high-value-added design and assembly work itself but outsources the making of parts to leading companies from advanced countries—parts such as jet engines from GE and avionics from Honeywell, both from the U.S.A., wing stubs and pylons from Kawasaki of Japan, door and fuselage parts from France, Spain, and Belgium, and so on. With reverse outsourcing, Embraer benefits from alliances with companies at the forefront of technology, speedy development, and lower costs compared to its fully integrated competitors[35] (see also Chapter 3, Figure 3.4).

One of the most far-reaching reverse outsourcing deals between a developing-country firm and a developed-country firm was negotiated by India's largest telecom operator, Bharti Airtel, with IBM Global Business Services (and other foreign IT companies) in 2004. Under this 10-year deal, valued at over $2 billion, IBM took responsibility for supplying, installing, and managing Bharti Telecom's end-to-end IT infrastructure, integrating a wide range of customer-facing and back office processes. All client-specific investments in the infrastructure and its management were made by IBM, allowing Bharti to focus its energies on marketing and branding. In return, IBM was paid a share of Bharti's telecom revenues. (Bharti renegotiated its agreement with IBM in 2014, bringing some IT tasks in-house and giving some to other IT services vendors in India, with a deal value of $400 to $500 million over five years.)

Along with the outsourcing of the IT infrastructure to IBM, Bharti Airtel negotiated outsourcing agreements with Ericsson, Nokia, and Siemens in 2004 to obtain network capacity and a full range of managed services, such as network design, optimization, operation, and field maintenance. Payment for network capacity to the vendors was to be made only when the capacity was actually used by Bharti's customers. Bharti was not responsible for paying for unused capacity at any time, even though the ownership of the assets created by the vendors providing that capacity rested with it.[36] Bharti later utilized the same outsourcing model in South Africa, while other telecom operators in India, such as Idea Cellular and Vodaphone (of the U.K.), did the same.

What Is Different about Globalization Today than in Earlier Eras?

If globalization has been evolving for thousands of years, what is different about it today than in earlier eras? We have already seen how today's world is much more integrated than it was just 10 or 15 years ago through the processes of globalization, convergence, and role reversal—aided by technologies and networks. In Chapter 1, we also saw how the role and influence of emerging economies in global business and world affairs had been rising. In this section, we will attempt to see how else today's world is different from that in earlier time periods, which may also provide a window into what might be expected in the future.

A McKinsey Global Institute[37] study on cross-border flows of trade, finance, and people shows how connected the world is now compared to, say, 10 or 20 years ago. According to the study, while cross-border flows have been behind the growth of globalization since the earliest periods, cross-border exchanges today have exploded in scope and complexity. In addition to the globalization forces discussed earlier, the study highlights two major forces that are accelerating the growth of cross-border flows. They are "increasing global prosperity" and the "growing pervasiveness of internet connectivity and spread of digital technologies." Some key findings of the study are presented below.[38]

- Cross-border (global) flows are growing and contribute to GDP growth. The value of flows of goods, services, and finance in 2012 was $26 trillion, or 36 percent of global GDP, one-and-a-half times as large, relative to GDP, as they were in 1990.
- The McKinsey Global Institute's "Connectedness Index" shows that developed economies are much more connected than emerging economies, though the level of connectedness in the latter is rising rapidly.
- The knowledge-intensive portion of global flows increasingly dominates the capital- and labor-intensive flows and is growing faster than them. In the past, global flows were dominated by labor-intensive, low-end manufacturing and commodity flows. Now, knowledge-intensive cross-border flows account for half of all global flows and are growing more dominant.
- Cross-border flows are enabled by digitization and by the consequent reduction in the marginal costs of production and distribution.
- Networks of cross-border flows are broadening and deepening as emerging economies join in. They are becoming important as both consumers and

31

producers in the global economy and now account for 38 percent of global flows, nearly triple their share in 1990.

- As global supply chains become more fragmented and countries specialize in the production of intermediate goods, flows of intermediate goods (as opposed to flows of final goods) are rising.
- Companies, entrepreneurs, and individuals now have the opportunity to participate in the global economy, once the preserve of governments and major MNEs. Today, even the smallest company or individual entrepreneur can be a "micro-multinational" that sources, produces, and sells its products, services, and ideas across borders, courtesy of digital technologies (consistent with Tom Friedman's Flat World construct).

A Transformed World?

Early in this chapter, we distinguished among many kinds of globalization, though this book is focused mostly on economic globalization, i.e., on the growing economic integration and interdependence between nations. However, the other kinds of globalization, such as the globalization of environmental concerns and terrorism, have also been bringing the world together, in both positive and not-so-positive ways.

First, the not so positive: An editorial in *The World in 2015*, The Economist's annual publication, sounds the alarm.

> Optimism is in short supply as thoughts turn to 2015. Two grand gatherings towards the end of the year, the UN's meeting to set "sustainable development goals" and a get-together in Paris to combat climate change, will show whether countries can agree on ways to tackle some of the planet's biggest issues. But for much of 2015 it will be the world's divisions—economic, political and cultural—that will draw most attention... In 2015 international cooperation on many issues will suffer from the strength of nationalism.

Now, the positive: The editorial in *The World in 2015* continues... "The noise surrounding these divisions will stop many people noticing progress in all sorts of areas in 2015. ... Indeed, there will be magic moments to suit all tastes in the year ahead. ... For all its divisions, the world will have a chance to join together in wonder." Bill Gates, in the same publication, offers hope for humankind in 2015 and beyond in the globalized world. The number of children who die has dropped by half, from 12.7 million in 1990 to just over 6 million in 2014. And, the percentage of very poor people in the world has been cut by more than half since 1990.

These developments did not come about on their own. They are a result of the concerted global efforts of some 189 nations over the last 15 years, as well as the work of some philanthropic organizations, such as the Bill & Melinda Gates Foundation. In year 2000, 189 world leaders came together at the United Nations to design a roadmap for ending extreme poverty, disease, child mortality, and hunger and forging a partnership between governments and the private sector to promote economic development. Together, they created eight goals, the Millennium Development Goals (MDGs), and agreed to achieve them by 2015. In adopting the Millennium Declaration, the international community pledged to "spare no effort to free our fellow men, women and children from the abject and dehumanizing conditions of extreme poverty." While progress toward achieving the MDGs has been uneven across nations, literally all nations involved in the effort have made progress, some of it highlighted by Bill Gates above. This was an incredible effort of nations from almost the entire world coming together to end some of the most serious, dehumanizing conditions in the world.

In September 2015, leaders from these countries met in New York City to celebrate the progress that had been made toward achieving the MDGs and to set new goals, the Sustainable Development Goals (SDGs), for the next 15 years.[39] The SDGs are much more ambitious than the MDGs they replaced. The 17 new goals, with 169 specific targets, are intended to be achieved by 2030, include:

- End poverty in all of its forms everywhere.
- End hunger, achieve food security and improved nutrition, and promote sustainable agriculture.
- Ensure inclusive and quality education for all and promote lifelong learning.
- Ensure access to affordable, reliable, sustainable, and modern energy for all.
- Take urgent action to combat climate change and its impacts.

The Sustainable Development Goals represent a new universal agenda and plan of action for people and achieving prosperity for all.

It's a transformed (no, transforming) world!

Concluding Remarks

The chapter began with disparate views on globalization—globalization as the source of all evil to globalization as a panacea for many of the ills facing humanity. According to Nobel-Prize winning economist Amartya Sen, globalization "has enriched the world scientifically and culturally and benefited many people economically as well."[40] Another Nobel-Prize winning economist, Joseph Stiglitz, has been an ardent critic of globalization for perpetuating inequality in the world.[41] The truth is somewhere between the two extremes, especially because of the convergence unleashed by globalization itself (Chapter 1). The connected economy is seeing more and more of the reversal phenomena, such as the reversal of innovation, reversal of FDI, and even reversal of outsourcing and offshoring. The arrival of many emerging markets in the global arena in the 2000s has opened up opportunities (and challenges!) for MNEs not seen before. The combined actions being taken by most of the world leaders (e.g., the Millennium Development Goals and the Sustainable Development Goals) are good for not only humanity but for global business as well.

Notes

1 Jagdish Bhagwati, *In Defense of Globalization* (New York: Oxford University Press, 2007), p. 3.
2 Adam Smith, *An Enquiry into the Nature and Causes of the Wealth of Nations* (London: Methuen & Co., Ltd., 1776).
3 Thomas L. Friedman, *The World Is Flat: A Brief History of the Twenty-First Century* (New York: Farrar, Straus and Giroux, 2005).
4 For an even earlier perspective on the history of globalization, starting with the period when humans began moving out of Africa and dispersing throughout the world, see: Nayan Chandra, *Bound Together: How Traders, Preachers, Adventurers, and Warriors Shaped Globalization* (New Haven, CT: Yale University Press, 2008).
5 See the Silk Road chronology at http://www.silk-road.com/artl/chrono.shtml.
6 Peter Frankpan, *The Silk Roads: A New History of the Worlds* (London: Bloomsbury, 2015).
7 Based on description of Marco Polo's travels at the Silk Road Foundation website (http://www.silk-road.com/artl/marcopolo.shtml). See also Francis Wood, *The Silk Road: Two Thousand Years in the Heart of Asia* (Berkeley, CA: University of California Press, 2004) for a fascinating account of history and survey of the Silk Road over several thousand years.
8 Source: https://en.unesco.org/silkroad/content/what-are-spice-routes. For a history of the spice trade, including his own family's history as spice traders, from 3000 BC to the present, read University of Arizona professor Gary Paul Nabhan's recent book, *Cumin, Camels, and Caravans: A Spice Odyssey* (Berkeley, CA: University of California Press, 2014).
9 See, for example, Pankaj Ghemawat, *World 3.0: Global Prosperity and How to Achieve It* (Boston: Harvard Business Review Press, 2011).
10 The British East India Company ruled large parts of India from 1757 to 1858, when the British Crown assumed direct control of India as one of its colonies. British rule in India ended in 1947.
11 Source: *Encyclopedia Britannica*.
12 See specific references in Wikipedia: https://en.wikipedia.org/wiki/Dutch_East_India_Company.
13 See Chapter 1 for a discussion of Michael Spence's thesis about convergence.
14 Jagdish Bhagwati, *In Defense of Globalization* (New York: Oxford University Press, 2007).
15 Pew Research Center, "Faith and Skepticism about Trade, Foreign Investment" (September 16, 2014). http://www.pewglobal.org/2014/09/16/faith-and-skepticism-about-trade-foreign-investment/.
16 UNCTAD. *World Investment Report 2005: TNCs and the Internationalization of R&D* (Geneva, Switzerland: United Nations Conference on Trade and Development, 2005).
17 Barry Jaruzelski and Kevin Dehoff. "Beyond Borders: The Global Innovation 1000," *Strategy+Business*, Winter 2008: p. 4.
18 Vijay Govindarajan and Ravi Ramamurti. "Reverse Innovation, Emerging Markets, and Global Strategy," *Global Strategy Journal, 2011, 1(2)*.
19 This section based on: Vinod K. Jain and S. Raghunath, "Strengthening America's International Competitiveness through Innovation and Global Value Chains." In *Restoring America's Global Competitiveness through Innovation*, edited by Ben Kedia and Subhash Jain (Northampton, MA: Edward Allen, 2010).
20 Barry Jaruzelski, Volker Staack, and Brad Goehle, "Global Innovation 1000: Proven Paths to Innovation Success," *Strategy+Business*, Winter 2014.

21 Source: *UNCTAD World Investment Report, 2014.*
22 Quoted in *The Economist*, January 25, 2014, p. 19.
23 See, for instance, articles by Joel Backaler in *Forbes* magazine: "10 Chinese Companies Going Global in 2015," January 14, 2015, and "14 Chinese Companies Going Global in 2014," January 10, 2014.
24 The author was a visiting professor at Nottingham University Business School China during the 2012–2013 academic year.
25 See also Evan Osnos, *Age of Ambition: Chasing Fortune, Truth, and Faith in the New China* (New York: Farrar, Straus and Giroux, 2015).
26 Daniela Wei and Stephanie Wong, "China's Haier to Buy GE's Appliance Unit for $5.4 Billion," Bloomberg Business, January 14, 2016. Accessed from www.bloomberg.com.
27 Joel Backaler, "5 Reasons Why Chinese Companies Go Global," *Forbes*, May 6, 2014.
28 Ravi Ramamurti and Jitendra V. Singh, "Indian Multinationals: Generic Internationalization Strategies." In *Emerging Multinationals from Emerging Markets,* edited by Ravi Ramamurti and Jitendra V. Singh (New York: Cambridge University Press, 2009).
29 Vinod K. Jain and Kamlesh Jain, *How America Benefits from Economic Engagement with India* (Silver Spring, MD: India-US World Affairs Institute, 2010).
30 For the list of Tata's mergers and acquisitions, visit: http://www.tata.com/htm/Group_MnA_CompanyWise.htm?sectid=Mergers-and-acquisitions.
31 For business and financial market sophistication, India ranked very high among all countries, not just among developing countries, in the World Economic Forum's Global Competitiveness Index for 2009–2010.
32 Jain and Jain, 2010, p. 10.
33 The Economist, "Latin America and Spain: Shoe on the Other Foot," *The Economist*, January 25, 2014.
34 Vinod Sreeharsha, "British Food Delivery Giant Forms Joint Venture in Brazil," *The New York Times*, September 19, 2014.
35 Antoine van Agtmael, *The Emerging Markets Century: How a Breed of World-Class Companies Is Overtaking the World* (New York: Free Press, 2007).
36 Various sources including Bharti Airtel, IBM, and Ericsson websites and Everest Group research reported in LiveMint, an online publication: http://www.livemint.com/Companies/v0BPytPnOJMAalnMRWRDAM/Bharti-Airtels-evolving-outsourcing-strategy.html.
37 The McKinsey Global Institute is the business and economics research arm of McKinsey & Company. It was established in 1990 to develop a deeper understanding of the evolving global economy.
38 McKinsey Global Institute, "Global Flows in a Digital Age: How Trade, Finance, People, and Data Connect the World Economy," McKinsey Global Institute, 2014.
39 Source: https://sustainabledevelopment.un.org/sdgs.
40 Amartya Sen, "Ten Theses on Globalization," published online, June 28, 2008, DOI: 10.1111/0893–7850.00430.
41 See, for instance, Joseph Stiglitz, *Globalization and Its Discontents* (New York: W.W. Norton & Company, Inc., 2002).

3

GLOBALIZATION OF INDUSTRIES AND FIRMS

I would define globalization as the freedom for my group of companies to invest where it wants when it wants, to produce what it wants, to buy and sell where it wants, and support the fewest restrictions possible coming from labour laws and social conventions.

—Percy Barnevik, CEO and later Chairman,
Asea Brown Bovery Group (1988–2002)

What is the one industry that you believe has had the greatest impact on the globalization of business in the post-World War II era? Aircraft? Automobiles? Energy? Information technology? Telecommunications? Or ...? These are all good answers, but the single industry that enabled the globalization of industries that sell physical goods is the shipping industry. Currently, some 86,000 ships carry over 9 billion tons of cargo around the world each year, or about 90 percent of all world trade in goods. According to Lori Ann LaRocco and Matthew McCleery in, *The Shipowners and Financiers Who Expanded the Era of Free Trade*, "[F]rom refrigerated freighters and container ships to car carriers and supertankers, the world's shipping industry has played an incredibly key role in transporting 90 percent of the world's food, products and energy while helping transform the global economy along the way." Further, the shipping industry "raised standards of living virtually everywhere by shuttling products and commodities from where they're most efficiently produced to where they are most profitably consumed."[1]

The shipping industry owes much of its prominence in recent decades to the invention of the container—a uniform metal container of standard size. The first container was designed by Malcom McLean in 1956 to replace the previous method of handling bulk dry goods for transportation on trucks, railroads, and ships. The International Standards Organization standardized the measurements of containers between 1968 and 1970 (8-foot high, 8-foot wide, and 20-foot long), which has had a profound economic and social impact worldwide. For instance, containerization has reduced cargo handling costs by over 90 percent, thus slashing a major cost component for firms trading goods internationally. Cities for which shipping had been their mainstay for decades lost ground to newer centers of industry and trade, causing huge worker dislocations. While container shipping "killed off" some cities of the old economy, it helped create a new economy—in true Schumpeterian fashion. In Schumpeter's own words (1942):

> The opening up of new markets, foreign or domestic, and the organizational development from the craft shop to such concerns as U.S. Steel illustrate the same process of industrial mutation—if I may use that biological term— that incessantly revolutionizes the economic structure from within, incessantly destroying the old one, incessantly creating a new one. This process of Creative Destruction is the essential fact about capitalism.[2]

According to Marc Levinson, the author of *The Box: How the Shipping Container Made the World Smaller and the World Economy Bigger*, "the standard container has all the romance of a tin can." However, the container "is at the core of a highly automated system for moving goods from anywhere to anywhere, with minimum of cost and complication. The container made shipping cheap, and by doing so changed the shape of the world economy." For instance, "factories in Malaysia could deliver blouses to Macy's in Herald Square [New York City] more cheaply than could blouse manufacturers in the lofts of New York's garment district."[3]

Containerization has had major impacts on many levels, not just on the cost of loading and unloading. It has significantly reduced inventory-carrying costs and losses due to theft (since containers are sealed at the factory before being shipped out), which, in turn, reduced insurance costs. It has also led to higher labor productivity, easier inland distribution by trains and trucks, and so on. For instance, the cost of loading/unloading loose cargo before containerization was $5.83 per ton but only $0.16 per ton after containerization. The cost of capital tied up in inventory during transit, say, between Hamburg and Sydney, fell by half, and dockworkers could load 30 tons per hour on a cargo ship by 1970, compared to only 1.7 tons per hour in 1965.[4]

Containerization not only made shipping cheaper but has also had a huge impact on the global economy, individual countries, industries, and communities. The cost of international freight in the 1950s and 1960s was so high, as much as 25 percent of the cost of the goods being exported, that exporting for some products was not even worthwhile. Now, with substantially lower freight costs, companies that did business only in domestic markets became international companies. Manufacturers are able to source their inputs from the lowest-cost locations with the assurance that the goods will arrive when needed—giving rise to JIT (just-in-time) manufacturing. This led to huge increases in the import/ export of intermediate goods by companies doing business worldwide and the lengthening of supply chains. Retailers and wholesalers are able to purchase their merchandise from almost anywhere with the assurance that goods will arrive when needed, in time for Christmas sales, for example. Poor countries benefited as companies began to look for low-cost sources of inputs and supplies, enabling them to have access to global value chains.

With the rise of container shipping, cities that had based their economies on maritime commerce for centuries found their economic base vanishing. Their place was taken by cities such as Seattle and Busan (South Korea) that converted their existing port infrastructures to handle container ships. Producers no longer have to manufacture close to their major markets now that the whole world is accessible to them due to lower-cost, easier, and faster transportation of their inputs and intermediate and finished goods.[5]

In addition to the significantly reduced cost and time for handling and shipping goods, one of the factors behind the early growth of container shipping was the Vietnam War, when America needed to ship large quantities of war supplies to Vietnam in the late 1960s and early 1970s. The U.S. armed forces picked up the cost of the entire two-way journey for the shipment of war supplies. Rather than returning empty to the U.S., cargo ships would stop in Japan and pick up consumer electronics, automobiles, and other goods for sale in the U.S. The easy and cost-effective entry of Japanese goods into the U.S. market explains, at least in part, the rise of Japanese business in the 1970s and 1980s.

The growth of the shipping industry, leading to the diffusion of economic activity around the world, parallels the globalization of competition in recent decades—a process that began thousands of years ago. As we saw in Chapter 1, Arab traders had been traveling to spice-producing regions (the East Indies) by boat as early as 4000 to 5000 years ago. Competition for spices became very intense between the various "East India Companies" in the 17th century as explorers (and armies) from many European countries discovered sea routes to the spice-producing regions. Competition for product markets[6] occurs mostly within industries and between firms in those industries. It is industries where competitive advantage is won or lost.[7] We will therefore now explore the globalization of competition in industries and firms.

Figure 3.1 A Container Ship
Source: www.adobe.com.

38

The Globalization of Industries

An *industry* is a collection of firms offering goods or services that are close substitutes of each other. Alternatively, an industry can be defined as consisting of firms that directly compete with each other. An industry can be defined rather broadly (e.g., the beverage industry) or more precisely (e.g., the carbonated soft drink industry). For analyzing competition, it is generally a good idea to circumscribe industry boundaries as narrowly as possible. For example, in discussing competition between soft drink companies like the Coca-Cola Company and PepsiCo, one would want to define the boundaries of the carbonated soft drink industry rather than that of the beverage industry.[8] Once the industry is defined as the "carbonated soft drink industry," other beverages (water, milk, juices, beer, wine, etc.) can be treated as *substitutes* in competition analysis.[9]

Over the years, practically all industries have been becoming more and more global in their geographic scope, some more slowly than others. An industry begins to have "global" characteristics if firms can derive some competitive advantage by spreading and integrating their activities on a worldwide basis. For instance, if a firm has operations in three countries and can benefit from configuring and coordinating its activities across the three countries, it will begin to approach its market as a global market. *Configuration* means where in the world a firm performs its value-creation activities, and *coordination* means how like activities are coordinated with each other across different countries (more on configuration and coordination in Chapter 5).

Patterns of International Competition

Competition in some industries is restricted to within individual countries, i.e., what a company does within a country is generally not impacted by (or impacts) what it does in other countries. Such industries are called *multidomestic industries*, where competition and competitive advantage tend to be country-specific. Some examples of multidomestic industries are: cement, hospitals, consumer finance, and utilities such as electricity generation and distribution. Globalization is an option for firms in such industries but not a strategic imperative. A firm in a multidomestic industry can consider globalization if it has some core competencies or advantages that it could profitably leverage in other countries.

There are also industries in which what a company does in one country is impacted by (or impacts) what it does in the other countries where it competes. These are *global industries*, where a company's competitive position in one country is impacted by its competitive position in the other countries where it competes. Some examples of global industries are fast-moving consumer goods (FMCGs), automobiles, many industrial goods, and services that can be digitized. Such industries often face *multi-point competition*, which means that they tend to meet the same global competitors in different national markets. Companies in global industries must therefore integrate (coordinate) their activities across markets in order to develop competitive advantage. Globalization is generally a strategic imperative for firms in such industries.

The pattern of international competition can be visualized as a continuum ranging from multidomestic to global. However, there are no industries that are purely multidomestic or purely global. Most exhibit elements of both, though some may be more multidomestic and some more global. For instance, services that can be digitized and FMCGs are much more global than, say, automobiles; they can be traded across borders much more easily.

Multidomestic   ←——————————————→   Global
Industries   Industries

What Drives this Pattern of International Competition?

Firms in multidomestic industries face *local responsiveness* pressures due to differences in customer tastes, preferences, and needs across nations; differences in levels of economic development; differences in distribution channels; differences in infrastructure and use conditions; and host-government demands. As a result, firms in multidomestic industries tend to offer customized goods and services to suit local needs and requirements in the countries where they do business. They also customize their competitive strategy to suit each market in which they do business. Firms in multidomestic industries may indeed be multinational; however, their approach to doing business in a specific country and competitive advantage tend to be country-specific. Competitive advantage developed in one country may not travel to other countries.

Firms in global industries face *cost reduction* pressures arising from the commoditization of goods and services and the existence of competitors based in low-cost locations. Firms in global industries often produce everyday products,[10] or universal products, which are widely needed and available around the world. Thus, global industries in a country typically consist of large numbers of firms, both domestic and foreign, and the products they sell tend to behave like commodities, i.e., they are bought and sold based on price more than on features. The term "commodity" here refers to any product, even a manufactured product, that is so commonplace and offered by so many sellers that it begins to behave like a real commodity (such as wheat or pork bellies)—as distinct from a "differentiated" product, which sells because it has certain features that at least some customers prefer and for which they are willing to pay a premium price. Firms in global industries thus face a strong pressure to keep their costs low. They do that by standardizing products across markets or by having fewer versions of the same product available in different markets—to leverage economies of scale and scope—as well as standardizing their competitive strategy. Price is of course always a factor in competition, but it is a much stronger consideration in global industries than in multidomestic industries. See Box 3.1 about the globalization of markets proposed by Theodore Levitt in 1983.

Box 3.1 The Globalization of Markets

Harvard Business School professor Theodore Levitt forcefully introduced a new phrase into the business lexicon with his 1983 article on "The Globalization of Markets."[1] He suggested that consumer tastes and preferences had been converging toward some common norms that resulted in "global markets." This meant that companies no longer needed to customize their products to suit the tastes and preferences of customers in different national markets. Instead, they should offer standardized products across national markets and thereby achieve savings in the cost of production, marketing, and management of their multinational enterprises. In his own words:

A powerful force drives the world toward a converging commonality, and that force is technology.... The result is a new commercial reality—the emergence of global markets for standardized consumer products on a previously unimagined scale of magnitude. Corporations geared to this new reality benefit from enormous economies of scale in production, distribution, marketing, and management. By translating these benefits into reduced world prices, they can decimate competitors that still live in the disabling grip of old assumptions about how the world works.... Gone are accustomed differences in national or regional preference.... The globalization of markets is at hand. With that, the multinational commercial world nears its end, and so does the multinational corporation.

Levitt defined the "multinational corporation" as a company "operating in a number of countries, adjusting its products and practices in each—at relatively high costs." He contrasted the multinational corporation from what he called a "global corporation," a company that "operates in different countries without adjusting its products and practices—and at relatively low costs." His article unleashed a great deal of thinking about marketing strategy among companies of the mid-1980s and 1990s, and some began to view the world as a huge, single market with similar tastes and preferences across national boundaries. A good example is the Coca-Cola Company, which, under its former CEO Robert Goizueta adopted the "think global–act global" mantra in the mid-1990s. Coca-Cola's global strategy at the time emphasized "international growth, scale economies, statelessness, ubiquity, and centralization and standardization."[2]

Levitt was ahead of his time in suggesting a global approach for most consumer products. Companies that heeded his advice have had to rethink their strategy, and even Coca-Cola has gone through several attempts over the years to resolve the local-global dilemma. There is, though, some evidence of the globalization of markets in the connected economy of the

41

2010s—the trend that Levitt wrote about in 1983. Tastes and preferences for many consumer products have been becoming more cosmopolitan, notwithstanding cultural and other differences across nations. It's a result of globalization, growing convergence between developed and developing nations, advances in communication and transportation technologies, and greater movement of people across borders. For such products, a global or regional approach to strategy might be warranted.

1 Theodore Levitt, "The Globalization of Markets," *Harvard Business Review*, May–June 1983.

2 See an extended case study of The Coca-Cola Company's changing global strategy under different CEOs in Pankaj Ghemawat, *Redefining Global Strategy: Crossing Borders in a World Where Differences Still Matter* (Boston, MA: Harvard Business School Press, 2007), pp. 17–31.

Nestlé of Switzerland competes in both multidomestic and global industries worldwide. Its products range from customized products, such as Maggi Noodles, to global products such as Perrier bottled water that are essentially the same worldwide. Nestlé's Maggi is a soup-and-sauce product available in most countries of the world, with local and regional variations. By introducing Maggi Noodles in India in 1983, Nestlé created a new food category, a dry noodle cake product, not a sauce or a soup, that can be prepared within two minutes and which appeals to the local palates. Over the years, Maggi Noodles became a staple of urbanites, and especially the younger people in India. Maggi Noodles has now been repackaged and repositioned as a 99 percent fat-free food product in Australia and some other countries. In food products, the company's *mantra* is to be very local. Even Nescafé instant coffee (a seemingly global product), which may look the same and has similar-looking packaging around the world, actually tastes different in Bangalore, Berkeley, and Buenos Aires. In fact, according to Peter Gumbel writing in *Time* magazine, "the company makes about 200 different types of Nescafé, ranging from the 'three-in-one' sachets on sale in parts of Asia—which contain the supposedly perfect mix of coffee, milk and sugar for local taste—to the considerably more expensive jars of freeze-dried Colombian coffee aimed at French coffee snobs.... The key to prosperity in the food business, it turns out, is being local (but not too local) at the same time as being global (but not only global)."[11]

Comparative and Competitive Advantage

The concept of "comparative advantage" refers to a *country's* advantage in a certain industry in international trade. The theory of comparative advantage[12] suggests that a country should specialize in the production and export of goods that it produces most efficiently, while importing goods from other countries that it produces (comparatively) less efficiently, even if it could produce them more efficiently itself. For the sake of simplicity, assume that there are two countries (Switzerland and China) and two goods (high-end watches and DVDs). Now assume that Switzerland is more efficient than China in producing both high-end watches and DVDs. Assume also that the difference in productivity between Switzerland and China in producing watches is greater than the difference in producing DVDs. So, Switzerland is comparatively more efficient in producing watches than DVDs, even though it is more efficient than China in producing both products. According to the theory of comparative advantage, it will be in Switzerland's interest to specialize in the production and export of high-end watches and to import DVDs from China even though it could produce DVDs more efficiently itself.

So, if a country exports goods that it produces (comparatively) more efficiently, and then imports goods from other countries that they produce more efficiently, they all benefit from trade. That is, free trade (trade unhindered by tariff and non-tariff barriers) is a positive-sum-game for all countries involved in it. See Box 3.2 for an example of comparative advantage in practice.

Box 3.2 Comparative Advantage in Practice

Imagine there's a baseball player who is the best pitcher as well as the best batter on his team. Should the team use him for pitching or for batting? Obviously, doing both pitching and batting would tire him out so much that he would be able to do neither very well. This question can be answered by looking at his performance as a pitcher *relative to* the performance of other pitchers on the team and his performance as a batter *relative to* the performance of other batters on the team. If the performance difference between him and the next best batter in the team is greater than the performance difference between him and the next best pitcher in the team, he should be batting more than pitching. He has a *comparative advantage* in batting over pitching.

This actually happened in the case of Babe Ruth, one of the greatest batters in the history of baseball. What is not well known is that he was also one of the greatest pitchers of all time. However, he stopped pitching after 1918 and began batting and set record after record in batting. "Although Ruth had an absolute advantage in pitching, his skill as a batter relative to teammates' abilities was even greater: His *comparative* advantage was at the plate. ... To exploit Ruth's *comparative* advantage, the Red Sox [Boston's baseball team] moved him to center field in 1919 so that he could bat more frequently."[1]

1 Paul Krugman, Maurice Obsfeld, and Marc J. Melitz, *International Economics: Theory and Policy.* 10th Edition (Boston: Pearson, 2015), p. 33. See also Edward Scahill, "Did Babe Ruth Have a Comparative Advantage as a Pitcher?," *Journal of Economic Education*, 21(4), Fall 1990: 402–10.

The concept of "competitive advantage" refers to the advantage possessed by a *company* in relation to its competitors. A company has competitive advantage if it has higher profitability, or the potential to have higher profitability, than competition in its industry. A firm's competitive advantage typically arises from one of two sources—low cost or differentiation. It can achieve competitive advantage by either performing its value-creation activities at lower cost or in a unique way compared to competition.[13]

Tradable and Non-Tradable Goods

Tradable goods are those that can be sold in locations distant from where they are produced, either within the country or across national borders. On the other hand, non-tradable goods can only be sold in the locations where they are produced. Many services can only be performed close to the customer, e.g., a haircut. Similarly, many goods can only be sold where they are produced because of low value relative to the cost of transportation (low value-to-weight ratio) or because they could get spoiled if shipped to distant places, e.g., prepared food. With the rise of container shipping, including refrigerated containers, some formerly non-tradable goods have now become internationally tradable. Cement is an excellent example of a good that was non-tradable until a few decades ago but is now a tradable good. Cement is generally produced in relative close proximity to where it is sold and used—for reasons such as cost of shipping (very low value-to-weight ratio) and because it can get easily spoiled through moisture if not shipped in sealed packages. Cement companies like CEMEX of Mexico, which typically manufacture the product in close proximity to where it is sold to final customers, now derive a large share of their revenue from trading cement across borders.

Products with high value (relative to weight) are likely to be traded more heavily internationally than products with low value-to-weight ratio. According to the DHL Global Connectedness Index for 2012, the industry with the highest value-to-weight ratio among the traded industries included in the Index is the electronic integrated circuit industry. This is followed by the mobile phone, pharmaceutical, footwear, and car industries (Table 3.1). The value-to-weight ratio for most commodities, including cement, is less than $1 per kilogram.[14]

Table 3.1 Value-to-Weight Ratio Comparison, 2010

Industry	*Approximate Value of Traded Merchandise in U.S. Dollars per Kilogram*
Electronic Integrated Circuits	$40,000
Mobile Phones	$391
Footwear	$14
Cars	$13

Source: Adapted from DHL Global Connectedness Index, 2012, Figure 3.4.

Sometimes it does not make sense for a firm to export its product to a country due to low value-to-weight ratio, due to high tariffs, because it might get spoiled during transportation or because the distribution system there is not yet well developed. In such situations, the firm would choose FDI (or licensing or franchising) instead of exporting as a means of doing business in that country (see also Chapters 4 and 5).

Drivers of Industry Globalization

In Chapter 2, we explored the factors behind the growth of globalization, such as multilateral institutions, governments, and MNEs. In this subsection, we will explore drivers of the globalization of industries. In a later subsection, we will explore the drivers of the globalization of firms. Two prominent approaches to the study of globalization of industries are George Yip's drivers of industry globalization and Michael Porter's competitive advantage of nations.

Yip's Drivers of Industry Globalization

According to George Yip, there are four sets of factors that must be analyzed to determine an industry's potential for globalization: Market drivers, cost drivers, government drivers, and competitive drivers.[15] In this typology, Yip makes a distinction between multidomestic and global industries. His drivers of industry globalization present a list of factors that are typically outside an industry's or a firm's control. If all of these factors are favorable for an industry, it will have good potential to be a global industry—an industry producing standardized products that are sold (exported) worldwide. Recall that firms in a multidomestic industry can also be competing in many countries but must customize their offerings and strategy on a country-by-county basis.

MARKET DRIVERS

These include factors such as similarities of customer tastes and needs across nations, existence of global customers (who desire an identical product wherever they are), similarity of global distribution channels, and transferability of marketing know-how. For instance, if customer tastes and needs across nations tend to be similar for an industry, companies within that industry can simply standardize their products, manufacture them in one or two or a few locations, and then export them worldwide. Thus, such an industry will have higher potential for going global than an industry for which customer tastes and needs differ greatly from nation to nation.

COST DRIVERS

Industries for which cost is not a major consideration, such as industries with high value relative to transportation cost (high value-to-weight ratio) or low trade barriers are likely to be global industries. This category also includes industries with high potential for economies of scale; so a company could manufacture its products in large quantities in one or two or a few locations to take advantage of economies of scale. For instance, the Intel Corporation manufactures its wafers (microprocessors and chip sets) in 11 fabrication plants (fabs) in four countries, with 8 fabs in the U.S. and one each in China, Israel, and Ireland. The majority of Intel's wafers are then assembled and tested at facilities in Malaysia, China, Costa Rica, and Vietnam, from which they are exported worldwide.

GOVERNMENT DRIVERS

Industries for which different national governments have specific standards (e.g., technical standards) or regulations (e.g., trade barriers, local content requirements, etc.) are not likely to have high globalization potential. Firms in such industries must customize their offerings for each country or region where they do business to be able to meet industry standards and government regulations.

COMPETITIVE DRIVERS

Industry structure, differences in industry structure (concentration) across nations, and the feasibility of protecting intangibles such as intellectual property (IP) also impact the globalization potential of industries. The globalization potential of fragmented industries is likely to be higher than that of concentrated industries. In IP-intensive industries, if firms are able to protect their IP in foreign markets, then they are also good candidates to go global.

Porter's Competitive Advantage of Nations

In the 1980s, Michael Porter studied 100 industries in 10 leading trading nations to try and identify the factors that led industries in specific countries to become internationally competitive.[16] His research identified four sets of factors that indicate the "competitive advantage of a nation" in a certain industry: factor conditions; demand conditions; related and supporting industries; and business policy and rivalry (Figure 3.2). An industry in a nation that has all four factors at a favorable level will likely become internationally competitive. Thus, Porter's model (Porter's Diamond) can be used to assess an industry's globalization potential. While Yip's globalization drivers are all outside firms' control, many of Porter's factors are within firms' control.

FACTOR CONDITIONS

These are the business inputs available in a nation and are essential for an industry to exist and to excel. Porter makes a distinction between *basic factors* such as natural resources and demographics and *advanced factors* such as those created

46

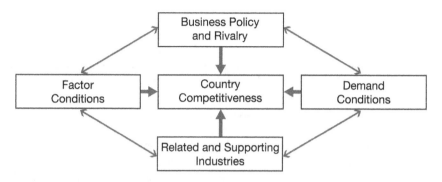

Figure 3.2 Determinants of International Competitiveness at Industry Level
Source: Adapted from Michael E. Porter, "The Competitive Advantage of Nations," *Harvard Business Review*, March–April 1990, pp. 73–97.

by individuals, companies, and the nation through their own efforts. The latter includes skilled labor, communication infrastructure, research and higher education institutions, high technology, etc. While the basic factors can provide an initial advantage to a nation in an industry, they must be supported by advanced factors for it to achieve and sustain international competitiveness. Advanced factors are created by government policy as well as by corporate action.

DEMAND CONDITIONS

For an industry to excel internationally, its home market must consist of demanding and sophisticated customers. The existence of demanding and sophisticated customers in the domestic market encourages firms to be innovative and to build appropriate capabilities that can then be the foundation for competing successfully in international markets.

RELATED AND SUPPORTING INDUSTRIES

No industry can become internationally competitive on its own; it's typically a cluster of industries that together become internationally competitive. Therefore, the existence of related and supporting industries in a nation or region that are internationally competitive is essential for an industry to become internationally competitive itself. (See Box 3.3 for an example of California's wine cluster.)

BUSINESS POLICY AND RIVALRY

Finally, for an industry to become internationally competitive, it must consist of firms that have a long-term corporate vision and a management ideology that encourages investment and sustained upgrading through innovation and capability building. The domestic market must also have open and vigorous

Box 3.3 The California Wine Cluster

A *cluster* is a collection of interconnected companies, specialized suppliers, service providers, trade associations, universities, governments, and other institutions present within a specific geographic region.[1] For instance, California's wine cluster consists of grape-growing and wine-making industries, as well as an extensive array of industries that support grape growing and wine making. "On the growing side, there are strong connections to the larger California agricultural cluster. On the winemaking side, the cluster enjoys strong links to both the California restaurant and food preparation industries (complementary products) and the tourism cluster in Napa and other wine-producing regions of the state."[2]

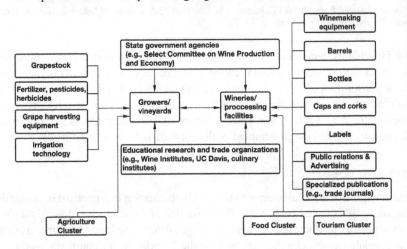

Figure 3.3 The California Wine Cluster

Source: Michael E. Porter, "Clusters and Competition: New Agendas for Companies, Governments, and Institutions." In Michael E. Porter, *On Competition*, Boston: Harvard Business School Publishing, 2008, pp. 213–303. Reprinted with permission.

Notes

1 Michael E. Porter, "Clusters and Competition: New Agendas for Companies, Governments, and Institutions." In *On Competition*, edited by Michael E. Porter (Boston: Harvard Business School Publishing, 2008), pp. 213–303.

2 Porter, 2008, pp. 217–18.

competition, supported by appropriate laws and regulations, such as antitrust laws, that are vigorously enforced. Strong domestic rivalry presses firms to become more innovative in meeting customer needs, which, in turn, can make them stronger international players.

Porter's theory of the competitive advantage of nations predicts the pattern of international trade that is often observed in the world today. A country where all four components of the diamond are favorable in a specific industry will export its products to other countries, while importing products of industries where the components are not favorable. Thus, industries where all four components are favorable have the highest globalization potential. In Porter's own words: "A nation's competitiveness depends on the capacity of its industry to innovate and upgrade. Companies gain advantage against the world's best competitors because of pressure and challenge. They benefit from having strong domestic rivals, aggressive home-based suppliers, and demanding local customers."[17]

The Globalization of Firms

Industries globalize when firms within those industries go global, i.e., when they begin spreading and integrating their activities on a worldwide basis.

What's a Global Firm?

A multinational enterprise (MNE) is a firm that has operations in two or more countries. On the other hand, a global firm (also an MNE) has operations in many more countries and exhibits globalization of supply chain, globalization of market presence, globalization of capital base, and globalization of the corporate mindset.[18]

A global firm sources its inputs from wherever it can best obtain them cost effectively and in a timely manner—from its own foreign subsidiaries, from third-party vendors, or from the global marketplace. Internationally active firms, such as Caterpillar and Ikea, derive their competitive advantage through participation in global value chains.

A global firm sells its products worldwide and also sources its capital from global capital markets. A number of foreign multinationals, such as Infosys of India, Telefonos de Mexico of Mexico, and Waterford Wedgwood of Ireland, have listed their stock on NASDAQ in the United States. Some companies even launch their initial public offerings (IPOs) in the U.S., even though they are quite "local" in their own home markets—sourcing their inputs locally and selling their products locally. They do not fit our definition of a global firm. For instance, China's Alibaba Group launched the biggest IPO in U.S. history on the New York Stock Exchange in 2014, raising over $25 billion, even though it has little business presence in the U.S., sources the bulk of its goods in China, and also has the greatest share of its sales in China.

The final characteristic of a global firm is globalization of the corporate mindset—the extent to which the senior and top management of a company understand the opportunities and challenges coming from outside their home market and are able to strategize bearing the global nature of their business and the world around them in mind. VeriFone Systems Inc. is a good example of a company that has successfully cultivated a global mindset. Founded in Hawaii in 1981 and now headquartered in San Jose, California, VeriFone's products include devices and point-of-sale (POS) systems that process all kinds of payment transactions, whether in person at a retail outlet or online. VeriFone has headquarters in each of its global areas of operations—San Jose, California; Miami, Florida; London, U.K.; and Singapore. From these headquarters and other regional locations, VeriFone has local presence in over 45 countries.[19] In 2014, the company changed its informal name from VeriFone to Verifone.

During the tenure of Verifone's former CEO, Hatim Tyabji (1986–1998), the top management of the company met for five days every six weeks at a different location around the world. The corporate philosophy manual, written by Tyabji himself, was issued in a number of languages, including English, Chinese, French, German, Japanese, Portuguese, and Spanish. The CEO's letter to shareholders, in annual reports, was also published in multiple languages. Verifone recruited employees on a global basis. Furthermore, one of the company's core competencies is its ability to access and leverage knowledge from throughout its multinational enterprise network to serve its customers everywhere.[20]

Why Do Firms Go Abroad?

Firms invest abroad for one or more of four reasons: resource seeking, market seeking, efficiency seeking, and asset seeking.[21] Firms can also go abroad through non-equity entry modes such as exporting/importing, licensing, franchising, etc.; more about that later in the chapter. Speaking pragmatically, and in general, firms go abroad (via FDI and other means) for reasons that range from the strategic to the tactical. This is true whether a firm is going abroad for the first time or expanding its global footprint in a specific market.

Strategic Reasons

DESIRE TO CONTINUE TO GROW

A common reason for firms to start exploring foreign markets is that their domestic market isn't growing as quickly as they would like or is getting saturated through competition. At the same time, they may find great opportunity in some foreign markets, such as emerging markets, which encourages them to go abroad. There are literally thousands of MNEs from advanced countries that have entered emerging markets over the last one/two decades to specifically tap the potential there.

SMALL DOMESTIC MARKET

Another reason for many firms to go abroad is that their domestic market is very small. Some small countries have traditionally been home to major multinational enterprises, simply because their domestic market is too small for them to achieve their corporate objectives. For example, Switzerland is home to several major MNEs, including ABB Group, Nestlé, Novartis, and Zurich Insurance

Group—all of which do much more business overseas than at home. Nestlé, for instance, derived only about 1.6 percent of its $100 billion sales in 2014 from Switzerland. Of Nestlé's 339,000 employees worldwide, only 3.3 percent are in Switzerland, and of its 442 factories worldwide, only 2.5 percent are in Switzerland. So, companies like Nestlé and Novartis that come from small countries must necessarily go abroad as a strategic imperative.

Even large countries may have small markets for specific industries, and firms wanting to grow in those industries must necessarily explore foreign markets. For products like jet aircraft, no single country market will provide the economies of scale needed for their design, development, manufacture, and sales. For instance, Brazil's regional jet maker Embraer sells its products to airlines worldwide and also sources its inputs through reverse outsourcing to, and innovative risk-sharing arrangements with, major multinationals from developed countries. The Embraer 170/190 family of commercial jets has been sold to airlines in over 35 countries, including Air France, Alitalia, British Airways, Finnair, Saudi Arabian Airlines, and US Airways. Embraer developed its 170/190 jet family through a risk-sharing partnership with 16 partners and 22 main suppliers. "Embraer is responsible for the design and development of the aircraft, manufacture of the forward fuselage, fuselage center section II, wing-to-fuselage fairings, wing assembly and whole aircraft integration. Other companies responsible for structural sections of the aircraft include Kawasaki Heavy Industries from Japan, Sonaca of Belgium, Latécoère of France and Gamesa of Spain. The U.S.-based C&D Aerospace is supplying the passenger cabin and cargo compartment interiors of the aircraft. The main systems partners include General Electric (engines and nacelles), Hamilton Sundstrand (tail cone, auxiliary power unit, air management and electrical systems), Honeywell (avionics)."[22] All of these companies have created subsidiaries in Brazil for the local manufacture of parts, components, and systems for Embraer. The risk-sharing partners responsible for designing and supplying the structural segments of the aircraft's main systems invest their own resources for research and development and share the risk and success of their products with Embraer (Figure 3.4).

OBTAINING ACCESS TO VALUABLE RESOURCES

Some firms go abroad to access valuable resources—knowledge, technology, capital, talent, and management expertise—that they may lack or are unable to access in their home market. Information technology (IT) firms from many countries have been coming to the U.S., especially to Silicon Valley, for the abundant knowledge, technology, and talent that exists there. We saw earlier that firms may list their stocks in foreign stock exchanges to have access to capital there. This is especially true for firms from emerging markets. One of their motivations for going to highly developed countries is to have access to lower-cost capital; capital in developing countries tends to be in short supply and much more costly than in developed countries. For example, Mexico's CEMEX, when it decided

A Worldwide Partnership Project

EMBRAER 170/175 Suppliers

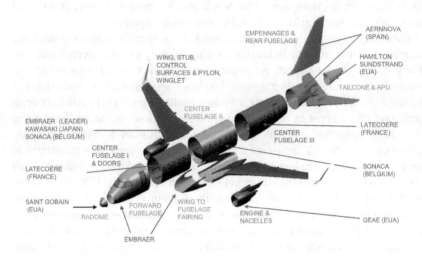

Figure 3.4 Embraer's Risk-sharing Partnerships for the ERJ 170/190 Program
Source: Embraer Company. Reprinted by permission.

go abroad in the early 1990s, acquired two competitors in Spain (Valenciana and Sanson) and set up an international division there. It was then able to access lower-cost capital through its Spanish subsidiary.

In 1984, Toyota of Japan entered into a joint venture with General Motors to set up a car assembly plant, NUMMI (New United Motor Manufacturing Inc.), in Fremont, California with a desire to learn about the American marketplace (which closed down in 2010). While GM was able to find use for its 20-year old plant that had been closed down, Toyota's motivation for the JV was much more strategic. "For Toyota, this was its first major manufacturing investment in the United States. What better way to learn about the peculiarities of the U.S. automotive market than from GM? Toyota learned how to adapt its famed Toyota Production System to work with U.S. suppliers, U.S. government regulations, and, most importantly, the UAW [United Auto Workers union]. After just two years in school with GM, Toyota invested in its first wholly-owned plant in the U.S.A.; this new plant in Kentucky eventually became Toyota's largest outside of Japan."[23]

EFFICIENCY REASONS

Another strategic reason for firms to go abroad, especially to developing countries (but not just to developing countries), is to try and reduce their costs, i.e., to seek operational efficiencies. Multinational enterprises from developed countries

	Domestic (Onshore)	Overseas (Offshore)
Make	Onshore (In-house)	Offshore (Captive Center)
Buy	Domestic Outsourcing	Offshore Outsourcing

Figure 3.5 The Basic Sourcing Models

have been outsourcing manufacturing to developing countries for decades to benefit from their comparative advantage in labor costs and increasingly to be close to their key markets. For instance, East Asia has been a choice location for the offshoring of intermediate and final goods production for at least two decades. What is relatively new is that, since the arrival of the digital economy in the 1990s, MNEs from developed countries also began offshoring a variety of corporate services functions, such as software development and customer relationship management, to developing and middle-income countries, including India, China, and countries in Central and Eastern Europe. These were (and are) the countries that offered highly skilled workers at low cost. In the 2000s, rising costs, competitive pressures, and a lack of adequate talent at home led many developed-country MNEs to offshore even core innovation, engineering, and research and development (R&D) work to such countries—to leverage not just low costs but also the skills and talent available there. Just like for offshoring of manufacturing, MNEs offshore services functions by setting up wholly owned foreign subsidiaries (captive centers) or by outsourcing to third-party vendors in foreign markets. Figure 3.5 shows different sourcing models used by firms—both within their home countries and in other countries.

FOLLOWING CUSTOMERS

Some firms go abroad because their key customers are located there. This was a major reason for the globalization of Cisco, which makes Internet networking equipment. As countries began investing in cyber infrastructure, it became imperative for Cisco to be there—to not only meet the emerging demand for networking equipment but also to educate customers and prospective future employees about their offerings. Some firms go abroad following their global customers, who require identical goods and services everywhere. Citigroup, the leading global bank, often went abroad following their customers. For instance, whenever Coca-Cola opened a subsidiary in a new country, Citibank followed, sometimes even preceding the client to facilitate its foreign-market entry through introductions to government and other officials, trade associations, etc. The author had an account with Citibank, then the First National City Bank, when he worked for the Coca-Cola Export Corporation in India in the late 1960s. Sometimes global customers require the identical products from their suppliers in their foreign operations as are needed in the home country. For instance, there are some 400 Japanese automotive transplants (U.S. subsidiaries of Japanese companies) in Ohio, and dozens more elsewhere in the U.S., that provide the same parts and components to Honda, Nissan, and Toyota automotive factories in the U.S. as they do in Japan. Similarly, when Mercedes-Benz opened its U.S. factory in Tuscaloosa County, Alabama, dozens of its German suppliers set up factories there.

EXCHANGE RATES AND TRADE BARRIERS

Another strategic reason some firms invest abroad is to counter unfavorable exchange rates or to circumvent actual or threatened trade barriers in those markets. This is exactly what happened in the case of Japanese automakers' manufacturing investments in the United States during the 1980s. Honda established its first auto assembly plant in the United States in Marysville, Ohio, in 1980. The yen had appreciated against the dollar from an average of 240 yen to a dollar in December 1979 to 209.79 yen to a dollar in December 1980, which would have made Honda's exports almost 13 percent costlier for its U.S. customers.

Honda's initial investment in the U.S. was followed by Nissan in 1983 and Toyota in 1986. Two other Japanese automakers, Subaru and Mitsubishi, also set up assembly plants in the U.S. These companies have other manufacturing plants in the U.S. as well—making motorcycles, engines, transmissions, and other automotive components. From an exchange-rate perspective, investing in the United States turned out to be a very good decision on the part of the Japanese automakers. As shown in Figure 3.6, the yen rose by almost 40 percent against the dollar, from an average of 240 yen to a dollar in December 1979 to 143.62 yen to a dollar in December 1989, and has almost consistently remained below 140 yen to a dollar ever since.[24] In fact, the yen recorded its highest-ever value against the U.S. dollar at 75.74 yen to a dollar in October 2011.

Another reason for Japanese automakers' entry into the United States was the threat of punitive tariffs being imposed against the import of Japanese vehicles in the early 1980s. With the rise of Japan Inc. in the 1970s and 1980s, Americans were getting very concerned about Japanese imports, especially of automobiles, the most visible symbol of high-value imports from Japan. Calls for protectionism were rising, and it was believed that the U.S. government would impose punitive tariffs against automotive imports from Japan. To circumvent such an eventuality, the Japanese automakers voluntarily agreed to restrict their exports to the U.S. to 1.68 million vehicles per year in 1981. This is called Voluntary Export Restraint, a quota on exports imposed *voluntarily* by the exporting country, often at the request of the importing country. The export quota was raised

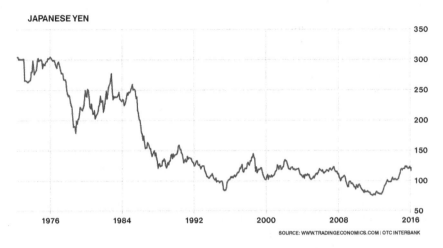

Figure 3.6 Japanese Yen – U.S. Dollar Exchange Rate, 1972–2015
Source: www.tradingeconomics.com. Reprinted with permission.

to 1.85 million Japanese vehicles a year in 1984 and allowed to expire in 1985, though the Japanese government indicated that they would continue to restrict exports of vehicles to the U.S. at the prevailing level at least for some time.[25]

Tactical Reasons

PURCHASE OF COMPANIES IN DISTRESS

In contrast to making strategic investments abroad, which require a proactive approach to exploring and identifying investment opportunities, sometimes companies expand their presence abroad opportunistically, as and when an acquisition opportunity becomes available. This is especially true for companies that find themselves financially stretched and thus become an attractive acquisition target. In 2005, Indegene Life Sciences, India's largest pharmaceutical communication and education company at the time, acquired Medsn Inc. of New Jersey, U.S.A., for $15.5 million. Medsn, which was funded with an initial venture capital (VC) investment of $39 million, had been operating at a loss for seven years when acquired by Indegene. In 2006, Indegene acquired MedCases LLC, also of New Jersey, for $800,000 when it was on the verge of filing for bankruptcy. With these two acquisitions, the Indigene worldwide group significantly expanded its U.S. presence in continuing medical education and related fields.[26]

Foreign acquisitions of distressed U.S. companies became somewhat commonplace during the global financial crisis of 2008–2010. However, opportunities to acquire distressed companies are also available in Europe and even in emerging markets such as China and Brazil, which have lately been experiencing slower growth rates, and especially in China, which also experienced a stock market meltdown in mid-2015 and January 2016. In fact, the Blackstone Group LP raised a $5 billion fund in 2014 to finance distressed businesses in the United States and Europe. KKR & Co., another buyout firm, raised $2 billion for a global fund to invest in failing Indian companies and banks through equity investment and by restructuring their loans. By February 2014, KKR had invested $1.6 billion of private-equity funds in India and lent a similar amount to local companies through its India-based finance company.[27]

PURCHASE OF COMPANIES IN BANKRUPTCY

Bankruptcy sales are another method of making an opportunistic foreign acquisition, typically at a substantially lower cost than acquiring a going business. Like all investments, however, purchasing a company out of bankruptcy has risks, including the added risk of dealing with bankruptcy court and possibly having to renegotiate long-term labor or other contracts.[28] For instance, Bharat Forge Ltd. of India, the second largest forging company in the world, bought Federal Forge Inc., of Lansing, Michigan, out of bankruptcy in 2005. The $9.1 million acquisition provided Bharat Forge with manufacturing presence in North America, further strengthening its global manufacturing footprint. The sale of Federal Forge was approved by the U.S. Bankruptcy Court and concluded after successful renegotiation of its existing UAW contract.[29]

Another good example is the 2014 purchase of Baltimore, Maryland-based Hedwin Corporation by Fujimori Kogyo Co. Ltd. of Japan for $22.2 million. The purchase was approved by the United States Bankruptcy Court in May 2014.[30] Hedwin is an industrial plastics packaging company whose operations were disrupted by a June 2013 fire in its plant, which, along with other factors, pushed the company into Chapter 11 bankruptcy. Fujimori had been making Hedwin containers in Japan for over 50 years as a Hedwin licensee and was in an ideal position to make the acquisition, though it is more common for a licensor to acquire a licensee rather than the other way around.[31]

Actually, the acquisition of distressed firms and firms in bankruptcy may sometimes be quite strategic since some firms systematically research and target potential acquisitions, a process that may last years. They target a firm whose performance has been going down, often in a downward spiral, and time their acquisition bid to when the target's performance has gone down enough, as judged by its share price or the financial difficulties it may be having, such as making required payments on borrowed money, obtaining trade credit, or raising additional debt to meet its working capital needs.

FOLLOWING COMPETITORS

Some firms go abroad when they find that their major competitors are going to a certain foreign market; they just follow them because of the fear that by not going they might miss out on an emerging opportunity they had overlooked. The Asian financial crisis, which began in 1997 in Thailand, and then spread to other Southeast Asian nations (Indonesia, Philippines, Malaysia, and South Korea, etc.), presented a great opportunity for foreign firms to make acquisitions in the region. For instance, during 1998–1999, practically all of the major global cement producers made acquisitions in Southeast Asia, one after the other (Table 3.2).

In another example of foreign market entry following competitors, South Africa has lately been experiencing a surge in the fast food restaurant business, with several U.S. restaurant chains entering or on schedule to enter the market during 2015–2016. This is no doubt a result of the growing popularity of fast foods in South Africa and the success that KFC and McDonald's have had there. The Yum! Brands' KFC chain has been in South Africa since 1971 and is currently the market leader with 771 restaurants, while all other international chains entered (or re-entered) the market after the end of apartheid in 1994. Table 3.3 shows the number of existing restaurants and year of entry into South Africa for the existing fast food chains as of mid-July 2015.

The fast food chains that have recently announced plans to enter the South African market during 2015–2016 are Starbucks, Domino's Pizza, Dunkin Donuts, Krispy Kreme Donuts, and Hardee's. Starbucks has signed a licensing agreement with Taste Holdings, which will have the exclusive rights to develop and operate Starbucks restaurants in South Africa starting in 2016. Through another agreement with Domino's Pizza, Taste Holdings plans to have 150 Domino's outlets by the end of 2015. Dunkin Donuts has announced plans to

Table 3.2 Global Cement Companies' Acquisitions in S-E Asia during 1998–1999

Company	Home Country	No. of Acquisitions	Acquisitions in	Total Investment (US$ Million)	Total Cement Capacity Acquired
CEMEX	Mexico	5	Indonesia (3) Philippines (2)	$811 M	25.9 M Tons
Lafarge	France	4	Indonesia (1) Philippines (2) South Korea (1)	$712 M	13.9 M Tons
Blue Circle	U.K.	8	Philippines (5) Malaysia (3)	$671 M	12.6 M Tons
Holderbank	Switzerland	5	Philippines (2) Malaysia (1) Thailand (1) China (1)	$433 M	23.1 M Tons
Italcementi	Italy	2	Thailand (2)	$206 M	6.4 M Tons

Source: Adapted from Pankaj Ghemawat, "The Globalization of CEMX," Harvard Business School Case Study No. 9–701–017, November 2004, Exhibit 8.

Note: Blue Circle was acquired by Lafarge in 2001, and Holderbank (which later changed its name to Holcim) merged with Lafarge in 2014 to form LafargeHolcim.

Table 3.3 Fast Food Chains in South Africa, July 14, 2015

Restaurant Chain	No. of Restaurants	Year of Entry (Re-Entry)
KFC	771	1971
Mcdonalds	200	1995
Subway	17	1996
Burger King	44	2013
Pizza Hut	10	2014

Source: Adapted from Staff Writer, "The Biggest Fast Food Chains in South Africa," BusinessTech, July 14, 2015. http://businesstech.co.za/news/lifestyle/93156/the-worlds-biggest-fast-food-chains-in-south-africa/

enter the market through its Baskin-Robbins ice cream chain, with the donut chain to follow. Similar announcements have been made by Krispy Kreme Donuts and Hardee's.

What Challenges do MNEs Face in Foreign Markets?

Firms new to foreign markets, even firms that have gone abroad before but are entering a new foreign market, often face challenges arising from a lack of managerial, organizational, and financial resources needed for successful exploration of foreign markets. Other challenges include the inability to modify products, strategy, and approach to doing business to suit the host market; the additional cost of operating in an unfamiliar market; a lack of understanding of the market, including culture and business practices; a host of geopolitical, social, and regulatory challenges in the host market; existing competitors, both indigenous and foreign; or simply because they are a foreign company, known as the *liability of foreignness*. Some of the challenges get accentuated when a developed-country firm goes to a developing country and vice versa.

Challenges Faced by Developed-Country Firms in Developing Countries

Some of the most common challenges faced by developed-country firms in developing countries include the lack of cross-cultural understanding, the importance of relationships (e.g., *guanxi* in China), a lack of understanding of business practices and government regulations, and inadequate infrastructure and under-developed institutions, such as rule of law, there.

Sometimes a developed-country firm makes assumptions about a prospective developing country that may not be quite valid, such as an assumption that the cost of operating in a developing country will be low just because the cost of living there is low. In fact, the cost of buying or renting real estate in cities like Mumbai and Moscow can be as high, or higher, than in London or New York. There may also be additional fees and expenses that are uncharacteristic of business expenses in the home market, such as the cost of having a private security service in some countries. The typical cost of sending an expatriate manager or a technical professional to an emerging market is often two to three times the cost of having the same individual in the home market and orders of magnitude higher than the cost of someone hired locally for the same position. Firms may also underestimate the extent of entrenched competition in a host market—competition from local firms, state-owned enterprises, and foreign firms already established there.

Then, there are obvious mistakes, such as in branding and advertising that even smart companies with years of international experience make. IKEA once marketed its products in Thailand with Swedish names that meant "sex" and "getting to third base" in the Thai language. KFC's "finger licking good" fast food was translated into Chinese as "eat your fingers off."[32] A friend of the author who worked for Standard & Poor's many years ago went on a business visit to China and had his business card translated into Chinese. The company name got translated into Chinese as "Average & Bankrupt."

Challenges Faced by Developing-Country Firms in Developed Countries

Some of the challenges listed above, such as lack of cross-cultural understanding, lack of understanding of business practices and government regulations, entrenched competition, and liability of foreignness, are also likely to be faced by developing-country firms entering developed markets. The additional challenges they may face include difficulties accessing distribution channels, the lack of brand image and reputation, and the high cost of operating in a developed country.

Mini Case Study: The Experiences of American Companies in China

The American Chamber of Commerce in Shanghai (AmCham Shanghai) conducts an annual survey of its members doing business in China. These findings are indicative of the kinds of experience foreign firms have lately been having in China. The case of American firms in China is instructive, though not necessarily generalizable to other emerging markets or to MNEs from other countries doing business in China.

According to AmCham Shanghai's 2015 China Business Report,[33] American businesses in China were generally quite optimistic about their prospects there, with some 45 percent of the respondents reporting an optimistic outlook for the next five years, though there was a drop in optimism of 10 percent from 2014 to 2015. They also reported facing many operational and legal/regulatory challenges in the country (taken almost verbatim from the 2015 report). The top three *operational challenges* found by the 2015 Survey included rising costs, human resources (HR) constraints, and domestic competition for the third straight year. Corruption and fraud, especially by employees, also featured as major concerns.

Ninety-one percent of respondents indicated that rising costs were their main business challenge, a finding consistent with data from last year's survey. (Low cost was the reason many companies came to China in the first place!) Among the many factors that contribute to rising costs, the cost of labor remains the most significant concern, with 86 percent of companies reporting this as their primary cost issue. Rising costs are most keenly felt by the manufacturing sector, particularly in the automotive, electronics, energy, and chemicals industries.

HR constraints—attracting, developing, and retaining staff—remain a perennial issue for U.S. companies in China. Respondents indicated that the talent environment had worsened in the past year in all three categories surveyed, especially for managers and executives. Recruiting and retaining skilled workers and professionals, and to a lesser degree technical staff, became more difficult. This is partly a result of domestic companies becoming more attractive to prospective local hires.

Ranked as the number three business issue, domestic competition from both state-owned enterprises (SOEs) and private Chinese companies continued to affect the success of U.S. companies in China. Focus group interviews suggested that Chinese companies from all sectors no longer competed on price alone, but increasingly relied on quality and product differentiation, along with speed to market and breakthrough business models (especially in consumer goods and e-commerce).

Regarding *legal and regulatory challenges*, an unclear regulatory regime, the difficulty of enforcing contracts, and tax administration ranked as the top concerns. Other widespread concerns were difficulty obtaining required licenses and the increasing impact of laws and regulations favoring domestic companies.

This year, 78 percent of respondents said that an unclear regulatory environment hinders their business, making this the number one legal and regulatory challenge for U.S. businesses in China, up from last year's 72 percent. More than half the respondents (54 percent) believe that the regulatory environment favors local companies, with this perceived bias being more pronounced in the services sector. This high response rate has held steady for the past three years. Companies also reported that the lack of regulatory transparency was increasingly impacting their business.

U.S. companies this year reported increased difficulty enforcing contract terms, rating this as the second most challenging issue in the legal and regulatory environment—a jump from its rank as the number five issue last year. Additional analysis of survey data reveals that retail sector companies are more likely to rate this challenge as a serious hindrance to business than are companies from the manufacturing and services sectors.

Tax administration rounded out companies' top three legal and regulatory challenges issues this year, keeping the same ranking as last year. Recently, China's State Administration of Taxation reported that it will more closely monitor tax payments and the profitability of foreign firms. President Xi Jinping also supports China's participation in global tax collection regimes. Taken together, this suggests that tax administration will rise in complexity and impact for international companies in future years. This year, the Survey also asked companies to give their views on anti-monopoly and anti-corruption investigations. Not surprisingly, in a year of high-profile cases, these investigations are fueling perceptions that Chinese regulatory authorities are targeting foreign firms.

Concluding Remarks

This chapter made the distinction between multidomestic industries and global industries, which will form the basis for designing and implementing strategies for foreign markets in future chapters. The chapter also distinguished between comparative advantage and competitive advantage, concepts that are sometimes misused as synonyms. The drivers of globalization of industries and firms have implications for how industries and firms become internationally competitive, an important theme of the book.

Key Issues Facing Firms as They Begin To Go Abroad

Firms starting out on their internationalization journey, or even those expanding their presence abroad, typically face a variety of questions, which sometimes are not adequately explored. Thoughtful consideration of questions such as those shown below can make the difference between successful and unsuccessful internationalization.

1 Why go abroad?
2 Which country (countries) to enter?
3 Which product(s) to internationalize?
4 When to enter? What should be the scale of entry?
5 How to enter foreign markets?
6 How to compete and grow in foreign markets?
7 How to implement global strategy?

The theories, frameworks, and concepts included in this book are intended to help the reader research and answer such questions. The first five questions are covered in the next chapter, Question 6 in Chapters 5–6, and the remaining in Chapters 7–10.

Happy exploration!

Notes

1 Lori Ann LaRocco and Matthew McCleery, *Dynasties of the Sea: The Shipowners and Financiers Who Expanded the Era of Free Trade* (Stamford, CT: Marine Money, Inc., 2012). Quoted in Barry Glassman, "Shipping: Globalization's Lifeblood," *Forbes*, January 2, 2013.
2 Joseph Schumpeter, *Capitalism, Socialism, and Democracy*, 3rd Edition (1942. New York: Harper and Brothers, 1950), p. 83.

3 Marc Levinson, *The Box: How the Shipping Container Made the World Smaller and the World Economy Bigger* (Princeton, NJ: Princeton University Press, 2008), p. 3.

4 The Economist, "The Economist Explains: Why Have Containers Boosted Trade So Much?," *The Economist*, March 21, 2013.

5 This section is based on Marc Levinson, 2008.

6 We use the term "market" to refer to both product markets and geographic markets. A product market is akin to our definition of "industry."

7 Michael Porter, "Changing Patterns of International Competition," *California Management Review*, Winter 1986.

8 Coca-Cola and PepsiCo now also sell other beverages, like water, juices, etc. So, if one is analyzing competition in the market for juices, then the industry should be defined to include only juices.

9 One of the most popular ways of performing competition analysis is Michael Porter's five forces analysis model, a staple of most strategy textbooks. The five forces model defines a "substitute" in the manner used here.

10 We use the term "products" to refer to both goods and services.

11 Peter Gumbel, "Taste Test: Same, but Different," *Time*, June 14, 2007.

12 The Theory of Comparative Advantage was advanced by David Ricardo in 1817 and provides the rationale for countries to engage in free trade, or trade without artificial controls imposed by the trading countries.

13 Michael Porter extended the concept of competitive advantage from companies and industries to countries with his 1990 book, *The Competitive Advantage of Nations* (New York: Free Press); this is discussed later in this section.

14 The DHL Global Connectedness Index is prepared biennially by Pankaj Ghemawat and Steven A. Altman for DHL: http://www.dhl.com/content/dam/flash/g0/gci_2012/download/dhl_gci_2012_complete_study.pdf.

15 George S. Yip and G. Tomas M. Hult, *Total Global Strategy*, 3rd Edition (Upper Saddle River, NJ: Prentice Hall, 2012).

16 Michael Porter, 1990.

17 Michael Porter, "The Competitive Advantage of Nations." *Harvard Business Review*, March–April 1990: 73.

18 Anil K. Gupta, Vijay Govindarajan, and Haiyan Wang, *The Quest for Global Dominance: Transforming Global Presence into Global Competitive Advantage* (San Francisco: Jossey-Bass, John Wiley Sons, 2008).

19 Source: http://www.verifone.com/company/.

20 Gupta et al., 2008. See for more details 1994 Harvard Business School case study, "VeriFone: The Transaction Automation Company (A), Product Number: 195088-PDF-ENG.

21 This taxonomy of FDI motivations was proposed by John Dunning in *Multinational Enterprise and the Global Economy* (Harlow, U.K.: Addison-Wesley, 1993).

22 Embraer 170, Brazil: http://www.aerospace-technology.com/projects/embraer_170/.

23 Ben Gomes-Casseres, "NUMMI: What Toyota Learned and GM Didn't," *Harvard Business Review*, September 1, 2009.

24 The U.S. dollar had been rising, rather unexpectedly, against major world currencies from 1980 to 1985 despite a large and growing U.S. trade deficit. The growing trade deficit led to calls for protectionism in the United States. In September 1985, the Group of Five nations (the G5: United States, U.K., Germany, France, and Japan) met at the Plaza Hotel in New York City and jointly agreed to stop the rise of the dollar through active intervention in the foreign exchange market; this later became known as the Plaza Accord. The G5 agreement led to the expected depreciation of the dollar against those currencies. When the dollar had fallen quite a bit against the other currencies, the G5 finance ministers met again to try and stop the dollar's

decline. They met in Paris in February 1987 and agreed to help stabilize exchange rates at current levels (the Louvre Accord).

25 Charles W.L. Hill, *International Business: Competing in the Global Marketplace*, 9th Edition (New York: McGraw-Hill/Irwin, 2013), Chapter 7.

26 Vinod K. Jain and Kamlesh Jain, *How America Benefits from Economic Engagement with India* (Silver Spring, MD: India-US World Affairs Institute, Inc., 2010).

27 George Smith Alexander, "Kravis Says KKR to Fund Distressed India Firms Amid Slowdown," *Bloomberg Business.* http://www.bloomberg.com/news/articles/2014-02-20/kkr-to-invest-in-distressed-indian-firms-and-banks-amid-slowdown.

28 See also Nicholas E. Williams, "Opportunistic Acquisitions: Buying Assets through Bankruptcy," October 14, 2014. http://www.martindale.com/mergers-acquisitions-law/article_Foley-Lardner-LLP_2180238.htm.

29 Donelly Penman & Partners, "Federal Forge Inc. Has Been Acquired by Bharat Forge Ltd." http://www.donnellypenman.com/pdf/2005FederalForgeSummary.pdf.

30 Joanna Sullivan, "Japanese Company Wins Bid for Hedwin Corp., Nearly 300 Jobs May Be Saved," *Baltimore Business Journal*, May 9, 2014. http://www.bizjournals.com/baltimore/news/2014/05/09/japanese-company-wins-bid-for-hedwin-co-nearly300.html.

31 Jim Johnson, "Fire Adds Woes Forcing Hedwin into Chapter 11, Forced Sale," *Plastics News*, April 9, 2014. http://www.plasticsnews.com/article/20140409/NEWS/140409897/fire-adds-to-woes-forcing-hedwin-into-chapter-11-planned-sale.

32 See many more examples at: http://www.inc.com/geoffrey-james/the-20-worst-brand-translations-of-all-time.html. See also David A. Ricks, *Blunders in International Business*, 3rd Edition (Malden, MA: Blackwell Publishing, 1999).

33 AmCham Shanghai, "2015 China Business Report, American Chamber of Commerce in Shanghai." http://www.amcham-shanghai.org/ftpuploadfiles/Website/CBR/2015/2014-2015-China-Business-Report.pdf.

Part II

STRATEGY FOR INTERNATIONAL MARKETS

4

HOW TO ENTER FOREIGN MARKETS

I believe it is a mistake to open a factory overseas without first having a sales and marketing system established and knowing the market very well. My view is that you must first learn about the market, learn how to sell to it, and build up your corporate confidence before you commit yourself. And when you have confidence, you should commit yourself wholeheartedly.
— Akio Morita, Co-founder, Sony Corporation (1921–1999)

On December 31, 2010, Bobbie Johnson, then the European editor for Gigaom, a prominent emerging technologies research firm, wrote a piece about Netflix at gigaom.com with the title: "Will Netflix Go Global in 2011? Maybe, but It Won't Be Easy."[1] The U.S.-based Netflix had just entered Canada in September 2010 and had hinted about global expansion in the years to come. Johnson was questioning whether Netflix would be able to enter other foreign markets.

He outlined three reasons Netflix's global expansion would not be easy. First, Netflix would face entrenched local competition in the markets in which it might be interested. For example, in Britain it would face LoveFilm,[2] a successful DVD rental firm that had been preparing defensively against Netflix's possible entry into the country by launching its own streaming services and making deals with major movie studios and the retailer, Tesco. Second, it would face a lot of red tape in each country it tried to enter. Finally, Netflix's biggest issue going abroad would be cultural divide, considering that several U.S. firms, such as Craigslist and Yelp, faced difficulties in foreign markets. Johnson concluded, "None of this is to say that Netflix can't succeed, just that it will certainly not be an easy ride... global expansion requires a sales operation, a backbone and an infrastructure." Some of the readers at gigaom.com suggested other issues that Netflix might face such as the need to localize its content and services in each foreign market.

Fast forward to December 2015. Netflix "is the world's leading Internet television network with over 70 million members in over 190 countries enjoying more than 125 million hours of TV shows and movies per day, including original series, documentaries and feature films."[3] Netflix is still not available, however, enter China and some countries where the U.S. government restricts companies from doing business, such as Syria, Crimea, and North Korea.[4] Netflix localizes its content and marketing materials for each major market and even personalizes its offerings for individual subscribers based on user-specific choices such as language, viewing behavior, and taste preferences.

After entering its first foreign market, Canada, in September 2010, Netflix entered other markets in quick succession—Latin America in September 2011, U.K. and Ireland in January 2012, Nordic countries in October 2012, the Netherlands in September 2013, and so on. Netflix offers DVD video rental as well as online streaming services in the U.S., but only the online streaming services in foreign markets. It streams its own content, e.g., its phenomenally successful original series, "House of Cards," and the content it licenses from other media companies, such as Disney, Sony, Turner Broadcasting, Warner Brothers Television Group, and DreamWorks Animation.

How could an editor at a respected research firm be so wrong about a company's globalization prospects? Well, it was not the first time and won't be the last. Predicting the future is a very risky business. Netflix's approach to globalization is instructive, and we will have a chance to return to Netflix again in the rest of the chapter.

Key Issues Facing Firms as They Begin to Go Abroad

The last chapter ended with a series of key issues that firms face as they begin, or continue, their internationalization journey.

1 Why go abroad?
2 Which country (countries) to enter?
3 Which product(s) to internationalize?
4 When to enter? What should be the scale of entry?
5 How to enter foreign markets?
6 How to compete and grow in foreign markets?
7 How to implement global strategy?

This chapter explores the first five of these issues, while the remaining issues will be the subject matter for Chapters 6–10. We discuss each of these five issues separately below, though there is a fair amount of interaction among them. For instance, the mode of entry (how to enter foreign markets) depends a good deal on the country (countries) selected for entry. Countries have all kinds of regulations relating to trade and investment. Some countries allow foreign direct investment only as joint ventures, while others may have other restrictions relating to industries open to FDI and amount of foreign ownership allowed among others.

Why Go Abroad?

The previous chapter identified a number of reasons a firm may want to go abroad, such as the need to grow, to seek resources that may not be available in the home market, to create operational efficiencies, and so on. These are all good reasons, and the firm must seek to explore foreign markets for a valid reason, not for hubris. Thoughtful consideration of the reasons for going abroad will have an impact on the competitive strategy to be adopted and can make a difference between successful and unsuccessful internationalization.

As for Netflix, global expansion had become the company's strategic objective by 2015—for reasons such as the need to continue to grow, to become more efficient, and to source content for its streaming services from the entire world. Though Netflix derived three-fourths of its global revenues in the United States with a high growth rate, its growth in the U.S. domestic market had begun to slow down by December 2014. At the same time, its international growth was rising. For instance, Netflix signed up more subscribers internationally in the third quarter of 2013 than in the U.S. for the first time since its launch in U.K. and Ireland in January 2012. The company needs to grow revenues quickly to be able to develop and license more content, do so cost effectively, and maintain growth—not just because of stock market expectations. Content providers typically license Netflix to stream their content on a country-by-country basis, which is very expensive and time consuming. So, to gain efficiencies as its global network expands, it wants to be able to license content on a global basis. Having new and varied content, especially for local markets worldwide, is essential for Netflix to hold on to its existing subscriber base and to continue adding new subscribers in its existing and new markets—enabling it to benefit from network effects.[5]

Netflix's stated goal is to be in 200 countries by 2016, which is practically the entire world, and to reach annual revenues of $10 billion. Netflix was already available in 190 countries by the end of 2015, according to the company website. In their January 2015 letter to shareholders, as part of the company's Q4 earnings report, Reed Hastings, CEO, and David Wells, CFO, stated:

> Our international expansion strategy over the last few years has been to expand as fast as we can while staying profitable on a global basis. ... With the growth of the Internet over the next 20 years, there will be some amazing entertainment services available globally. We intend to the one of the leaders.[6]

Which Country (Countries) to Enter?

Foreign market selection is a critical step in any firm's internationalization, whether it is starting out on its internationalization journey or planning to enter new markets after having been abroad for some time. Oftentimes, firms' first foreign forays are into markets for reasons of proximity and/or cultural affinity. As an example, Netflix's first entries were into Canada and Latin America. When Walmart decided to go global in the early 1990s, it entered the largest markets in Latin America—Mexico (1991), Brazil (1994), and Argentina

STRATEGY FOR INTERNATIONAL MARKETS

(1995). The same was true for France's retailer Carrefour, whose first international entry in 1973 was into Spain. Similarly, when the Mexican cement giant, CEMEX, decided to go abroad, it chose Spain for reasons of cultural and language affinity.

Another major factor in country selection for Netflix was market size as judged by the extent of Internet adoption and the availability of fast broadband speeds in different countries. Accordingly, among the first foreign markets that Netflix entered outside North America were Western European countries including Britain, Germany, France, and the Nordic countries, all of which have large and growing Internet populations and fast broadband speeds. See also the mini case study on Costco e-commerce (Box 4.1).

Box 4.1 Costco e-Commerce

Costco Wholesale Corporation is a U.S.-based membership warehouse club offering a huge variety of goods and services in the United States and eight foreign countries, including Canada, Mexico, Japan, Taiwan, South Korea, Spain, and the U.K. The company has 672 warehouses (stores) and 72 million members and is the fifth largest retailer in the U.S. and sixth worldwide, with 2014 revenues of $112.6 billion.[1]

While Costco had been selling online in the U.S. and Canada, only in early 2012 did it begin to explore the possibility of selling online in other foreign markets. Costco management was concerned about the challenges the company might face in foreign markets, the additional cost of selling online, whether online operations might cannibalize warehouse sales, whether it might distract local managers from growing their warehouse business, regulatory issues, and so on. The Costco Internet Business Solutions Group (IBSG) was given the responsibility of exploring the online business opportunity, analyzing key countries' online markets, and prioritizing country rollout.

As part of its research, the IBSG interviewed several global e-commerce pioneers, major retailers, consulting firms, and suppliers to understand the best practices in e-commerce rollout and management. These expert interviews revealed that Costco should prioritize its country rollout based on the size of its existing business and the overall size and maturity of the e-commerce market, in prospective countries.

Based on IBSG's findings, Costco decided to launch its e-commerce operations in the U.K. in October 2012. It did so for four main reasons: (1) Costco already had high sales and membership in the country, with presence since 1993; (2) as of 2012, the U.K. was the second largest e-commerce market in the world and was growing very quickly; (3) the U.K. had a sophisticated e-commerce infrastructure, which, along with its supplier network, could be leveraged relatively easily; and (4) having e-commerce operations located in the U.K. could help Costco reach out to online customers on the continent as had been the experience of some other U.K.-based retailers.

Costco's entry into online retailing has been slow relative to the expansion of its physical warehouses worldwide. After its entry into Britain's online market, it began selling online in Mexico and expects to add one more market by 2015. Costco also began selling online in China in October 2014; however, it does so through Alibaba's online marketplace, Tmall.com, China's largest online shopping site, rather than through its own e-commerce site.

During fiscal year 2014 (ending in August), Costco's online sales represented only 3 percent of total revenues but were growing much more quickly and were more profitable than warehouse sales. For instance, online sales during the last quarter of 2014 grew by 21 percent compared to only 6 percent at its physical warehouses.[2]

1 This case study is based on information taken from the company website and: "Costco. com Successfully Expands into United Kingdom in Record Time," Cisco.com, 2013. Accessed from https://www.cisco.com/web/about/ac79/docs/retail/Costco-com_UK.pdf.
2 Stefany Zaroban, "Costco Grows Web Sales 18% in Its Most Recent Quarter and Fiscal Year", *Internet Retailer*, October 13, 2014. Accessed from https://www.internetretailer. com/2014/10/13/costco-grows-web-sales-18-its-most-recent-quarter-and-fis.

Over the years, a number of approaches have been suggested to help companies make the foreign-market-selection decision. These range from PEST, PESTEL, and PESTLE to the CAGE framework. All of these approaches, while making the selection process more systematic than before, suffer from some basic deficiencies in that they are limited in terms of the factors they consider in foreign market selection. For instance, most such models rarely consider "market potential" or "resources," the two factors critical in foreign-market-selection decisions.

The PEST (Political-Economic-Social-Technological) framework helps organizations scan and make sense of the external environment they face in their home market or might face in a prospective foreign market. The factors contained in the PEST framework are essentially beyond a firm's control but are still factors on which the firm must keep an eye during its business operations in foreign markets.[7] Some analysts and consulting firms added other factors to the PEST framework, such as Legal factors (to make SLEPT) and Environmental factors (to make PESTEL or PESTLE), while some others added even more factors to include Ethics and Demographics (to make STEEPLE and STEEPLED, respectively).[8]

A detailed discussion of many of the factors contained in some of these tools is deferred to later in the chapter when the PRISM model is discussed; it has some of the same factors and many more that are relevant for decisions relating to foreign market selection.

The CAGE Framework

In 2001, Pankaj Ghemawat, then of the Harvard Business School, developed the CAGE (Cultural-Administrative-Geographic-Economic distance) framework, which can be used for comparing markets from the perspective of a company in a specific country.[9] For instance, a company from Germany exploring the possibility of going to Argentina versus Brazil can use the framework to see how distant these two countries are from Germany in terms of the CAGE factors. The idea is that the country that is closer to Germany in terms of CAGE factors is the one the company should select for its foreign market entry. According to Ghemawat, "most of the costs and risks [of foreign market entry] result from barriers created by distance."[10] In addition to the geographic distance between countries, Ghemawat is referring to the cultural, administrative, and economic distances between the home and host countries. So, the CAGE framework is about the "distance" of foreign markets from the internationalizing firm's home market along the four dimensions—cultural, administrative, geographic, and economic.

The CAGE Framework: Attributes Creating Distance

Cultural distance: Different languages; different ethnicities; lack of connective ethnic or social networks; different religions; different social norms.

Administrative distance: Absence of colonial ties; absence of shared monetary or political association; political hostility; government policies; institutional weakness.

Geographic distance: Physical remoteness; lack of a common border; lack of sea or river access; size of country; weak transportation or communication links; differences in climate.

Economic distance: Differences in consumer incomes; differences in the cost and quality of natural resources, financial resources, human resources, infrastructure, intermediate inputs, and information or knowledge.

We contend that the CAGE framework misses out on some really important dimensions, especially dimensions related to market potential and competition. Market potential is a most important consideration in foreign market selection, but the CAGE framework does not consider market factors, such as market size, growth rate, market structure, and competition. It does include differences in consumer incomes (e.g., per capita GDP), which is an important attribute, but "market size" may imply something other than GDP for specific industries. In the two cases discussed above, market size was measured by the extent of Internet adoption and broadband availability (for Netflix) and the size of the e-commerce market (for Costco) in prospective countries. The CAGE framework also does not make a distinction between basic and advanced resources à la Michael Porter.[11]

As an alternative to the CAGE framework, presented below is the author's PRISM framework, which uses the prism metaphor to convey an understanding of the differences between nations and how they impact decisions relating to foreign market selection and entry. However, no single framework, no matter how comprehensive, can incorporate every possible factor relevant for foreign market selection for every firm. The PRISM framework incorporates the most important factors relevant in a large variety of situations.

The PRISM Framework

The PRISM framework of foreign market selection (Table 4.1) has the following elements.

P: Political economy
R: Resources
I: Institutions and infrastructure
S: Society and culture
M: Market potential

The PRISM framework does not include "risk" as a specific factor since risk can arise from any of the five factors (P, R, I, etc.). While evaluating the PRISM dimensions, one should always explore the risks posed by each.

Table 4.1 The PRISM Framework

Factor	Description
P	**Political economy**: Political and economic systems, along with the formal institutions embedded within them
R	**Resources**: Basic and advanced resources
I	**Institutions**: Formal and informal institutions **Infrastructure**: Physical, telecommunication, energy, and Internet infrastructure
S	**Society** and **culture**
M	**Market potential**: Market size and growth rate, industry structure, competition, capacity utilization, exports/imports, etc.

P: Political Economy

The term political economy has had many interpretations over the last two centuries. Today, it typically refers to interdisciplinary studies incorporating political science, economics, and law to explain how political and economic systems and legal institutions influence each other. All of these are key factors in evaluating the suitability of a foreign market for entry. Under "P" here, we are concerned with political and economic systems in a country, while the legal institutions are contained in the "I" (Institutions) of the PRISM framework.

Political Systems

A political system is the system of government in a nation, i.e., the formal and informal structures representing a nation's sovereignty (power) over its territory and people.[12] A nation's political system shapes its economic and legal systems, and all three systems present opportunities and risks for businesses operating in the nation. See, for instance, the mini case study on American companies' experiences in China in Chapter 3. Political systems have been classified in many ways by scholars from different disciplines. For our purpose, we classify political systems by the degree to which they are democratic or totalitarian (Figure 4.1).[13]

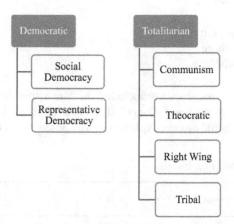

Figure 4.1 A Classification of Political Systems

DEMOCRATIC

A democratic form of government implies a system in which the nation is governed by the people through elected representatives. A *social democracy* is a system whereby a nation attempts to achieve socialist goals through democratic as opposed to authoritarian means (as in communism). In a social democracy, some industries are nationalized, giving rise to state-owned enterprises (SOEs), while the others are left to private enterprise.

In a *representative democracy*, the government is run by the people through their elected representatives—a "government of the people, by the people, for the people" as famously stated by Abraham Lincoln in his Gettysburg Address on November 19, 1863. In a representative democracy, most industries are privately owned and managed. In a democracy, citizens generally enjoy a number of constitutionally guaranteed rights, such as the right to free speech, free media, and limited terms of elected representatives.

TOTALITARIAN

The freedoms enjoyed by citizens in democratic societies are typically denied to citizens in totalitarian regimes. Under totalitarianism, one person, a group of people, or one political party exercises total control over all aspects of human life, and opposition political parties are not allowed. Scholars have identified four types of totalitarian regimes, viz. communist, theocratic, right-wing, and tribal, though the more important for our purpose are states run on communist or theocratic principles.

In a *communist* society, the people in power believe that socialist goals can only be achieved through violent revolution (that's how they came into power) and an authoritarian regime. During the late 1970s, more than half of the world's population lived under communist rule. Today, there are only a few countries that practice communism, such as China, North Korea, Vietnam, and Cuba.

Theocratic totalitarianism is practiced in countries, such as Saudi Arabia, where an individual, group, or a religious sect governs the nation according to religious principles. Citizens in a theocratic state generally do not enjoy the freedom of political and religious expression.

In a *right-wing* totalitarian state, citizens do not have political freedom but have the freedom to pursue their own economic interests. Such a state may be backed or dominated by the country's military. The term "right wing" has also had meanings in history that are different from our definition. In the U.S., for instance, "right wing" refers to the conservative movement in politics. According to our definition, the countries that could be classified as having had a right-wing political system in the 1970s/1980s were South Korea, Singapore, and the Philippines, among others. Today, however, there are practically no right-wing states.

Under *tribal* totalitarianism, a specific tribe in a country with multiple tribes or a political party dominated by a specific tribe, exercises political power and control over its people. A few states in Africa, for instance, have a one-party government—such cases often are instances of tribal totalitarianism.

Economic Systems

An economic system is a system of production and consumption of goods and services as well as the allocation of resources in a nation. The economic systems prevalent in the world today range from (free) market economies to command economies, with an intervening position taken by mixed economies. Economic systems can be visualized as a continuum as shown in the figure below.

Command ←——————————————————→ Market
Economy   Economy

In a *market economy*, all economic decisions (such as what to produce, how to produce, how much to produce, and for whom to produce) are decided by private entrepreneurs and corporations acting in their own interest. What and how much to produce is determined by consumer preferences, how to produce is determined by private producers seeking profit, and for whom to produce is determined by consumers' purchasing power. In other words, all production and resource allocation decisions are determined by market forces. Accordingly, all business is privately owned. The concept of "the invisible hand," proposed by Adam Smith in his 1776 seminal work, *The Wealth of Nations*, is a useful concept to evoke. Smith suggested that if everyone were to pursue his own self-interest, it would be as if there were an invisible hand of the market which would ensure that individuals' actions benefit the society more than if the actions were directly intended to benefit society.

In a *command economy*, the government makes all economic decisions, generally guided by central planning. This is why a command economy is also referred to as a centrally planned economy. All businesses are owned by the state and run as state-owned enterprises (SOEs)—in the interest of the people—and all property is owned by the state.

In a *mixed economy*, some sectors of the economy are state owned and some are privately owned. Today, there's no *pure* market economy or *pure* command economy. All economies are mixed economies, though the balance between private and public sectors varies widely. In some countries, such as the U.S., much of the economic activity is controlled by private interests; as such, the U.S. would be positioned toward the far right of the continuum shown above and is effectively a free-market economy. In China, while the government has been giving a good deal of economic freedom (but not political freedom) to its citizens, the economy is still largely controlled by it. Under these conditions, China would be positioned toward the left side of the continuum, though no longer positioned at the extreme left.

Implications of Political Economy in Foreign Market Selection

While performing PRISM analysis for a country, the analyst should explore questions such as those listed below. This is not a comprehensive list; the specific questions to be explored will depend on the country being analyzed and the prospective entrant's line(s) of business. The idea of the exercise is to identify potential opportunities and risks in host markets and to understand how different they are from the firm's home market.

- What kinds of political and economic systems does the country have? What are the implications for business, especially for foreign companies doing business in the country?
- Who are the major power brokers in the country, and what are their views on foreign business?
- How stable is the country politically and economically?
- Does the country face any potential political or economic threats—internally or externally?

R: Resources

The resources available in a foreign market can be classified in many ways, e.g.,

- Tangible, intangible, and human
- Physical, technological, capital, human, etc.
- Basic and advanced factors (as in Porter's Diamond)

Why do so many multinational firms set up manufacturing plants in China or in-house IT service centers in India? They do so partly because of the availability of specialized human resources and talent there, not simply any human resources. The *mantra* for smart companies today is "we go where the talent is," not just "we go where the market is." For at least two decades, California's Silicon Valley has been a magnet for IT firms from through-out the world. It offers many of the resources that IT firms need, such as talent (the IT workforce in the Silicon Valley region), capital (most of the prominent venture capital firms have operations there), technology, and pre-mier research and higher education institutions (Stanford University and University of California at Berkeley—to name just two) that are a continu-ing source of technology and talent. Besides, Silicon Valley has successful diaspora populations from several nations (e.g., India, China, Taiwan, Korea) that can be tapped by prospective entrants from those nations. In fact, accord-ing to AnnaLee Saxenian, Dean and Professor in the School of Information at Berkeley, "Silicon Valley is known as the home of the IC, or integrated circuit. But when local technologists say 'Silicon Valley is built on ICs,' they refer not to chips, but to Indian and Chinese engineers."[14] Some of the other frameworks cited earlier, such as PEST and PESTEL, do not consider resources at all in their formulations.

As discussed in the previous chapter, Michael Porter makes the useful distinction among basic resources, such as a country's demographics and nat-ural resources, and advanced resources that are created through the efforts of governments, industries, firms, and individuals.[15] While exploring the potential of different markets, looking at demographics (e.g., population and socioeconomic indicators) and natural resources is not quite enough; skilled labor, technology, research and higher education institutions, and other *man-made* resources must be considered as well. The kinds of resources to be assessed in PRISM analysis depend on the industry in which the firm operates. For instance, a firm in the automotive industry would want to know whether the country/region being targeted has the kinds of skilled shop-floor manpower and engineering talent it would need, high quality engineering schools, certification agencies, and other kinds of human resources needed for an automotive-industry firm. The firm would, of course, also need business development, sales, marketing, finance, and many other professionals, which are often more readily available than engineers.

In performing PRISM analysis, it is useful to list the specific resources (e.g., talent, technology, capital, and research and higher education institutions) available in a prospective host market, especially those sought by the entrant.

I: Institutions and Infrastructure

INSTITUTIONS

Institutions provide the context for individual and corporate behavior in societies and nations and must be considered while making foreign-market-selection decisions. Institutions are the "rules of the game" often devised by people in positions of power or authority, such as a nation's parliament or the ruling political elite. They may incorporate economic incentives so that people (and organizations) are encouraged to follow them, as well as penalties to discourage people from violating them. Thus, institutions both enable and constrain behavior. They tell prospective entrants how to conduct business in a host market and provide them with definitive information on what they might expect there.

The term "institutions," which has had a long history in social sciences, has been defined variously by scholars from different disciplines. Two of the prominent definitions are by Douglas North and Geoffrey Hodgson. According to North, institutions are the "rules of the game in society, or, more formally, are the humanly devised constraints that shape human interaction."[16] And, according to Hodgson, institutions are the "durable systems of established and embedded social rules that structure social interactions rather than rules as such. In short, institutions are *social rule systems*, not simply rules"[17] (emphasis in the original).

Institutions arise in politics (e.g., "rules" codified in a nation's constitution), economics (e.g., property rights and contract enforcement), and law (e.g., various laws and regulations). Needless to say, a firm doing business in a foreign market must familiarize itself with, and follow, the rules, laws, and regulations of the host market. Institutions can be "formal" (e.g., rules codified into laws and regulations, such as laws against corruption) or "informal" (e.g., unwritten rules or folkways). Formal institutions (codified rules) are central to the functioning of a society, and violations can invite serious consequences. Informal rules or folkways, on the other hand, are the unwritten conventions of everyday life in a society, such as dress code and social manners. An example of the latter is the practice of siesta in some countries. They often have no moral significance and violations are generally not serious.[18]

Tarun Khanna and Krishna Palepu of the Harvard Business School proposed an innovative definition of "emerging markets." According to them, an emerging market is one that does not have strong institutions or where institutions are not adequately enforced, a nation with "institutional voids." The existence of factors such as corruption, excessive red tape, inability to enforce contracts, inability to enforce one's intellectual property rights, etc., can lead to persistent difficulties in doing business in a host market. On the other hand, "in developed markets, a range of specialized intermediaries provides the requisite information and contract enforcement needed to consummate transactions."[19]

For a company planning to enter an emerging market, knowing about its institutional environment and the opportunities and risks it might entail before actual entry is absolutely essential. For instance, a firm whose core competence is its intellectual property (IP) should think hard before entering a country that has a poor record of safeguarding foreign companies' IP rights, or perhaps enter using an entry mode (such as greenfield investment, rather than a joint venture or licensing) that may pose a lesser risk of loss of IP.

While performing PRISM analysis, some of the institutions-focused questions to be considered are:

- Are there any specific regulations (regarding FDI, local content requirements, corporate social responsibility, customer protection, taxation, IP, etc.) that could impact a foreign firm's business in the country? Could any pending legislations have material impact on foreign firms' business there?
- How well developed are the country's laws relating to property rights, corruption, etc., and how effectively are they enforced?

INFRASTRUCTURE

In a proposed host market, the second "I" of the PRISM framework is also very important and includes the usual dimensions (transportation and communication networks, utilities, telecommunication networks, etc.) that are critical for the success of most businesses. In specific situations, firms should be concerned about the availability of the infrastructure elements important to them. For example, a company selling fast moving consumer goods (FMCGs) or machine tools will want to know whether a prospective country has adequate road, railroad, and port infrastructures. A company like Netflix is concerned about the availability of fast broadband in prospective foreign markets. A company wanting to locate its data center in a foreign market is concerned about the continuous availability of electric power there because data centers consume huge amounts of electric power. A *New York Times* study in 2012 found that data centers consume vast amounts of energy, of which 90 percent or more is wasted since they run the centers at maximum capacity, 24/7, irrespective of actual demand. "Worldwide, the digital warehouses use about 30 billion watts of electricity, roughly equivalent to the output of 30 nuclear power plants, according to estimates industry experts compiled for The Times."[20]

The institutions/infrastructure analysis will include both qualitative and quantitative measures. The analyst must also identify any "institutional voids" that might exist in a country. If an institutional void exists with respect to a specific (political/economic/legal) institution, it is usually manifested as a lack of some intermediaries related to that institution. For instance, institutional voids in a nation's product market infrastructure can be assessed through questions such as:[21]

- Can companies easily obtain reliable data on customer tastes and purchase behavior?
- How strong is the logistics, transportation, and ICT infrastructure?
- Is it difficult for multinationals to collect accounts receivables from local retailers?
- What recourse do consumers have against false claims by companies?

S: Society and Culture

A country's social fabric and culture (or cultures) are important factors in foreign market selection since they have a major impact on entering firms' business practices and their competitive and growth strategies there. Most models (PEST, PESTEL, CAGE, etc.) include this dimension. Cross-cultural and cross-national understanding *and* sensitivity are crucial for international business, as they are in fact for any business anywhere in today's connected world.

The term *culture* represents "a system of values and norms that are shared among a group of people and when taken together constitute a design for living."[22] More broadly, culture consists of values, norms, customs, attitudes, and the beliefs of a group of people, and which distinguish it from other groups. A *society* is a group of people who share the same culture.

There is no one-to-one correspondence between society and nation state. A nation may contain a single society or several societies, and a specific society may span across several nations. For instance, we may talk about the Arab society, which exists across most countries in the Middle East. Similarly, a country may have several societies within its borders. In the U.S., for instance, there are German-Americans, Irish-Americans, Chinese-Americans, Indian-Americans, Mexican-Americans, and so on, each representing a specific society. The People's Republic of China has over 55 officially recognized ethnic groups, each with a more or less distinct identity, though the Han group represents about 92 percent of Mainland China's total population, and even more in Hong Kong.

In exploring why the cultures of Russia and the United States are different, Professor Maria Carlson[23] of the University of Kansas makes the following observations:

- Russians have specific geographical conditions and logistic problems (different from ours), and they solve them differently;
- Russians have their own historical record (what happened to them didn't happen to us, and vice versa); thus their religion, political structures, social evolution, and cultural development are different;
- Russians have their own values, beliefs, and priorities that arise from their record, their language, their experience, and their conditions (none of which we share).

Further, Carlson says that, "in order to understand why things are this way now, we have to go back and understand the context from which they emerged. Because context and continuity are everything."

High-Context vs. Low-Context Cultures

To describe the social and cultural context of a nation, it is useful, especially from a business perspective, to identify the nation as having a "high-context" or a "low-context" culture.[24] Some cultures are high-context cultures, like Chinese, Arabic, Slavic, and Spanish, while some are low-context cultures, like Anglo-American, German, and Scandinavian. Most countries can be placed somewhere along the high-context–low-context continuum shown below.[25]

Low-Context
Cultures

High-Context
Cultures

This is a very broad-brush distinction, however, and not everyone and every interaction in a particular culture could be described by the kinds of characteristics (stereotypes) described below. Besides, each culture has both high-context and low-context elements. India, for instance, will be positioned somewhere toward the high-context end of the continuum.

HIGH-CONTEXT CULTURES

A high-context culture evolves when a group of people have had a very long history together, forging close connections over long periods of time, so much so that not everything in their daily interactions needs to be explicit. Most people know how to behave and what to expect of others from years of interactions with each other, as if they have been living in a small town where everyone knows everyone else. In other words, they can "read between the lines." History, tradition, and language are important in high-context cultures. "In our relationship with them, *we* cannot ignore *their* history, since they themselves do not view any single event in their personal, communal, professional, or national lives as an isolated event; everything is contextualized by shared history, shared experience, shared kinship, shared friendship, shared enmities, and/or shared prejudices…. In high-context cultures, written contracts and formal agreements are of lesser importance; the culture itself provides alternative enforcement mechanisms (Russian culture, for example, uses shame, fear, personal friendship, honor, loyalty, and obligation to enforce agreements)."[26]

LOW-CONTEXT CULTURES

In a low-context culture, people have also had many connections, but of shorter duration, and some could indeed be impersonal in nature. People tend to play by the rules, which are often explicit and public—with the task being often more important than relationships. They think of the present and the future, rather than of the past. Written agreements and contracts are more important than verbal agreements, and, in fact, form the basis for future transactions between companies from different countries.

A low-context culture may be easier to enter for a company than a high-context culture because an outsider can get on with the task at hand rather than first trying to develop deep relationships. For instance, in a high-context culture like in France or Japan, business dealings are often preceded by much wining and dining. In China, a high-context culture, the role of *guanxi* (connections or relationships) is pre-eminent in business dealings. In a low-context culture like Germany or the United States, business can be done without first getting to know each other very much (though it is always a good idea to get to know prospective partners, customers, etc., before beginning to interact with them).

Hofstede's Cultural Dimensions

Another framework for diagnosing culture was suggested by Geert Hofstede, a Dutch social psychologist who worked for the IBM Corporation where he conducted an employee attitude survey at company locations worldwide between 1967 and 1973. Based on this research, which included some 100,000 survey respondents, Hofstede concluded that a nation's culture could be classified into four dimensions: power distance, individualism vs. collectivism, uncertainty avoidance, and masculinity vs. femininity. His research provided quantitative estimates for these dimensions for 50 countries and was later extended to include two more dimensions—long-term orientation vs. short-term orientation, and indulgence vs. restraint. Though dated and often criticized, this is the most comprehensive study of cultures ever undertaken and has been used by scholars in thousands of research studies see Table 4.2 for data on the four dimensions.[27]

POWER DISTANCE

Reflects people's attitudes toward inequality in their society or country. It is the extent to which the less powerful members of a society expect and accept unequal distribution of power, such as between superiors and subordinates, between teachers and students, and so on. In a high power-distance country, subordinates may accept their superiors' orders without question, and companies tend to use centralized decision making. The power-distance scale ranges from zero in countries with practically no power distance among its people to 100 in countries where power distance is at the maximum.

INDIVIDUALISM VS. COLLECTIVISM

In countries high on individualism, people tend to be self-directed and take personal initiative. They work better as individuals than as part of teams and prefer their employers to offer incentives based on individual performance instead of team-based incentives. In a collectivist country, people belong to groups and look after each other in exchange for loyalty. The individualism-collectivism scale ranges from zero in countries high on collectivism to 100 in countries high on individualism.

UNCERTAINTY AVOIDANCE

Uncertainty avoidance in a country reflects peoples' desire to avoid ambiguous situations and risks. They tend to have a high need for security and prefer written rules and instructions to unstructured work assignments. In a low uncertainty-avoidance country, people tend to be more ambitious and exhibit greater willingness to take risks. The uncertainty-avoidance scale ranges from zero in countries where people are willing and able to handle ambiguous situations to 100 in countries where people exhibit the greatest level of uncertainty avoidance.

MASCULINITY VS. FEMININITY

Hofstede defines countries high on masculinity as those where the dominant social values are money, success, and possessions. People tend to place great importance on recognition, challenge, and wealth. Work roles tend to be sharply differentiated by gender. In countries high on femininity, the dominant social values are quality of life and caring for others, and work roles are not differentiated by gender. People tend to place great importance on cooperation and friendly work and life environment. The masculinity-femininity scale ranges from zero in countries very high on femininity to 100 in countries very high on masculinity.

Table 4.2 provides quantitative estimates for the four Hofstede dimensions for a selection of both developed and developing nations. Check to see if these numbers seem to match your understanding of cultures of these countries.

Table 4.2 Hofstede's Dimensions for Selected G20 and EU Countries

Country	Power Distance	Uncertainty Avoidance	Individualism	Masculinity
Argentina	49	86	46	56
Australia	36	51	90	61
Brazil	69	76	38	49
Canada	39	48	80	52
China	80	20	66	30
Denmark	18	23	74	16
France	68	86	71	43
Germany	35	65	67	66
India	77	40	48	56
Indonesia	78	48	14	46
Italy	50	76	75	70
Japan	54	92	46	95
Mexico	81	82	30	69
Netherlands	38	53	80	14
Russia	93	39	36	95
Saudi Arabia	95	80	25	60
South Korea	60	85	18	39
Spain	57	86	51	42
Sweden	31	29	71	5
Turkey	66	85	37	45
United Kingdom	35	35	89	66
United States	40	46	91	62

Source: Accessed from http://geert-hofstede.com/.

M: Market Potential

No firm can expect to enter and be successful in a foreign market without an in-depth understanding of market potential and market dynamics in the host nation. Measures to assess the market potential of a prospective foreign market include market size and growth rate, industry structure, competition and rivalry, level of economic development, capacity utilization, exports/imports, etc. These factors are missing in the foreign-market-selection models (PEST, CAGE, etc.) mentioned earlier.

It is appropriate to use a country's population size or GDP to measure its market potential for some products. However, for a lot of goods and services, market size must be defined differently. For instance, for a company selling machine tools, market size could be defined as the number of companies in the foreign market that could potentially use its machine tools in their own production processes. Official statistics for many countries provide such information. As we saw earlier, market size could be defined as the number of Internet users in a country for companies like Costco and Netflix. The analyst will need to be creative in finding the correct measure for market size for the specific industry under consideration. Along with market size, it is also important to know how fast the market is growing in the host country (see Box 4.2 for a mini case study of Mary Kay Cosmetics' entry into Japan and China).

Box 4.2 Mary Kay Cosmetics Inc.

In 1992, Mary Kay Cosmetics Inc. (MKC) was a billion dollar company, with about 11 percent of its annual revenue derived from foreign markets, compared to 55 percent of the $3.6 billion in revenue for its major competitor, Avon Products Inc., which also relied on the direct-selling method. MKC executives were evaluating further expansion into Asia, specifically entry into Japan and/or China. (The company had previously entered Thailand in 1988 and Taiwan in 1991.) Japan was an established market for cosmetics but was growing at only three percent a year, while China represented a very small but rapidly growing market for cosmetics. Japan's population in 1992 was 124 million with high purchasing power, compared to China's 1.139 billion with very low purchasing power. The total market size for cosmetics in Japan was $9.3 billion, versus $825 million in China. Avon was the only direct-selling company that had entered China by then, and its sales had doubled from $4 million in 1991 to $8 million in 1992. In addition to market size and growth rate, MKC executives also considered other factors in foreign-market-selection decisions, such as competition, cost of entry, and the acceptance and potential success of their party plan method of direct selling.[1] Based on much analysis, MKC decided to enter both Japan and China—Japan in 1994 and China in 1995.

Fast forward to 2008. Over half of Mary Kay Inc.'s (MKI's) total sales of $2.8 billion came from abroad, with China as its second most important national market. MKI exited the Japanese market in 2001 because of legal restrictions, cultural mismatch, the need to reformulate (customize) its products, and because low prices did not quite appeal to the Japanese market. (Avon also exited the country for somewhat similar reasons, but in 2010.) When the Chinese government banned direct selling in 1998, MKC was the only direct-selling company to survive the ban (which was lifted in 2005).[2] The moral of the story is: Market size and growth rate are both important in foreign-market-selection decisions, and a country's population and GDP are often poor indicators of market size or potential.

1 John A. Quelch and Nathalie Laidler, "Mary Kay Cosmetics: Asian Market Entry (A)," Harvard Business School Publishing Case Study, 1994 (Revised June 2009). Product Number: 9-594-023.
2 John A. Quelch, "Mary Kay Inc.: Asian Market Entry (B)," Harvard Business School Publishing Case Study, 2009. Product Number: 9-509-067.

The term *industry structure* refers to the number and size distribution of firms in an industry. The number of firms in an industry in a country may run into hundreds, thousands, or more. If all firms in an industry are small in size, relative to the size of the industry, it is a *fragmented* industry. If a few firms control a large share of the industry's output or sales, it is a *consolidated* (or *concentrated*) industry, often referred to as an oligopoly. Industry structure between "fragmented" and "consolidated" can be visualized as a continuum, with different industries positioned at different points on the continuum. On the extreme left side of the continuum are industries with literally hundreds or thousands of firms, each taking a negligible share of the market; these are referred to as *perfectly competitive* industries or markets.[28] On the extreme right side of the continuum are industries dominated by a single seller or by monopolies. Oligopolies are industries positioned toward the right end of the continuum.

Fragmented   Consolidated
Industries   Industries

A good, intuitive measure of industry structure is the **four-firm concentration ratio**, denoted as **CR4**, which is the combined share of market held by the four largest firms in the industry. A CR4 of 40% or higher represents a consolidated industry, or an oligopoly. The larger the value of CR4, the more consolidated the industry.

Another measure of industry concentration is the **Herfindahl-Hirschman Index** (HHI), which actually provides a better understanding of industry concentration than CR4. The HHI is computed using the sum of squares of the market shares of all firms in an industry, typically the largest 50 firms in the industry. The HHI ranges from zero to 10,000 points, with a score of zero for a completely fragmented industry (a perfectly competitive market) and 10,000 for a monopoly. It is the measure used by the U.S. Federal Trade Commission (FTC) and the Department of Justice to decide on merger and acquisition applications in the United States. Their objective is to make sure that, with the combination of two competing firms, the industry structure does not get so consolidated that the combined firm could hurt consumer or competitor interests. These agencies generally consider markets in which the HHI is between 1,500 and 2,500 points to be moderately concentrated, and markets in which the HHI is in excess of 2,500 points to be highly concentrated.[29] A CR4 of 60 percent or more (HHI of 2,000 or more) represents a tight oligopoly with significant opportunities for dominant firms to exercise market power. A CR4 of 90 percent or more (HHI of over 8,000) represents a highly consolidated industry, with one firm being effectively the market leader.

In the United States, the U.S. Census Bureau does an economic census of industries every five years and publishes concentration ratios (e.g., CR4 and

Table 4.3 Concentration Ratios and HHI for Selected Manufacturing Industries, 2007 (Based on the Value of Shipments)

NAICS Code	Industry Description	No. of Companies	CR4 (%)	CR8 (%)	HHI (50)
311	Food Manufacturing	21,355	14.8	22.8	102.1
311111	Dog and Cat Food Manufacturing	199	71.0	83.5	2,325.1
311230	Breakfast Cereal Manufacturing	35	80.4	91.9	2,425.5
339	Miscellaneous Manufacturing	30,934	10.1	15.4	52.4
339920	Sporting and Athletic Goods Manufacturing	1,808	27.0	37.7	253.4
339992	Musical Instruments Manufacturing	580	32.2	49.4	404.6

Source: 2007 Economic Census of the United States, accessed from https://www.census.gov/econ/concentration.html.
Note: The NAICS Codes are based on the industry classification system used in North America.

CR8) and the HHI (based on the largest 50 companies in the nation) for all industries—manufacturing, trade, services, etc. Such measures may also be available for many other countries. Table 4.3 shows a sampling of manufacturing industries and their concentration ratios as well as the HHI for the latest available year.

Analyzing the structure of an industry reveals a good deal about competition, rivalry, entry barriers, and other aspects of competitive dynamics in that industry. For instance, the type of competition in fragmented industries is generally very different from that in consolidated industries. Consolidated industries are often mature industries with a few dominant firms and high entry barriers.

Along with market size, growth rate, and industry structure, identifying who the actual competitors are (e.g., domestic, foreign, SOEs), the values of imports and exports of the industry in question, capacity utilization, and other factors relevant for assessing market potential in the country being analyzed are also very important.

A Systematic Approach

The PRISM framework is a systematic and comprehensive approach for analyzing foreign markets. It can be customized for use in practically any industry and for any host-home country pair. Firms that explore foreign markets systematically, prior to entry, have a greater chance of success than those that do not. In a study of 68 firms that went abroad, Yip, Biscarri, and Monti found that firms that approached internationalization using a systematic methodology had stronger performance compared to those that did not.[30]

Given how comprehensive the PRISM framework is, no firm would want to use it as a preliminary step in its search for markets to enter; rather a three-step process for identifying the market(s) for future entry is recommended.

Step 1

Initial screening—designed to narrow down the number of markets to 2–3 countries to be included in Step 2 (PRISM) analysis. This can be done through brainstorming within the management team, learning from the experiences of other firms in the industry that went abroad, active participation in industry trade association activities, and participation in international trade fairs, among other possible approaches.

Step 2

Apply the PRISM framework to the 2–3 countries identified in Step 1, comparing them with the home country, and ranking them in terms of market potential and risk in each.

Step 3

Since foreign market entry is a very costly and often risky decision, the final step should ideally involve actual visits to the selected countries and matching company resources and capabilities with the market opportunities and risks presented by them.

The Appendix to this chapter provides an annotated list of key data sources that can be utilized to assess the factors included in the PRISM framework.

Which Product(s) to Internationalize?

Most firms today have multiple products or product lines and must decide which of those products to consider internationalizing when going abroad for the first time or entering a new market after having been abroad for some time. The decision can be easy as in the case of Netflix when it began its internationalization journey in 2010. Netflix had (and still has) only two products[31] in the U.S. market—a DVD video rental service and online streaming of television and other video programs. The DVD video rental service requires huge investments in inventory and logistics, which would be very expensive and difficult to manage in foreign countries. So, when Netflix decided to go abroad, it decided to only offer online streaming. For most other companies, however, the choice is not so simple.

Haier, a $30 billion home appliance company from China that sells a full range of appliances in the kitchen, home entertainment, laundry, and home comfort (e.g., air-conditioning) categories, is now almost a household name in dozens of countries in the Americas, Europe, Asia, and Australia. However, merely two decades ago, the company was little known outside China. Haier began internationalization in the early 1990s as a contract manufacturer (an original equipment manufacturer or OEM) for multinational brands in the U.K., Germany, France,

88

and Italy. The company's *mantra* was if you can succeed in highly competitive developed markets, it will be easy to succeed in lesser developed markets. Haier began selling refrigerators in Germany as an OEM for the Liebherr brand in 1991. When the refrigerators manufactured by Haier for Liebherr beat out Liebherr brand refrigerators in a blind test, the company decided to start marketing the product under its own brand name.

Haier entered the U.S. market in 1994 with a niche product—compact refrigerators for student dormitories and offices—a category neglected by the existing competitors. The entry into the U.S., designed to avoid head-on competition with the entrenched companies making major home appliances, was as an OEM for Welbilt Appliances of New York. Once the compact refrigerator became successful, Haier began to introduce its other products in the U.S. market. In 1999, Haier entered into a joint venture with Welbilt to sell a broader selection of Haier products in the U.S. and, encouraged by its continuing market success, established a $40 million industrial park and refrigerator factory in South Carolina in 2001. The U.S. eventually became Haier's most important foreign market. "After we were successful in the niche products, then we started to introduce regular products to the U.S., like the full-sized refrigerator freezers, air-conditioners, and washing machines," according to Diao Yunfeng of Haier's Overseas Promotion Division.[32]

When Sony Corporation entered the U.S. market in the early 1950s, they entered with a transistor radio that could fit in a pocket, a product initially developed in the U.S. but which no one else was making. According to Sony's co-founder Akio Morita in a 1971 *Time* magazine interview, "I knew we needed a weapon to break through to the US market, and it had to be something different. Something that nobody else was making."[33]

This strategy whereby a company enters a foreign market with a niche product so as to not get in the way of major competitors there, and then slowly expands its product range once its initial offering becomes successful, makes a lot of sense. Future success depends on "first impressions" in a market, as in a job interview or going on a date. Making a very good first impression with a quality product and smart strategy, before considering expanding the product portfolio in a foreign market, is essential for future success.

Companies with significant managerial, organizational, and financial resources, however, do not necessarily need to enter a foreign market with a niche product. If they have the resources and the mindset, they should consider a stronger entry once they have learned enough about the market. Obviously they should take only those products to a foreign market for which there's sufficient demand there. Questions relating to whether and to what extent a product and a company's strategy should be customized for each foreign market are discussed in the next chapter, under "the globalization-localization dilemma."

A novel approach to deciding which product to internationalize is to identify if a prospective host market suffers any institutional voids that it could fill with its own products. Institutional voids are not only challenges a company faces in a foreign market but also a source of potential opportunity it could leverage.[34]

Learning About Foreign Markets

As Akio Morita says in the opening quote to this chapter, a firm must learn much about a foreign market before making a commitment to it. Entering and succeeding in foreign markets is a race to learn; the firm that learns the most and the fastest has the best chance of success. So, how can a firm embark on a learning journey about a foreign market?

Going on a trade delegation to, or attending a trade fair in, a prospective host market is one of the best means of learning about the market. This offers an opportunity to see what exists there and even an opportunity to talk to competitors, wholesalers, etc., in an *incognito* mode if so preferred. Much information about a host market can also be gained from trade magazines and online sources such as trade association websites in the host market, as well as other online sources.

The commerce departments in the home country at national, state, and local levels are usually excellent sources of information about foreign markets. The U.S. Department of Commerce, for instance, is perhaps the world's most valuable resource for companies everywhere, not just for U.S. companies. In addition to providing much valuable information about foreign markets, it offers low-cost services for American companies interested in exploring foreign markets. For instance, its Gold Key Matchmaking Service helps arrange prescreened introductions and meetings for U.S. companies in foreign markets—at a nominal cost. Similarly, joining an international trade association, or a bilateral chamber of commerce in the home country, can be an excellent means of learning about specific foreign markets.

Another approach to learning about a foreign market is to engage a consultant to research the foreign market for its products or do its own research and analysis. It should also try to learn what its home-based competitors are doing in the foreign market of interest to it (see also Chapter 8).

When to Enter? What Should Be the Scale of Entry?

After deciding which market(s) to enter, and with which specific product(s), the company must now decide the timing of entry (as an early mover or a late mover) and the scale of entry (foothold versus toehold entry). Each option has both positives and negatives.

Timing of Entry

Foreign market entry is early if a firm enters a market ahead of other foreign firms or before there is established demand for its products there. Entry is late if the firm enters after other foreign firms are already established in that market. Entering early in a market bestows first-mover advantages on the firm. These include the ability to preempt potential rivals from capturing customers and demand, ability to preempt valuable resources (e.g., key employees) from access by rivals, establishing brand equity and market position, building marketplace relationships, and creating other entry barriers for later arrivals into the market. Early entry also offers an opportunity for the firm to build capacity, even ahead of demand, and thus derive economies of scale and learning curve benefits.

Early entry is especially valuable for products that exhibit network effects and/ or for products with more or less certain demand growth. Cisco Systems of the United States, the maker of Internet and telecommunication networking equipment, entered foreign markets early because of public and private investments in Internet infrastructure worldwide and the liberalization of the telecom industry in the 1990s. Cisco products also enjoyed network effects. As a result, the demand for Cisco products was certain to grow. Starting in 1997, the company began establishing Cisco Networking Academies in practically all of its markets as a means of educating the nascent IT workforce. Currently, more than 9,000 educational institutions in over 170 countries that offer the Networking Academy curriculum.

However, being a first mover also has disadvantages such as that the first mover must incur pioneering costs (e.g., the cost of educating customers and building a distribution system for entirely new products), face a greater risk of failure (since the firm may lack understanding of the "rules of the game" in an unfamiliar territory), risk piracy of its intellectual property, and risk latecomers' taking a free ride on its investments in educating customers and developing a distribution system. If the market does not develop as expected, or if the first mover is not able to successfully leverage the opportunity, it may also suffer from a "lock-in/lock-out" effect. Since foreign market investments are generally major investments that are difficult, if not impossible, to reverse without much cost, the first mover may be locked into a foreign market and get locked out of other potential opportunities that may arise later. While Cisco has done extremely well internationally, being a first mover it did suffer some of the disadvantages. The company's success gave rise to competitors, such as Huawei of China, who took a free ride on Cisco's investments. Huawei was also able to lure engineers trained by Cisco and was even charged with infringing upon some of Cisco's intellectual property.[35]

Scale of Entry

Along with timing of entry, the firm must also decide whether it wants to make a major commitment to a foreign market with the aim of achieving a foothold in the market or treat it more as a learning opportunity through a small, toehold investment. Making a significant investment in a foreign market is often associated with superior performance there. For instance, "industrial economists have demonstrated that costly-to-reverse commitments to durable, specialized factors are necessary for sustained differences in the performance of competing organizations."[36] Apart from the possibility of achieving superior performance, the advantage of a major commitment is that it sends a signal to the host government, to competitors, and to other stakeholders about its intentions for the market. Most jurisdictions welcome foreign direct investments, which typically lead to jobs and taxation revenues, among other benefits of inward FDI.

As an example of a major commitment, DuPont of the United States (E.I. du Pont de Nemours and Company) announced plans in the early 1990s to make major investments in manufacturing facilities in Spain during the decade. This was also a signal to competitors to stay off the Spanish market, unless they were willing to match DuPont's proposed billion dollar investment there. For DuPont, Spain offered an attractive investment opportunity in light of its membership of the European Union (EU), which it had joined in 1986 (then called the European Economic Community), and because it was still a lower-cost country compared to most other EU member states at the time.

DuPont's first investment in Spain was in a flagship plant to manufacture synthetic fiber in Asturias, Northern Spain, accomplished with assistance from the Spanish government and the EU. The investment reinvigorated a formerly declining region in Spain and reinforced DuPont's commitment to the EU market as well as to environmental sustainability; DuPont arranged to plant some 160,000 trees and shrubs to restore the region's original habitat. Later, in 1996 and 1999, two more plants were added in the region. Because Asturias offered easy access to the rest of the EU market, DuPont made it a center for specialty services and corporate finance. According to the company website, much of the success in Spain is attributable to DuPont's community relations efforts. The mid-1990s also saw DuPont making record profits after several years of declining profits (from $2.5 billion in 1989 to $0.6 billion in 1993); profits in 1996 rose to $3.6 billion. The company's stock price also surged, from a low of about $15 in 1990 to a high of almost $50 in 1996. This was a result of several factors, including major corporate restructuring and international investments such as those in Spain.[37]

A toehold entry on the other hand has the advantage of allowing a firm to learn about a new foreign market, without opening itself up to significant risks, and can also set the stage for it to increase its commitment to the market in the future. A toehold entry can be accomplished via exporting/importing, purchasing of a very small percentage of the stock of a potential future acquisition target, a minority joint venture, and licensing, among other possible entry mode choices. There is a good deal of research in M&A literature about toehold investments in prospective acquisition targets, which is beyond the scope of this book.

How to Enter Foreign Markets

Finally, we come to the topic of entry strategy for foreign markets. The possible entry mode choices available to a prospective entrant are: exporting (and importing); licensing; franchising; foreign direct investment, including both partly and wholly owned subsidiaries; and strategic alliances. Exporting/importing, licensing, franchising, and strategic alliances are non-equity modes of foreign market entry (i.e., a company going abroad through such modes does not have to necessarily invest in physical assets in a host market). Foreign direct investment, whether a joint venture or a wholly owned subsidiary, by definition implies investment in physical assets abroad. FDI is the costliest and the riskiest means of doing business abroad, because it can take a significant amount of time to accomplish it, and anything can potentially go wrong during that time, and because such investments are typically large and mostly non-reversible. Each approach has its pluses and minuses, which are briefly discussed below.

Exporting/Importing

This is often the first approach many companies take when they begin their internationalization journey. It is a cost-effective, low-risk approach to internationalization and offers opportunities for a firm to get its feet wet in a foreign market and start learning the nitty-gritty of doing business there. This is especially true if the company is involved in *direct* exporting/importing rather than *indirect* exporting/importing; the latter implies using a third party to consummate the actual transactions. It is a non-equity entry mode, unless the firm decides to invest in setting up its own branch office, a buying office, and/or a servicing operation in a foreign market. If successful, it can set the stage for further commitment to the market. Exporting/importing is beneficial when the value-to-weight ratio of a product is high and when there are low trade barriers (in the host market for imports and in the home market for exports).

Disadvantages can arise when using an agent or a distributor (indirect exporting/importing) over whose actions the firm may have little control. Host-country regulations regarding international trade, such as tariffs and as local content requirements, can also pose challenges for foreign firms.

The Carlsberg Group of Denmark, the fourth largest brewer in the world, has a major presence in Western Europe, Eastern Europe, and Asia. It started exporting beer to China in the mid-19th century and strengthened its presence in the country through a range of investments from 1980s to 2010. Other than Western Europe, Eastern Europe, and Asia, the company competes in the rest of the world through exporting and licensing agreements.

Licensing

A cross-border licensing agreement gives a foreign company the right to produce and sell the parent firm's goods in its market. Under licensing, a company (the licensor) grants the rights to its intellectual property (patents, trademarks, copyrights, designs, etc.) to another company (the licensee) for a certain period of time in return for royalties. The royalties can be payable as a one-time lump sum or as a percentage of sales (which is more common) by the licensee during the term of the license. A licensing agreement typically specifies the geographic area where the licensee can sell the products manufactured under license using the licensor's brand name. Since it does not involve an investment by the licensor, it can be an easier, less risky means of foreign market entry for some products, especially if a host market restricts inward FDI, if the company does not have the managerial, organizational, and financial resources to invest in foreign markets, or for other strategic reasons. For instance, Britain's PPS Rotaprint Ltd. recently licensed an Indian company, Swifts Limited, to manufacture small offset printing machines for sale in India.

Licensing can pose serious risks for the IP owner if a licensee misuses the IP rights granted to it by the owner or produces a shoddy product giving the brand a bad name. The licensor cannot generally keep tight control over the actions of its foreign licensees. There is also always a risk that by licensing its IP, a company might be creating a future competitor. As such, licensing is not advisable for companies whose core competence is technology and knowhow. Box 4.3 has the interesting case of Volkswagen acquiring Rolls Royce in 1998, but, mistakenly, without the Rolls Royce brand name.

Box 4.3 Volkswagen and BMW Spat Over Rolls-Royce

The Rolls-Royce PLC of the U.K. was the manufacturer of aircraft engines, the second largest in the world; luxury cars; and equipment for the marine and energy industries during the late 1990s. The cars were made by its Rolls-Royce Motor subsidiary in its legendary factory in Crewe, England. In 1998, Volkswagen of Germany purchased Rolls-Royce Motor Cars Ltd., along with its two luxury brands, Rolls-Royce and Bentley, and the Crewe factory for $917 million, for which BMW had also bid. However, the VW deal did not include Rolls-Royce's most valuable assets, the "Rolls-Royce" brand name and the "RR" logo, which by some quirk of fate had been sold by the Rolls-Royce aircraft company to BMW for $78 million. Now, even though VW could make cars that looked and performed like Rolls-Royces, it could not call any car it made a Rolls-Royce.

After protracted negotiations between VW and BMW, the latter allowed VW to use the brand name and logo on its cars for a significant sum of money, though only until December 31, 2002. Now, VW makes the Bentley at the Crewe factory and BMW the Rolls-Royce in West Sussex, England.

Another type of licensing, which is actually more common, is when a company allows (licenses) other companies to use its trademark on their products, such as t-shirts, caps, etc.—the idea being that consumers will be more likely to buy a product if it has a well-known trademark (brand). For instance, while Calvin

Klein does design and make some ready-to-wear clothing, much of its revenue and profit come from licensing the Calvin Klein brand name for dozens of products manufactured and sold worldwide, including watches, shoes, hosiery, even furniture. Licensing of their IP results in nearly costless income for the trademark owners. There can be many other kinds of licensing, such as a physician receiving a license to practice as a medical professional. These last two types of licensing are, however, beyond the scope of this book.

Franchising

While licensing typically involves manufacturing, franchising is almost always done for services. Under franchising, a franchisor sells its intangible property to another company (the franchisee) for an initial franchise fee and a certain percentage of its sales during the period of the franchise agreement. A franchise agreement often includes the obligations of both parties to the agreement, with the franchisor agreeing to offer a variety of continuing services to the franchisee, such as fulfilling its supply chain needs and advertising support, and the franchisee agreeing to follow the operating policies (the business model) of the franchisor. Franchising, like licensing, also allows a company to expand abroad without necessarily making much (or any) investment. Some disadvantages of franchising include the possibility of poor quality control at a franchisee's location and potential legal problems if a franchisee fails to meet the terms of the franchise agreement. Enforcing such agreements in foreign countries can be very expensive and time-consuming, especially in countries that may lack strong contract enforcement mechanisms. Even in a highly developed market such as the United States, a foreign company interested in franchising its business model faces challenges such as a highly regulated business environment, fierce competition, diverse demographics, and generally high investment requirements. Yet, dozens of foreign companies have found franchising success in the U.S., including Le Pain Quotidien, a restaurant company from Belgium, and Kumon, an education company from Japan.

U.S.-based McDonald's is one of the most popular fast food franchises in the world. When the company gives a franchise to an individual entrepreneur or a company, McDonald's requires the individual or company to follow its business model quite precisely—in terms of store layout, signage, menu, food preparation, supply chain, accounting, etc. Over 80 percent of the 35,000 McDonald's restaurants worldwide are owned by independent franchisees. The start-up cost of establishing a McDonald's franchise ranges between $950,000 and $2.3 million, depending on location, restaurant size, selection of kitchen equipment, décor, and landscaping. In addition to these costs, McDonald's charges an upfront franchise fee of $45,000 and an ongoing monthly service fee of 4 percent of gross sales, as well as rent, which is a percentage of monthly sales. In return, the company provides many services to its franchisees. McDonald's even has a Hamburger University, a huge corporate university located outside Chicago, which offers training in restaurant operations and leadership to McDonald's franchisees and employees.

Foreign Direct Investment

As indicated earlier, foreign market entry via direct investment is the costliest and the riskiest means of doing business abroad, yet it is the second most popular mode of entering foreign markets after exporting/importing. FDI is costliest because it necessarily involves creating a physical presence, and all that it entails, in a foreign market. It is riskiest not only because of the significant investment involved, but also because FDI can take one, two, or more years before becoming fully functional, and anything can happen (government regulations, political change, competition, etc.) during the intervening period. However, FDI also has advantages for the company making the investment, such as the ability to have tight control over foreign operations, ability to transfer its organizational routines and core capabilities to the foreign subsidiaries, ability to better serve local customers, less risk of losing technological competence to others, and learning in the host market. A company can make FDI via a partly owned enterprise, i.e., a joint venture, or a wholly owned subsidiary via mergers and acquisitions (M&As) or greenfield investment. FDI through partly and wholly owned subsidiaries will be discussed in greater detail in Chapter 5, and briefly explored below.

A joint venture is an arrangement whereby two (or more) companies invest financial and other resources to set up a new legal entity in the home or host market. The new entity, a joint venture (JV), can be set up with equal investment by both parties, as in a 50:50 JV, or a majority JV where one of the partners invests more than 50 percent of the total investment. As discussed in the previous chapter, NUMMI (New United Motor Manufacturing Inc.) was a 50:50 JV between Toyota of Japan and General Motors of the U.S. to assemble both Toyota and GM cars in Fremont, California. In 1956, the Xerox Corporation of the United States (then, Haloid Photographic) set up a 50:50 JV in the U.K. (called Rank Xerox) with the Rank Organization to manufacture and sell photocopying equipment. In 1962, Xerox (through its British JV, Rank Xerox) set up a 50:50 JV in Japan, Fuji Xerox, with the Fuji Photo Film Company. Refer also to Chapter 1 (under Reverse FDI) for examples of JVs between firms from developed and developing countries.

A wholly owned foreign subsidiary is one where a firm sets up a new 100-percent-owned legal entity in a foreign market. It can do so through M&A by acquiring or merging with an existing enterprise in the foreign market or by establishing a greenfield enterprise from the ground up. A wholly owned enterprise set up as a greenfield operation offers the best opportunity for a firm to learn the most about a foreign market.[38] For example, Honda of America Manufacturing, Inc. is a wholly owned subsidiary of Honda of Japan in the United States, set up as a greenfield entity starting in 1977. In 2002, South

African Breweries of the U.K. merged with the Miller Brewing Company owned by the U.S.-based Altria Group to form SABMiller PLC. Google of the U.S., which derives over half its revenues from overseas, has made dozens of acquisitions abroad and continues to do so. In May 2014, Google reported to the U.S. Security and Exchange Commission that it would spend $20 billion to $30 billion of its accumulated international profits to acquire foreign companies and technology rights. Some of the foreign companies Google acquired just in 2014 are: Vision Factory, an artificial intelligence company from the U.K., SlickLogin, an Internet security company from Israel, and mDialog, an online advertising company from Canada.

Strategic Alliances

A strategic alliance is a partnering arrangement between two or more companies sharing resources in the pursuit of a common goal, while remaining independent. A strategic alliance can be formed with suppliers, customers, universities, government agencies, even with direct competitors, and is generally intended to enter new markets, strengthen a specific skill, share the cost of a major project, develop technology, and so on. Not all strategic alliances are "strategic." Jason Wakeam of the Hewlett-Packard Company has identified several alliance types that have the potential to be truly strategic. These are alliances critical to the success of the partners' core business objective, alliances critical to the development or maintenance of their competitive advantage, alliances that block a competitive threat or mitigate a significant business risk, and alliances that help the partners maintain strategic choices open to them.[39]

In June 2012, Dr. Reddy's Laboratories Ltd of India and Merck Serano, a division of Merck KGaA of Germany, announced the formation of a strategic alliance to co-develop a portfolio of biosimilar compounds in oncology. The alliance includes joint technology development, manufacturing, and commercialization of the compounds so developed around the world, excluding some specific countries. Under the agreement, Dr. Reddy's will lead early product and complete Phase I development, with Merck Serano taking up manufacturing of the compounds and leading Phase III development. The agreement involves full R&D cost sharing. Further, Merck Serano is to be responsible for commercialization of the compounds globally, outside certain emerging markets for which Dr. Reddy's will have exclusive rights. In the U.S., the two companies will jointly commercialize the products on a profit-sharing basis.

Stefan Oschmann, Merck Serano's CEO, highlighted the importance of the alliance to both companies: "Our expertise in developing, manufacturing, and commercializing gives us a clear advantage in the biosimilars field, and the partnership with Dr. Reddy's will bring their first-in-market experience in biosimilars, as well as their expertise in generics and Emerging Markets, to the table. Sharing know-how, risks and rewards is the right approach to enter the emergent biosimilars market and will be a win-win for both parties."[40] A strategic alliance may or may not involve equity investment by either party. If equity investment is involved and the two parties form new legal entity, it is a joint venture.

This chapter presented approaches companies might use to enter foreign markets, However, that is just a beginning. The next two chapters are about competing and growing in foreign markets.

Concluding Remarks

This chapter is about the nitty-gritty of doing business abroad and posed and answered several questions a firm must consider at the start of its internationalization journey, such as why go abroad, which country (countries) to enter, which product(s) to internationalize, when to enter and what should be the scale of entry, and, finally, how to enter foreign markets. Such questions are also appropriate for firms entering a new market after they had been abroad for some time. The PRISM framework of foreign market selection offers a major advance by incorporating most of the factors a firm should consider while deciding on which country (countries) to enter. The Appendix to this chapter provides an annotated listing of the various data sources that can be used to apply the PRISM framework. The PRISM framework and the Appendix evolved over a number of years during research and teaching and have been tested in dozens of real-life student projects. No other book on strategy, global strategy, or global business offers this level of in-depth information on how firms should go about selecting foreign markets to enter. The chapter also covers other important topics such as institutional voids and how to profit from them and how to learn about foreign markets before entry.

Part II of the book presents a variety of strategy frameworks, starting with frameworks for foreign market selection and for how to enter foreign markets in this chapter. The strategy frameworks for competing and growing in foreign markets are to be covered in the next two chapters.

Appendix: Selected Information Sources
for PRISM Analysis

This annotated list offers suggestions on the kinds of information sources that can be used to conduct the PRISM analysis for foreign market selection. Some information sources, such as the World Bank and OECD, provide a range of statistics and information that could fit under several dimensions of the PRISM model. The brief descriptions and the website links below will help readers navigate these and other sites and find with ease what they are looking for. This list of sources is quite comprehensive, and not all of these sources will be needed for a specific project. The language below is adapted from the descriptions on the websites of the organizations highlighted here.

P: Political Economy

Country Profiles

Several organizations offer "country profiles," which are excellent sources of information about most countries in the world, including information on their political and economic systems and much else. Most of the country profiles/ reports shown below are updated regularly.

BBC

BBC Country Profiles

http://news.bbc.co.uk/2/hi/country_profiles/default.stm

These profiles provide an instant guide to the history, politics, and economic background of countries and territories, as well as background on several key multi-lateral institutions. Also included are audio and video clips from BBC archives.

CENTRAL INTELLIGENCE AGENCY

CIA World Factbook

https://www.cia.gov/library/publications/the-world-factbook/

The World Factbook provides facts on every country, dependency, and geographic entity in the world, including information such as the history, people, government, economy, energy, geography, communications, transportation, military, and transnational issues.

U.S. DEPARTMENT OF STATE

Background Notes

http://www.state.gov/r/pa/ei/bgn/

This is a series of short, factual pamphlets with information on a country's land, people, history, government, etc., for practically all countries in the world. For "Background Notes" for years up to 2012, refer to archives: http://www.state.gov/outofdate/bgn/.

THE WORLD BANK

Country Profiles

http://data.worldbank.org/data-catalog/country-profiles

These country profiles present the latest development data drawn from the World Development Indicators (WDI) database, the World Bank's primary database for cross-country comparable development data for practically all countries in the world. The list of topics covered includes Agriculture & Rural Development,

Aid Effectiveness, Climate Change, Economy & Growth, Education, Energy & Mining, Environment, External Debt, Financial Sector, Gender, Health, Infrastructure, Labor & Social Protection, Poverty, Private Sector, Public Sector, Science & Technology, Social Development, Trade, and Urban Development.

Development Indicators

http://data.worldbank.org/indicator

This is absolutely the most comprehensive source of data on dozens of time series (see list of topics above).

Note: See also OECD resources under R: Resources.

Political Risk

Political risk is the risk faced by international businesses arising from the decisions of governments and the broader stability of the political system and could negatively impact a firm's operations in foreign markets. Below is the list of some potentially valuable sources for keeping tabs on political and terrorism risk.

THE PRS GROUP

Political Risk Index (PRI)

https://www.prsgroup.com/category/risk-index

The PRI is the overall measure of risk for a given country, calculated by using several risk components, including turmoil, financial transfer, direct investment, and export markets. The Index provides a basic, convenient way to compare countries directly and also to analyze changes over the past five years.

EURASIA GROUP

Top Risks 2016

http://www.eurasiagroup.net/pages/top-risks-2016

The Eurasia Group is the world's largest political risk consultancy, with 500 experts in some 90 countries. Their Group Global Political Risk Index (GPRI) is a qualitative comparative political and economic risk index designed specifically to measure stability in emerging markets. The Top Risks 2016 report (see link above) identifies the key geopolitical areas to watch for global investors, business leaders, and other market participants. Eurasia Group services, such as the GPRI, require a paid subscription.

AON'S POLITICAL RISK MAP

http://www.aon.com/2015politicalriskmap/index.html

Aon PLC is a leading global provider of risk management, insurance and reinsurance brokerage, and human resources solutions, with presence in some 120 countries worldwide. Aon has developed two dedicated analytics tools allowing managers to analyze a country historically and compare different countries against each other over time and with respect to different risk factors. These tools allow users to plot their organizations' exposures and review the potential risks they may face as they look to invest, grow and diversify their investments. Some of the Aon services require a paid subscription.

Marsh's Political Risk Map for 2015

http://usa.marsh.com/Portals/9/Documents/Growing%20Political%20Risk%20in%20the%20Year%20Ahead%20and%20Beyond-Marsh%27s%20Political%20Risk%20Map%202015.pdf

The Marsh Political Risk Map 2015 provides an overall country risk score for 185 nations, based on the three categories of political, macroeconomic, and operational risks to stability over a short- and long-term time horizon. See also www.businessmonitor.com.

Terrorism and Political Violence Risk Map 2016

http://www.aon.com/chile/attachments/mapaterorismoaon2016.pdf

R: Resources

Resources can be classified in many ways. A useful classification is the one suggested by Michael Porter in "Competitive Advantage of Nations" discussed in Chapter 3. Porter's Diamond defines factor conditions (input factors or resources) as basic and advanced—the basic factors being demographics and natural resources, and advanced factors being those created through public and private efforts.

Basic factors can be measured by a country's demographics, such as population, workforce, age distribution, distribution into socio-economic groups, etc., and the extent of natural resources available in the country. The latter may be of interest to a firm interested in specific commodities, such as oil and gas. Data on such measures are often available from official statistics of the countries being analyzed (see also country profiles listed under P: Political Economy).

However, most firms going abroad will be interested in resources like skilled workforce (with the "skills" categories, such as scientists and engineers, to be defined by the prospective entrant), capital, technology, higher education institutions, etc. Such information is also often available from official statistics sources in the countries of interest, and even from sources such as Wikipedia. For instance, a quick google search for "higher education in Romania" provided a good deal of information on this topic on Wikipedia and other websites.

Human Capital

One of the best means of assessing a country's human capital is the *Human Capital Index* published by the World Economic Forum.

THE WORLD ECONOMIC FORUM

The Human Capital Report 2015

http://www.weforum.org/reports/human-capital-report-2015

The Human Capital Index measures countries' ability to maximize and leverage their human capital endowment. The index assesses learning and employment outcomes across five distinct age groups for 124 countries, on a scale from 0 (worst) to 100 (best).

Technology

A good approach for assessing a country's strengths in terms of technology is to look at the IP being generated in that country in the technology domains of interest to the prospective entrant. This is available from the World Intellectual Property Organization (WIPO) for practically all countries.

WORLD INTELLECTUAL PROPERTY ORGANIZATION

Statistical Country Profiles

http://www.wipo.int/ipstats/en/statistics/country_profile/

The statistical country profiles provide information on patents, utility models, trademarks, and industrial designs for the period 1999–2013. They cover different dimensions of IP activity, including incoming and outgoing filings, the share of filings in different technological fields, total patents in force, and the use of international IP systems by applicants.

Capital

One measure of capital in a country is gross capital formation, i.e., the net additions to the (physical) capital stock in the country, the capital actually used for investment purposes and not held as savings or consumed. The following three organizations provide statistics on capital formation in different countries as well as much other relevant data.

THE WORLD BANK

Gross Capital Formation as % of GDP

http://data.worldbank.org/indicator/NE.GDI.TOTL.ZS

Gross capital formation consists of outlays on additions to the fixed assets of an economy plus net changes in the level of inventories. Fixed assets include land improvements (fences, ditches, drains, and so on); plant, machinery, and equipment purchases; and the construction of roads, railways, and the like, including schools, offices, hospitals, private residential dwellings, and commercial and industrial buildings. Inventories are stocks of goods held by firms to meet temporary or unexpected fluctuations in production or sales, and "work in progress."

IESE BUSINESS SCHOOL AND EMLYON BUSINESS SCHOOL

The Venture Capital & Private Equity Country Attractiveness Index 2015

http://blog.iese.edu/vcpeindex/ranking-2015/

The index measures the attractiveness of a country for investors in Venture Capital and Private Equity limited partnerships.

Regional and country profiles (http://blog.iese.edu/vcpeindex/profiles/) allow comparisons with country peers along six dimensions: the level of economic activity, depth of capital markets, taxation, investment protection and corporate governance, human and social environment, and entrepreneurial opportunities.

ORGANIZATION FOR ECONOMIC COOPERATION AND DEVELOPMENT (OECD)

The OECD is a valuable resource for economic, social, political, and other valuable information for OECD and many non-OECD countries.

Main Reference

http://www.oecd-ilibrary.org/statistics;jsessionid=3mknvj9hhwop.x-oecd-live-02

An excellent source for statistics on OECD countries (and occasionally for major non-OECD countries). Some specific OECD sources are highlighted below.

Country Statistical Profiles

http://www.oecd-ilibrary.org/economics/country-statistical-profiles-key-tables-from-oecd_20752288

The key tables by country statistical profiles include a wide range of indicators on economy, education, energy, environment, foreign aid, health, information and communication, labor, migration, R&D, trade, and society.

Entrepreneurship at a Glance 2013

http://www.oecd-ilibrary.org/industry-and-services/entrepreneurship-at-a-glance-2013_entrepreneur_aag-2013-en;jsessionid=3mknvj9hhwop.x-oecd-live-02#statlinks

Entrepreneurship at a Glance, a product of the OECD-Eurostat Entrepreneurship Indicators Programme, presents an original collection of indicators for measuring the state of entrepreneurship, along with key facts and explanations of the policy context. This third issue provides country-level information on 24 dimensions such as new enterprise creation, bankruptcies, self-employment rates, enterprises by size, and gazelle rate (gazelles are high-growth enterprises).

Main Economic Indicators

http://www.oecd-ilibrary.org/economics/data/main-economic-indicators_mei-data-en

Up-to-date statistics on earnings, labor, prices, sales, production, balance of payments, consumer opinion, exports/imports, leading indicators, employment, labor cost, and finance for OECD and major non-OECD countries.

I: Institutions and Infrastructure

Institutions

For the purpose of PRISM analysis, one of the most comprehensive set of indicators to analyze the existence and strength of institutions in different countries is the World Bank's World Governance Indicators (WGI) database. Given below also are some specialized indexes that are relevant for analyzing specific institutions in different countries.

THE WORLD BANK

World Governance Indicators, 1996–2014

http://info.worldbank.org/governance/wgi/index.aspx#home

The WGI database offers aggregate and individual governance indicators for 215 countries and territories over the period 1996–2014 for six dimensions of governance: (1) voice and accountability, (2) political stability and absence of violence, (3) government effectiveness, (4) regulatory quality, (5) rule of law, and (6) control of corruption. The aggregate indicators combine the views of a large number of enterprise, citizen, and expert survey respondents in industrialized and developing countries. The individual data sources underlying the aggregate indicators are drawn from a diverse variety of research institutes, think tanks, non-governmental organizations, and international organizations.

In addition to the above, the following indexes may also be of interest for specific institutional analyses.

Doing Business 2016

http://www.doingbusiness.org/reports/global-reports/doing-business-2016

This is the 13th in the World Bank's series of annual reports measuring the regulations that enhance business activity and those that constrain it. *Doing Business* presents quantitative indicators on business regulations and the protection of property rights that can be compared across 189 economies—from Afghanistan to Zimbabwe—and over time.

Doing Business measures regulations affecting 11 areas of business life in countries. Ten of these are included in this year's ranking on the ease of doing business: starting a business, dealing with construction permits, getting electricity, registering property, getting credit, protecting minority investors, paying taxes, trading across borders, enforcing contracts and resolving insolvency. *Doing Business* also measures labor market regulation, which is not included in this year's ranking.

TRANSPARENCY INTERNATIONAL

Corruption Perceptions Index, 2015

https://www.transparency.org/cpi2015

The annual *Corruption Perceptions Index (CPI)* ranks 168 countries by their perceived levels of corruption, as determined by expert assessments and opinion surveys. The CPI indicates the perceived level of corruption in countries on a scale of 0 (highly corrupt) to 100 (very clean). A poor score may signal widespread bribery, lack of punishment for corruption, and public institutions that do not respond to citizens' needs.

THE HERITAGE FOUNDATION

The Index of Economic Freedom 2015

http://www.heritage.org/index/ranking

This 21st edition of the Index evaluates 186 countries in four broad policy areas that affect economic freedom, viz. the rule of law, the intrusiveness and size of government, regulatory efficiency, and the openness of markets. The Index ranks and grades countries on 10 specific aspects of economic freedom: property rights, freedom from corruption, fiscal freedom, government spending, business freedom, labor freedom, monetary freedom, trade freedom, investment freedom, and financial freedom.

FREEDOM HOUSE

The 2015 Freedom in the World—Country Reports

https://freedomhouse.org/report-types/freedom-world#.VcgUr_nkPLI

Freedom in the World is the Freedom House's flagship publication offering a comparative assessment of global political rights and civil liberties. Published annually since 1972, the publication offers ratings and narrative reports on 195 countries and 15 related and disputed territories.

Infrastructure

THE WORLD BANK

Development Indicators: Infrastructure

http://data.worldbank.org/indicator#topic-9

This is a very comprehensive source of data on various infrastructure elements, including air transportation, container port traffic, broadband subscriptions, ICT goods imports and exports, Internet users, mobile phone subscribers, motor vehicles, rail lines, roads, energy consumption, etc.

WORLD TRADE ORGANIZATION

Country Services Profiles

http://stat.wto.org/ServiceProfile/WSDBServicePFHome.aspx?Language=E

"Country Services Profiles" contain basic data on "Infrastructure services" for WTO member states such as:

Transportation: Number of international airports, airplane fleet size, maritime merchant fleet size, rail network in km, and road network in km.

Telecommunications: Numbers of telephone subscribers, mobile phone subscribers, Internet users, broadband Internet subscribers, and secure Internet servers.

S: Society and Culture

Society

OECD

Country Statistical Profiles

http://www.oecd-ilibrary.org/economics/country-statistical-profiles-key-tables-from-oecd_20752288

This link provides access to information on a variety of social indicators, such as education, employment, health, and migration for OECD and many non-OECD countries (see also "country profiles" under P: Political Economy).

Culture

Culture, etiquette, manners, cross-cultural, and cross-national communication have become critical for success in international business and government. Here are some sources of information on such issues.

Wikipedia

https://en.wikipedia.org/wiki/High-_and_low-context_cultures

For a quick classification of countries along the high-context/low-context framework, refer to this entry in Wikipedia.

HOFSTEDE'S DIMENSIONS OF CULTURE

http://geert-hofstede.com/countries.html

Working for IBM in the late 1960s and early 1970s, Geert Hofstede developed the following four dimensions of culture at workplace through a very large sample survey: power distance, individualism, uncertainty avoidance, and masculinity. His research provided quantitative estimates for these dimensions for 50 countries, which were later extended to cover many more countries. This is rather old research, and organizational and national cultures do change. However, these data seem to have some face validity; the readers can decide for themselves whether to use this research for analyzing their companies' prospects in different countries or not.

KWINTESSENTIAL CROSS CULTURAL SOLUTIONS—GLOBAL GUIDE TO CULTURE, CUSTOMS AND ETIQUETTE

Country Profiles—Global Guide to Customs, Culture, and Etiquette

http://www.kwintessential.co.uk/resources/country-profiles.html

This link offers information for selected countries on: language, useful phrases, the society, culture, and business and social etiquettes.

CULTUREGRAMS

http://www.culturegrams.com/

These short, priced publications provide concise and up-to-date information on the cultural, customs, and traditional life in over 200 countries, each U.S. state, and all 13 Canadian provinces and territories.

M: Market Potential

To assess the market potential of a product, the factors to be considered are: market size and growth rate, industry structure, competition, capacity utilization, and exports/imports. Sources for some of these dimensions are given below.

Market Size and Growth Rate

Market size can be measured by a nation's demographics or GDP for some products. However, for a lot of goods and services, market size must be defined differently. For instance, for a company selling machine tools, market size could be defined as the number of companies in the foreign market that could potentially use its machine tools in their own production processes. Official statistics for many countries provide such information. A good measure of market potential in a country is the level of imports in the country for the product in question. Refer to the section below on FDI and Trade for data on exports/imports.

UNITED NATIONS

International Human Development Indicators

http://hdr.undp.org/en/countries/

A common indicator of economic development (a proxy for market potential) in a country is per capita GDP or per capita GNI (Gross National Income). However, such indicators measure only the richness of an economy, not the quality of human life there. Nobel Laureate Amartya Sen suggested that development should be measured by the opportunities and the choices that people enjoy rather than just by per capita GNI. Accordingly, the United Nations developed the Human Development Index to measure and emphasize that people and their capabilities should be the ultimate criteria for assessing the development of a country, not economic growth alone. It is thus an important measure of market potential for many kinds of goods and services. The variables included in the HDI are: per capita GNI (at purchasing power parity), life expectancy at birth, mean years of schooling, and expected years of schooling.

Industry Structure

Measures of industry structure for a country include concentration ratios (e.g., CR4) and the Herfindahl-Hirschman Index (HHI). In the U.S., the primary source for CR4 and HHI for most industries is the Census Bureau.

2007 Economic Census of the U.S.

https://www.census.gov/econ/concentration.html

For other countries, similar data may be available from their official statistics offices.

Competition

WORLD ECONOMIC FORUM

Global Competitiveness Report, 2014–2015

http://www.weforum.org/reports/global-competitiveness-report-2014-2015

The Global Competitiveness Report's main competitiveness ranking is the Global Competitiveness Index (GCI) for some 144 countries, developed by the World Economic Forum. The GCI is based on 12 pillars of competitiveness, providing a comprehensive picture of the competitiveness landscape in countries at all stages of development. The 12 pillars include: Institutions, Infrastructure, Macroeconomic Stability, Health and Primary Education, Higher Education and Training, Goods Market Efficiency, Labour Market Efficiency, Financial Market Sophistication, Technological Readiness, Market Size, Business Sophistication, and Innovation.

Market potential can be assessed using the World Economic Forum's Global Competitiveness Report, among other sources.

WEF has also published other research reports, such as the Africa Competitiveness Report, The Travel and Tourism Competitiveness Report, The Global Information Technology Report, and so on. Interested readers should explore the WEF website for complete details.

FDI and Trade

UNITED NATIONS CONFERENCE ON TRADE AND DEVELOPMENT (UNCTAD)

World Investment Report 2015

http://unctad.org/en/pages/PublicationWebflyer.aspx?publicationid=1245

The *World Investment Report* provides time series data on FDI at region and country levels for the period 1990–2014. County fact sheets contain data on FDI, M&A, and greenfield investment. Inward FDI is a good indicator of country attractiveness for investment.

See also: UNCTAD's World Investment Prospects Survey 2013–2015, which provides an outlook for future trends in FDI by the largest transnational corporations:

http://unctad.org/en/PublicationsLibrary/webdiaeia2013d9_en.pdf

WORLD TRADE ORGANIZATION

International Trade Statistics, 2015

https://www.wto.org/english/res_e/statis_e/its2015_e/its15_toc_e.htm

International Trade Statistics 2015 provides a detailed overview of the latest developments in world trade, covering merchandise trade, services trade, as well as trade measured in value-added terms (i.e., trade in global value chains). Data up to 2014 are available for downloading in both EXCEL and PDF formats.

Statistics Database

http://stat.wto.org/Home/WSDBHome.aspx?Language=E

Country Trade Profiles contain data on trade policy (e.g., tariff rates) and merchandise and services trade for the latest available year. Also included are services profiles and tariff profiles for WTO member countries.

UN COMTRADE DATABASE

http://comtrade.un.org/

The UN Comtrade is a repository of official trade statistics and relevant analytical tables. It contains annual trade statistics starting from 1962 and monthly trade statistics since 2010.

Notes

1 Bobbie Johnson, "Will Netflix Go Global in 2011? Maybe, but It Won't Be Easy," Gigaom.com December 31, 2010. Accessed from https://gigaom.com/2010/12/31/netflix-global-expansion/.
2 LoveFilm was later acquired by Amazon in 2011.
3 Source: company's website: http://ir.netflix.com/.
4 Drew Harwell, "Netflix's Global Goals Have Hit the Great Wall," *The Washington Post*, January 8, 2016.
5 Several sources, including company website and: http://www.trefis.com/stock/nflx/model/trefis?easyAccessToken=PROVIDER_6cb527391292b79c31c4a1ee6e20e2c9ae8e6504.
6 Netflix Letter to Shareholders, January 20, 2015. Accessed from http://files.shareholder.com/downloads/NFLX/0x0x804108/043A3015-36EC-49B9-907C-27960F1A7E57/Q4_14_Letter_to_shareholders.pdf.
7 For a detailed look at the PEST framework, refer to "PEST Analysis: Identifying "Big Picture" Opportunities and Threats" at: http://www.mindtools.com/pages/article/newTMC_09.htm.
8 Refer to Wikipedia for a brief discussion of these and other similar mnemonic devices: https://en.wikipedia.org/wiki/PEST_analysis.
9 Pankaj Ghemawat, "Distance Still Matters: The Hard Reality of Global Expansion," *Harvard Business Review*, September 2001. See also, Pankaj Ghemawat, *Redefining Global Strategy: Crossing Borders in a World Where Differences Still Matter* (Boston: Harvard Business School Press, 2007).
10 Ghemawat, 2001, p. 138.
11 Michael Porter, *The Competitive Advantage of Nations* (New York: Free Press, 1991).
12 Charles W.L. Hill, *International Business: Competing in the Global Marketplace.* 9th Edition (New York: McGraw-Hill/Irwin, 2013), Chapter 2, and R.J. Rummel, *Understanding Conflict and War: The Conflict Helix.* v.2 (New York: John Wiley & Sons, 1976), Chapter 31. Accessed from https://www.hawaii.edu/powerkills/TCH.CHAP31.HTM#31.2.
13 This section is based on: Hill, 2013, Chapter 2.
14 AnnaLee Saxenian, "A Valley Asset: Chinese, Indians Creating Businesses, Jobs, Wealth As Successful Entrepreneurs," *San Jose Mercury News*, June 21, 1998.
15 Porter, 1991.
16 Douglas C. North, *Institutions, Institutional Change, and Economic Performance* (Cambridge, MA: Harvard University Press, 1990), p. 3.
17 Geoffrey M. Hodgson, "What Are Institutions?" *Journal of Economic Issues*, 2006 (XL): 13.
18 Hill, 2013, Chapter 4.
19 Tarun Khanna and Krishna G. Palepu, *Winning in Emerging Markets: A Roadmap for Strategy and Execution* (Boston: Harvard Business School Press, 2010), p. 14.
20 James Glanz, "Power, Pollution, and the Internet," *The New York Times*, September 22, 2012.

21 These are adapted from Khanna and Palepu, 2010, Toolkit 2–3, pp. 45–50. See the original reference for the complete toolkit.

22 Hill, 2013, p. 101.

23 Maria Carlson, "Culture and History Matter: Russia's Search for Identity after the Fall." Lecture at University of Kansas, April 10, 2007. Accessed from http://kuscholarworks.ku.edu/bitstream/handle/1808/1368/halllecturecarlson10apr07.pdf?sequence=3.

24 This distinction was suggested by Edward T. Hall in *Beyond Culture* (New York: Anchor Books, 1976).

25 Much of this discussion in this sub-section is adapted from Carlson, 2007.

26 Carlson, 2007, p. 5.

27 Geert Hofstede, *Culture's Consequences: International Differences in Work-Related Values* (Newbury Park, CA: Sage Publications, 1980).

28 In economics, a perfectly competitive market is one that has many sellers, each taking a negligible share of the market, and many buyers, each taking a negligible amount of the market's output. Some other characteristics of perfectly competitive markets are the existence of a homogenous product, free entry and free exit, perfectly available market information to all market participants, and so on.

29 Source: The U.S. Department of Justice: http://www.justice.gov/atr/herfindahl-hirschman-index.

30 George S. Yip, Javier G. Biscarri, and J.A. Monti, "The Role of Internationalization Process in the Performance of Newly Internationalizing Firms," *Journal of International Marketing*, 2000 (8): 10–35.

31 Recall that we use the term "product" to refer to both physical goods and services.

32 Tarun Khanna, Ingrid Vargas, and Krishna G. Palepu, "Haier: Taking a Chinese Company Global," Harvard Business School Publishing Case Study, 2012. Product Number 9–712-408, p. 6.

33 Akio Morita profile accessed from Public Broadcasting System website: http://www.pbs.org/transistor/album1/addlbios/morita.html.

34 Refer to Khanna and Palepu, 2010, Chapter 3 for a detailed discussion on how to leverage institutional voids in foreign markets.

35 Michael Lee, "Cisco Issues Legal Challenge to Huawei, Tiptoes US-China Dispute," ZDNet, October 12, 2012. Accessed from http://www.zdnet.com/article/cisco-issues-legal-challenge-to-huawei-tiptoes-us-china-dispute/.

36 Pankaj Ghemawat, *Commitment: The Dynamics of Strategy* (New York: The Free Press, 1991), p. xi.

37 This information is taken from various DuPont websites, including: http://www2.dupont.com/Phoenix_Heritage/en_US/1993_a_detail.html#more.

38 Vinod K. Jain, *Evolution of International Investment Strategy: The Case of Foreign MNEs in the United States*. Unpublished Ph.D. dissertation, University of Maryland, College Park, 1994.

39 Jason Wakeam, "The Five Factors of a Strategic Alliance," *Ivey Business Journal*, May-June 2003.

40 Press release from Dr. Reddy's Laboratories: "Dr. Reddy's Laboratories Ltd. and Merck Serano Announce Collaboration to Develop and Commercialize Biosimilars," June 6, 2012. Accessed from http://www.drreddys.com/media/press-releases/june06-2012.html.

5

HOW TO COMPETE
IN FOREIGN MARKETS

*You have no choice but to operate in a world shaped by globaliza-
tion and the information revolution. There are two options: adapt
or die.*

—Andrew S. Grove, former COO, CEO,
and Chairman, Intel Corporation

A firm is judged by its stakeholders for the value it creates for them. Different
stakeholders of course have different expectations of the firm in which they have
(or claim to have) some stake. From a *shareholder* perspective specifically, a firm
creates value when it makes an economic profit, i.e., when its goods and services
are valued more highly by its customers than the cost of producing them and when
it gives high returns on their investment. Global strategy is concerned with how
firms create value through international operations. This chapter is about the strategies a firm might employ to create value by competing internationally. The focus
of the chapter is on value creation in foreign markets through actual presence
there, i.e., through FDI, rather than through exporting, importing, licensing, or
franchising, which do not necessarily require physical presence in foreign markets.

Studio Moderna Holdings B.V., an Amsterdam, Netherlands, registered company, started out as a single-product company in Slovenia in 1992. Today, Studio
Moderna is the leading multi-channel retailer with over 6,000 employees in Central and Eastern Europe (CEE) and Russia. The company targets over 300 million consumers in 21 countries, utilizing a vertically integrated, multi-channel
sales, marketing, media, and distribution strategy. The company's selling
platform includes: 130 localized e-commerce websites; 6 proprietary 24-hour
home-shopping television channels; over 300 hours of direct response television
(DRTV) advertising (infomercials) through 300 TV channels every day; over 300
company-owned and franchised retail outlets; thousands of retail and wholesale
partners; print sales through newspapers, magazines, and 25 million catalogues
issued annually; and over 70 million calls handled each year through the company's own 22 Customer Management Centers in 20 countries. Studio Moderna's 5,000+ products include proprietary products (that's how the company got

its start), products licensed from other manufacturers, and products from the world's largest DRTV product suppliers[1] (see Box 5.1 for timeline of Studio Moderna's foreign market entries).

How did it get here from being a single-product no-name company selling only in Slovenia a little over two decades ago? The previous chapter suggested that firms entering new foreign markets should do so with niche products, thus avoiding head-on competition with entrenched incumbents, unless of course they have the resources to meet competitors on their own terms. These are not the only ways to enter and compete in foreign markets. A company can also successfully compete in foreign markets using a strategy different from others' strategies. The key here is to have a differentiated approach compared to what others are doing.

So, what did Studio Moderna do differently from both domestic and foreign companies selling in the CEE? According to Studio Moderna CEO and co-founder, Sandi Češko:

> We decided to do the opposite of the Western DRTV companies when they applied the American business model to the European market. They outsourced all critical functions; we insourced everything. They centralized decision-making; we gave authority to the country managers. They sent American executives to set up and manage operations; we used local talent.[2]

Box 5.1 Studio Moderna's Globalization Timeline

Year of Entry	Country
1992	Slovenia
1993	Croatia
1995	Macedonia
1996	Bulgaria; Serbia
1997	Slovakia; Poland
1998	Hungary
1999	The Czech Republic
2002	Russia; Kosovo
2003	Lithuania; Latvia; Estonia; Albania; Romania
2004	Ukraine
2005	Azerbaijan (exited)
2006	Turkey (exited)
2010	Montenegro; Moldova
2011	Kazakhstan

Studio Moderna did a number of things right in its strategy for its home and foreign markets, including the following.

Capability building. Studio Moderna built up resources, capabilities, and competitive advantages studiously over more than two decades. These included the ability to localize products and strategy to meet the needs of each country and local market; the ability to derive synergies from a mix of sales channels with each supporting the other; the ability to handle cross-border logistics in multiple currencies; almost 10 million customer records; superior customer service; a "return policy" unheard of in the CEE region prior to Studio Moderna; and media power.

Localization. The company's localization strategy ranged from offering customized products for local markets, launching localized e-commerce websites, and hiring local staff to having an organizational structure that delegated decision-making authority to country and other local managers for quick response in local markets.

Leveraging IT. Starting in 1999, the company started digitizing all business processes with a view to creating a better control mechanism for its fast-growing footprint in the CEE—building its own IT system. According to Češko, "because there were no proper SW applications on the market in 1999 for such a complex and dynamic organization (SAP like programs would kill our entrepreneurial spirit and our disruptive business model) we have decided to build our own application. ..."[3]

Leveraging institutional voids. Studio Moderna adopted a vertical integration strategy from the very beginning—mainly because the critical support functions it needed, such as reliable call centers and delivery services, simply did not exist in the newly independent CEE region in the 1990s. Institutional voids in emerging markets often create problems for Western companies doing business there. However, like many other successful emerging-market firms, Studio Moderna found ways to circumvent or take advantage of the institutional voids by developing its own intermediaries, some of which became profit centers in their own right.

Deriving synergies. The company not only created multiple sales channels, but also derived synergies from them. "For example, Studio Moderna's DRTV media were geared to drive viewers to Studio Moderna's Internet sites. Internet presence and DRTV media helped strengthen Studio Moderna's TopShop brand, which in turn had a positive impact on Studio Moderna's retail and wholesale channels. Whereas in an infomercial viewers might see only two Dormeo mattresses displayed, when they went to a shop to try out the mattresses, they would encounter the entire Dormeo line of over two dozen mattresses and accessories. Presence in retail and wholesale points of sale in turn increased the credibility of the company's DRTV products."[4]

Building trust. From the very beginning, Studio Moderna attempted to win the trust of customers and to remove the negative image of selling products on television that existed in the CEE at the time. For instance, it offered a 45-day return policy, no questions asked, which sometimes even exceeded the return policies of its Western competitors. Call center operators spoke with existing and prospective customers in the local language and not only tried to upsell them but also helped build trust with them.

Media power. In addition to trust, the success of a company selling DRTV products depends on factors such as the availability of high-speed broadband in the market and having access to TV channels and media time. The company worked hard to negotiate access to television channels in all countries where it did business, even setting up joint ventures with TV companies in some major markets. Where it could not get good access to media, as in Azerbaijan, it exited the market.

Organization design. Studio Moderna created a matrix organizational structure and pushed decision-making authority down to executives in foreign subsidiaries. The structure encouraged the emergence of an *internal market* within the company, whereby country and functional managers negotiated exchanges of goods and services with each other as if in a real market. The overall organization consisted of three companies formed in such a way as to minimize tax liability. For instance, one of the group companies, Studio Moderna Operations SA of Switzerland, is the sole company in charge of buying and order fulfilment for all Studio Moderna products. It is also the only company responsible for selling the products to operating companies, thus minimizing the overall tax burden. Finally, an important aspect of how the company's organization design worked is its control system. Key performance indicators are established for all entities, including the corporate headquarters and individual country subsidiaries, and systematically and continuously monitored. The digitization of all processes enabled the management to provide access to critical data to operating managers throughout the organization. According to Češko, "today more than 1500 decision makers in the company are using these [IT] applications and are running the company."[5]

Growth strategy. Studio Moderna grew mostly organically by setting up foreign subsidiaries through greenfield investments. It did set up two joint ventures with leading television companies in Poland and Hungary (Box 5.1) but later acquired them.

Global mindset. Last, but not least, are the CEO Sandi Češko's global mindset, continuing investments in intangibles (people, IT, and innovations) and confidence in the growth of broadband penetration and the potential of the CEE market.

In recent years, Studio Moderna also entered Western markets, including the U.K. and the U.S., selling only Dormeo mattresses there. These entries are not included in Box 5.1. Some Studio Moderna products are available through online channels (such as amazon.com), but these are typically offered for sale by its distributors, not directly by the company.

The Globalization-Localization Dilemma

Companies competing internationally want to be both global and local—to have the reach and the power of a global company but also the ability to serve the needs of customers in individual foreign markets as a local company. According to Theodore Levitt, writing in the *Harvard Business Review* in 1983, "the world's needs and desires have been irrevocably homogenized. This makes the multinational corporation obsolete and the global corporation absolute."[6] This meant that companies could design and produce standardized products (because customers' needs and desires the world over were becoming essentially quite similar), manufacture them in one, two, or a few optimal locations, and export them worldwide. Levitt was ahead of his time in 1983 to suggest that all business was global business. In the 21st century, however, his prognostication is proving to be correct, though only for some goods and services (see also Chapter 3, Box 3.1).

Using Levitt's terminology, being *global* means standardized products, economies of scale, greater efficiency, and the ability to access resources and value chains globally—for improved profitability—but little attention to the needs of customers in individual local markets. On the other hand, being *local* means that a firm can cater to the specific needs and desires of customers in each individual market, but at a much higher cost and lower profitability. To be global or local is a key challenge of competing globally.

What Is Behind Globalization?

Several factors are leading companies and managers to thinking and acting *globally*, enabled by developments in information and communication technologies (ICTs).

Convergence of Needs, Tastes, and Preferences

As globalization progressed, and as discussed in the introductory chapter, there is growing convergence between the developed and developing countries. However, convergence is much more pervasive than simply in the levels of economic development. There is now also greater convergence in consumer tastes, preferences, and needs between different national markets—at least for some goods and services. For many consumer goods (e.g., fast food, clothing, and consumer electronics), customer tastes and preferences are quite similar in many parts of the developed and developing worlds, especially in major towns and metropolitan areas. For a lot of intermediate, industrial goods, such as parts and components, the needs of customers (companies producing final goods) are essentially identical worldwide. The same is true for many service providers, whose global customers need similar, if not identical, services wherever they are. This has led to the globalization of, for example, advertising agencies, management consulting firms, and firms providing architectural services. An advertising agency must no doubt follow the laws of the land, but the basic craft (the craft of persuasion) and the media (print, television, and Internet) are essentially the same wherever it operates. When customer needs converge to some global norms, a firm no longer has to design and produce customized products for each market; it can simply offer standardized products the world over.

Harmonization of Technical and Regulatory Standards

Many previously country-specific technical and regulatory standards are becoming harmonized to "global standards" in many parts of the world, leading to, for example, internationally accepted product specifications and business processes, which enable companies to do business worldwide without having to make major changes to their processes and products. For instance, since countries have historically had their own accounting standards (such as the Generally Accepted Accounting Principles, or GAAP, in the U.S.), a company doing business in different countries must prepare its annual statements according to the accounting principles of the countries in which it does business. Now, with over 110 countries having adopted the International Financial Reporting Standards (IFRS), accounting standards are becoming increasingly harmonized, and a company doing business in these countries can now prepare its annual statements using the common IFRS standards.

Standardization of Business Practices

With the globalization of business and management thinking, business practices such as strategic planning and just-in-time (JIT) inventory management are now almost standard practices adopted by companies all over the world.

Globalization of Science, Technology, and Innovation

The decentralization of "big science" (such as the Genome project), the increasing complexity and cross-disciplinary nature of frontier scientific research, and the increasing mobility of scientists and engineers across national and organizational boundaries are leading to the globalization of science, technology, and innovation.

All of these factors are behind many companies' desire to adopt a *global* approach to business. The benefits of such an approach include economies of scale, which arise from the design, production, marketing, and distribution of standardized goods and services, higher profitability, and the opportunity to create a consistent brand image worldwide. Some examples of companies that have leveraged the advantages of a global approach are: IKEA (furniture, furnishings, and housewares), Burger King (fast food restaurant), and Sony (consumer electronics), among others.

A Problem with the Global Approach

As we saw in Chapter 4 (the PRISM framework), countries differ along many dimensions, such as political economy, resource endowments, institutions and infrastructure, society and culture, and market characteristics. All of these factors impact customer tastes, preferences, and needs. Thus, products for which customer tastes, preferences, and needs differ from market to market are not likely to be good candidates for applying a global approach to business.

Ford's attempts to develop a "world car" over the last several decades provide a good example of why a global approach may not work. The Ford Motor Company has been at the vanguard of developing a car that would appeal to customers worldwide and has introduced a succession of such vehicles in the past—the Ford Fiesta launched in the 1970s, the Ford Escort launched in the U.S. in 1981[7] and the Ford Mondeo (called a *global car*) launched in Europe in the early 1990s. The Mondeo was launched in the United States in the early 1990s, but as Ford Contour/Mystique. Ford introduced another global car in the U.S. in the late 1990s, the Ford Focus. The rationale for developing a world car or a global car is quite attractive, namely, the possibility of achieving huge economies of scale through a globally integrated organization and mass production of a standardized vehicle, or at least mass production of the bulk of the parts and components that go into making a car. According to Louis Ross, the vice chairman and head of international operations for the Mondeo/Contour/Mystique program, "We'd say to suppliers, 'Listen this isn't 250,000 units, this is 700,000 units annually, and you're going to have it all.' The goal was to save $75 per car. We came closer to $150. On 700,000 units that will be $100 million a year."[8]

The development cost for the Mondeo/Contour/Mystique global car turned out to be $6 billion, and it took twice as long to design the car compared to Ford's other new car models. Industry analysts estimated that a cumulative production volume of 2 million cars would be required just to recoup the initial fixed cost, whereas actual production was much below that level. Over the years, Ford faced a variety of challenges with the world-car project, e.g., the need to overcome cross-national logistics barriers, divergent U.S. and European engineering standards, design changes during the long period of time it took to design the world car, currency fluctuations, and the need to create uniform standards for raw materials procurement and manufacturing of individual parts in different countries. Consumer tastes and preferences also differed considerably between countries, even between Europe and the U.S., such that Ford's subsidiaries in different countries specified many design changes to accommodate varying tastes and manufacturing preferences. There were difficulties all around in designing and manufacturing one car that would appeal to customers in Europe and America, let alone the entire world.

Clearly, even for a utilitarian product like a car, which serves the same basic needs the world over, a total global approach may not quite work. However, a car could be so designed that some of the parts and components for a specific model sold in different markets are standardized and manufactured to derive economies of scale. The only true example of a world car is perhaps the classic Volkswagen Beetle.

A solution to deal with such challenges is to adopt a local approach to doing business, or localization, as exemplified by the opening Studio Moderna case study.

What Is Behind Localization?

The basic factors behind the need for localization are customers' needs, tastes, and preferences in host markets. Besides, as noted earlier, countries do differ along many other dimensions, which also make it imperative for firms to be more local in their strategy for foreign markets.

Localization involves making a product linguistically and culturally appropriate for the target market where it is sold and used—to meet the specific needs, tastes, and preferences of the customers there. A *local* approach to business also means that the company's marketing, operations, and strategy comply with the laws and regulations of host markets and are appropriate for local distribution channels.

Approaches to Localization

How a company should think about localization goes beyond making a product linguistically and culturally appropriate for its target markets. Localization is actually a two-stage process: localization of marketing strategy and localization of the company's overall business strategy, i.e., its business model.

LOCALIZATION OF MARKETING STRATEGY

A company's marketing strategy or marketing mix refers to the famous four Ps of marketing: **Product, Price, Promotion,** and **Place**—the factors that are within a firm's control (as opposed to factors outside its control such as demographics, government regulations, or weather).

The **Products** a company sells are the first element of its marketing strategy for any market, and a company selling abroad must decide whether to sell the same products overseas that it sells at home or to customize its products for each foreign market—the globalization-localization dilemma. Most companies actually do customize their products for foreign markets to a lesser or a greater extent. Even companies with a global approach like IKEA and Burger King have had to adapt their products to suit the host markets. For instance, IKEA, the world's largest furniture retailer—selling essentially standardized Scandinavian furniture, furnishings, and housewares in 370 warehouse stores across

50 countries—entered the U.S. market in 1985. It experienced difficulty building traction in the market with its standardized products during the first few years.

Americans were visiting IKEA stores but not buying much there. One reason was that the dimensions of IKEA products did not suit American customers. The mattresses sold by IKEA did not fit American beds, which were larger in size. The drawers of bedroom furniture were not deep enough, and European style sofas were not large enough for American tastes. Similarly, bedsheets and curtains were designed for European homes, not American homes. Starting in the early 1990s, therefore, IKEA management decided to start customizing their products for the U.S. market, and about one-third of all products had been customized for American tastes by the year 2000. Today, the U.S. is IKEA's second largest market after Germany. Moral of the story: When the demand in a country market is large enough to enable achieving economies of scale, it makes sense even for a global firm to customize its products and strategy for that market.

Price, of course, depends a great deal on the market, the level of economic development, and competition, among other factors. For instance, when IKEA entered China, it not only customized its store layouts, products, and geographic positioning within cities, but also deep-discounted its prices—by as much as 70 percent for some products compared to the prices of the same products outside China.

Promotion involves both paid advertising and publicity, the latter being promotional content or an event (such as a press release or sports sponsorship) that is presented by the media free of cost because they think it is newsworthy. While many companies do both, research has shown that publicity often has greater impact on consumers' buying choices than paid advertising. What is of interest for us is the localization and contextualization of marketing and promotional content: product labels, user manuals, and warranty information; point-of-sale (P-O-S) materials; advertising; websites; etc. IKEA, which utilizes a global approach to business by and large, does customize many elements of its marketing strategy as needed. The IKEA website, for instance, is presented in over three dozen languages, and the IKEA catalog is printed 17 languages in 38 editions.

Place refers to the distribution channels used by a company—the place where customers can get access to its products. Localization is the rule when it comes to distribution channels. To be successful, a company must attempt to use the distribution channels that exist in a foreign market, rather than to try and develop its own.

LOCALIZATION OF THE BUSINESS MODEL

Most marketing textbooks end discussion of the globalization-localization dilemma with the 4 Ps of marketing (the marketing mix). The question of globalization or localization (standardization or customization) affects all functions of a business enterprise, including not only the marketing mix, but also operations, R&D, finance, procurement, and organizational structure—in fact the firm's overall strategy for foreign markets, its business model. The Honda Motor Company of Japan, for instance, localizes its strategy for all its major foreign markets. Each foreign subsidiary is an autonomous entity, with a full complement of business functions, including R&D, engineering, procurement, finance, manufacturing, and sales and marketing, and is run mostly by people hired locally. It attempts to become a local company wherever it has operations.

Groupe Danone (the Dannon Company in the U.S.), a French food products company, presents an excellent example of how to go about localizing products to suit the tastes of consumers in 140 foreign markets. Danone's turnover in 2014 was 21 billion euros, of which over 60 percent came from outside Europe and 90 percent from outside France. Of its four food product categories (fresh dairy, water, early nutrition, and medical nutrition), Danone is #1 or #2 worldwide in three (#1 in fresh dairy and #2 in waters and early nutrition). About 80 percent of Danone's fresh dairy products are made in the country where Danone is the market leader. In foreign markets, Danone adapts and designs its products to the tastes, habits, and nutritional needs of consumers there. For instance, Activia, Danone's probiotic yogurt product intended to improve digestive health, is sold in over 70 countries and tailored to consumer tastes—vegetable flavors in Japan, cactus in Mexico, kefir in Russia, and "Greek style" in the United States. Given the size and the diversity of the U.S. market, Activia is actually marketed in the U.S. in six varieties—Activia, Activia Light, Activia Greek, Activia Greek Light, Activia Fiber, and Activia Drinks.

For the water category, Danone uses a global approach for its Evian brand, though many other water brands are specific to the countries where they are manufactured and sold, e.g., Aqua in Indonesia and Bonafont in Brazil and Mexico.[9]

A Problem with the Local Approach

Localization is a very costly strategy as it involves customizing a firm's entire business model for each of its foreign markets. It can also result in an inconsistent brand image. Besides, attempts to localize a firm's strategy for each local market place huge demands on managers to not only understand the key differences between markets but also to leverage such differences to the firm's benefit.

A Potential Solution

The "think global, act local" *mantra* is often suggested as a solution to the global-local dilemma. Companies have sometimes attempted to adopt a global-local (or, simply *glocal*) approach for competing in foreign markets; however, the mantra is easier recited than implemented.[10] The strategic choices available to companies range from global, where a company applies the same strategy in all markets, to local, where strategic tools are country-specific, or to something in between. Coca-Cola, for example, shifted its stance, unsuccessfully, between "think global, act global" and "think local, act local" during the tenures of three different CEOs in the late 1990s and early 2000s.

Roberto Goizueta, Coca-Cola's famous Chairman and CEO from 1980 until his death in 1997, firmly believed that the world's markets are essentially similar and hence a global approach would work well. He considered Coca-Cola to be a truly global company that just happened to be headquartered in the United States. He adopted a "think global, act global" approach for doing business worldwide. "Goizueta engaged in an unprecedented amount of centralization and standardization. Divisions were consolidated, and regional groups headquartered in Atlanta. Consumer research, creative services, TV commercials, and most promotions were put under the supervision of Edge Creative, Coke's internal ad agency, with the idea of standardizing these marketing activities. ..."[11] No one questioned Goizueta's approach since the company's stock price had risen by 7,100 percent during his 16-year tenure.

After Goizueta's death, Douglas Ivestor became the Chairman and CEO and continued the strategy set by his predecessor, which had so far done extremely well for the company. However, a number of global events led to serious issues for Coca-Cola's performance in the late 1990s and early 2000s, as they did for many other multinationals. These included: the Asian currency crisis of 1997–1999, which had a wide-ranging impact on several emerging markets from Thailand to Brazil; the world's second largest economy (Japan) was in deflation by 1997; Russia defaulted on its debt in 1998; Germany was "the sick man of Europe" due to labor market rigidities and high costs; and the dot-com bust in America in early 2000.[12] Coca-Cola's stock price fell from $80.50 on July 1, 1998 to $61.31 on July 3, 2000, and to $44.60 on July 2, 2001, in line with major declines in the stock prices of most U.S. firms.

Douglas Daft took over as Chairman and CEO of Coca-Cola in 1999, and completely changed the company's approach to global business—it moved from "think global, act global" to "think local, act local." He led a major restructuring of the company with huge layoffs at the corporate headquarters in Atlanta and pushed decision making to local levels in foreign subsidiaries. A big change was made for global marketing at the corporate headquarters, which had total control over worldwide advertising under his predecessors. Daft delegated advertising decisions and budgets to executives in local subsidiaries overseas. This, however, did not stop Coca-Cola's performance decline, so much so that *The Wall Street Journal* declared in March 2002, "The 'think local, act local' mantra is gone. Oversight over marketing is returning to Atlanta."[13]

The potential solution to the globalization-localization dilemma suggested above, "think global, act local" is not necessarily a panacea for companies competing globally. Some companies like Nestlé and Groupe Danone have wisely chosen a global approach for some products (e.g., Nescafé and Evian), and a local approach for other products (such as Maggi soups/sauces and Activia) where consumer tastes and preferences predominate their buying decisions. Hence, it is not just a case of either global or local. A company can attempt both, but for different products. The Chinese have a term for it—*yin and yang*—indicating how apparently opposite choices could actually be complementary to each other. And, even for a global product, a company should localize its strategy for markets that are large enough to enable minimum-efficient-scale operations.

Which Products and Functions Are More Global Than Others?

Products that tend to be more global, or more tradable, are those with high value-to-weight ratio, such as computer chips and pharmaceuticals, or which do not get damaged or spoiled during transportation.[14] However, as we noticed in the case of CEMEX, even cement is traded across countries, in fact, across continents—a direct outcome of containerization and the significantly reduced cost of shipping. Similarly, services are global or tradable when they can be performed remotely, i.e., away from where the service recipient is located. In the connected economy, digital goods, such as a software package, and services, such as reading x-rays, which can be performed anywhere in the world, are most global.

Furthermore, some functions are more global than others, such as R&D, software development and maintenance, and many back office functions, e.g., accounting, insurance claim processing, and customer relationship management. Essentially, any activity that can be digitized is global and can be performed anywhere.

The Global Integration and Local Responsiveness Framework

One way to get past clichés like "think global, act local" and "think global, act global" is to utilize a systematic framework to help think about strategies for foreign markets. One such approach is the **global integration and local responsiveness framework**.

As noted earlier, firms want to be both global and local. The globalization-localization challenge arises partly because of the competitive environment they face in foreign markets. If they find customer needs, tastes, and preferences to be similar across markets, they are likely to find intense competition in those markets, because of the "commodity" nature of the product (implying too many sellers in the market selling similar products) and also because buyers are powerful and can easily switch between sellers. In such a situation, firms would have a strong need to keep costs low. On the other hand, if they find customer needs, tastes, and preferences varying significantly from market to market, they would have a strong need to be responsive to local markets. This leads us to the global integration and local responsiveness framework, along with three strategies for competing in foreign markets, shown in Figure 5.1.[15]

Multidomestic Strategy

Companies facing a high need for local responsiveness (because customer needs, tastes, and preferences differ from market to market and other considerations) must adapt their marketing strategy and business model to each of their markets. This is the multidomestic (or localization or multinational) strategy, whereby a firm localizes (customizes or adapts) its marketing strategy and its overall business model to suit customer needs, tastes, and preferences in each national market. Competitive strategy tends to be country-specific, without necessarily having any strategic linkages among a firm's different country markets. Most value-creation functions, such as R&D, procurement, manufacturing, and marketing, are delegated to country subsidiaries. Groupe Danone's Activia yogurt, Nestlé's Maggi soups and sauces, and Studio Moderna follow a multidomestic strategy for foreign markets.

Global Strategy

When companies face similar needs, tastes, and preferences as well as intense competition in foreign markets, they do not need to adapt their business model to each market. Instead, they should offer standardized products across markets. Global strategy involves the mass production of a standardized product in one, two, or a few optimal locations to take advantage of economies of scale and then to export the product worldwide. The "optimal" locations are decided based on the comparative advantages of nations, discussed in Chapter 3, and other factors such as those included in the PRISM framework of Chapter 4. Key organizational functions, such as R&D, marketing, and procurements are centralized in one or two (or a few) worldwide locations, typically at the corporate headquarters, with foreign subsidiaries being responsible for customer-facing functions

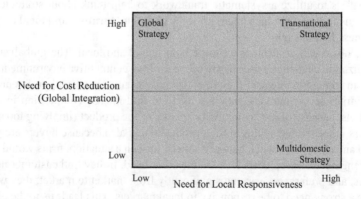

Figure 5.1 The Global Integration and Local Responsiveness Framework

Source: Charles W.L. Hill and G. Tomas M. Hult, *Global Business Today.* 9th Edition. New York: McGraw-Hill Education, 2016. Reprinted with permission.

such as sales, service, and customer relationship management. Of course, if a specific market is large enough, previously centralized functions, such as manufacturing and marketing, can also be decentralized to the market.

Global strategy is the global integration strategy—in the sense that the company must integrate its operations and strategy on a worldwide basis. That is, what it does in one country impacts, and is impacted by, what it does in other countries. This is because intense competition and standardized products often involve *multipoint competition*; that is, the company encounters the same global competitors in different product, country, or regional markets. Attacking a competitor in one market may have the unintended effect of the competitor attacking it in other markets, even in its home market. However, "[A]lthough multipoint competition provides more opportunities for competitive interactions and retaliation, paradoxically it results in less intense rivalry owing to mutual familiarity and deterrence. Empirical research provides substantial support for the 'mutual forbearance hypothesis' that multipoint competition reduces price and non-price rivalry and improves performance."[16] In such a situation, firms in an industry will collectively do well to compete on non-price factors, such as advertising and product features, and refrain from competing vigorously on price. Groupe Danone follows a global strategy for Evian, and so does Nestlé for Nescafé and other global brands.

Transnational Strategy

As firms compete increasingly in markets characterized by both high need for cost reduction and high need for local responsiveness, strategy scholars have suggested that they should employ a transnational strategy—a strategy whereby they can be both efficient and responsive, i.e., both global and local.[17] To do that, they must try to simultaneously achieve low costs through economies of scale, leveraging optimal locations for performing value-creation activities, and adapt their marketing strategy and business model to customer needs in individual country markets. Since knowledge and capabilities can reside anywhere within a firm's multinational enterprise system, they must also leverage such knowledge and capabilities irrespective of wherever they arise. In fact, a company must always leverage knowledge and capabilities throughout its global network, not just for transnational strategy, irrespective of where they arise. Implementing a transnational strategy entails conflicting demands and can be quite challenging for companies. Several approaches for implementing a transnational strategy are presented in the next section.

Generic Strategies in International Competition

Extending the discussion above, four **generic strategies**[18] can be identified for competing in foreign markets—multidomestic (or local), global, transnational, and regional.

Multidomestic Strategy

As indicated above, the multidomestic (localization) strategy involves customizing a firm's marketing strategy (the 4 Ps) and its overall business model to suit customer needs, tastes, and preferences in each national market. In addition to customer needs, a multidomestic strategy is called for to meet the requirements, design and engineering standards, and other regulations in host markets. There may also be country-specific geographic and climatic conditions that necessitate changes in marketing strategy. Most governments have specific requirements and regulations relating to product packaging, labeling, advertising, etc. There may also be price controls for certain products, such as pharmaceuticals, in certain markets. Furthermore, how developed a nation's distribution system is will dictate what products can actually be sold there. For instance, frozen desserts cannot be sold in a country that does not have adequate refrigeration facilities or where the refrigerated transport market is under-developed.

Firms following a multidomestic strategy often start with the core products and capabilities that made them successful in the home market and leverage them in foreign markets that may lack them. Therefore, only firms with a distinctive set of products and capabilities that are transferable abroad are likely to be successful with a multidomestic strategy. This is actually true for all strategies for competing in foreign markets, not just for multidomestic strategy. Firms like Procter & Gamble (P&G) of the United States and Unilever of the Netherlands and the U.K. typically entered foreign markets by creating a mini-P&G or a mini-Unilever, selling products there that had been successful in their home market, and utilizing brand management and marketing skills that had been honed at home. A similar strategy was adopted by Studio Moderna as it entered one CEE market after the other. Netflix entered foreign markets with online streaming service but customized its offerings in each market to suit the interests of customers there by licensing content from local media owners. Netflix not only localizes its content and marketing materials for each major market but even personalizes its offerings for individual subscribers based on user-specific choices such as language, viewing behavior, and taste preferences. All of these companies were typically either the first or early movers in the markets they entered.

Once a foreign subsidiary becomes an established entity in a foreign market, and after it has absorbed the initial transfer of products and capabilities from the parent corporation, it is given greater autonomy to become a fully functional business enterprise in that market, with a full range of value-creation activities and resources. By now, companies like P&G and Unilever have many well-established major subsidiaries in dozens of countries around the world, though, as we will see later in the chapter, their strategic approaches have changed over the years. Automotive firms like Ford, Honda, and Toyota similarly have a full range of R&D, production, procurement, marketing, and service infrastructures in all of their major markets to better serve local customers there. A multidomestic firm can indeed achieve economies of scale in individual country markets where demand is large enough to support scale-efficient operations.

Another interesting example can be found in the strategies of major players in India's IT services industry that have set up operations in the city of Dalian, China. Given its strategic location in Northeast China, close to Japan and South Korea, Dalian has a special place in the strategies of many IT services firms from India and elsewhere that have clients in Japan and/or South Korea. (Dalian is closer to Seoul than to Shanghai.) Some 870,000 speakers of the Japanese language and two million Koreans live in China, many in the Dalian region. Therefore, many large Indian IT players (including TCS, Infosys, Wipro, and Genpact) have set up operations in Dalian to benefit from its language and cultural affinity to their clients in Japan and South Korea, as well as to arbitrage the relatively low wages in Dalian compared to Tier-1 cities like Beijing and Shanghai.[19]

Foreign subsidiaries receive autonomy over their own affairs and are accountable for their own performance. They are able to leverage the power, the products, and the capabilities of the parent corporation but operate independently of each other. As such, a subsidiary's performance is typically not affected by the performance of other subsidiaries.

The fact that a multidomestic strategy implies a relatively low need for cost reduction does not mean that cost is not a factor. Cost considerations are always a factor in business, and no firm can overlook costs. This starts with designing products and processes for maximum efficiency, reducing duplication between subsidiaries, and taking advantage of economies of scale and scope wherever possible.

Global Strategy

Firms following a global strategy favor global efficiency over local responsiveness, create standardized products for all markets, and use the same business model worldwide. They take advantage of global economies of scale and scope by concentrating key operations in one, two, or a few optimal locations, from which the product is exported to other markets. If a firm's demand justifies manufacturing in more than one location, i.e., if the firm can achieve minimum-efficient-scale (MES) production levels in more than one location, then it should consider manufacturing in more than one location to benefit not only from scale economies but also from locational advantages and to be close to customers (see also Box 5.2). For instance, the Intel Corporation makes its chips, a standardized product, in nine fabrication plants ("fabs") in four countries (China, Ireland, Israel, and the United States), with about 75 percent of the production coming from the U.S. After the chips are manufactured, they are sent for assembly and testing to facilities in Malaysia, China, Costa Rica, and Vietnam. From there, they are exported to countries worldwide. If a global firm has scale-efficient operations in a specific country, it should also try and adapt its marketing strategy (the 4 Ps) to the market.

The foreign subsidiaries of a firm following global strategy act in an integrated manner, i.e., what a particular subsidiary does impacts (and is impacted by) what other subsidiaries do. Intel's highly integrated manufacturing system is enhanced by the fabs and other facilities—constantly sharing information with each other to improve product performance while continuing to fine-tune the manufacturing process.[20]

Although Sweden's IKEA designs its own products, it does not manufacture most of what it sells (the only manufacturing done by IKEA is through its Swedwood subsidiary, which supplies about 10 percent of the furniture sold by IKEA). Most IKEA products are manufactured and supplied by some 1,220 contract manufacturers in 55 countries, each restricted to producing only some products to be able to achieve global economies of scale. For instance, the Swedwood factory in Danville, Virginia, manufactures only the LACK, EXPEDIT, and BESTA brand lightweight panel furniture and storage systems (Box 5.2 has a brief discussion of the economies of scale concept).

Box 5.2 Economies of Scale

The concept of economies of scale is very important in economics, strategy, operations, marketing, and many other business functions. Essentially, a firm has *economies of scale* when its average cost of production (i.e., cost per unit) declines as output rises (Figure 5.2). Some sources of economies of scale are: fixed costs of operations get spread over a larger volume, the firm receives discounts for larger input purchases, and increased productivity of variable inputs. As a firm continues to increase its output in a single plant, its cost per unit continues to decline—until it reaches its lowest level, called the *Minimum Efficient Scale* (MES). MES is the production level at which the firm achieves the lowest cost per unit. When an established firm in an industry functions at the MES, it acts as a high-entry barrier for new entrants into the industry.

There is, however, a limit to economies of scale; beyond a certain size, a bigger firm may not always be the most efficient firm in its industry. If the firm continues to expand its production level beyond its MES level, it may encounter *diseconomies of scale* as the cost per unit begins to rise. Diseconomies of scale can arise when the project becomes so large that the management gets overwhelmed by the enormity of the task and

---

specialized resources get spread out too thin and because employee wages
are generally higher in larger firms than in smaller firms.

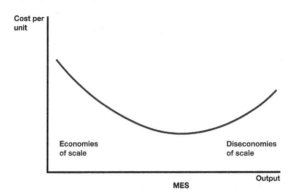

Figure 5.2 Economies of Scale Curve

Transnational Strategy

The transnational strategy involves attempts to simultaneously balance the need
for cost reduction and local responsiveness, while leveraging knowledge and
skills from throughout a firm's multinational enterprise system. Being globally
efficient and locally responsive are essentially contradictory goals for a firm to
achieve; however, that contradiction is not necessarily true. Such goals can be
achieved by leveraging the power of flexible manufacturing technologies and
information technologies as the following approaches show.

Mass Customization

One approach to implementing a transnational strategy is to use mass customization to satisfy local market needs, while not suffering the cost disadvantages of
short-run manufacturing (as compared to mass manufacturing). With the help of
flexible-manufacturing and IT technologies, a company can produce customized
products quickly for niche markets, even for individual customers, almost as cost
effectively as mass manufacturing. Mass customization processes often utilize
computerized numerical controlled machines (CNC machines), which combine
many types of manufacturing equipment, such as lathes, mills, and grinders
needed for producing a specific product, into a single machine tool. The CNC
machines are programmed to manufacture a product without someone having to
manually change the equipment set up from one manufacturing stage to another.
Such end-to-end integration of manufacturing is achieved through computer-aided

129

design (CAD) and computer-aided manufacturing (CAM) software programs. A CNC machine can produce 1,000 pieces of one item or one piece each of 1,000 items at low cost because the process is automatic and controlled by computers. CNC machines are relatively easily programmable and permit rapid changes to the manufacturing process, without human intervention (even software changes can be pre-programmed), and can respond quickly to marketplace changes. CNC machines have been around since at least the 1980s and can today be found in most manufacturing industries.[21] One implication of using CNC machines is the reduced importance of economies of scale in manufacturing.

Modular Design

Firms can also use modular design or modular architecture to combine the advantages of standardization and customization in designing a product, whether a mechanical device, an integrated circuit, or a software program. The idea is to divide a product into smaller parts, called modules, which can be independently produced and then combined to create different products. Each of the modules can be produced in large quantities to obtain economies of scale, and then various modules can be combined to make customized products for different markets. Lego bricks, which can be combined in different ways to make thousands of different objects, provide an excellent analogy for modular design. Dell, one of the largest computer technology firms in the world, uses modular design to customize the computers it sells to its customers. Dell realized that a computer is essentially a collection of parts (modules), such as disk drives, screen displays, memories, power packs, motherboards, etc., each of which can be produced in large quantities and then combined to make the computer. Using its make-to-order approach, Dell offers customized computers to its customers' specifications—the computers they "design" themselves while placing their orders—cost effectively.

Caterpillar of the United States, which makes diesel engines and earthmoving, mining, and other equipment and sells its products through dealerships worldwide, utilizes a modular design to respond to the need for cost reduction as well as local needs. Different climatic conditions, host government regulations, construction practices, and levels of economic development in different markets make it imperative for Caterpillar to differentiate its products for different markets. At the same time, Caterpillar must keep its costs low, especially because of the competitive pressures it faces from major competitors like Komatsu of Japan and Deere & Company of the United States. Therefore, for any piece of equipment, such as a bulldozer, it manufactures the basic module in large quantities in one, two, or a few locations to benefit from economies of scale and locational advantages and then ships it to manufacturing plants close to local markets where they add peripherals and other features to customize it for local needs. Caterpillar also designs its products to include as many identical components as possible, which it produces in a few large-scale plants around the world.

Platform Design

The idea of platform design is somewhat similar to that of modular design in the sense that a product platform also consists of one or more standardized components. The difference, however, is that the same platform is shared among different products, whereas the basic module in modular design can only be used to make a specific product, e.g., a bulldozer in the case of Caterpillar. The concept of platforms is common in the IT industry, e.g., Apple's iOS and Google's Android platforms, which have spawned thousands of apps. Car companies have traditionally shared the same platform for different brands and models. A car platform consists of the underbody, suspension, and axles, plus components such as the steering mechanism, engine, and powertrain. Using such a platform, a car company can design several distinct car models to suit different customer groups—with substantial cost savings in product development and through large-scale manufacturing of common platform components. The German automaker Volkswagen (VW) uses the same *Modularer Querbaukasten* (MQB) platform to make several car brands and models, including the Audi A3, the VW Polo, Golf, Passat, and Tiguan, as well as Seat León and Škoda Octavia, with claimed savings of 20 percent in materials cost and 30 percent in the cost of tooling and facilities.[22]

Some of the major Indian IT services firms have been investing in R&D and creating their own platform-based services since their traditional IT services business is quickly getting commoditized. IT services firms typically invoice their clients for services provided to them on a time-and-materials (T&M) revenue model, but with new, emerging competitors from even lower-cost geographies, India's IT services firms have come under a great deal of pressure. Businesses built on platforms are IP-led businesses, and revenue comes from licenses or fees for software as a service (SaaS). For instance, "Infosys Edge" is a family of some 20 IP-based products and business platforms, hosted and managed by Infosys, India's second largest IT services firm. The same platform can be used by multiple clients for multiple applications, which is cost effective for both Infosys and its clients.[23]

3D Printing

Three-dimensional (3D) printing is the latest development in manufacturing technologies. It involves *additive* manufacturing—building a three-dimensional object from a digital model one layer at a time—as compared to the traditional (*subtractive*) manufacturing, which takes a piece of solid material and uses processes such as cutting, drilling, and machining to remove material from it to make a product. 3D printing has been used in hundreds and thousands of applications, including jewelry, footwear, industrial components, medical implants, human organs, and even a fully functional car. Three-dimensional objects are formed using a process similar to that used by an inkjet printer, except that a 3D printer continues to place layer after layer of "ink" over the other to make an object. 3D printers use a variety of materials instead of "ink," such as metals, plastics, and even organic materials such as live cells.

According to Vivek Srinivasan of Computer Sciences Corporation's Leading Edge Forum, "3D printing can make objects with a complex internal structure that would be almost impossible using traditional methods. There's no large factory and no retooling of an entire assembly line. The same printer that creates a piece of art can be used next to print a bike part. And that printer can be kept close to the point of consumption, which has implications for logistics."[24]

Traditional manufacturing requires quite a bit of preparatory work, such as setting up plant and machinery, making tools, molds, etc., before manufacturing can actually take place. As such, the lead time for producing something with traditional manufacturing, when plant and machinery are already available, can take from 1–2 weeks to 2–3 months before the first items start coming off the production line. With 3D printing, however, the needed items can be printed almost on demand without need for much ramp-up or tooling in as little as 2–3 days and without need for major investment in manufacturing plants and equipment. It can also enable an organization to develop and test prototypes for quick customer feedback before taking up full manufacturing.

There are still limitations in 3D printing, mainly that not all materials can be used in a 3D printing process. As the technology matures, more and more materials are being used for 3D printing. 3D printing technology is fast evolving, though it is still far from replacing factories that mass-produce identical products quickly and at low cost. However, it is already being used for mass customization where a product is designed and produced for individual customers or for groups of customers. A 3D printer can indeed make (print) hundreds or thousands of identical products. Still, as of now, these products are made at a higher cost per unit, even though they take much less time to make than traditional manufacturing.

Regional Strategy

The regional strategy is an intermediate stage between multidomestic and global, or between multidomestic and transnational, strategies. Many firms that compete abroad operate only within certain regions rather than on a global basis, and for which a regional strategy that takes advantage of intra-regional similarities is more appropriate. Furthermore, a global firm might find it beneficial to adopt a regional strategy for different regions to leverage both intra-regional similarities and inter-regional differences to its advantage. Generally, however, it is a multidomestic firm that finds itself overwhelmed by competition in different markets due to its high cost structure and then decides to move toward a global or a transnational strategy via a regional approach.

A regional strategy involves grouping countries with similar characteristics into regions and then following a consistent strategy within each region. A firm following a regional strategy attempts to take advantage of scale economies within each region due to intra-regional similarities, while at the same time customizing its marketing and overall strategy for different regions. The regional strategy is adopted by firms that expand their footprint beyond their home market to the immediate region in which they operate, as well as by firms that find their multidomestic strategy under assault by competition and want to achieve at least some benefit of economies of scale.

Procter & Gamble of the United States is an excellent example of how a firm had to move from a multidomestic strategy in Europe to a pan-European (regional) strategy in the late 1970s and 1980s when it faced growing competition in its European markets. P&G established its first foreign subsidiary in England in 1930, and set up *mini-P&Gs* in most West European countries during the 1950s and 1960s. Each of these mini-P&Gs was an autonomous entity within the P&G corporate umbrella and followed a multidomestic strategy. The European subsidiaries sold many of P&G's products that had been successful in the U.S. market, including personal care products and laundry and cleaning products. An R&D center, called the European Technical Center (ETC) was established in Brussels, Belgium, in 1963 to serve the European market. Walter Lingle, P&G's overseas vice president in the mid-1950s, set policies for foreign subsidiaries, saying "Washing habits... vary widely from country to country. We must tailor products to meet consumer demands in each nation. We cannot simply sell products with U.S. formulas. They simply won't work. They won't be accepted." And, "The best way to succeed in other countries is to build in each one as exact a replica of the U.S. Procter & Gamble organization as it is possible to create."[25] Besides, national regulations regarding product formulation and advertising as well as competitive conditions varied considerably from country to country, which also necessitated customizing products for each national market. Each subsidiary had a sizable R&D staff responsible for adapting products brought from P&G headquarters to their own markets, seeking assistance from the ETC on technical matters as needed. The result was a good deal of marketing-strategy and business-model customization at the subsidiary level.

In addition to these many differences, consumers in different countries preferred washing their clothes at different temperatures. Accordingly, P&G and other detergent makers offered different versions of the same products in different countries. P&G's Ariel laundry detergent powder, for instance, came in nine different versions for Europe.

All such customization, however, meant much duplication in product development, manufacturing, and marketing among P&G's European subsidiaries and high costs since demand in no single country was large enough to achieve economies of scale (minimum efficient scale) in any of these functions. And, with growing competition and lower profitability by the late 1970s, P&G Europe's management began to explore products and technologies that had the potential to be sold throughout Europe—with the idea of developing Europe-wide (pan-European) brands and marketing approaches. Vizir, a new heavy duty liquid (HDL) laundry detergent, was being evaluated as a test case for Europe-anization in the early 1980s.

The Vizir HDL laundry detergent had been developed to be marketed throughout Europe as an all-temperature detergent, with expected savings to come from the large-scale manufacture of a standardized detergent, along with standardized packaging, multilingual labels, flexibility in sourcing inputs, and reduced inventory levels. Vizir was P&G's first pan-European brand since the company's market research indicated some convergence in consumer laundry habits among different countries. However, a major motivation for developing and marketing a pan-European brand was to pre-empt competitive entry into this newly created product category (HDL), which P&G's major competitors had also been eyeing.

After several months of test marketing, Vizir was launched in June 1981 in Germany, Europe's largest market for laundry detergents, and in several other West European countries within the year. Germany was designated as the "lead country" for Vizir and given the responsibility of exploring further opportunities for the standardized product, its packaging, and promotion, and to help eliminate any duplication in brand management between countries.

By the 1970s, 1980s, and 1990s, as competition developed, the competitive situation faced by P&G Europe was also faced by many other MNEs that had previously been successful in foreign markets with multidomestic strategies. Companies such as Unilever, Philips, and Nestlé were also forced to move away from a multidomestic to a regional strategy as an intermediate step to eventually become global or transnational corporations over the coming decades.

Unilever's Changing Strategy

The case of Unilever of Britain and the Netherlands is especially instructive as it transitioned from a multidomestic to a global and finally to a transnational strat-egy over a period of about three decades. Unilever had historically been orga-nized on a decentralized basis, with national subsidiaries worldwide responsible for production, sales, marketing, and distribution in their respective markets. However, Unilever, with 17 autonomous subsidiaries in Western Europe by the early 1990s, was finding itself unable to compete with strong multinationals like P&G and Nestlé, which had already moved on to regional or even global strat-egies, building successful regional and global brands. Its decentralized, multi-domestic structure was a high-cost structure unable to benefit from economies of scale or global branding. In order to change its approach for the European market, it had to change its decentralized structure. Therefore, in 1996, Unilever introduced an organizational structure based on regional business groups as a precursor to employing a regional strategy, with each business group responsible for several products or product lines within the group. For instance, the European

Business Group consisted of product divisions such as detergents and ice cream and frozen foods. In Europe, the number of manufacturing plants making soap was reduced from 10 to 2, product sizes and packaging were standardized, and unified pan-European advertising was implemented. The 17 European subsidiaries were tasked to develop and execute a consistent pan-European strategy for their products.[26]

A pan-European strategy also made sense with growing European integration. For instance, the Single European Act of 1987 was intended to remove all frontier controls within the European Community by December 31, 1992, with mutual recognition of product standards in all member countries, removal of barriers to competition in banking and insurance, and removal of restrictions on foreign exchange transactions. As of February 1992, the European Community came to be known as the European Union (EU), which now consists of 28 member states.

Unilever's pan-European strategy of the 1990s actually turned out to be an intermediate step as it moved toward a global strategy by the early 2000s. In 2000, Unilever reduced the number of divisions to two global product divisions—a food division and a home personal care division—with each division organized by geography (Figure 5.3). The number of manufacturing plants was reduced from 380 to 280 by 2004, and the number of brands was reduced from 1600 to 400. The brands were then marketed on a regional or a global basis.

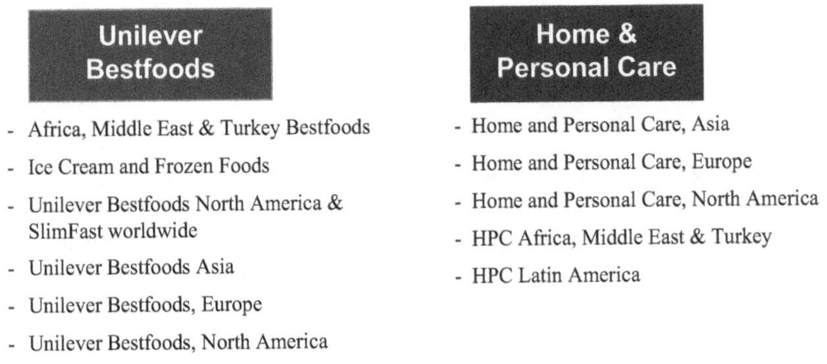

Unilever Bestfoods	Home & Personal Care
- Africa, Middle East & Turkey Bestfoods	- Home and Personal Care, Asia
- Ice Cream and Frozen Foods	- Home and Personal Care, Europe
- Unilever Bestfoods North America & SlimFast worldwide	- Home and Personal Care, North America
- Unilever Bestfoods Asia	- HPC Africa, Middle East & Turkey
- Unilever Bestfoods, Europe	- HPC Latin America
- Unilever Bestfoods, North America	

Figure 5.3 Unilver's Organizational Structure, 2000

Configuration and Coordination

Strategies other than a multidomestic strategy involve spreading a firm's value-creation activities in multiple countries or locations. (A firm following a multidomestic strategy performs most value-creation activities within the countries in which it operates, with no need to configure or coordinate its activities between countries.) Configuration for global, transnational, and regional strategies involves decisions such as where in the world to perform which value-creation activity and whether a specific activity should be centralized in one location or decentralized to many locations. If the decision is to decentralize an activity to many locations, the question would then be how many locations. Coordination involves processes by which dispersed activities are coordinated within a firm's multinational enterprise system or network.[27]

Decisions regarding where to locate specific activities are best made based on the comparative advantages of nations, as well as on factors such as those included in the PRISM framework. Furthermore, an activity should be performed in as many locations as can support minimum efficient scale (MES) operations because if plant size at a specific location increases beyond MES, diseconomies of scale can arise and lead to higher costs.

Centralizing manufacturing operations in one, two, or a few locations is appropriate when[28]:

- the manufacturing processes involve high fixed costs and high minimum efficient scale relative to global demand;
- there are major differences in input costs and other factors that impact the overall cost structure between countries;
- trade barriers are low, so that a company can produce its goods in a few locations and export them worldwide;
- the value-to-weight ratio for the goods being produced is high, and when the goods do not get damaged or spoiled during shipping and transportation; and
- exchange rates are relatively stable.

Concluding Remarks

The preceding discussion identified four generic strategies for how companies create value through international operations: multidomestic, global, transnational, and regional. They are *generic* in the sense that they are applicable to most firms competing internationally. Recall that this chapter has been concerned with strategies for firms competing in foreign markets by having actual presence there, i.e., through FDI, rather than through exporting, importing, licensing or franchising, which do not necessarily require physical presence in foreign markets. We revert briefly to these approaches in the next chapter. It should also be noted that firms generally do not follow the pure form of any of these strategies. For instance, global firms like IKEA, Pizza Hut, and other fast-food companies do customize some of their products to meet customer needs in foreign markets, though their overall strategy (global strategy) remains unchanged. Pizza Hut, for instance, is a sit-down restaurant with waiter service in Poland and has rice dishes on the menu in India for people who don't eat pizza. Krispy Kreme offers eggless donuts in India, and KFC expects one-third of its sales in India to come from vegetarian dishes.

Firms following a multidomestic strategy can indeed benefit from economies of scale in markets where demand is large enough to support minimum efficient scale operations. P&G and Unilever, which traditionally went abroad with a multidomestic strategy, did benefit from economies of scale in major markets such as India. A firm may follow different strategies for the same product at different times during their internationalization journey, and sometimes can benefit from using different strategies for different products at the same time. Netflix localizes its content and marketing strategy for each foreign market; however, the bulk of its content for all markets (e.g., movies and its own series, House of Cards) is fairly standardized except for language dubbing or use of subtitles.

Following is a list of seven action items for the internationalizing firm irrespective of the strategy (multidomestic, global, etc.) it adopts. Refer to Table 5.1 for the distinctive features of each.

- A firm's strategy for foreign markets should begin with the identification of the distinctive products and capabilities that provided it competitive advantage in its home market. Then, explore which of these products/capabilities are transferable to foreign markets, and which foreign markets might have a need for them.
- Expand your international footprint by leveraging your distinctive products and capabilities in foreign markets; consider being a first or an early mover.
- Leverage the learning and experience gained in markets entered as a first or an early mover for other markets later on.
- Take advantage of economies of scale and scope in countries/regions where demand justifies setting up minimum efficient scale (MES) operations. Note, however, that flexible manufacturing technologies and information and communication technologies have lessened the importance of economies of scale for many goods.
- Tap optimal locations for performing value-creation activities, such as R&D, procurement, operations, and marketing. Optimal locations are those that offer the most cost-effective resources, based on the comparative advantages of nations, and lowest risk. (However, the globalization of value chains and ICTs have allowed firms to match or even circumvent the comparative advantages of nations in some cases as they are able to source many inputs from anywhere in the world cost-effectively.)
- As a firm's product range broadens, the core activities for some products may best be located in other countries to leverage their comparative advantages. For a major product, such as Google's AdWords product, while teams from many countries work cohesively to develop and maintain the product, it is not *headquartered* in any single country.
- Leverage learning, capabilities, and innovation throughout your multinational enterprise system irrespective of where such knowledge comes from.

Table 5.1 One More Time—How to Create Value through International Operations

Strategy	How to Create Value
Multidomestic	Adapt your products to meet customer needs in each foreign market.
	Delegate most value-creation activities to foreign subsidiaries, giving them a fair amount of autonomy over their own affairs.
Global	Offer standardized products in all foreign markets—produced in one, two or a few optimal locations, and exported worldwide.
	Exploit economies of scale and scope by centralizing various functions (R&D, procurement, operations, marketing, etc.) in locations wherever they can be best performed; many core functions are, however, often kept at the corporate headquarters.
	Coordinate strategies between subsidiaries, especially in view of multipoint competition.
Transnational	All of the above.
	Use mass customization, modular design, platform design, and/or 3D printing to achieve both global efficiency and responsiveness to local market needs.
	Leverage knowledge and skills from throughout the multinational enterprise system.
Regional	Group countries with common characteristics into regions and then follow a consistent strategy within each region.
	Adapt your products to meet customer needs in each region.
	Take advantage of intra-regional similarities (by offering standardized products within each region) and inter-regional differences (by locating value-creation activities wherever they can be best performed).

Notes

1 Source: http://www.studio-moderna.com/. Accessed August 26, 2015.
2 A good deal of information for this introductory mini case study is taken from the company's website, author's phone and email communications with CEO Sandi Češko, and the Harvard Business School Publishing case study: Daniel Isenberg, "Studio Moderna—A Venture in Eastern Europe," Harvard Business School Publishing Case Study Number 9-808-110, July 21, 2009.
3 Private email communication to the author.
4 Isenberg, p. 7.
5 Private email communication to the author.
6 Theodore Levitt, "The Globalization of Markets," *Harvard Business Review*, May-June 1983: 92–102.
7 Ford Escort was launched in Europe in 1968 and in the U.S. in 1981.
8 The discussion of Ford's world car project is based on several sources, including: Alex Taylor III and Wilton Woods, "Ford's $6 Billion Baby," *Fortune*, June 28, 1993, from which this quote is taken; and Maria Isabel Studer Noguez, *Ford and the Global Strategies of Multinationals: The North American Auto Industry* (New York: Routledge, 2003).

9 Source: www.danone.com and www.dannon.com.

10 "Mantra" in Hinduism and Buddhism is a sacred word or utterance that is repeated frequently to help one concentrate or meditate. Hence, we use the term "recite" rather than "speak."

11 This discussion of Coca-Cola is based on Pankaj Ghemawat, *Redefining Global Strategy: Crossing Borders in a World Where Differences Still Matter* (Boston: Harvard Business School Press, 2007). The quote is from p. 20.

12 The Economist, "The World Economy in 2015 Will Carry Troubling Echoes of the Late 1990s," *The Economist*, December 20, 2014.

13 Quoted in Ghemawat, 2007, p. 22.

14 Recall that we use the term "product" for both physical goods and services.

15 C.K. Prahalad and Yves L. Doz, *The Multinational Mission: Balancing Local Demands and Global Vision* (New York: Free Press, 1987).

16 Javier Gimeno, "Multipoint Competition." In *The Palgrave Encyclopedia of Strategic Management*. (Basingstoke, UK: Palgrave, 2014).

17 Christopher Bartlett and Sumantra Ghoshal, *Managing across Borders: The Transnational Solution* (Boston: Harvard Business School Press, 1998).

18 Michael Porter defined two main generic strategies, cost leadership and differentiation. These typically pertain to domestic business, i.e., these are the strategies by which a firm could create value or competitive advantage in its home market. In this section, we are defining generic strategies in international competition, i.e., how a firm could create value through international operations. These are "generic" in the sense that they are applicable to most industries. When in a specific foreign market, Porter's generic strategy framework still applies.

19 Vinod K. Jain, "Capability Building and Innovation in the IT Services Industry in India and China," research for Institute of Emerging Market Studies and funded by E&Y, September 29, 2013.

20 Source: Intel Global Manufacturing Facts, accessed from http://download.intel.com/ newsroom/kits/22nm/pdfs/Global-Intel-Manufacturing_FactSheet.pdf.

21 The author's first exposure to a CNC machine was in the early 1980s when he worked for the Indian subsidiary of a British MNE, Molins PLC.

22 Dan Neil, "At Geneva, the Promise and Perils of Sharing," *The Wall Street Journal*, September 9, 2012.

23 Jain, 2013.

24 CSC, "How 3D Printing Will Turn Manufacturing on Its Head," Computer Sciences Corporation, 2012. Accessed from http://www.csc.com/townhall/insights/94525-how_3d_printing_will_turn_manufacturing_on_its_head#summary.

25 For more information, please refer to Christopher A. Bartlett, "Procter & Gamble Europe: Vizir Launch," Harvard Business School Case Study, 1989, Number 9-384-139. The quotes appear on pp. 3–4.

26 This discussion of Unilever is based on: Charles W.L. Hill, Gareth R. Jones, and Melissa A. Schilling, *Strategic Management Theory: An Integrated Approach*, 11th Edition (Nashville, TN: South-Western Publishing, 2014). Chapter 13.

27 Michael E. Porter, "Competing across Locations: Enhancing Competitive Advantage through a Global Strategy." In Michael E. Porte, *On Competition* (Boston: Harvard Business School Publishing, 2008), pp. 305–44.

28 Adapted from Charles W.L. Hill, *International Business: Competing in the Global Marketplace*, 9th Edition (New York: McGraw-Hill/Irwin, 2013, Chapter 17).

6

HOW TO GROW IN FOREIGN MARKETS

Coca-Cola has a long-term business plan and vision, based on our
permanent investment commitment.... We, as a system, have been
investing [in Mexico] an average of $1 billion every year for the
last ten years, and we are reaffirming this commitment until 2020.
—Francisco Crespo, President, Coca-Cola
Mexico, July 16, 2014

The previous two chapters were about entering and competing in foreign markets. This chapter is about growing in foreign markets—not growing internationally, what may be called a firm's internationalization journey, but growing
within the foreign markets entered earlier. Netflix expanded its global footprint
by entering successively into dozens of new markets since September 2010,
as part of its high-octane internationalization journey. Honda Motor Company
Ltd. of Japan also entered many new markets over the last several decades, but
systematically strengthened its presence in its major markets such as the United
States. Honda currently has 22 automotive assembly plants in 13 countries
outside Japan, including four in the United States, its largest foreign market
(Box 6.1). In the U.S., Honda also has an auto engine plant in Anna, Ohio, its
largest engine plant in the world, as well as major R&D facilities in California,
Florida, North Carolina, and Ohio. (Box 6.1 shows only Honda's automotive
assembly plants in different countries, not its other investments.) In each market, Honda also established a distribution system by appointing dealerships and
consumer finance operations.

Much of Honda's expansion worldwide was achieved through foreign
direct investment—mostly through wholly owned greenfield investments, but
also through some joint ventures (JVs), such as its 2003 Honda Automobiles
(China) Company JV with Dongfeng Motor Corporation and Guangzhou
Automotive Group Co., Ltd. of China. Joint ventures and mergers and acquisitions (M&As) are two of the most common methods of growing in foreign
markets.

140

Box 6.1 Honda Motor Company's Assembly Plants Outside Japan

Region	Country/Location	Year Opened
Asia	**China**	
	Guangzhou	1998
	Wuhan	2003
	India	
	Noida, Uttar Pradesh	1995
	Bhiwadi, Rajasthan	2009
	Indonesia	
	Jakarta	1976
	Karawang	2003
	Pakistan	
	Lahore	1992
	Taiwan	
	Pingtung County	2002
	Thailand	
	Ayutthaya	2000
	Turkey	
	Gebze	1992
Europe	**United Kingdom**	
	Swindon	1992
North America	**Canada**	
	Allison, Ontario	1986
	United States	
	Marysville, Ohio	1982
	East Liberty, Ohio	1989
	Lincoln, Alabama	2001
	Greenburg, Indiana	2008
South America	**Argentina**	
	Florencio, Varela	2006
	Campana	2011
	Brazil	
	Manaus, Amazonas	1976
	Sumaré, São Paulo	1997
	Mexico	
	El Salto, Jasilco	1995
	Celaya	2014

In July 2014, Coca-Cola Company announced that, following its $5 billion investment over the previous five years, it would invest another $8.2 billion in Mexico through 2020. The new investment is designed to strengthen Coca-Cola's manufacturing, refrigeration equipment, and marketing and distribution infrastructure in Mexico. Coca-Cola has been in Mexico for almost 90 years and is one of the nation's largest employers, accounting for over 90,000 direct and some 800,000 indirect jobs.[1] The July announcement came shortly after PepsiCo's announcement in January 2014 that it would invest $5 billion in Mexico over the next five years to strengthen its food and beverage business there. This is in addition to the $3 billion it had already invested in the country since 2009. PepsiCo has been in Mexico, its third largest market in the world, for over a century. In 2014, Switzerland's Nestlé also announced a $1 billion investment in Mexico to build an infant nutrition factory and a pet food factory and to expand its breakfast cereal factory in the country.[2] Food products companies like Coca-Cola, PepsiCo, and Nestlé have been increasing their investment in Mexico despite the introduction in January 2014 of an 8 percent tax ("fat tax") on high-calorie foods such as potato chips, ice cream, and chocolate, and a 12 percent tax on soda in the country.

Not just food products companies are investing in Mexico. Some of the other companies expanding their presence in Mexico are automakers Volkswagen, the Daimer-Nissan joint venture COMPAS, and BMW; auto-parts supplier Delphi; and home-improvement retailer Home Depot.[3] After a sharp decline in 2012, FDI in Mexico, Latin America's second-largest economy, has been rising as a result of the lower cost of doing business, a relatively low corporate tax rate (30 percent, compared to 34 percent in Brazil and 39 percent in the U.S.), a fast growth rate, growing affluence, a young population, and business-friendly policies.

How to Grow in Foreign Markets

The approaches for expanding a firm's business in a specific foreign market are essentially the same as for expanding its business in its home market— diversification, vertical integration, and geographic expansion.[4] These typically fall within the purview of a firm's *corporate strategy*, which involves identifying a set of businesses with which to compete and following the logic that doing so will create greater value than individual firms will competing as stand-alone businesses.[5] Corporate strategy is about expanding a firm's scope—horizontal scope, vertical scope, or geographic scope (or decreasing a firm's scope through divestment).

Diversification

Diversification involves strategies to add to a firm's existing line(s) of business in a market. Haier of China, the world's second-largest home appliance maker, entered the U.S. market in 1994 with a compact refrigerator suitable for college dorms and small offices (Chapter 4). Once its compact refrigerator became successful, Haier expanded its U.S. presence by diversifying into *related* products such as full-sized refrigerators, freezers, air-conditioners, and washing machines. In 2001, it set up a $40 million industrial park and refrigerator factory in South Carolina. Many of Haier's expansions in its foreign markets were achieved through M&As and joint ventures, but also through greenfield investments such as the one in South Carolina. Sometimes firms diversify into *unrelated* product markets, though they rarely attempt unrelated diversification in foreign markets.

Vertical Integration

Vertical integration involves expanding a firm's business in a market by extending its value chain in the country—going upstream by getting into the business of its suppliers (backward vertical integration) or going downstream by getting into the business of its customers (forward vertical integration). Tysons Foods Inc. of the United States is one of the world's largest processors and marketers of meat and poultry, with about 30 percent of its $38 billion worldwide sales coming from poultry. For decades, Tyson bought chickens from independent farmers worldwide for processing and sales to its customers—supermarkets, wholesalers, restaurant chains, meatpackers (such as companies that make sausages), and others. For instance, in the U.S., its largest market, Tyson contracts with some 4,000 farmers to each raise about 100,000 chickens at a time. However, in China, which has mostly small farmers and where food security has been a continuing issue, Tyson decided in the early 2010s to set up its own chicken farms, a case of backward vertical integration. By 2015, it is expected to have 90 such farms in China that will supply company-raised chickens to its processing plants there. With fast-growing poultry sales, China overtook the U.S. as the world's largest consumer of chickens in 2012, encouraging Tyson and other food companies to increase their investment in the country. For instance, Cargill Inc., another food products company from the United States, established a chicken-processing plant in China in 2012 and has been opening its own farms to raise chickens as part of a $250 million investment in the country.[6]

Consider Coca-Cola Company's acquisition of its bottlers as a case of forward vertical integration. The Coca-Cola Company makes soft drink concentrate, which it sells to bottlers who add water and other ingredients to it to make the soft drinks sold in supermarkets, restaurants, and elsewhere. Independent bottlers are responsible for about 72 percent of the company's global sales volume, with the rest coming from company-owned bottlers. In the early 1980s, Coca-Cola Co. began acquiring some of its independent bottlers, such as the Coca-Cola Bottling Company of New York, the Associated Coca-Cola Bottling Company, and the bottling operations of Beatrice Foods and the Lupton Family. This led to the formation of Coca-Cola Enterprises (CCE), later spun off by the company in 1986 as an independent entity. For the next 24 years, CCE operated as Coca-Cola's main bottler in North America and Western Europe. In February 2010, Coca-Cola reversed its long-standing strategy of keeping its bottling operations, which are more capital-intensive and less profitable than concentrate production, separate from its core concentrate business by acquiring CCE's North American operations. Reacquiring its bottling operations was intended to give the Coca-Cola Company greater flexibility in adapting to changing customer tastes and greater control over its downstream operations (and over profits).

Sometimes a company has to necessarily adopt vertical integration since the intermediaries it needs do not exist in its market. That was the case with Studio Moderna's expansion into Central and Eastern Europe. It set up its own call centers and delivery services since such intermediaries did not yet exist in the newly independent CEE region in the 1990s (Chapter 5).

Geographic Expansion

Involves expanding a firm's geographic footprint in a market after initial entry and success there. The Carlsberg Group of Denmark, the fourth largest brewer in the world, has a major presence in Western Europe, Eastern Europe, and Asia. Carlsberg, which had been exporting beer to China since the mid-19th century, officially began its operations in Greater China in 1978. It opened the Carlsberg Brewery in Hong Kong in 1981, which formed the basis for its expansion into the eastern part of mainland China. In 1995, Carlsberg acquired a majority stake in a brewery in Huizhou, Guangdong Province, and moved all production from Hong Kong to Huizhou by 1999. Carlsberg's geographic expansion into the huge Western part of the country began in 2003 with the acquisition of Kunming Huashi Brewery and the Dali Beer Group in the Yunnan Province. With several other investments in the region during 2004–2010 (Box 6.2), Carlsberg is today the leading brewery group in West China.[7]

Growth Mechanisms

As highlighted by the examples discussed above, companies typically expand in their existing foreign markets through greenfield investments (or internal development), mergers and acquisitions, and joint ventures. Firms, in fact, have many options available to them to enter, compete, and grow in foreign markets, ranging from exporting/importing, licensing/franchising, to foreign direct investment and joint ventures and strategic alliances. Chapter 4 has a brief discussion of each of these approaches. Exporting/importing and licensing are often more appropriate for entering new markets than for expanding into

144

Box 6.2 Carlsberg Group's Expansion into West China

2003	Carlsberg acquires 100% shareholding in Kunming Huashi Brewery and Dali Beer Group in the Yunnan Province
2004	Carlsberg acquires major shareholding in Lhasa Brewery in the Tibet Autonomous Region
2004	Carlsberg acquires major shareholding in Lanzhou Huanghe's three breweries in the Gansu Province
2004	Together with local partners, Carlsberg invests in greenfield brewery in Qinghai—with production starting in 2005
2004	Carlsberg acquires 34.5% shareholding in Wusu Brewery in Xinjiang Autonomous Region
2005	Carlsberg increases shareholding in Wusu Brewery Group to 50% and, later, via Xinjiang Hops Co. Ltd holds 10% of Wusu
2006	Through a joint venture with Ningxia Nongken Enterprise Group, Carlsberg establishes a greenfield brewery in Ningxia Autonomous Region; Carlsberg owns 70% of the joint venture
2008	Carlsberg becomes the 2nd largest shareholder of Chongqing Brewery Co. Ltd by holding 17.5% shareholding
2010	Carlsberg increases stake in Chongqing Brewery Co. Ltd to 29.71%

Source: http://www.carlsberggroup.com/Markets/asia/Pages/China.aspx.

existing markets. Fast food and service firms typically use franchising to enter, compete, and expand in foreign markets. The rest of this chapter focuses on the Build|Buy|Ally framework that represents the options available to firms to grow their business in foreign markets via internal development, M&As, and alliances and joint ventures (Figure 6.1).

Figure 6.1 shows the strategies a multinational firm employs to expand its business in a foreign market. A firm may adopt any of these strategies, use different strategies for different products, or use different strategies for the same product at different times or in different markets.

Build (Greenfield Investment or Internal Development)

Companies sometimes prefer making a greenfield investment (a *build* strategy) to other options for expanding in their existing foreign markets. This could be due to habit or hubris or for strategic reasons such as the opportunity to safeguard their intellectual property, maintaining full control over operations, the ability to transfer their organizational routines and corporate culture to the foreign subsidiary, and learning in the host market. As mentioned in Chapter 4, a greenfield operation offers companies a greater opportunity to learn about a foreign market compared to any of the other options. Companies will want to

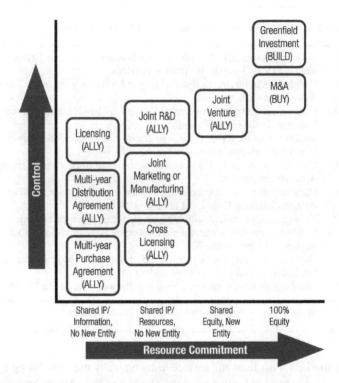

Figure 6.1 MNE Growth Strategy: The Build|Buy|Ally Framework

use the greenfield strategy if they have the time and in-house expertise needed to build or if they need the foreign subsidiaries tailored to their exact needs. Since a greenfield investment can take two, three, or more years to become operational, firms must not be in a great hurry to strengthen their presence in the foreign market. Otherwise they should consider acquiring another firm or entering into a joint venture. A company also might take up greenfield investment if no clear acquisition targets are available in the market.

Making greenfield investments has often been the *modus operandi* of automotive firms like Toyota, Mercedes-Benz, and Hyundai as they *expanded* their business in the United States. Toyota, after exporting cars to the U.S. for many years, entered into a joint venture with General Motors, NUMMI, in 1984 to set up an auto assembly plant in Fremont, California, that made both Toyota and GM cars (Chapter 3). After learning the ropes of doing business in America, Toyota established its own assembly plant in the U.S. in 1986 (Box 6.3 is a mini case study, General Motors in Poland).

The build strategy, however, has some major disadvantages. It almost always requires a high commitment of the company's managerial, financial, and organizational resources. (If the company is seeking such resources in a foreign market, it would be better to pursue a joint venture or an acquisition.) The company has to bear the full cost and risk of investing in the foreign market, and, since this is a time-consuming approach, the realization of competitive and financial benefits is usually much delayed. (In a merger/acquisition situation, the company also has to bear the full cost and risk of investing in the foreign market but has the potential of deriving benefits much sooner.) Besides, since the process may take several years, anything can happen to subvert the company's designs for the market and expose it to unnecessary risk. Finally, since the company making a greenfield investment will necessarily take market share from the existing play-ers (the incumbents), it will risk stronger retaliation from them compared to if it were to make an acquisition in the country.

Box 6.3 General Motors in Poland

General Motors of the U.S. entered Poland in May 1991, shortly after the fall of the Soviet Union and the beginning of a market economy in Central and Eastern Europe. GM started its business in Poland by importing Opel cars from its other plants in Europe. In 1992, GM entered into a majority joint venture with FSO, a heavily indebted state-owned enterprise, invest-ing $75 million, with FSO providing land and building. In 1994, the JV started assembling the Opel Astra model cars from semi-knocked down (SKD) parts and components imported from GM's other subsidiaries. The JV ended in 2000 when the Polish government wanted GM to acquire the remaining shares of the JV, but the two parties could not agree on deal terms. FSO was sold to Daewoo Motor Company, Ltd. of South Korea, which itself was acquired by GM in 2001.[1]

In 1994, GM decided to establish a greenfield automotive assembly plant in Poland and selected a site in the Katowice Special Economic Zone (SEZ) in Gliwice, in Southern Poland (see map below). Construction of the Opel plant began in 1996 and was completed in a record 22 months. Production at the state-of-the-art plant (Opel Polska) began in 1998 with the Astra Classic model. Over the years, other models were added.

The author, who had visited the Opel assembly plant in Vienna, Austria, in 1998, visited the Opel Gliwice plant in 2005. At the time, the plant had a capacity of producing 180,000 cars a year. On the question of why GM selected Gliwice as the location for its major investment in Poland, two of the senior executives interviewed by the author gave the following reasons:

- The region had an industrial tradition, and it would be easy to find workers used to the factory environment.
- Two of the largest technical universities in the country were in Gliwice and nearby Krakow, which meant that the company would not have difficulty finding qualified engineering and technical staff.

147

- The City of Gliwice and the Katowice region had decided to invest in infrastructure, e.g., to extend the A4 Motorway westward toward Wroclaw and eventually to Germany, and the region already had a good rail system and good IT and power infrastructure.
- The Katowice SEZ offered many incentives to GM.
- The operating costs in the region were quite low, including low wage rates. The region, a former mining hub, had a very high unemployment rate.

GM also reviewed the City's offer and its management to see if it would be able to fulfill the promises it made to the company. GM management had its eye on the larger EU market with the expectation that the country would eventually join the EU and that it would then be able to export vehicles to the rest of the EU without trade barriers. (Poland joined the EU on May 1, 2004.)

General Motors Manufacturing Poland in 2015

GM has invested over €700 million in Poland since its initial entry into the country. Its Polish subsidiary manufactures passenger cars in Gliwice and engines in Tychy and has 63 main dealerships (and 29 satellite sales points) and 72 servicing facilities (and 27 satellite servicing stations). The annual production capacity is 207,000 vehicles, of which 98 percent is exported. The Gliwice plant has 3,000 employees working in two shifts and is the leading Astra plant in Europe. The current automobile line-up includes Astra Hatchback, Astra Sedan, Astra Classic Sedan, Astra GTC Coupe, Astra OPC, and Opel Cascada, a luxury convertible.

In 2014, the company announced an additional investment of €250 million to expand its Opel diesel engine plant in Tychy, as part of Opel's plan to invest four billion euros in Europe through 2016 to develop vehicles and engines that meet EU's exacting emission standards. Once completed, the Tychy plant, which currently employs 550 people, will have the capacity to produce 200,000 engines annually. In December 2013, General Motors announced that it will pull most of its Chevrolet brands from the European market—except for the Corvette—and will replace them with more cars from its Opel and Vauxhall brands. According to the announcement, "The company's Chevrolet brand will no longer have a mainstream presence in Western and Eastern Europe, largely due to a challenging business model and the difficult economic situation in Europe."[2]

General Motors continues to contribute to the Polish economy and society through employment, exports, employee development, supply chain development, protection of the environment, bringing in modern methods of management and production, and much else. The company's integrated quality system and environmental management system both have ISO certifications. GM has been a model corporate citizen in Poland and has received numerous awards over the years, including the "employer of the year" award several times, the prize for the best foreign investment in Poland every year from 1989 to 2004, and the Economic Prize of the President of Poland.

Figure 6.2 Map of Poland
Source: https://commons.wikimedia.org/wiki/File:NowaMapaA4.svg#/media/File:Nowa MapaA4.svg.

Notes
1 Sources include the author's personal interviews at the Opel plant in Gliwice in 2005; Wikipedia; company website (http://www.opel.pl/poznaj-opla/gmmp-gliwice/fabryka-opla-w-gliwicach/start.html); Stephen Engelberg, "G.M. Agrees to Build Opel Cars in Poland," *The New York Times*, February 29, 1992; Anna Chudzik, "The Polish GEM of GM—General Motors," *Manufacturing Journal* (http://www.manufacturing-journal.net/company-profiles-home/54-automotive/1922-general-motors); and Automotive News, "GM to Spend $342 million Expanding Diesel-Engineer Plant in Poland," *Automotive News*, February 11, 2014.
2 Aaron Smith, "GM to Discontinue Chevrolet Brand in Europe," CNN Money, December 5, 2013. http://money.cnn.com/2013/12/05/news/companies/gm-chevrolet-europe/

Buy (Mergers and Acquisitions)

Making a merger/acquisition to grow in a foreign market (a *buy* strategy) is often companies' preferred choice when they are seeking resources they lack, they want to broaden their product line, or want to achieve quick market access and quick results. During the dot-com boom days of the late 1990s, companies sometimes acquired other companies simply because they had the software engineers with the requisite skills and the capabilities they needed. India's Tata

Motors acquired Jaguar Land Rover from Ford Motor Co. of the United States in 2008 to enter the premium-car segment and expand its geographic footprint.

AMEC (now, AMEC Foster Wheeler PLC), a British engineering services and project management company, made numerous acquisitions from the 1980s onwards, obtaining engineering expertise to expand its capabilities and geographic footprint. In November 2014, AMEC acquired Foster Wheeler of Switzerland for $3.2 billion and began trading on both the London and the New York Stock Exchanges. AMEC's acquisition of Foster Wheeler has been described as "transformational" for the company since it provided AMEC with expertise and capacity downstream in both the oil and petrochemical industries, complementing its upstream strengths, as well as the potential of achieving double-digit growth in earnings. In fact, according to the AMEC CEO, Samir Brikho, interviewed by *The Wall Street Journal*, the Foster Wheeler acquisition "rescued" the company: "Our upstream side of the business would be finding it hard in the current market because it is not getting as many orders it used to; the main driver is the downstream side of the business that is coming from [the] Foster Wheeler [side of the business]." AMEC Foster Wheeler now has 40,000 employees, serving clients in the oil and gas, clean energy, environment and infrastructure, and mining industries in the Americas, AMEA (Asia, Middle East, and Africa), Southern Europe, Northern Europe, and CIS (Commonwealth of Independent States of the former Soviet Union), much of it achieved through M&As. (Foster Wheeler itself has had an interesting history. Founded in New York City in 1927, Foster Wheeler relocated to New Jersey in 1987, to Bermuda in 2000, and then to Switzerland in 2008.)[8]

Sometimes, a buy strategy is more practical than a build strategy, especially when an attractive acquisition target becomes available, as in the case of the AMEC-Foster Wheeler deal; Foster Wheeler had been put up for sale the previous year. It also may often be more economical to buy than to build, unless the company gets involved in a bidding war for an attractive target or if the target has large nonfinancial assets (such as goodwill) that do not show up on its balance sheet. Expanding quickly in a market through M&A can help prevent, or at least delay, competitive entry into the market, and, as mentioned earlier, it entails a lesser risk of retaliation from the existing players than a build strategy. One of the main reasons advanced by companies for undertaking a merger/acquisition is that it will generate synergies that could be realized from economies of scale and scope, asset rationalization, layoffs, and by adopting the best practices, routines, and capabilities of the two companies.

A prospective acquirer can sometimes benefit even if the M&A deal falls through. In June 1997, antitrust regulators in the United States blocked the proposed merger of two of the three major office supplies superstore chains at the time—Staples and Office Depot—with the contention that their combination would give the combined company near-monopoly pricing power. Staples, which had spent more than $20 million and 10 months performing due diligence on Office Depot and to defend the merger with the regulators,[9] did benefit even though the merger could not take place. During all this time, it had access to a good deal of Office Depot's competitive information, which proved beneficial after the merger deal fell through.

In 2013, Office Depot acquired the third largest office supplies superstore chain, OfficeMax, in a deal that was not contested by U.S. antitrust regulators. Fast forward to February 2015: With a much-changed competitive landscape, when both Staples and Office Depot faced intense competition from online retailers as well as from big-box chains like Walmart and Target that sell many of the same office supplies, but for less, Staples announced that it would acquire Office Depot for $6.3 billion in cash and stock. According to Staples' Chairman and CEO Ron Sargent, the deal is expected to bring savings of a billion dollars as the combined company reduces its global expenses and optimizes its retail footprint. This time the deal is being looked at by both the U.S. Federal Trade Commission and the European Commission in the E.U. In December 2015, the FTC said that it would attempt to block the merger because, in its view, not much had changed since the late 1990s when the two companies had attempted a merger; they are still each other's closest competitors, and the proposed deal could potentially raise prices for customers. Staples and Office Depot both said that they will fight for the deal.[10]

Merger or Acquisition?

While we often talk about mergers and acquisitions in the same breath, which is more common, mergers or acquisitions? Over 95 percent of cross-border M&As are acquisitions, and less than 5 percent mergers.[11] In an acquisition, one company (the acquirer) completely takes over the assets and operations of another company (the target), which then becomes a unit of the former. The target company sometimes retains its branding as part of the acquirer's business. For instance, in 2005 P&G acquired the Gillette Company, which is now a part of P&G; however, P&G continues to sell Gillette products under the Gillette brand name. The L'Oréal Group of France, which acquired a number of beauty products companies during the 1980s and 1990s, including Ralph Lauren Fragrances, Helena Rubenstein, and Maybelline, continues to sell these products under their original brand names. The acquirer typically retains its own name for the combined firm after the acquisition, though there have been some interesting exceptions. In 2002, South African Breweries of South Africa (listed on the London Stock Exchange) acquired Miller Brewing Company of the U.S. and changed its name to SABMiller PLC. In 2005, Southwestern Bell Company acquired AT&T but decided to take the target's name and branding, and changed its name to AT&T, which had been a household name in the U.S. for over a century.

A merger, on the other hand, is a consolidation of the assets, operations, and management of two or more companies to establish a new legal entity. In 2015, for instance, the three independent bottlers of Coca-Cola in Europe

(Coca-Cola Enterprises Inc., Coca-Cola Iberian Partners of Spain, and Coca-Cola Erfrischungsgetränke AG of Germany) agreed to a three-way merger, forming a new, London-based company, Coca-Cola European Partners PLC.

The distinction between a merger and an acquisition is often not clear, and media reports sometimes refer to mergers as acquisitions and vice versa. (In this chapter, we have also sometimes used the two terms interchangeably.) Even in a *merger of equals*, in which two companies, sometimes of about equal size, combine their assets, operations, and management, and with no cash changing hands, it is generally the stronger company that ends up controlling the combined entity, unless the merger ends up in a failure, which is quite common. The 1998 merger between Daimler-Benz of Germany and Chrysler Corporation of the United States had been billed as a merger of equals. That it was effectively a Daimler acquisition became clear when the Daimler Chairman, Jürgen Schrempp, announced in 2000 that they had called it a "merger of equals" for psychological reasons to sell the deal to Chrysler employees and that he had always intended Chrysler to be a division of Daimler.[12] (The "merger" ended in 2007.) Alan Brew, a founding partner of BrandingBusiness, provides examples of failed mergers of equals, including the merger of advertising giants Omnicom Group of the United States and Publicis Groupe of France in July 2013 that ended in less than a year. Omnicom blamed the failure on cultural differences and Publicis on a sense of "inequality." George Sard, chief executive of Sard Verbinne, a strategic communications firm, says, "Mergers of equals have long been among the most challenging deals from a communications perspective, because of the internal politics involved and because nobody believes there really is such a thing."[13]

M&A Waves

Given a poor performance record of mergers and acquisitions, companies still make M&As, a lot of M&As. In fact, M&A activity seems to come in waves. According to KPMG, quoting research from Canada's York University (Table 6.1), the world has experienced six M&A waves since the late 1800s, and we may currently be in the midst of the seventh wave.[18] M&A activity rises and falls with the economy's growth and decline. For instance, the second wave of the 1920s ended with the Great Depression, the fifth wave with the dot-com bust, and the sixth wave with the worldwide recession. The fifth and sixth waves grew and ended with the rise and temporary decline of the global connected economy.[19]

During the current M&A wave, technology companies, especially IT companies, have been the most prominent acquirers of both domestic and foreign firms (Table 6.2).[20] Google, in fact, has been on a shopping spree for technologies and businesses almost since its founding in 1998. For instance, it acquired over 180 companies from 2001 to mid-July 2015, including almost 50 from abroad. These range from mobile software and applications (20 acquisitions), social

152

Table 6.1 M&A Waves, 1890s–2008

Wave	Time Period	Types of M&A
First Wave	1893–1904	Horizontal mergers & acquisitions
Second Wave	1919–1929	Vertical mergers & acquisitions
Third Wave	1955–1970	Diversification; birth of conglomerates
Fourth Wave	1974–1989	Hostile takeovers, corporate raiders, leveraged buyouts
Fifth Wave	1993–2000	Mega deals caused by globalization and deregulation
Sixth Wave	2003–2008	Mega deals, private equity, shareholder activism
Seventh Wave	2011–?	Mega deals in healthcare, technology, consumer goods, etc.

Source: Adapted from KPMG, "The Seventh Wave of M&A," www.kpmg.com, May 31, 2011.

Table 6.2 The Top 8 Technology Acquirers by Number of Deals, 2007–2012

Company	Google	IBM	Oracle	Cisco	MSFT	VMware	Dell	HP
# Deals	52	44	40	30	25	20	18	17

Source: www.capitaliq.com (quoted by Lakshmikanth Ananth, www.kauffmanfellows.org).

applications (16), online advertising (12), robotics (7), search (5), security (5), artificial intelligence (4), and so on. Google, which derives over half its revenues from abroad, told the U.S. Securities and Exchange Commission in May 2014 that it would spend up to $30 billion of its accumulated international profits to acquire foreign companies and technology rights.[21]

M&A PERFORMANCE

An M&A strategy has many drawbacks, which often lead to poor performance of the combined firm. Like the greenfield strategy, it requires a huge investment of resources—managerial, financial, and organizational—and the company bears the full financial risk. Safeguarding intellectual property (IP) could be an issue since many executives and technical people may leave the company shortly after the merger/acquisition. A company may end up overpaying for the acquisition if a bidding war escalates. Synergies are often over-hyped during merger/acquisition talks and typically not fully achieved. Finally, integrating an acquired company into its structure after the merger/acquisition is often the biggest challenge an acquirer faces. Post-merger integration requires integration of the two companies' operations, cultures, systems, routines, and policies, which is a difficult and time-consuming process. (See the section on post-merger integration later in this chapter.)

In fact, making a merger/acquisition has been likened to going to Las Vegas—a few win, but most lose. Studies of mergers and acquisitions estimate their failure rate at 70 to 90 percent.[14] Based on a wealth of academic research, Peter Clark and Roger Mills concluded that as many as two-thirds of all M&As fail, i.e., they do not deliver the benefits promised when the deals were struck.[15] McKinsey & Company refer to M&As as the winner's curse, with most of the value created by the M&A going to the acquired firm, not the acquirer.[16] Harvard Business School professor Michael Porter, who researched the performance of both domestic and cross-border M&As, concluded, "I studied the diversification records of 33 large, prestigious U.S. companies over the 1950–1986 period and found that most of them had divested many more acquisitions than they had kept. The corporate strategies of most companies have dissipated instead of created shareholder value."[17]

Some Reasons for M&A Poor Performance or Failure

Mergers and acquisitions "are often the largest capital expenditure most firms ever make, they are frequently the worst planned and executed activities of all."[22] Integration, people, and cultural issues are often the most cited reasons for M&A poor performance or failure. When a company pays a big premium for an M&A target, its future earnings will have to be so substantial that the acquisition does not capitalize all future earnings; this places a huge focus on profits at the cost of other important considerations. Some M&As fail because the synergies they expected could not be realized. Some 47 percent of senior executives of the acquired company leave the company within one year of the acquisition, 75 percent within three years. In fact, according to KPMG's Chris Gottlieb, "Once executive recruiters hear of a merger, the light bulbs start going off. The pressure is on the management team because that is a time when, on average, companies are vulnerable to losing people."[23] And, when performance begins to go down, it is like a downward spiral, leading management into a perpetual fire-fighting mode, instead of focusing on the business of the company.

There have been many spectacular acquisition failures in high-technology, high-velocity industries for reasons such as fast-changing technology, the acquirer's inability to fully integrate the acquired company into its structure, or for other reasons. In 2006, Rupert Murdoch's News Corp. purchased MySpace, the hottest social network at the time, for $520 million. The acquisition did quite well for News Corp. for about two years. However, by 2008, MySpace had been overtaken by Facebook, and News Corp. eventually sold the company for $35 million in 2011. In 2005, EBay purchased Skype Technologies SA of Luxembourg for $2.6 billion, but sold it for $1.9 billion four years later. The acquisition did not pan out, according to press reports, because the two companies were not able to successfully integrate their technologies.

Improving M&A Performance

During the pre-merger/pre-acquisition phase, a company should perform due diligence as if the future of the company depended on it because it does. Potential targets should be evaluated for both strategic and organizational fit with the firm, and the synergies likely to result from the merger/acquisition should not be overestimated. Do not pay too much for a target; set limits on how much to pay for a target, and, in case of a bidding war, be prepared to walk away. Be prepared to deal with any roadblocks that may be placed by people whose jobs or power may be threatened by the acquisition. Have a plan to address their concerns before, during, and after the acquisition.

After the merger/acquisition, the company should treat post-merger integration as a core competence and accord it appropriate importance in its strategy. (See the next section on post-merger integration.) Do everything possible to retain key employees and important customers. Address the concerns of all key stakeholders as they arise. In fact, anticipate their concerns through regular surveys and take action as needed. In this respect, the experience of IBM, which has made dozens of acquisitions in the last two decades (Table 6.2), is valuable. IBM has a small team of employees who work full-time on pre-merger due diligence and post-merger integration issues. They send team members to perform due diligence at the company being acquired and to assess its culture and the strengths of its key employees. Then, during the first 30 days after acquisition, IBM brings in the acquired company's managers for discussion about IBM's culture and how to succeed in the company. Six months after the first meeting, the managers of the acquired company return to IBM and, along with managers of other acquired companies, provide their perspectives on IBM's management, leadership, culture, and products and services. The idea is to not only have an open dialogue but also to build a bond with the leaders of the acquired companies.[24]

Post-merger Integration

Cross-border M&As have been on the rise for decades, not only between firms from developed countries but also between firms from developing and developed countries, as well as between firms from developing countries. (A few such cases were highlighted in the preceding discussion.) It is also known that the success rate of M&As has been woefully low, anywhere between 15 percent and 35 percent. Having a well-designed and well-executed post-merger integration (PMI) approach, such as the one discussed above for IBM, improves the chances of merger/acquisition success. Most consulting firms (BCG, Bain & Company, Booz & Company, Deloitte, McKinsey, and others) have their own PMI processes that they use for consulting assignments. The following summary of the key steps involved in a good PMI process is adapted from Bain & Company and other sources.[25]

1   The success of a PMI process depends a good deal on the leaders selected to lead the integration team. They must be senior enough in the organization to have decision-making authority, as well as expertise in strategy and the functional areas involved in the merger; they are potentially the company's rising stars. During the integration process, they will be spending up to 90 percent of their time on this activity, with their normal responsibilities being handled by their superiors or others in the company.

2   Structure the integration team around the key sources of value creation, with a clear understanding of where synergies will come from and what the risks are. Identify, with the help of the integration team, the financial and non-financial results expected and by when. Get their commitment to the results and time frames.

3   A merger/acquisition always creates a good deal of uncertainty and anxiety among people in both companies about their future roles and how they will fit into the combined organization, especially if the merger involves creation of synergies, which often implies layoffs. Identify and select the people from both companies who are enthusiastic about the merger and its vision for important roles. Fill the top levels of the combined company quickly because the longer it is delayed, the greater the chance that key employees leave and important customers are poached by competition. Then, select key employees at the next organizational levels and get on with the integration process.

4   Integrating the two companies' systems and policies (e.g., IT systems and people policies) and business functions, will likely take considerable time. Not all functions may, of course, need to be integrated, depending typically on the objectives of the acquiring (or the dominant) firm. Table 6.3 presents some of the common organizational arrangements that might emerge after the acquisition/merger. Examples include the acquisition of Ritz Carlton Boston by Taj Hotels (Tata Group) of India and the acquisition of Anheuser-Busch by InBev of Belgium.

5   Maintain momentum in the core business of both companies and monitor performance continuously. Integrating two organizations is not just the task of the integration team, but also of top management. However, top management should not get distracted from doing its primary job, i.e., managing the business, by the integration process. While the integration team will spend up to 90 percent of its time on integration, top management should be spending up to 90 percent of its time on managing the business.

6   Culture is often the most difficult issue to manage during a merger/acquisition, especially in a cross-border merger where not only the corporate cultures of the two companies may be different but also their national cultures. There are dozens of potential areas of cultural conflict or misunderstanding between the two organizations, including how they make decisions, how they conduct meetings, and how they communicate. Diagnosing cultural misalignment can range from candid conversations and observations of

Table 6.3 Typical Organizational Arrangements after M&A

Organizational Arrangement	Extent of Integration	Target's Identity after M&A	Relationship of the Target with the Acquirer
Hold	Separate business units	Target remains autonomous	Cash moves between firms
Retain	Combine back office, but keep product lines separate	Target's external identity remains, but the internal identify changes to that of the acquirer	Transfer of culture and best practices to the target
Absorb	Target absorbed into the acquirer firm	Target assumes acquirer's identity	Takeover
Merge	A new company created	New company begins to develop its own identity	Merger

Source: Adapted from Lipi Patel and L.J. Bourgeois, "Note on Postmerger Integration," Darden Business Publishing, University of Virginia, Product No. UV1024, 2009.

the two organizations to formal cultural diagnosis through employee surveys. Once points of cultural differences become known, they should form the basis for deciding how the organization will help reduce such differences through a systematic change effort. The integration process offers the opportunity to decide the kind of culture the combined entity will have— the culture of the acquiring (or the dominant) company, the culture of the acquired company, a "best of both worlds," or something quite new.

7 Communicate-communicate-communicate... starting on the day the merger is announced, if not earlier. This will help remove any misgivings or anxieties members of the two organizations, their customers, and other stakeholders may have. Communicate timelines, goals, and the next steps involved in the PMI process. The merger needs to be "sold" internally in both organizations as well as externally.

8 Learning what works and what does not work during and after integration will be valuable in future integrations. Codify everything—processes used, integration team members and their specific expertise, results achieved, and time frames—so that the process can be improved and repeated the next time an acquisition is made.

Ally (Alliances and Joint Ventures)

As discussed in Chapter 4, a strategic alliance is a partnering arrangement between two or more companies sharing resources in the pursuit of a common goal while remaining independent. An alliance can be formed with suppliers, customers, universities, government agencies—even with direct competitors—and is generally intended to enter new markets, acquire a resource, strengthen a specific skill, share the cost and risk of a major project, develop technology, and so on. An ally strategy offers the opportunity to enter a new product or geographic market more quickly than a build or a buy strategy. The first six blocks in Figure 6.1 all refer to alliances; the seventh represents joint ventures. Alliances and JVs also have many drawbacks, including a perceived lack of control by either partner, the risk of losing IP or core competence to the partner, and the need to share profits with the partner. Shared ownership also can sometimes lead to conflict if the goals of the two partners do not align. An alliance is a race to learn; the partner who learns the fastest often ends up controlling the alliance.

As mentioned in Chapter 4, not all strategic alliances are "strategic." An alliance is strategic if it is critical to the success of the partners' core business objectives, helps develop or maintain their competitive advantage, blocks a competitive threat or mitigates a significant business risk, or helps the partners maintain strategic choices open to them. An alliance may or may not involve equity investment by either party. If both parties in an alliance make an equity investment and join together to form a new legal entity, it is a joint venture. A JV is also an alliance, though involving equity investments by both partners and culminating in a new legal entity. Hence, much of what we discuss in this section applies to both alliances and JVs.

In the connected economy, alliances are increasingly common in industries such as life sciences, IT, automation, renewable energy, and automotive. In fact, more and more companies in both the old and new economies are seeking resources and capabilities externally rather than developing them just internally. This is because of the disintegration of value chains through digitization and globalization, the emergence of specialist, intermediary firms that can take up specific parts of the formerly vertically integrated value chains, and the emergence of crowdsourcing platforms, such as freelancer.com and innocentive.com, through which a firm can access expertise and resources worldwide. Chapters 8 and 9 present more on capability building and innovation, respectively, utilizing both internal and external resources.

Alliances are quite common in the airline industry, with most airlines having code-sharing agreements with other airlines. United Airlines of the U.S., for instance, has code-sharing agreements with 39 airlines worldwide, including 26 partners in its Star Alliance. In life sciences, major pharmaceutical firms often license other companies' drugs and compounds to market through their global networks. "Externally sourced, midstage drug candidates can represent as much as 50 percent of the largest pharmaceutical companies' total pipelines."[26] Many pharmaceutical firms, in fact, have lists of compounds and drugs on their websites that they are interested in licensing from others. For example, Takeda Pharmaceutical Company Ltd. of Japan lists dozens of areas on its website in which it is interested: "Takeda is seeking pre-registration, registration and in-market late stage opportunities in our core therapeutic areas: cardiovascular/ metabolic, immunology and respiratory, oncology, central nervous system, GI, renal, general medicine and vaccines. For commercial stage assets, we consider single-country as well as regional deals or agreements covering the globe. Our goal is to identify opportunities that allow us to leverage our global infrastructure to bring products to market that address unmet patient needs. We are interested in opportunities for both ethical and over-the counter medications. In the United States, our interest is in ethical compounds only."[27]

In January 2014, CSC (Computer Sciences Corporation) of the U.S. formed a strategic alliance with its rival IT services provider, HCL Technologies of India. The alliance is designed to deliver application-modernization services—utilizing CSC's strength in hosting applications on its cloud platform and HCL's strength in modernizing legacy applications—from delivery centers in Bangalore and Chennai in India. According to Kiranjeet Kaur and Pallavi Saxena of Everest Group, "Buyers place a high value on application modernization. While clients acknowledge the value of cloud adoption in order to transform their operating models and save costs, cloud-incompatible legacy applications limit the ability to harness this value. ... CSC and HCL, exploring mutual synergies, will theoretically be able to lower the risks and costs for clients transitioning to cloud. ... Like shrewd warring factions, CSC may have just married its enemy, turning it into an ally."[28, 29] It looks like a win-win alliance for two former rivals in the IT services domain, as well as for their clients.

In July 2015, CSC and HCL Technologies entered into a joint venture agreement to form CeleritiFinTech, a banking software and services company addressing the multi-billion-dollar, global core banking software market. Representing the firms' prior respective history with the banking industry, the JV is intended to help the industry modernize its business environments through advanced core banking software platforms and a broad suite of services.[30]

In September 2014, the British online food-ordering giant, Just Eat, formed a joint venture with iFood of Brazil, owned by Movile Internet Movel S.A. of São Paulo. The joint venture, IF-JE Participações Ltda., is 25 percent owned by Just Eat, 50.02 percent by Movile, and the balance, 24.98 percent, by iFood's original founders. Both Just Eat Brazil (Just Eat's Brazilian subsidiary) and iFood contributed all of their share capital to the IF-JE joint venture, with Just Eat providing an additional $5.7 million to finance it. According to press reports, Just Eat decided to join its competitor rather than to continue fighting it.[31]

Performance Record of Alliances

Like for M&As, the failure rate of alliances/JVs also is very high, with 30 to 70 percent of all alliances failing to achieve the objectives of one or both partners. Some of the most commonly cited reasons for alliance failure are "unclear strategies, poor partner choice, weak or unbalanced alliance economics, dysfunctional governance, clashing corporate cultures and goals, and lack of sufficient operating staff skills and parent commitment."[32] Problems in any of the areas can lead to a lack of trust and breakdown of communication between the partners and, eventually, to poor performance or outright failure.

Given the poor record of alliances, even alliances between existing partners may not always succeed. This is especially true for fast-evolving high-tech industries. In February 2011, BMW of Germany and PSA Peugeot Citroën of France entered into a 50:50 joint venture to develop and manufacture hybrid components for the electrification of their respective vehicle ranges. The JV was named BMW Peugeot Citroën Electrification, with the management and the workforce drawn from both companies (plus new hires), and with key management positions shared equally by them. BPCE comprised an R&D center in Munich, Germany, and manufacturing plant in Mulhouse, France. Both companies had been successfully cooperating with each other for several years on automotive engines. However, just 18 months after the signing of the JV agreement, the alliance ended, with BMW buying Peugeot's 50 percent stake. Concerned about their partner's finances and the ability to remain fiscally viable, BMW decided to pull the plug and, instead, collaborate with Japan's Toyota, the maker of Prius hybrid cars, to develop components for electric cars. Peugeot Citroën, in the meantime, had decided to pursue its R&D efforts with its new alliance partner, GM of the United States. Philippe Varin, the CEO of Peugeot Citroën, told a French parliamentary committee in July 2012 that the needs of BMW regarding specifications for cars to be sold in the U.S. and China and of Peugeot were not coinciding "so that the conditions that prevailed 18 months ago are no longer the same."[33]

Improving Alliance Performance

With the growing popularity of strategic alliances over the last two to three decades, much has been written by both scholars and alliance practitioners on how to improve alliance performance. Professors Prashant Kale and Harbir Singh suggest several drivers of alliance success during the three phases of its life cycle: (a) alliance formation and partner selection, (b) alliance governance and design, and (c) post-formation alliance management.[34] Figure 6.3 presents the factors critical to success at each phase of an alliance's life cycle.

Consultants Jonathan Hughes and Jeff Weiss suggest five principles for improving alliance performance based on over 20 years of experience working with both successful and unsuccessful alliances, as well as six years of systematic research. Their thesis is that, while carefully structuring an alliance arrangement and documenting it in a detailed contract are helpful, what is really needed to improve the chances of success is setting a strong foundation for trust and collaboration between the partners. The following five principles for alliance management are adapted from Hughes and Weiss.[35]

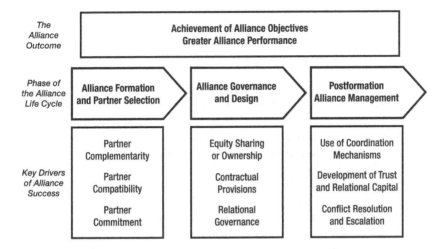

The Alliance Outcome	Achievement of Alliance Objectives Greater Alliance Performance		
Phase of the Alliance Life Cycle	Alliance Formation and Partner Selection	Alliance Governance and Design	Postformation Alliance Management
Key Drivers of Alliance Success	Partner Complementarity	Equity Sharing or Ownership	Use of Coordination Mechanisms
	Partner Compatibility	Contractual Provisions	Development of Trust and Relational Capital
	Partner Commitment	Relational Governance	Conflict Resolution and Escalation

Figure 6.3 Alliance Key Success Factors

Source: Prashant Kale and Harbir Singh, "Managing Strategic Alliances: What Do We Know Now, and Where Do We Go from Here?" *Academy of Management Journal,* August 2009, p. 48.

PRINCIPLE 1

Focus less on defining the business plan and more on how to work together.

Hughes and Weiss found that a lack of trust and breakdown of communication between the partners was a more common reason for alliance failure than planning and written contracts. While the partners may agree to foster mutual trust and respect for each other, what transpires in practice may be anything but. To achieve better communication, each partner must know how the other operates, its corporate culture, and its organizational policies and procedures. Such knowledge can help develop guidelines for effectively working together. All parties must invest time to jointly define the kind of relationship they want and work at it consistently.

PRINCIPLE 2

Develop metrics to measure not only the achievement of specific goals, but also how the alliance is progressing.

The metrics alliance partners adopt are often about costs, revenues, and market share. Most alliances take time, sometimes a year or more, to begin producing the kinds of end results the partners may desire. If the partners are anxious for the alliance to begin producing quick results, chances are that they will feel discouraged and lose confidence in the alliance. Hughes and Weiss suggest that companies should use "leading indicators," i.e., interim metrics of how the alliance is progressing, not just "end results." These include qualitative measures relating to things like information sharing between the partners and development of new ideas, which can be assessed through ongoing surveys of managers and employees involved in the alliance.

PRINCIPLE 3

Leverage differences between the partners, rather than to try and reduce them.

Companies often have different corporate cultures and organizational policies and routines as they form an alliance, especially companies from different countries. So, which partner's culture, policies, and routines should the alliance adopt? A dominant company may want to impose its own way of doing business on the alliance. However, it is best to let the alliance develop its own "personality," its own policies and organizational routines, while leveraging the respective strengths of each partner. This is particularly important in the case of joint ventures, where a new legal entity is created by the partners. Corning, Inc., a U.S. manufacturer of glass, ceramics, and related materials, which has entered into dozens of alliances over the last several decades, has a *mantra* for alliance management: "Don't Corningize the alliance."

PRINCIPLE 4

Encourage collaborative behavior, even more than what the partners' formal governance structure prescribes.

Formal governance structures in strategic alliances typically prescribe a variety of means, such as joint steering committees and oversight committees, to encourage collaboration, which is good. However, no formal structures can effectively engender real cooperation and collaboration between members of the two organizations at different levels involved in an alliance. If things go wrong, a typical reaction of each side may be to blame the other. What is needed is for both partners to jointly diagnose the problem rather than trying to figure out who is at fault. The focus should be on diagnosis, not on finger-pointing that can make one or the other partner defensive and withhold information from the other. Hughes and Weiss provide a set of "working rules" that were adopted by an alliance between the pharmaceutical company, Aventis (which later merged with Sanofi-Synthélabo in 2004 to form Sanofi-Aventis), and the biotechnology company, Millennium Pharmaceuticals, that resulted in both organizations achieving their respective goals for the alliance. (See Box 6.4 for a sampling of some of these working rules.)

PRINCIPLE 5

Managing internal stakeholders is as important as managing the relationship with the alliance partner

Each of the companies involved in an alliance consists of multiple stakeholders, including business units, business functions, and others, who may have

---

Box 6.4 Working Rules for Alliances (Aventis and Millennium Pharmaceuticals)

We agree to escalate issues [communicate them to senior executives for resolution] jointly, rather than unilaterally up our own management chains.

We agree to share information regarding internal strategic [and] business environment changes, so we can discuss their potential impact on the alliance.

[When discussing challenges] we will present possible solutions, not just problems.

We will use objective criteria to decide among multiple possible options—criteria that set good precedent for solving problems going forward.

We will strive to generate multiple, creative options for mutual gain.

We will share with one another complaints we hear from internal constituents [people within our own company] with the understanding that a) we are not defending or accusing but sharing information, b) we agree that we will jointly decide when something is significant enough to take action, c) we will collect data together about the situation, analyze and draw joint conclusions, and develop jointly any actions or plans in response to the problem.

We will hold regular weekly phone calls even if there are not critical issues at hand.

Source: Adapted from Jonathan Hughes and Jeff Weiss, "Simple Rules for Making Alliances Work," *Harvard Business Review,* November 2007.

---

different views about, or expectations of, the alliance and should not be treated as a homogeneous entity with a single voice. During the lifetime of an alliance, the different stakeholders within each partner organization can be sending out different messages to the other side or may have differing levels of commitment to the alliance. This calls for ongoing management of the internal dynamics within the organization, not just managing the alliance, the other partner in the alliance, or its external stakeholders.

Characteristics of an Ideal Alliance Partner

An ideal partner is one whose assets and goals are complementary to your own, who shares your vision for the alliance, and whose geographic and product markets have low overlap with yours. Though it may be difficult to assess in a cross-border situation, the partner should be one who will not try to exploit the alliance opportunistically for its own purpose and should not have a history of failed alliances with others. Good due diligence is generally able to identify such issues in advance.

A well-designed alliance agreement, with a "pre-nuptial" clause, can help avoid misunderstandings and opportunistic behavior by the partners and so can seeking a credible commitment from a prospective partner, such as cross-licensing valuable technologies with each other. This is exactly what Cisco Systems did in its recent partnership agreement with Blackberry when the two companies signed a long-term patent cross-licensing agreement. According to Dr. Mark Kokes, vice president of intellectual property and licensing at Blackberry, "With the agreement in place, Blackberry and Cisco can focus on innovation and continued technical cooperation, allowing our companies more freedom to create leading products and services for customers without the potential of patent disputes." And, according to Dan Lang, vice president of intellectual property at Cisco, cross-licensing is "an effective way for companies to assure freedom of operation and help remove concerns about lawsuits." Cisco had previously also signed cross-licensing agreements with Google and Samsung in 2014.[36]

The following is a mini case study of Cisco Systems' growth strategy, an example of the use of the Build|Buy|Ally framework. In particular, Cisco has been making acquisitions and alliances for over 20 years and has accumulated a great deal of experience and expertise in both domains. Most of Cisco's acquisitions and alliances have been successful, though some also ended prematurely. These include Cisco's 2009 acquisition of Pure Digital Technologies for $590 million, which closed down in 2011 as part of corporate restructuring, and its alliances with Motorola and Ericsson, which ended when the alliance partners became competitors because of their own acquisitions. However, the fact that an alliance ends does not necessarily mean that it is a failure. Although its alliances with Motorola and Ericsson ended, Cisco continues to work with them in other business areas, just like BMW and Peugeot Citroën continue to collaborate in technology areas other than parts for hybrid cars.

Mini Case Study: Cisco's Growth Strategy—Build|Buy|Ally

Cisco Systems, Inc., a quintessentially connected-economy firm, designs and sells a broad line of products and services to connect networks around the world—connecting people, things, and technologies to each other and to the Internet. With FY 2015 revenues of $49.2 billion, Cisco has over 70,000 employees in 400+ offices in almost 100 countries. As its network continues to evolve into a platform for automating, orchestrating, integrating, and delivering IT-based products and services, Cisco has been expanding into new markets that are a natural extension of its core networking business (Switches and Routing). Currently, Cisco's product lines include Switching, Next-Generation Network (NGN) Routing, Collaboration, Service Provider Video, Data Center, Wireless, Security, and Other Products, with the core Switching and Routing businesses accounting for over 35 percent of total revenues. Services account for 23 percent of total revenues.[37]

Cisco has divided its worldwide market into three regions—the Americas; Europe, Middle East, and Africa (EMEA); and Asia-Pacific, Japan, and China (APJC). The share of the three regions in its 2015 revenues was 60 percent, 25 percent, and 15 percent, respectively, with a gross margin of 60 percent to 63 percent in each. The company has been experiencing growth across almost all of its technology domains and geographies.

Cisco's growth strategy employs the Build|Buy|Ally framework, though with a greater focus on external sourcing through M&A and alliances than on internal development. Figure 6.4 represents the criteria the company uses to choose among the three alternatives (build, buy, or ally)—criteria such as risk, the speed of expansion required, and the availability of in-house resources and capabilities to pursue growth in specific situations. Cisco uses the build strategy in fields where it is the pioneer and can patent the technology, especially in its core businesses. However, much of its growth has come from acquisitions and alliances and joint ventures since the early 1990s.

The fact that Cisco's growth has often come from M&As and alliances does not mean that it is not involved in internal development. The company currently has a portfolio of over 19,000 patents, of which 12,000 came from its labs in the U.S. During 2013–2015, Cisco spent over $6 billion each year on R&D. Consistent with changing market dynamics, Cisco has been transforming its business model in the last few years—from a company selling networking boxes to one selling architectures, solutions, and business outcomes. This represents a growing role for services in the company's product portfolio, services such as consulting, software-subscription business, and software-as-a-service.

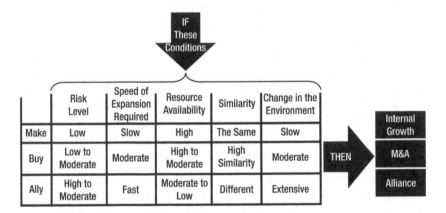

	Risk Level	Speed of Expansion Required	Resource Availability	Similarity	Change in the Environment		
Make	Low	Slow	High	The Same	Slow		Internal Growth
Buy	Low to Moderate	Moderate	High to Moderate	High Similarity	Moderate	THEN	M&A
Ally	High to Moderate	Fast	Moderate to Low	Different	Extensive		Alliance

Figure 6.4 Cisco Systems' Decision Criteria to Choose Among the Build|Buy|Ally Strategies

Source: Joe Deklic, "Build, Buy or Ally: Growth Strategies for Business," Cisco Systems Inc. presentation, 2009. Reprinted with permission. Courtesy of Cisco Systems, Inc. Unauthorized use not permitted.

Mergers and Acquisitions

Founded in December 1984, Cisco has been making acquisitions since 1993, when it acquired Crescendo Communications, a manufacturer of Ethernet switches. Since then, it has made over 120 acquisitions ranging from small startups to large, established firms to grow, as well as some divestments to optimize its portfolio. For instance, it acquired Linksys in March 2003 for $500 million but sold it to Belkin 10 years later for an undisclosed amount. Some of the "milestone" acquisitions made by Cisco included Crescendo Communications, Scientific Atlanta in the service-provider market, and WebEx in collaboration. Collaboration is now Cisco's third largest business segment, after Switching and NGN Routing, with revenue of $4 billion in fiscal 2015. Cisco made 10 strategic acquisitions in 2013, 6 in 2014, and 6 in 2015 (with an additional four acquisitions listed as "intent to acquire" on Cisco website as of November 2015).

Cisco segments its acquisitions into three categories—market acceleration, market expansion, and new market entry.[38] The company seeks acquisitions for talent, technology, mature products and solutions, and new business models, especially acquisitions that have the potential to reach a billion-dollar market. For instance, Cisco entered the data center market with the 2008 acquisition of Nuova Systems in data-center networking equipment and the 2009 acquisition of Tidal Software, which offered intelligent application management and automation solutions. Data Center is now a $3.2 billion business for Cisco.

Over the years, Cisco has accumulated a great deal of expertise in post-merger integration. With multiple acquisitions occurring each year, Cisco has developed a PMI approach that is consistent throughout the company, repeatable with each new acquisition, and adaptable to both small- and large-scale acquisitions involving different technologies and business models. The result has been very many successful acquisitions, with benefits such as: "(a) ability to realize acquisition value and pursue diverse acquisition types, (b) faster, smoother integration of acquired companies, (c) high levels of employee retention, (d) continuous development of integration expertise, and (e) efficient integration activity throughout the company."[39]

Alliances and Joint Ventures

Like M&A, making alliances has also been a core part of Cisco's growth strategy for two decades. Its list of some 70,000 alliance partners includes strategic alliances (and JVs), reseller partners, and technology-development partners, among others. Cisco derives many benefits from its alliances, such as faster entry into new markets; growth into existing markets at a reasonable cost; continuous learning about markets, business processes, and technologies;

and the ability to insert itself into pre-existing value chains, thus strengthening its competitive position. All of these have cemented Cisco's position as a thought leader in alliances and reputation as a best alliance partner.[40] The alliance partners also benefit from their relationship with Cisco. Cisco helps them transform their own businesses with leading-edge technologies and business practices and extend their capabilities through access to Cisco's other partners such as independent software vendors and Cisco Global Strategic Alliance Partners. Of particular importance to both partners are joint solutions they are able to offer to their customers. For instance, Cisco and its strategic alliance partner IBM have jointly developed industry solutions, such as telemedicine in healthcare, self-service banking kiosks in financial services, and mass notification in higher education.

As an example, Cisco India has over 2,500 "partners," including:

- 14 Gold Partners, such as Accenture Services Private Ltd., British Telecom India Private Ltd., Tech Mahindra, HCL Infosystems Ltd., IBM, Wipro, TCS, etc.;
- 7 Silver Partners, such as Locuz, PC Solutions, Allied Digital Services Ltd., etc.; and
- 4 Distributors: Ingram Micro, Redington, Computage, and Inflow Technologies.

Cisco has had a strategic alliance with Wipro Technologies of India since 1995, which has been expanding in scope over time. The relationship started with Wipro providing outsourced R&D services to Cisco, and today includes a broad range of services (R&D, Engineering and Development, IT, and Business Process Outsourcing) in various industry domains—combining Wipro's integration and IT consulting services with Cisco's technology products, platforms, and services. Wipro Technologies is now one of Cisco's Top 10 global system-integrator partners and has joint Centers of Excellence with the company in Bangalore, Mountain View, Houston, Singapore, and Australia. The Cisco-Wipro alliance has won numerous project awards in countries such as UAE, U.K., and the United States.[41] (In India, Cisco also has joint development centers with Infosys Technologies in Bangalore, HCL Technologies in Chennai, and Zensar in Pune, India.)

Cisco has a six-step process for creating successful alliances (Figure 6.5) that helps define the value proposition, alliance governance practices, success metrics, and ways to obtain a joint commitment from the alliance partners. The process is intended to ensure that the companies have a common view of the market and a shared strategy to be able to offer a joint value proposition to their customers.

Every individual alliance goes through a unique life cycle

Evaluate	Form	Incubate	Operate	Transition	Retire
Define Cisco strategy	Partnering value proposition	Structure alliance governance	Execute comms & boards	Review strategy & value prop	Conduct management discussions
Analyze portfolio	Secure sponsors	Build operations model	Business planning	Value curves & trends	Determine exit strategy
Evaluate ecosystem	Negotiations & agreements	Plan communication	Alliance solutions & initiatives	Update strategy goals	Build exit plans
Evaluate partner	Intellectual properties	Partner engagement model	Field engagement & marketing	Confirm joint commitment	Define activities & timeliness
Build business case	Announce alliance	New alliance launch marketing	Metrics & performance reporting	Determine future investment	Create messaging

Figure 6.5 Alliance Life Cycle at Cisco Systems

Source: Steve Steinhilber, "Strategic Alliance Update: Recent Developments and a View to the Future," Cisco Industry Analyst teleconference presentation, May 29, 2007. Reprinted with permission. Courtesy of Cisco Systems, Inc. Unauthorized use not permitted.

Concluding Remarks: Growing in Foreign Markets

This chapter was about how firms grow in foreign markets they entered previously. Growth strategies range from internal development to external sourcing through M&A and alliances and JVs, represented by the Build|Buy|Ally framework. Making FDI in a foreign market through a build or a buy strategy is costly and risky. While internal development can take a long time before any benefits are realized, and much can happen during that time to subvert a firm's designs for the market, M&As and alliances have a very poor success record. The cost and risk involved in alliances is the lowest of the three choices. Cost and risk are, of course, not the only considerations in making a choice about which growth strategy to adopt in a specific situation. Figure 6.6 presents a useful framework, by Renee Jansen of VantagePartners, to help companies choose among the three alternative strategies with greater confidence.

Chapters 4–6 presented key frameworks and strategies for entering, competing in, and growing in foreign markets. The remaining chapters in the book

168

Organizations should assess key internal and external conditions to understand how well a possible build-buy-ally solution meets its interests and fits within its constraints.

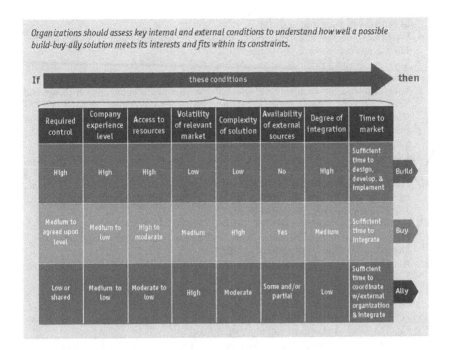

Figure 6.6 A Framework for Analyzing Build|Buy|Ally Alternatives

Source: Renee Jansen, "To Partner or Not to Partner: Best Practices for Making Decision to Ally," Vantage Partners. Accessed from www.vantagepartners.com. Reprinted with permission.

are about global strategy implementation and present information and ideas on how strategies are implemented, e.g., how a company's organizational structure changes as it pursues its internationalization journey from a domestic to a regional to a global firm. Other themes taken up in the remaining chapters include learning and capability building, innovation, and leveraging opportunities in the global connected economy.

Notes

1 Unbottled Staff, "Coca-Cola to Invest $8.2 Billion in Mexico by 2020," Coca-Cola Company's blog, Unbottled, July 17, 2014. Accessed from http://www.cocacolacompany.com/coca-cola-unbottled/coca-cola-to-invest-82-billion-in-mexico-by-2020/.

2 Mike Esterl and John Revill, "PepsiCo, Nestlé to Invest in Mexico," *The Wall Street Journal*, January 24, 2014.

3 William Boston, "Daimler, Nissan Investing $1.4 Billion in Mexico to Jointly Produce Cars," *The Wall Street Journal*, June 27, 2014.

4 Recall that this discussion is about growing a firm's business in the foreign market it entered earlier, not its globalization journey.

5 A firm's corporate strategy is distinct from its business strategy, the latter referring to approaches for competing in a specific business. So, corporate strategy is about

selecting a set of businesses in which to compete, and business strategy is about how to compete in a specific business.

6 David Kesmodel and Laurie Burkitt, "Inside China's Supersanitary Chicken Farms," *The Wall Street Journal*, December 9, 2013.

7 Source: Carlsberg in China, accessed from http://www.carlsberggroup.com/Markets/asia/Pages/China.aspx.

8 Sources include the company website (http://www.amecfw.com/); Kevin Baxter and Selina Williams, "Amec Rescued by Foster Wheeler Acquisition, Says CEO," *The Wall Street Journal*, November, 13, 2015; and Nils Pratley, "Amec's Foster Wheeler Buy May Deserve 'Transformational' Tag," *The Guardian*, January 13, 2014. The quote is from *The Wall Street Journal* article.

9 John M. Broder, "Office Depot and Staples Merger Halted," *The New York Times*, July 1, 1997.

10 Fortune Editors, "Staples to Buy Rival Office Depot for $6.3 Billion," *Fortune*, February 4, 2015. See also: Renae Merle, "GE Deal Off; Staples Deal under Fire," *The Washington Post*, December 8, 2015.

11 United Nations, *World Investment Report 2010* (New York: United Nations, 2000).

12 Danny Hakim, "Daimler Leader Explains Why He Called Deal Merger of Equals," *The New York Times*, December 11, 2003.

13 Alan Brew, "Why Corporate Mergers of Equals Almost Never Work," *Forbes*, June 5, 2014.

14 Clayton M. Christensen, Richard Alton, Curtis Rising, and Andrew Waldeck, "The New M&A Playbook," *Harvard Business Review*, March 2011.

15 Peter Clark and Roger Mills, *Masterminding the Deal: Breakthroughs in M&A Strategy and Analysis* (London: Kogan Page, 2013).

16 Scott Christofferson, Robert S. McNish, and Diane L. Sias, "Where Mergers Go Wrong," *McKinsey Quarterly*, May 2004.

17 Michael E. Porter, "From Competitive Advantage to Corporate Strategy," *Harvard Business Review*, May 1987.

18 KPMG, "The Seventh Wave of M&A," May 31, 2011. http://www.kpmg.com/za/en/issuesandinsights/articlespublications/transactions-restructuring/pages/seventh-wave-of-ma.aspx.

19 KPMG: The Seventh Wave of M&A: http://www.kpmg.com/za/en/issuesandinsights/articlespublications/transactions-restructuring/pages/seventh-wave-of-ma.aspx.

20 Lakshmikanth Ananth, "What Acquirers Want: An Insider Perspective on Getting Acquisitions Right," *Kauffman Fellow Report*, 2012. Accessed from http://www.kauffmanfellows.org/journal_posts/what-acquirers-want-an-insider-perspective-on-getting-acquisitions-right/.

21 Vinod Jain, "Google's Unprecedented Shopping Spree," Letters to the Editor, *The Washington Post*, August 16, 2015.

22 Thomas M. Grubb and Robert B. Lamb, *Capitalize on Merger Chaos: Six Ways to Profit from Your Competitors' Consolidation and Your Own* (New York: Free Press, 2001).

23 Kelley Holland, "Life after a Merger: Learning on Both Sides," *The New York Times*, June 24, 2007, p. 14.

24 Kelley Holland, 2007.

25 This section is based on: Ted Rouse and Tory Frame, "The 10 Steps to Successful M&A Integration," Bain & Company, 2009; Lipi Patel and L.J. Bourgeois, "Note on Postmerger Integration," Darden Business Publishing, University of Virginia, Product No. UV1024, 2009; and Peter Strüven, Chris Barrett, Niamh Dawson, Daniel Friedman, and Peter Goldsbrough, "Cross-Border PMI: Understanding and Overcoming the Challenges," *BCG Perspectives*, The Boston Consulting Group, 2010.

26 Laurence Capron and Will Mitchell, *Build, Borrow, or Buy: Solving the Growth Dilemma* (Boston, MA: Harvard Business Review Press, 2012), p. 68.
27 Source: http://www.takeda.com/partnership/opportunities/.
28 Kiranjeet Kaur and Pallavi Saxena, "CSC-HCL Partnership—A Big Deal or Much Ado about Nothing? Gaining Altitude in the Cloud," Everest Group, January 16, 2014. Accessed from http://www.everestgrp.com/2014-01-csc-hcl-partnership-a-big-deal-or-much-ado-about-nothing-gaining-altitude-in-the-cloud-12624.html.
29 Given India's ancient history, it is not at all unusual for an Indian company to "marry" an enemy. Chandragupta Maurya, India's greatest emperor who united India for the first time around 300 BCE, married the daughter of Seleucus Nicator, the ruler of Persia and West India, a former General of Alexander the Great, whom he had defeated in a war in 305 BCE. After defeating Seleucus, Chandragupta offered him a truce and alliance by giving him 300 war elephants and marrying his daughter and in return received his agreement to honor India's western boundary up to the current Afghanistan.
30 Source: http://www.celeritift.com.
31 Vinod Sreeharsha, "British Food Delivery Giant Forms Joint Venture in Brazil," *The New York Times*, September 19, 2014.
32 James D. Bamford, Benjamin Gomes-Casseres, and Michael S. Robinson, *Mastering Alliance Strategy: A Comprehensive Guide to Design, Management, and Organization* (San Francisco: Jossey-Bass, 2003), pp. 7–8.
33 Sources: BMW and Peugeot Citroën websites; David Pearson, "Peugeot Confirms Parts Venture with BMW is Over," marketwatch.com, September 24, 2012. Accessed from http://www.marketwatch.com/story/peugeot-confirms-parts-venture-with-bmw-is-over-2012-09-24.
34 Prashant Kale and Harbir Singh, "Managing Strategic Alliances: What Do We Know Now, and Where Do We Go from Here?" *Academy of Management Journal*, August 2009.
35 This section is adapted from: Jonathan Hughes and Jeff Weiss, "Simple Rules for Making Alliances Work," *Harvard Business Review*, November 2007.
36 Jessica Karmasek, "Cisco, Blackberry Agree to Cross-License Patents," Legal Newsline.com, June 30, 2015. Accessed from http://legalnewsline.com/stories/510593456-cisco-blackberry-agree-to-cross-license-patents.
37 Much of the information in this mini case study is from the Cisco website (www.cisco.com) and annual reports. Other sources used for this case study are also cited below.
38 The term "market" here refers mostly to product market rather than geographic market.
39 Cisco, "Business Management Case Study: How Cisco Applies Companywide Expertise for Integrating Acquired Companies." http://www.cisco.com/web/about/ciscoitatwork/business_of_it/acquistion_integration.html.
40 Steve Steinhilber, "Strategic Alliance Update: Recent Developments and a View to the Future," Cisco Industry Analyst teleconference, May 29, 2007.
41 Wipro Technologies, "Partnership Overview," Wipro Website: http://www.wipro.com/about-Wipro/Alliances/strategic-cisco/.

Part III

GLOBAL STRATEGY
IMPLEMENTATION

7

ORGANIZATIONAL DESIGN FOR GLOBAL OPERATIONS

When companies fail to deliver on their promises, the most frequent
explanation is that the CEO's strategy was wrong. But the strategy
itself is not often the cause. Strategies most often fail because they
aren't executed well.
    —Larry Bossidy and Charan Das, *Execution: The Discipline*
of Getting Things Done. Crown Books, 2002

The previous two parts of this book have been about the context of global business and strategies for entering, competing, and growing in foreign markets. The rest of the book is about implementing strategy in global business. It is not that designing strategies for foreign markets and implementing them are two separate, sequential activities; they are interdependent and proceed concurrently in most organizations most of the time. Strategy and implementation are presented in different parts of the book for the sake of clarity of presentation, and, in fact, no matter how great a company's strategy is, it is worthless unless its implementation is just as great.

A 2013 survey of over 3,500 global leaders, including 550 CEOs and 325 other C-suite executives, by Booz & Co., highlighted some of the challenges of strategy implementation. Almost two-thirds of the executives surveyed said that their biggest frustration in strategy execution was having too many priorities, and 64 percent of the executives did not believe that their company strategy would lead to success.[1]

This chapter is about designing a company's organizational architecture to successfully implement its strategy for foreign markets. Strategy is implemented through a properly designed organizational architecture consisting of five elements—the strategy itself, organizational structure, control systems, processes, and people (Figure 7.1). These five elements are closely interrelated, impacting (and being impacted by) each other and must be internally consistent. For instance, if a company adopts a localization (multidomestic) strategy, its organizational structure should be based on autonomous country subsidiaries, with a few centralized functions. Its control system should measure the contribution of each country subsidiary to the company's overall performance. If it adopts a global strategy with worldwide product divisions, it may be difficult to measure the contribution of each country to overall profitability, though it can be done.

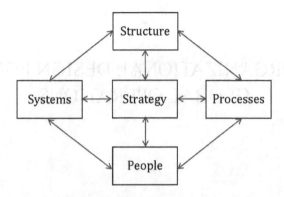

Figure 7.1 Strategy Implementation Framework

The company's organizational architecture must also be consistent with marketplace realities in each of its foreign markets. As the Volvo Group example below shows, the company changed its strategy and organizational structure to match evolving marketplace imperatives. For instance, in 2012, Volvo's growth strategy changed from a focus on M&As and JVs to organic growth, and its organizational structure from a long-standing matrix to a worldwide product division structure.

The Evolution of Organization at the Volvo Group

Sweden's Volvo Group, or AB Volvo (Aktiebolaget Volvo), is one of the world's leading manufacturers of trucks, buses, construction equipment, and marine and industrial engines and offers financing solutions for its customers. With 2014 annual revenue of SEK 282.95 billion (US$41 billion), the company has production facilities in 18 countries, 110,000 employees, and sales in more than 190 countries.[2]

Volvo started manufacturing cars in 1927, trucks in 1928, and buses in 1934 in a factory in Gothenburg, Sweden. Other products, such as engines and construction equipment, were added in later decades, and the company grew mostly through acquisitions and joint ventures. Major acquisitions made by the Volvo Group include Renault Trucks from France and Mack Trucks from the U.S., both in 2001, and Nissan Diesel (now, UD Trucks) from Japan in 2007. Volvo entered into a 70:30 joint venture with Shandong Lingong Construction Machinery Co. (SDLG) of China in 2006, a 50:50 JV with Eicher Motors Ltd. of India (Volvo Eicher Commercial Vehicles), and a 45:55 JV with Dongfeng Commercial Vehicles of China in 2015. SDLG manufactures low- and medium-end construction equipment that complements Volvo's high-end equipment. Eicher Motors is a leading manufacturer of commercial vehicles in India, and

Dongfeng Commercial Vehicles has a leadership position in both the heavy- and medium-duty commercial vehicle segments in China. Both these JVs are part of the Volvo Group's strategic refocus on commercial vehicles and represent a fundamental change in the company's potential in India and China.

The Volvo Group's two major divestments included the sale of its car division to the Ford Motor Company of the U.S. in 1999 (later acquired by Zhejiang Geely Holding Group of China in 2010) and of Volvo Aero to the British engineering group GKN PLC in 2012. The divestment of Volvo Aero, which made aircraft engines and aerospace components, was also part of the Group's strategic refocus on commercial vehicles.

The company grew through acquisitions and joint ventures from 1999 to 2011. Between 2012 and 2015, the Volvo Group management decided to refocus on its core business of commercial vehicles, grow organically, and improve efficiency through major cost reduction programs throughout the company—particularly in manufacturing, logistics, R&D, and selling and administrative expenses—with an anticipated cost reduction of SEK 10 billion from 2013 to 2016. A key goal for 2016 onwards is to improve profitability. Reorganization of the Group's structure played an important role in all these strategic initiatives.

The Volvo Group's organization had been based on a three-dimensional matrix for many years until 2011 (Figure 7.2A), which, according to CEO Olof Persson, served the company well during its acquisition phase (1999–2011). The three axes of the matrix were:

- Eight business areas, namely, Volvo Trucks, Mack Trucks, Renault Trucks, Volvo Buses, Construction Equipment, Volvo Penta, Volvo Aero, and Financial Services;
- Seven support functions serving the business areas, namely, Volvo 3P (Planning, Product Development, and Purchasing), Volvo Powertrain (engines, transmission systems, etc.), Volvo Parts (responsible for purchasing and product development of parts), Volvo Logistics, Volvo Business Services, Volvo IT, and Volvo Group Real Estate, and Volvo Technology; and
- The six geographies served (Western Europe, Eastern Europe, North America, South America, Asia, and Other Markets), not shown in Figure 7.2A.

Figure 7.2B shows the processes (support functions) and the business areas, highlighting how in a matrix most stakeholders are involved in most processes.

New Organization in 2012

The Volvo Group's new organization, launched on January 1, 2012, abandoned the matrix in favor of a worldwide product division structure (Figure 7.3). The product divisions are: Group Trucks (including Sales and Marketing, Operations, and

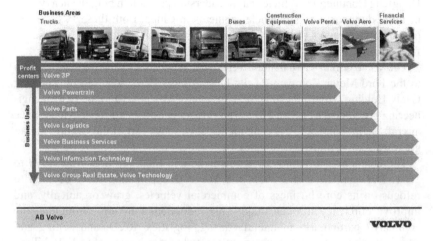

Figure 7.2A Volvo Group Matrix Organization, 2011

Source: Presentation by Olaf Persson, CEO, Volvo Group, at the Volvo Capital Market Day 2011. Reprinted with permission.

Brand positioning	Product strategies	Product planning	Product development	Sourcing	Assembly operations	Sales & Marketing
• Volvo Trucks	• Volvo Trucks	• Volvo Trucks	• Volvo Powertrain	• Volvo Powertrain	• Volvo Trucks	• Volvo Trucks
• Renault Trucks	• Renault Trucks	• Renault Trucks	• Volvo 3P	• Volvo 3P	• Renault Trucks	• Renault Trucks
• North American Trucks	• North American Trucks	• North American Trucks	• Volvo Parts	• NAP	• North American Trucks	• North American Trucks
• Trucks Asia	• Trucks Asia	• Trucks Asia			• Trucks Asia	• Trucks Asia
• Volvo Powertrain	• Volvo Powertrain	• Volvo Powertrain			• Volvo Powertrain	• Volvo Parts
• Volvo 3P	• Volvo 3P	• Volvo 3P			• Volvo Logistics	
		• Volvo Parts				

AB Volvo

VOLVO

Figure 7.2B Volvo Group Matrix Organization, 2011

Source: Olaf Persson Presentation at Volvo Capital Market Day 2011. Reprinted with permission.

Technology); Volvo Construction Equipment; and four Business Areas—Volvo Parts, Volvo Aero, Volvo Buses, and Government Sales. Under this new structure:

• Sales and marketing of all truck companies is now organized into three regions, the Americas (North and South America), EMEA (Europe, the Middle East, and Africa), and APAC (Asia Pacific), all reporting directly to the CEO;

178

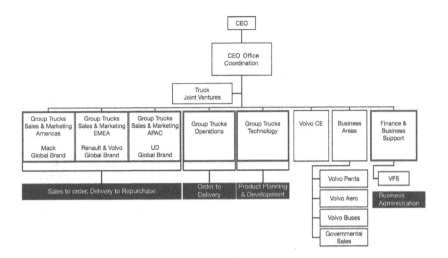

Figure 7.3 Volvo Group's New Organization, January 1, 2012
Source: Olaf Persson Presentation at Volvo Capital Market Day 2011. Reprinted with permission.

- The branded truck companies' operations, product planning and development, and manufacturing are now coordinated centrally, directly under the CEO; in the matrix, they operated as both independent units and as part of the broader Group structure;
- The Volvo CE (Construction Equipment) organization remains unchanged;
- Volvo Buses, Volvo Penta, and Volvo Aero are organized under the "Business Areas" unit, whose head reports directly to the CEO, rather than the head of each entity reporting to the CEO;
- The Finance and Business Support unit includes VFS (Volvo Financial Services), Volvo Business Services, Volvo IT, and Volvo Real Estate; and
- Volvo Group Truck Operations includes Volvo Logistics and Production.

What was the rationale for making such a major change in the Group's organizational structure in 2012? The company's management looked at emerging drivers in both developed and developing markets for the commercial vehicles business. For instance, according to the European Commission's estimates, the freight volume alone in Europe was expected to grow by 50 percent from 2010 to 2020, without a corresponding increase in transportation infrastructure. And, in developing and emerging markets, population growth, urbanization, and a rapidly growing middle class implied an increasing need for transportation. Next, climate change was creating a growing demand for sustainable transportation, a push away from fossil fuels, and restrictions on CO_2 emissions. Other emerging challenges included the safety of drivers, passengers, vehicles, and the goods being transported; demands for greener public transport, especially in cities impacted by congestion, pollution, and noise; and the Asia factor (e.g., the entry of new global competitors from low-cost Asian countries). In addition, the

Volvo Group was facing increasing cost pressures arising from not only competition but also its matrix structure.

The new structure is intended to achieve a greater customer focus (to respond to the increasing need for transportation, safety, and sustainability), improved efficiency (to respond to rising cost pressures), and a more agile organization to enable quicker decision-making and strategy execution. A number of cost-reduction initiatives have been launched to reduce costs by SEK 10 billion from 2013 to 2016, with the cost of the initiatives being about SEK 6–7 billion. These include a reduction in the number of white-collar employees and consultants, restructuring of the industrial structure in Europe and Japan, and restructuring of the trucks sales and service organization in Europe and of the spare-parts distribution system worldwide. Clear responsibility and accountability in the new organization is designed to remove functional overlaps and drive efficiencies throughout the organization, including manufacturing, logistics, purchasing, and R&D. For instance, cost savings in Group Truck Operations in Japan come from a 50 percent reduction in headcount, closure of 10 sites, and the divestment of one legacy plant and two non-core businesses (Figure 7.4A). The structural cost reduction in Global Truck Operations in Europe is shown in Figure 7.4B.

Revenue growth, which is to be accomplished by a greater focus on sales and marketing, branding, and leveraging the Asia opportunity, among others, goes alongside cost-reduction programs. Synergies are expected to arise from a global truck sales and marketing organization, common market footprint, common market capacity, common market logistics, and continuous improvement. For instance, medium-duty trucks have been organized into one line using the same platform, the same supply chain, and a common manufacturing process.

The push for organic growth, as compared to past growth through acquisitions and JVs, is planned to come from initiatives such as dual branding for construction equipment (Volvo and SDLG), development of over 55 new and upgraded Volvo CE products using technology from Volvo and low-cost solutions from SDLG of China, increased technical capacity at Volvo Eicher Commercial Vehicles (VECV) in India, and capability building.

New Organization in 2014

Figure 7.5 shows the Volvo Group's 2014 organizational structure after the sale of Volvo Aero in 2012 and with Volvo Construction Equipment now included as a Business Area reporting to the head of the Business Areas divisions rather than directly to the CEO. The three truck sales and marketing organizations are now a single global sales and marketing organization headquartered in Gothenburg, with one owner of all truck brands. In the past, there were three owners for the company's four wholly owned truck brands and three headquarters (Greensboro, Gothenburg/Lyon, and Tokyo). The new Group Truck Sales and Marketing organization allows global coordination of activities from a single, leaner headquarters, though with local strategy execution in seven regions worldwide.

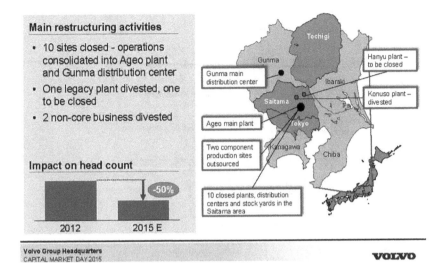

Figure 7.4A Structural Cost Reduction in Volvo Group Truck Operations, Japan

Source: Olaf Persson Presentation at Volvo Capital Market Day 2015. Reprinted with permission.

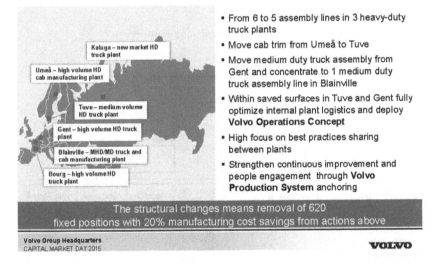

Figure 7.4B Structural Cost Reduction in Volvo Group Truck Operations, Europe

Source: Olivier Vidal Presentation at Volvo Capital Market Day 2015. Reprinted with permission.

New Organization in 2016

Figure 7.6 shows the Volvo Group's latest organizational structure, effective March 1, 2016, announced on January 27, 2016. The new structure is a brand-based organization designed to engender clearer accountability for the Group's

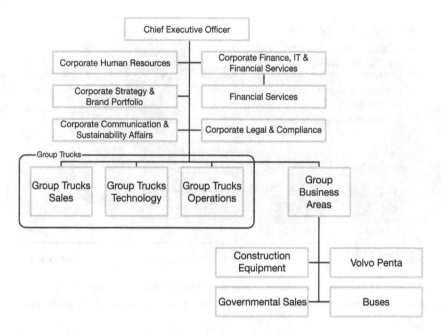

Figure 7.5 Volvo Group Organization, 2014

Source: Volvo Group Annual Report, 2014. Reprinted with permission.

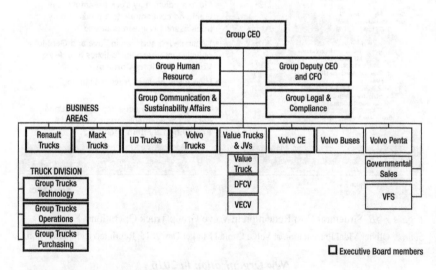

Figure 7.6 Volvo Group Organization, March 1, 2016

Source: Volvo Group Global Press Release, January 27, 2016. Accessed from: http://www.volvogroup.com/group/global/en-gb/newsmedia/_layouts/CWP.Internet.VolvoCom/NewsItem.aspx?News.ItemId=151446&News.Language=en-gb. Reprinted with permission.

four truck brands and six other business areas, each reporting directly to the Group CEO, Martin Lundstedt. The technology and product development and production functions for trucks remain responsible for the development and production of all four truck brands, as in the past. Under the new structure, purchasing for the truck operations forms a separate unit and joins the Group Executive Board. According to Martin Lundstedt, "This is an important change in how we conduct our truck business, with an expanded mandate for our sales organizations to control and develop their businesses with an explicit responsibility for profitability and organic growth. ... We will gain a simpler organization in which decisions are made more quickly and in closer cooperation with the customer, while each truck brand will be represented on the Group Executive Board with shared responsibility for optimizing Volvo Group's overall truck business."[3]

Organizational Architecture

As indicated at the start of the chapter, firms implement strategy through organizational architecture consisting of five elements—strategy, organizational structure, control systems, processes, and people (Figure 7.1). The rest of the chapter explores the different kinds of *organizational structures* and *control systems* multinational companies use.

Organizational Structures

A firm's organizational structure shows how the total organizational task is divided into various units and subunits (departments, sections, etc.) to facilitate the task's accomplishment. It has at least four characteristics. First, each unit or subunit is designed to bring together people with certain common skills, specialization, product, or geography, e.g., the finance department, the quality control department, or trucks (in the Volvo Group structure). Second, the formal division of an organization into units and sub-units is designed to show reporting relationships. Third, a structure establishes decision-making responsibilities and authorities within the organization. Finally, because the total organizational task has been divided into various components, a structure must also establish means of coordinating them, i.e., the organizational structure must also establish coordination or integration mechanisms.

No matter what kind of organization a company has, its structure almost always follows a hierarchy in which employees are shown in superior-subordinate relationships, with authority flowing from top to bottom. Figure 7.6, for example, shows the top two levels in the Volvo Group's hierarchy; each position in the chart also has its own hierarchy, shown below it. However, Zappos, an online shoe store owned by Amazon and run by its founder Tony Hsieh and based in Las Vegas, Nevada, operates without a hierarchy. Zappos has about 1,500 employees but has had no managers or bosses since 2014. "No one reports to anyone anymore." Employees manage themselves and belong to different decision-making circles, each composed of a few people who are expected to act like entrepreneurs. There are about 500 circles in the company. Hsieh calls it a "holacracy" and hopes that the circles will eventually develop new business lines or startups within the company. Since the launch of this new *non-structure*, about 14 percent of the employees took buyouts and left the company. Hsieh is hoping that Zappos will attract the kind of employees who would try and realize their entrepreneurial ideas inside the company rather than as independent entrepreneurs.[4]

Another interesting example of a non-traditional organizational structure is the one at W.L. Gore & Associates, a privately held American science and technology company best known for its Gore-Tex® fabrics. Its 10,000-plus employees working at some 50 locations worldwide are not organized in any formal hierarchy. The company has a team-based, flat lattice organization, with no traditional organizational charts, no chains of command, no predetermined channels of communication. Employees (called associates) communicate directly with each other and are accountable to fellow members in multi-disciplined teams. All associates are co-owners, and each decides what he or she wants to work on based on where they can contribute the most. Teams organize around opportunities, and leaders emerge. According to the company website, this unique corporate structure has proven to be a significant contributor to associate satisfaction and retention as well as company performance.[5]

Scholars and consultants have identified two other types of organizations that do not necessarily reflect a hierarchy—network organizations and virtual organizations. A *network organization* typically consists of the organization in question and its external partners, with organization members working in both internal and external relationships. According to businessdictionary.com, a network organization is "a group of legally independent companies or subsidiary business units that use various methods of coordinating and controlling their interaction in order to appear like a larger entity." However, there is no accepted definition of network organization or network structure, though the point is that it is an extended enterprise consisting of a central firm and its external partners working together for some common goal, and with the central firm acting something like a "systems integrator." Network organizations are common in manufacturing, where a group of closely interrelated firms comes together to design and produce a product, such as clothing (e.g., Benetton), cars (e.g., Honda), network hardware (e.g., Cisco), and commercial jet aircraft (e.g., Boeing), as well as services (e.g., Cisco). Greater collaboration with people inside as well as outside a company is a key feature of companies in the connected economy. For example, while Cisco has a hierarchical structure, it is also part of an extended enterprise or network consisting of Cisco and over 70,000 of its partners.[6]

A *virtual organization*, on the other hand, refers to an organization whose members interact with each other exclusively, or almost exclusively, through telecommunication. Indeed, they may never meet each other physically, or do so only sporadically.

The bases for creating an organizational structure are typically business functions, products, or geographies that give rise to functional, product, and geographic structures, respectively. As a company begins to go global, its strategy and organizational structure and systems also change; what worked when it was a domestic company may not work when it is a global company. The typical organizational structures adopted by MNEs are presented below.

Cisco uses an architectural approach, integrating mobility, video, and cloud to bring people together anytime, anywhere, on any device. Connect employees, customers, and suppliers to make decisions, resolve customer issues, or address supply-chain challenges. The architecture cost-effectively supports scalability, security, and accessibility. The Cisco collaboration strategy and architecture account for not only the technology, but also for what it means to your processes and culture.

International Division Structure

When a company begins to have a fair amount of international business or decides to go abroad in somewhat of a big way, it may add an "international division" to its existing structure under the control of a single executive reporting to the CEO. Creating an international division allows companies with international aspirations the opportunity to focus on some specific foreign markets. The executive heading the international division is typically responsible for all overseas sales, marketing, and manufacturing activities (if any). This structure has been used quite frequently by companies going abroad for the first time. According to a Harvard study, "60 percent of all firms that have expanded internationally have initially adopted it [the international division structure]."[7]

A good example of a company that adopted this structure is Walmart, which established an international division in 1991, the year it started on its internationalization journey. Its first international foray was into Mexico, a 50:50 joint venture with the largest retailing company there, Cifra. Located at the company's headquarters in Bentonville, Arkansas, the international division was intended to oversee Walmart's international expansion. Another good example is Mexico's largest cement company, CEMEX, whose first major investment abroad was into Spain in 1992. CEMEX acquired a controlling stake in two cement companies (Valenciana and Sanson) in Spain for $1.8 billion and set up an international division there to pursue future opportunities globally. The investment in Spain also offered the company entry into the European Union market as well as the ability to finance its global expansion at a significantly lower cost of capital than it could do from Mexico. (The cost of capital in developing countries is generally much higher than in developed countries.) Surprisingly, CEMEX's entry into Latin America came after its entry into Spain. The company made manufacturing investments in Latin America and Southeast Asia during the 1990s, the U.S. in 2000, the U.K. in 2005, and Australia in 2007, all through acquisitions.

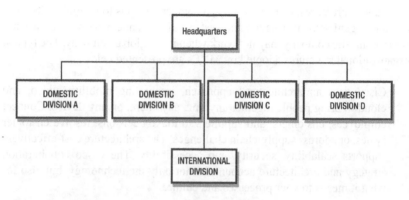

Figure 7.7 A Typical International Division Structure

A typical international division structure consists of the domestic operations and the international division, with the domestic operations organized by functions or products, and the international division by products or geographies (Figure 7.7). Unless a company has manufacturing operations overseas, the international division usually sells the products made by the parent company.

The international division structure worked well for both Walmart and CEMEX as it prepared the groundwork for embarking on significant international expansion. However, it can also pose challenges, such as the potential for conflict with the domestic divisions (e.g., when they both seek resources from the corporate headquarters), lack of coordination between the domestic and international divisions, and, if the international division is located away from corporate headquarters, it may have a lesser voice within the organization compared to the domestic divisions. Also, if a company's international operations continue to grow significantly, an international division structure may not be an ideal way to conduct business globally. For instance, if a company's international operations expand by adding new geographies, it would generally adopt a worldwide area division structure. And, if its international expansion is based on increasing product diversity, it will likely adopt a worldwide product division structure. However, if a company expands on both geographic and product dimensions, it will likely adopt a global matrix structure.[8]

Worldwide Area Division Structure

A worldwide area division structure is based on country, region, or continental borders but can also be based on factors such as cultural similarity or level of economic development. It is preferred by companies with a low degree of product diversity, such as CEMEX, which sells cement, ready-mix concrete, and aggregates intended for the construction industry (see Figure 7.8). The worldwide area division structure is also utilized by companies that follow a multidomestic strategy to facilitate local responsiveness. The advantages of this structure are that country or regional subsidiaries often have a fair degree of autonomy and operational authority, and the contribution of each country/regional subsidiary to corporate performance is clearly delineated. There is usually a clear demarcation between the responsibilities of country subsidiaries and those of corporate headquarters, with country managers having decision-making autonomy in most situations pertaining to their country. However, unless a company has a large enough global footprint, a worldwide area division structure may lead to duplication of functions among subsidiaries and reduced scale and synergies.

Figure 7.8 shows the worldwide area division structure for CEMEX, S.A.B. de C.V., an operating and a holding company within the CEMEX group that conducts its business through its subsidiaries. The chart also shows the direct and indirect percentage ownership for each subsidiary. It shows only the major operating and holding companies in the main countries where CEMEX does business and does not include all of CEMEX's intermediary holding and operating subsidiaries.[9]

Worldwide Product Division Structure

The worldwide product division structure is adopted by diversified firms with two, three, or more product lines. Since most MNEs are diversified firms, this structure is adopted more commonly than are any of the others. Each product division, sometimes also called a strategic business unit (SBU), is responsible for the company's business for the entire world. Business strategy and operating decisions in such organizations are the responsibility of the product divisions, while the corporate headquarters is typically responsible for corporate planning, budgeting, resource allocation, and oversight of the company's business. Similar to the worldwide area division structure, a key advantage of this structure is decentralized decision making and clear separation of responsibilities between the corporate headquarters and business units. When an organization uses a product division structure, it can facilitate knowledge sharing and transfer of core competencies within each division. However, country managers may have lesser importance within the corporate hierarchy than product division managers. A worldwide product division structure is preferred by multinationals following a global or regional strategy, which generally means a lesser focus on customer needs, tastes, and preferences in each local market than with the worldwide area division structure.

Sony Corporation CEO Kazuo Hirai announced new management and organizational structures for the company on February 18, 2015.[10] The new structures, shown in Figure 7.9A and 7.9B, are designed to achieve several key objectives—attribute responsibility and accountability more clearly within each business group, place greater emphasis on sustainable profit generation, and accelerate decision making and reinforce global competitiveness. (Figure 7.9A shows Sony's management structure and 7.9B its worldwide product division structure.) These strategic objectives are to be achieved by splitting out certain businesses as independent companies that were previously housed within the Sony Corporation.

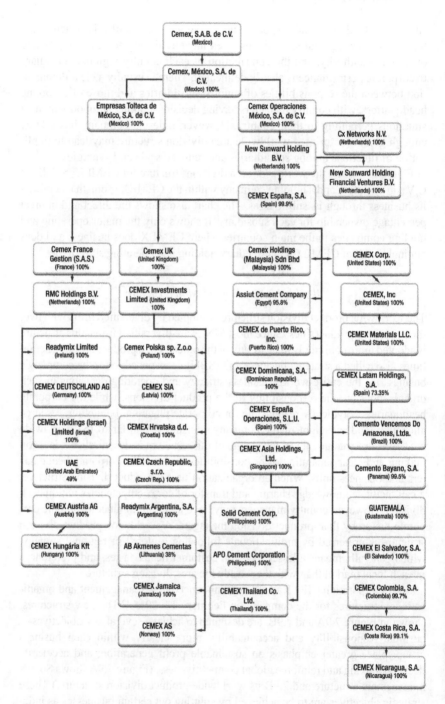

Figure 7.8 Organizational Structure of CEMEX, S.A.B. de C.V., December 31, 2014
Source: CEMEX 2014 Annual Report, SEC Form 20-F. Reprinted with permission.

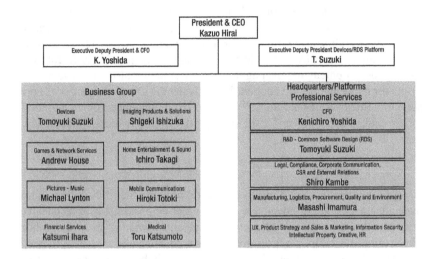

Figure 7.9A Sony Group's New Management Structure, November 1, 2015

Source: Sony Corporate Strategy Meeting, February 18, 2015: http://www.sony.net/SonyInfo/IR/strategy/2015.html. Reprinted with permission.

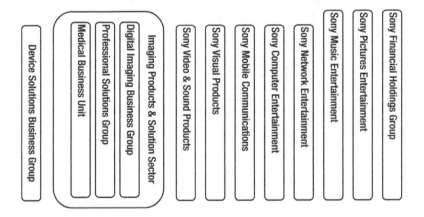

Figure 7.9B Sony Group Worldwide Product Divisions, January 1, 2016

Source: Sony Corporation website. http://www.sony.net/SonyInfo/CorporateInfo/Data/organization.html. Reprinted with permission.

Some businesses, such as Games & Network Services and Mobile Communications, had already been split out some time ago and are now operating as self-contained companies within the Sony Group. The new strategy is to split out other electronics businesses as well, thus giving them greater operational autonomy and creating a separate balance sheet for each. Each of the units so split out from the parent company will engage in its own R&D and human resource development, in addition to its usual business of making and selling products and services.

To achieve quicker decision making and to reinforce the competitiveness of the business groups, Sony management decided to eliminate some organizational layers within each group and to ensure greater transparency in sales and non-operational expenses. The leaner corporate headquarters is to focus on strategy development and oversight. The new structure also will have mechanisms for coordination and cooperation between the group companies "to preserve the integrity of One Sony."[11] (Kazuo Hirai announced the "One Sony" turnaround strategy in April 2012 shortly after taking over as the company's new CEO.)

Hybrid Structure

Both the worldwide area division and worldwide product division structures have advantages and disadvantages. The former emphasizes local responsiveness and the latter global integration. Companies wanting to leverage both dimensions may adopt a hybrid structure that contains elements of both geographies and products. Figure 7.10 shows Nestlé's hybrid organizational structure. The Nestlé Group is managed by geographies—EMENA (Europe, Middle East and North Africa), Asia/Oceania/Africa, and Americas—for most of the food and beverage businesses, except for Nestlé Waters, Nestlé Nutrition, and Nestlé Professional, which are managed as global product divisions.[12] Within each region are sub-regions consisting of countries that are geographically

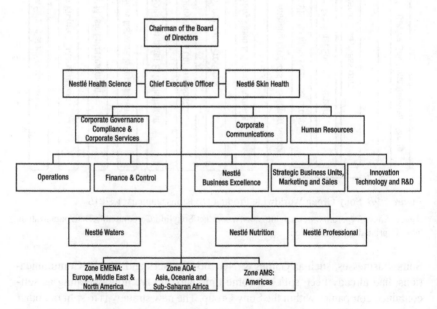

Figure 7.10 Nestlé's Hybrid Organizational Structure, December 31, 2015

Source: Nestle 2015 Corporate Governance Report. Reprinted with permission.

contiguous and have cultural/language affinity with each other. For instance, within EMENA, Nestlé's Nordic region consists of Denmark, Finland, Norway, and Sweden, with the regional headquarters in Copenhagen being responsible for marketing the nutrition and food businesses for the region.

Global Matrix Structure

The global matrix structure can be thought of as an extension of the hybrid structure, but with the distinction that in a matrix the firm is attempting to simultaneously leverage both the area dimension and the product dimension *for the same product*. (It will be recalled that Nestlé utilizes the worldwide area structure for most food product divisions but the worldwide product structure for other product divisions.) MNEs utilizing a matrix for their organizational structure do so to leverage both global integration and local responsiveness, as in transnational strategy. The matrix structure can involve two bases for differentiating the firm's total business in a two-dimensional matrix or three bases in a three-dimensional matrix. In a two-dimensional matrix, the bases for differentiating the organizational structure can be product divisions and business functions or product divisions and geographic regions. The matrix is a very complex structure, requiring well-designed and time-consuming coordination mechanisms. It can be costly to operate a matrix due to the duplication of functions among units as well as the difficulties of coordinating a very complex organization. Many employees have two bosses in a two-dimensional matrix and even three bosses in a three-dimensional matrix, which can make it difficult to assign accountability in performance evaluation and can also slow down decision making. We came across the three-dimensional matrix while discussing the evolution of the Volvo Group's organization (Figures 7.2A and 7.2B).

Many large MNEs have used the global matrix structure from time to time since the 1970s, though some abandoned it to pursue other structures as their corporate goals and strategies changed, due to difficulties encountered in managing a matrix, or in response to emerging marketplace realities. For instance, the Volvo Group abandoned its global matrix structure in 2012 in favor of a worldwide product division structure—in response to changing market dynamics. So did ABB (ASEA Brown Boveri), which had adopted a global matrix structure in 1988 but changed it to a worldwide product division structure 10 years later.

The Evolution of Organization at the ABB Group

ABB was created in 1988 through a merger of Sweden's ASEA and Germany's Brown, Boveri & Cie, and headquartered in Switzerland. It is now a global technology company in the power and automation sectors and serves customers in utilities, industry, transportation, and infrastructure. The ABB Group of companies operates in roughly 100 countries and employs about 135,000 people and had revenues of US$35.5 billion in 2015.[13]

ABB's organizational structure as of 1993 is shown in Figure 7.11, with regions and business areas representing the two axes of the three-dimensional matrix; the third axis (not shown in the figure) was "major projects" that involved both the regional and business area dimensions.[14] The horizontal axis is divided into three regions (EMEA, Americas, and Asia), composed of over 100 country holdings and comprising some 1,300 legally independent companies. The vertical axis is made up of four global product divisions, comprising about 50 global business areas. Overall, there were about 5,000 autonomous local units, each headed by a president and set up as a profit center. The regional dimension was responsible primarily for sales and intended to help satisfy customer needs in local markets, and the global product dimension was responsible for strategic direction, product distribution, global optimization, and R&D. The third dimension was major projects, which led to the development of permanent project structures—comprising both the product and regional dimensions. With about 5,000 local profit centers, the ABB matrix represented a high degree of decentralization, but also much duplication of functions such as accounting. It was intended to resolve the company's three "internal contradictions," as famously stated by the company's CEO at the time, Percy Barnevik, "We want to be global and local, big and small, radically decentralized with centralized reporting and control."[15]

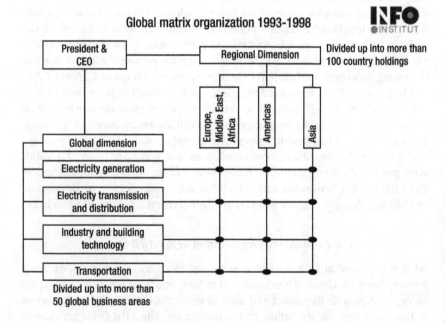

Figure 7.11 ABB's Global Matrix Structure, 1993

Source: Heinz Bierbaum et al., "Analysis of the Organizational Reorientation of the ABB Group," February 2001. Accessed from: http://www.willamette.edu/~fthompso/MgmtCon/ABB-Report. PDF. Reprinted with permission.

In 1998, ABB abandoned the matrix structure and adopted a worldwide product division structure—to simplify the management structure, reduce costs, and to respond to the incessantly globalizing world economy, which required a greater focus on global integration than on localization. Figure 7.12 shows the company's sector-based organization as of 2000.

The sector-based organization 1998-2001

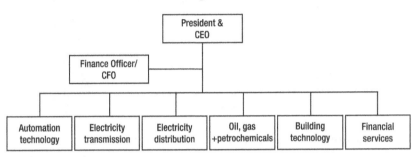

As of September 2000

Figure 7.12 ABB's Worldwide Product Division Structure, September 2000

Source: Heinz Bierbaum et al., "Analysis of the Organizational Reorientation of the ABB Group," February 2001. Accessed from: http://www.willamette.edu/~fthompso/MgmtCon/ABB-Report. PDF. Reprinted with permission.

In 2001, ABB changed its structure to a customer-oriented, sector-based organization, shown in Figure 7.13. This new organization comprises nine areas, including seven customer areas and two areas for optimum performance (Group Processes and Group Transformation). The seven customer areas are aimed directly at the end users. The product divisions are grouped into Electricity Technology products and Automation Technology products.

Fast forward to January 2016. As of January 1, ABB has realigned its worldwide product division structure from the existing five divisions to four divisions—Electrification Products, Discrete Automation and Motion, Process Automation, and Power Grids (Figure 7.14). Power products (Electrification Products; Power Grids) contribute about 55 percent of ABB's annual revenues, with the balance 45 percent being contributed by automation products (Discrete Automation and Motion; Process Automation). The January 2016 change in organizational structure (Figure 7.14), according to the company, was necessitated by changing customer needs and the need for greater operational efficiency. For instance, the new organization is expected to produce savings of $1 billion through savings in "white collar productivity" and release $2 billion in cash tied up in working capital by December 2017. Press reports, on the other hand, suggested that the reorganization was in response to activist investor Cevian Capital building up

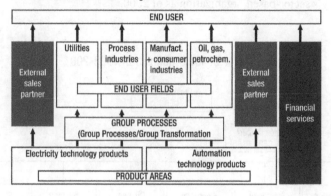

The new customer-based organization of the ABB Group

Figure 7.13 ABB's Customer-Oriented Product Division Structure, 2001

Source: Heinz Bierbaum et al., "Analysis of the Organizational Reorientation of the ABB Group," February 2001. Accessed from: http://www.willamette.edu/~fthompso/MgmtCon/ABB-Report. PDF. Reprinted with permission.

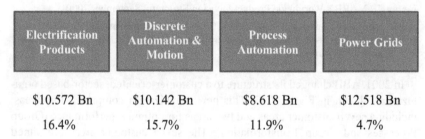

Electrification Products	Discrete Automation & Motion	Process Automation	Power Grids
$10.572 Bn	$10.142 Bn	$8.618 Bn	$12.518 Bn
16.4%	15.7%	11.9%	4.7%

Figure 7.14 ABB's New Worldwide Product Division Structure as of January 1, 2016, with 2015 Proforma Revenues and Operational EBITA Margin

Source: Based on information taken from ABB Group Corporate Presentation, February 5, 2016. Accessed from www.abb.com/investorrelations. Reprinted with permission.

its stake in the company to 5.1 percent, making it the second biggest investor in the company, and which could push for a break up of ABB.[16]

Coordination Mechanisms

Since designing a firm's organizational structure involves dividing the total organizational task into individual work units, the firm must also establish mechanisms for coordinating the work of the different units and subunits, especially if they are large, complex, and/or geographically distant from each other. The coordination (or integration) mechanisms can be formal or informal, ranging from taskforces, teams, a coordination department, a matrix, or simply the practice of managing by walking around (MBWA) made famous by Tom Peters and Robert Waterman in their 1982 bestseller, *In Search of Excellence*. A taskforce is a temporary unit created by an organization to deal with a specific coordination issue, e.g., responding to a request for proposals (RFP) for a major project that requires inputs from several departments or functions within the firm; the taskforce is dissolved once the RFP is submitted and its outcome becomes known. Consider the U.S. International Trade Commission (USITC), an agency of the United States Government responsible for investigating issues related to trade with other countries, such as dumping or IP rights infringement. For example, whenever the USITC receives a dumping complaint from U.S. companies, it sets up a taskforce of specialists from different parts of USITC and the U.S. Department of Commerce to research the complaint and issue a decision. Once a decision is reached, the taskforce is disbanded.

A team is a more permanent grouping of individuals who meet regularly for some specific purpose, such as a product development team composed of individuals from sales, marketing, operations, and R&D. Some large and complex organizations create a coordination department, or assign the responsibility to a single executive, to help coordinate the various units of the organization.[17] Alternatively, they may create liaison roles within the relevant units of the company with the responsibility of coordinating with each other on a regular basis. The matrix structure is the ultimate coordination mechanism used by companies where the need for coordination or integration is the greatest.

MBWA involves the practice of simply walking around the organization and occasionally stopping by at people's workstations to chat with them, getting a sense of how things are going, what they are thinking, and listening to whatever may be on their minds. It is especially important in today's life and work environment with e-mail and texting replacing face-to-face contacts.

Reorganization

Firms tend to reorganize their structure to cut costs or change organizational culture or when marketplace realities or their strategies change. However, the desire to improve performance is often the main cause behind reorganizations. For instance, the McDonald's Corp. announced in October 2014 that it was going to create a new organizational structure and eliminate management layers in its U.S. operations to respond better to customer tastes and to stem declining performance. A key reason for the change in organizational structure was one of the worst declines in McDonald's quarterly profits for the quarter ending September 2014, and the worst same-store sales since February 2003. According to McDonald's U.S.A. president, Mike Andres, "The reality is that our current U.S. structure is not optimized for the customer. What worked for McDonald's U.S. for the past is not sufficient to propel the business forward in the future." As part of the reorganization, McDonald's created four zones in the

U.S. (Northeast, South, Central, and West), replacing the earlier 3 zones, and gave leaders in its 22 U.S. regions greater autonomy in making local menu and marketing decisions.[18]

Interim Summary

Strategy is executed through a firm's organizational architecture, comprising strategy, organizational structure, control systems, processes, and people (Figure 7.1). The preceding discussion was about designing the firm's organizational structure. Multinational enterprises adopt different structures at different points during their internationalization journey, ranging from an international division structure, worldwide area division structure, worldwide product division structure, and a global matrix structure. Each of these structures has its own pluses and minuses. The role of the corporate headquarters is clearly distinct from that of the area or product divisions, with the corporate headquarters being responsible typically for corporate planning, budgeting, resource allocation, and oversight of the company's overall business, and the area/product divisions responsible for business strategy and operating decisions for their respective divisions.

The worldwide area division structure is often used by firms following a multidomestic strategy, i.e., to be more responsive to customer needs, tastes, and preferences in different country markets. This structure can be costly to operate due to the need to duplicate functions and activities in different markets, resulting in the firm's inability to leverage economies of scale and scope. However, if a firm has a large enough market in one or more countries, it may be able to achieve scale and scope economies there even with an area division structure.

The worldwide product division structure, which is by far the most common structure adopted by established MNEs, is appropriate for firms following a global or transnational strategy, especially when they face intense cost pressures in foreign markets and need to integrate their operations on a regional or a global basis. The product division structure enables firms to achieve economies of scale and scope and can facilitate knowledge sharing and transfer of core competencies within each global product division. However, a product division structure typically implies a lesser focus on customer needs, tastes, and preferences.

In fact, few firms have a *pure* international division, area division, or product division structure. They typically have mixed or hybrid structures with, for example, product divisions at the first level, and a functional or geographic structure at lower levels of the hierarchy.

The global matrix is the most complex of all organizational structures and is often used by firms facing both cost and local-responsiveness pressures, i.e., firms using a transnational strategy when they want to be both global and local. It is the most difficult structure for MNEs to manage due to complexity and higher costs, and sometimes firms abandon the matrix in favor of a worldwide product division structure. However, the matrix is alive and well and is indeed used by many MNEs throughout the world.

196

Control Systems

Performance is the *raison d'etre* for organizations of all kinds, for-profit, not-for-profit, government, and even non-governmental organizations (NGOs). Strategy and organizational architecture provide the roadmap for them to achieve superior performance. Chapters 4–6 were about strategy making, and the current chapter is about strategy execution via the firm's organizational architecture, including organizational structure and control systems (see also Figure 7.1). Having discussed the various types of structures MNEs may adopt at different points in their lifecycle, the rest of this chapter will focus on designing and implementing control systems to enable the firm to achieve the goals and objectives it sets for itself. Organizational structure and control systems are critical to achieving superior performance.

Far too often, articles and books on global strategy, even on strategy execution, have paid scant attention to control and measurement issues or treated them as an afterthought. If controls and performance metrics are actually considered, they often rely on financial measures, overlooking many other types of measures that are equally, if not more, important to the organization's current health and future success. (See also the discussion on "scorecards and dashboards" toward the end of the chapter for examples of measurement and visual display systems that incorporate non-financial measures.) Some organizations simply rely on feedback controls, which are good but do not offer a mechanism to take mid-course corrective action when things go wrong. If performance begins to go down, firms often have no means to trigger quick actions to stop the bleeding or to know in advance what might be in their future. These are the kinds of issues considered in this section.

The Seven Truisms of Superior Performance

1 Performance is in the eye of the beholder. Performance, like beauty, is not judged objectively, for what one person might consider good performance might not appeal to another. Organizations have multiple stakeholders. Different stakeholders often view organizational performance differently and may have different, even contradictory, views on what performance is, how it should be measured, and what should be considered "good" performance. Achieving superior performance in such a context raises the question: From whose perspective should performance be viewed? For instance, good performance from a customer perspective is quite different from that from a shareholder perspective.

2 Performance is multifaceted. The first objective of any (performance) control system is to define what performance is, what it should be, how it will be measured, and how control will be exercised. There are multiple types of performance (i.e., performance constructs), and each type of performance can be measured in multiple ways (through measures or

metrics). (See the section below on "constructs, measures, and standards of performance.") For instance, to assess the financial health (a construct) of an organization, one can utilize a number of measures, such as return on assets, profits, stock price, etc. To assess the performance of an organization, one can also use, depending on context, many other constructs, such as customer satisfaction, product quality, employee satisfaction, and growth potential. Each of these constructs can be measured using several metrics.

3 Performance must be validated externally. Whether or not an organization has superior performance can only be judged in comparison with other organizations facing the same context, e.g., firms in the same industry. Comparing actual results with targets or this year's performance with last year's performance is good, but not enough unless validated externally through competitive benchmarking or other means. As the Scottish poet, Robert Burns, wrote in 1786:

O wad some Pow'r the giftie gie us
To see oursels as ithers see us!
It wad frae mony a blunder free us ...

(Wikipedia translation:

And would some Power give us the gift
To see ourselves as others see us!
It would from many a blunder free us ...)

4 Superior performance is a journey, not a destination. Continuous improvement is a never-ending journey requiring an organizational culture that emphasizes such things as learning, goal-setting, performance measurement and feedback, open communication, employee empowerment, risk taking, experimentation, and benchmarking.[19]

5 Performance is outcomes, not just outputs. The difference between outcomes and outputs is more than mere semantics.[20] What stakeholders need are outcomes, such as customer satisfaction or student learning, not just what the organization produces, such as a quality product or classroom instruction. Classroom instruction or grades are not the same thing as student learning outcomes. Outputs or results are typically measured by hard, quantitative metrics, whereas outcomes are more difficult to measure and may not show up immediately after a project has ended. Outcomes are the benefits your stakeholders receive based on the results of what you do and should ideally be a part of firms' control systems.

6 Performance is not performance unless measured and validated. "What you measure is what you get" has become a cliché, but it is true. If something is not measured, one can never be sure if what one got is what one wanted to get.

7 Superior performance requires both controls and rewards. Each is a necessary condition for achieving superior performance, but neither is sufficient

on its own. Most organisms (human beings included) tend to do the things that are rewarded, sometimes to the exclusion of things that are not rewarded.[21] Peter Drucker said it best: "If a company is to obtain the needed contribution, it must reward those who make them. Decisions on people and especially its promotions affirm what an organization really believes in, really wants, really stands for. They speak louder than words and tell a clearer story than any figures."[22]

Constructs, Measures, and Standards of Performance

Designing a control system involves three key steps:

1 Define what performance is, i.e., the *constructs* or things that need to be measured, such as profitability, market share, customer satisfaction, learning outcomes, etc.
2 Determine the specific *measures* (metrics) to be used for each of the constructs. For instance, profitability can be measured by metrics such as return on equity, return on capital employed, and operating margin.
3 Set the *standards of performance* for each metric against which future performance is to be judged, e.g., an ROE of at least 5 percent, or customer complaints resolved within 24 hours.

Strategy as Control

A key part of strategy execution is the design and implementation of an appropriate control system that incorporates controls at most phases of the strategy process. Strategic control is an interplay among three types of control—feedback controls, concurrent controls, and feedforward controls—which, together, provide a holistic view of organizational performance as well as the means for taking corrective action, if and when needed and for performance improvement on an ongoing basis.

Feedback Controls

Feedback controls are the most common types of controls (measures) used in organizations, focusing on output measures, such as revenues, profits, expenses, inventory turnover, and market share. Feedback measures provide useful information on how the organization, or a specific subunit, did in the period just ended. For the organization as a whole, much of what is contained in its annual report is based on feedback measures. They are applied "after the fact" and can potentially improve future performance but are of little use for making mid-course changes or corrections to improve current performance. While fulfilling an important control function, they cannot by themselves be an answer to keeping the organization "on target." Using feedback measures alone is like driving a car by looking only through the rear-view mirrors.

Concurrent Controls

The use of concurrent controls involves taking ongoing measurements of various organizational activities or processes (e.g., recruitment and selection, software development, selling, team working, decision making, communicating, etc.) and phenomena (e.g., organizational culture, power structure, bureaucracy, employee morale, etc.) to ensure that things are going as planned. If not, concurrent controls alert the managers to potential problems in real time so that they may take corrective action before serious, or any, harm is done.

Concurrent controls are quite prevalent in manufacturing, where an operator takes ongoing measurements of some quality characteristic of products (such as the diameter of ball bearings) coming off a production line and plots them on a "control chart." The pattern of points on the control chart can indicate if the production process is "in control," i.e., if it is producing the product within allowed tolerances. If the process is not in control, the manager can stop the production line, look for potential causes, and take corrective action as needed. A control chart, also known as a statistical process control (SPC) chart, is an easy-to-implement statistical tool for assisting managers in monitoring and statistically controlling one or more variables in production processes. However, control charts are also extensively used for controlling non-manufacturing processes in real time, such as the time taken to resolve a customer complaint, or on-time flight arrivals for an airline.

Many companies conduct regular employee attitude and customer feedback surveys, which are essentially designed to identify potential problems in more or less real time so that corrective action can be taken as needed. Hospitals use concurrent controls to monitor key body functions, such as heart rate and blood pressure, for patients spending a night in a hospital ward. Patients are hooked up to monitoring devices that provide real-time measurements of body functions to staff at a nursing station so that they may take corrective action if and when needed.

Another example of concurrent control is GPS fleet tracking, whereby a manager monitors the movements of the company's vehicles in real time—movements such as where they go, when they get there, and how fast they travel. It helps the organization plan more efficient routes, adjusting them for exigencies in real time, such as traffic congestion or accidents.[23]

The Hyundai Motor Co. of South Korea, the world's fifth largest automaker, has perhaps gone the farthest in using concurrent controls. It has a Global Command and Control Center in South Korea that monitors every production line in its 27 plants worldwide, 24 hours a day, 365 days a year. "The production data is generated on the assembly lines and displayed on boards where team members can see it, and headquarters can see the same data at the same time. If the quality monitors spot errors or problems, they call the factory immediately."[24] (See also the next chapter for a mini case study of the Hyundai Motor Co.)

Feedforward Controls

Feedforward controls are designed to help managers take action before problems actually occur. They are early warning mechanisms that allow a process to be temporarily stopped in case of an impending problem so that a corrective action can be taken to forestall it. In fact, if the performance of a company begins to go down, or a process begins to show signs of going out of control, it is often like a downward spiral with no way to stop it unless quick action is taken in real time by the organization or the manager responsible for the process. The question is how to spot impending problems before they occur. Several approaches have been used for concurrent and feedforward control.

LEADING INDICATORS

In economics, a leading indicator is one that changes before the economy changes and which can, therefore, be used to predict where the economy is headed. Some examples are the unemployment rate, new business startups, stock prices, and money supply. Based on factors such as these, the Fed in the U.S. (the Federal Reserve System) decides whether to change interest rates. In the corporate world, a leading indicator serves a similar function. It is a measure that precedes some organizational outcomes, such as sales, profitability, or market share. For example, customer satisfaction is a leading indicator for market share, and satisfied and motivated employees can be thought of as a leading indicator for customer satisfaction. The order book[25] of a machine tools company or an aircraft manufacturer is a leading indicator of its future sales. The correct use of leading indicators is an effective means of achieving target performance, even improving performance. (Most financial measures are "lagging" indicators; they are the results of actions taken by companies in the past.)

CONTROL CHARTS

The use of statistical process control charts in both manufacturing and non-manufacturing processes was mentioned earlier. The distribution of points on a control chart can indicate whether the process is in control, out of control, or going to go out of control imminently. Each control chart tells a story.

Figure 7.15 shows the control chart of a process in control, where AVG is the target value of the characteristic being measured, e.g., the target diameter of ball bearings coming off a production line or the target time taken to resolve customer complaints. UCL and LCL are the upper and lower control limits—the engineering tolerances for the ball bearings or the allowable variation in the time taken to resolve customer complaints. The process shown in Figure 7.15 is in control, i.e., things are going as planned since all observations lie within the tolerances. It may come as a surprise to many people that even high-precision, automatic machines cannot produce output precisely at the target value; variation due to any number of causes, both random causes and assignable causes, always is present. Figure 7.15 shows a process in control though affected by random causes of

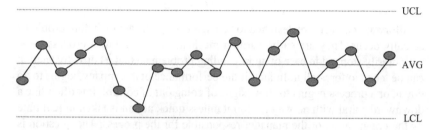

Figure 7.15 The Control Chart of a Process in Control

Source: SPC for Excel, "Teaching Variation to Leadership." www.spcforexcel.com.

variation. In non-manufacturing (non-automatic) processes, the range of potential causes of variation can be much greater since the human element is also involved.

How does an individual or organization assess whether a process is not in control or is going to go out of control imminently? Figure 7.16 below shows four control charts, each with a different story to tell. In Chart 1, seven of the observations fall above the target (AVG), though still within the tolerances. The same is true for Chart 2, except that the seven observations lie below AVG within control limits. If seven or more observations fall above or below AVG, but still within the control limits, it is no longer a case of random variation; an *assignable cause* must be present in the process. While the process seems to be in control, something seems to have happened to the process, needing management attention to find a potential cause for the variation. In a manufacturing situation, it might indicate a change in the quality of inputs into the process, a new worker, or something else. If the time taken to resolve a customer complaint goes down, indicating an improvement (as in Chart 2), the pattern of observations might suggest the effect of employee training or some other factors.

Chart 3, however, shows a downward trend of the seven measurements, as does Chart 4, which shows an upward trend. Even though the process seems to be in control, it is very likely that there is an assignable cause present and the process is likely to go out of control imminently. This "rule-of-seven test" is a powerful use of control charts—predicting potential problems before they occur. Control charts can pinpoint future trends and/or impending problems.

OTHER TYPES OF FEEDFORWARD CONTROLS

Preventive mechanisms are a special category of feedforward controls that are not based on errors in a process but designed to stop errors or variation from occurring before the process starts. Preventive maintenance of equipment is an obvious example. Poka-yoke, Japanese for mistake-proofing, is a mechanism that prevents mistakes from occurring. For example, when one exits a car with the keys still in the car, the car emits a beeping sound to warn the driver that something needs attention before the door is closed. This is a simple poka-yoke

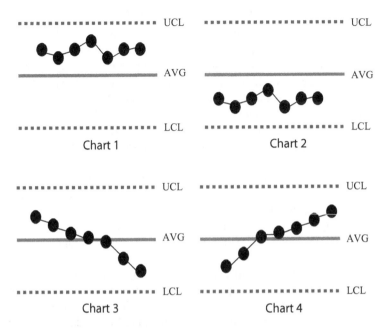

Figure 7.16 Control Charts: The Rule of Seven Tests
Source: SPC for Excel, "Teaching Variation to Leadership." www.spcforexcel.com.

device, but there are many, many uses for such devices in both manufacturing and non-manufacturing environments.

TRIGGER DEVICES

A trigger device is a mechanism to stop a process temporarily if things go hor-ribly wrong. As indicated earlier, if the performance of a company or a process begins to go down, it is often like a downward spiral with no way to stop it unless quick remedial action is taken. A trigger is a mechanism that is invoked to stop a process if its performance declines by a pre-defined amount. For instance, the New York Stock Exchange uses trading curbs or *circuit breakers* to trigger an action if the Dow Jones Industrial Average has a precipitous fall. NYSE halts trading for one hour if the Dow Jones falls 10 percent, for two hours if it falls 20 percent, and for the rest of the day if it falls 30 percent. The circuit breakers are designed to reduce market volatility caused by massive sell-offs and give traders time to reconsider their transactions. If the Dow Jones rallies by a signif-icant amount, NYSE applies no circuit breaker since such rallies are considered "good."[26] This exact situation took place in China during the first week of 2016, when the Chinese government stopped trading on the Shanghai Stock Exchange twice (on Monday and Thursday) when the market fell by 7 percent each time.

Dashboards and Scorecards

A *dashboard* is a visual display of an organization's strategy, goals, and up-to-date performance on a number of dimensions. According to Stephen Few, an expert in data visualization for sense-making and communication and principal at Perceptual Edge, "A dashboard is a visual display of the most important information needed to achieve one or more objectives, consolidated and arranged on a single screen so the information can be monitored at a glance."[27] Dashboards are intended to monitor and communicate an organization's progress toward its goals and milestones. They typically display a variety of financial and non-financial measures on one screen, frequently updated, even daily or in real time. Using color status indicators, such as red, yellow, and green, a dashboard can help draw attention to various levels of performance and potential problems.

Figure 7.17 presents the example of a dashboard that a CIO might employ to monitor day-to-day or month-to-month progress of different activities. The dashboard was designed by Stephen Few to provide key information to a Chief Information Officer on systems availability (uptime), expenses, customer satisfaction, CPU usage relative to capacity, major project milestones, and so on.

Figure 7.12 presents an example of a dashboard intended to provide month-to-month control information to a hospital CEO, designed by Katherine Rowell of Katherine S. Rowell & Associates of Brookline, MA, a data-visualization consultancy for healthcare organizations. The dashboard in Figure 7.18 presents metrics about such things as hospital occupancy rates, hospital quality, patient satisfaction, and revenues and expenses compared to budget. Up and down icons are used to alert the CEO to specific areas that may require further inquiry.

These two examples showcase the value of dashboards as a system for concurrent control. Dashboards like these can be designed using Excel spreadsheet software, though many software vendors now offer customized software to help design and update dashboards on a regular basis with the most current information.

The *Balanced Scorecard*, developed by Harvard Business School professor Robert Kaplan and David Norton in the early 1990s, is also a good approach for presenting a variety of control data. According to the Balanced Scorecard Institute, the Balanced Scorecard has been adopted by hundreds of organizations worldwide. It is a performance measurement and management system that specifically incorporates both financial and non-financial measures of organizational performance and attempts to show how different activities within an organization are inter-linked in cause-and-effect relationships. Many IT companies, including IBM and Oracle, provide software for operationalizing the Balanced Scorecard. The Balanced Scorecard incorporates measures along four perspectives that provide, according to the authors, a "balanced" view of organizational performance, namely, the learning and growth perspective, the business process perspective, the customer perspective, and the financial perspective (Figures 7.19A and 7.19B).

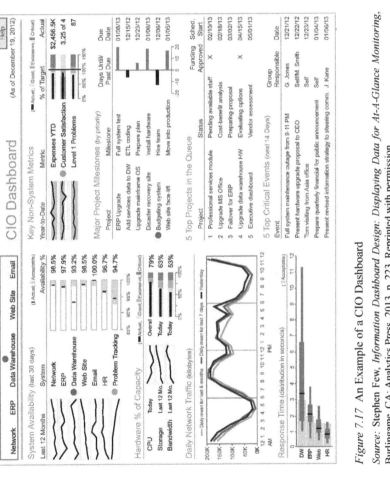

Figure 7.17 An Example of a CIO Dashboard

Source: Stephen Few, *Information Dashboard Design: Displaying Data for At-A-Glance Monitoring,* Burlingame, CA: Analytics Press, 2013, p. 223. Reprinted with permission.

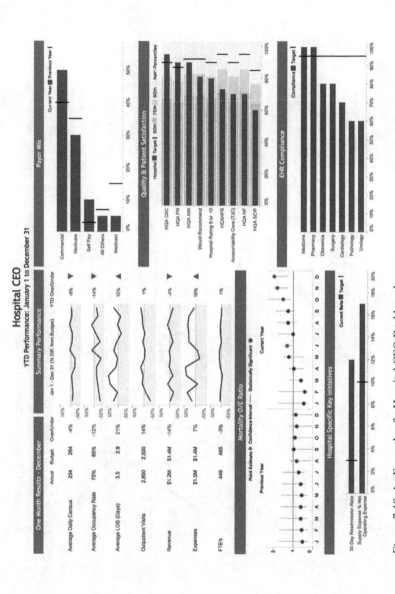

Figure 7.18 An Example of a Hospital CEO Dashboard

Source: Katherine S. Rowell & Associates and HealthDataViz, 2015. Reprinted with permission.

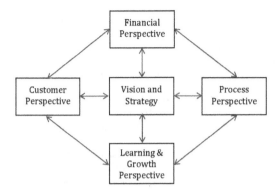

Figure 7.19A The Balanced Scorecard

Figure 7.19B Cause-and-Effect Relationships in the Balanced Scorecard

Figure 7.19A shows the basic Balanced Scorecard and Figure 7.19B the presumed cause-and-effect relationships within organizations. More than a visual display of performance information, the Balanced Scorecard is a performance management system that can help align a firm's vision and mission with customer requirements, manage and evaluate its strategy, and improve performance.[28]

Notes

1 Susan Adams, "Survey Suggests Executives Are in over Their Heads," *Forbes*, June 6, 2013.
2 Much of the information in this mini case study has come from the Volvo website (www.volvo.com), several annual reports, and presentations by the CEO at various fora.
3 Volvo Group Global press release, "Changes to Volvo Group Executive Board and Truck Organization with Clearer Commercial Accountability," January 27, 2016. Accessed from: http://www.volvogroup.com/group/global/en-gb/newsmedia/_layouts/CWP. Internet.VolvoCom/NewsItem.aspx?News.ItemId=151446&News.Language=en-gb.

4 Lillian Cunningham, "Tony Hsieh Got Rid of Bosses at Zappos and That's Not Even His Biggest Idea," *The Washington Post*, December 6, 2014, pp. G1, G4.
5 Source: Company website: www.gore.com.
6 Source for the quote on p. 185: http://www.cisco.com/c/en/us/solutions/collaboration/benefit.html.
7 Quoted from Charles W.L. Hill, *International Business: Competing in the Global Marketplace*, 9th Edition (New York: McGraw-Hill/Irwin, 2013), p. 454.
8 John M. Stopford and Louis T. Wells, *Strategy and Structure of the Multinational Enterprise* (New York: Basic Books, 1972).
9 Source: CEMEX submission to the U.S. Securities and Exchange Commission, Form 20-F, 2014 annual report.
10 Sony group's corporate Strategy Meeting on February 18, 2015, accessed from http://www.sony.net/SonyInfo/IR/strategy/2015.html.
11 Source: Much of this discussion is based on material taken from Sony Corporation website, www.sony.net.
12 Source: Company website, www.nestle.com.
13 Source: Company website, www.abb.com.
14 Much of the information in this mini case study up to 2001 is based on "Analysis of the Organizational Reorientation of the ABB Group" by Heinz Bierbaum and his colleagues at INFO-Institut, Saarbrücken, Germany, February 2001. Accessed from: http://www.willamette.edu/~fthompso/MgmtCon/ABB-Report.PDF.
15 William Taylor, "The Logic of Global Business: An Interview with ABB's Percy Barnevik," *Harvard Business Review*, March-April 1995, p. 95.
16 ABB press release, "ABB Accelerates Transformation: Stage 2 of Next Level Strategy," September 9, 2015, accessed from: http://www.abb.com/cawp/seitp202/a0400d533bc9c9e1c1257ead004eeaed.aspx. See also Alan Tovey, "ABB Restructuring Stokes Break-up Speculation," *The Guardian*, September 9, 2015.
17 The author once worked as a Coordination Manager for the Indian subsidiary of a British multinational that had two manufacturing plants and other operations in several locations in the country.
18 Julie Jargon, "McDonald's Plans to Change U.S. Structure," *The Wall Street Journal*, October 30, 2014.
19 Edwin A. Locke and Vinod K. Jain, "Organizational Learning and Continuous Improvement," *International Journal of Organizational Analysis*, 3, 1995.
20 Deborah Mills-Scofield, "It's Not Just Semantics: Managing Outcomes vs. Outputs," *Harvard Business Review*, November 12, 2012.
21 Steven Kerr, "On the Folly of Rewarding A, While Hoping for B," *Academy of Management Executive*, 9(1), 1985.
22 Source: Drucker Institute. Accessed from http://www.druckerinstitute.com/2012/04/the-behavior-we-reward/?lang=hi.
23 Eric Dontigney, "Examples of Concurrent Control in Management," Chron.com. Accessed from http://smallbusiness.chron.com/examples-concurrent-control-management-80471.html.
24 William J. Holstein, "Hyundai's Capabilities Play," *Strategy+Business*, Spring 2013, pp. 6–7.
25 An "order book" is a firm's list of open, unshipped, customer orders, normally time-phased and valued at actual individual item prices (adapted from Wikipedia).
26 See, for example, http://www.programtrading.com/curbs.htm.
27 Source: Stephen Few, "Dashboard Confusion," *Intelligent Enterprise*, March 20, 2004.
28 Balanced Scorecard Institute website: http://balancedscorecard.org/.

8

GLOBAL LEARNING, CAPABILITY BUILDING, AND THE MNE

We read, ask questions, explore, go to lectures, compare notes and findings, consult experts, daydream, brainstorm, formulate and test hypotheses, build models and simulations, communicate what we're learning, and practice new skills.

—Bill Gates

Learning, capability building, and innovation provide the foundation for strategy implementation and superior performance. (These are some of the characteristics included under "processes" in the strategy implementation framework of Figure 7.1.) The global connected economy offers MNEs the opportunity to leverage their knowledge, capabilities, and innovations in foreign markets. It also challenges them to acquire new learning, new capabilities, and new innovations from their own efforts, from multiple geographies, and from multiple sources, including customers, suppliers, subsidiaries, partners, competitors, universities, governments, trade bodies, and so on. They need all that and more to compete and grow in the hypercompetitive connected economy. Learning and capability are discussed in this chapter and innovation in the next chapter.

Survey after survey has highlighted the importance of learning, capability building, and innovation to performance in MNEs of all kinds. For instance, half of the 1,448 executives surveyed by McKinsey & Company in May 2014 ranked capability building as a top-three priority on their firms' strategic agendas. It is an even more significant priority among firms in India and China, with 62 percent and 58 percent ranking capability building as a top priority, respectively (Table 8.1).[1]

In a June 2013 survey conducted by Booz & Co. (also quoted in the previous chapter) of 3,500 executives from around the world, including 550 CEOs, only 21 percent said that their firms supported core capabilities in their strategy and operations. However, at firms where capabilities did support strategy, 47 percent of the respondents reported above-industry-average revenue growth. Unsurprisingly, though, only 14 percent of the respondents from firms where capabilities did not support strategy said that their revenues were growing at an above-average rate.[2]

Table 8.1 Percent of Respondents Rating Capability Building as a Top-Three Priority

Country/Region	Where Capability Building Falls on Organizations' Strategic Agendas			Total # Respondents
	Top Priority (%)	Top-3 Priority (%)	Total (%)	
Total	8	42	50	1,448
India	13	49	62	115
China	6	52	58	73
Europe	9	42	51	461
North America	9	40	49	428
Asia-Pacific	6	43	49	186
Developing Markets	6	41	47	184

Source: Adapted from McKinsey & Company, "Building Capabilities for Performance," McKinsey & Company, January 2015.

Learning, Capability Building, and Innovation at Hyundai Motor Group

The Hyundai Motor Group of South Korea, comprising Hyundai Motor Company, Kia Motors, and subsidiaries, is the world's fifth-largest automaker. Established in 1967, the company's sales revenue in 2014 was 89,256 billion Korean won (about US$80 billion) on sales of 4.8 million vehicles in over 200 countries. With over 80,000 employees worldwide, the company offers a full line of vehicles, including small, medium, and large passenger vehicles, SUVs, and commercial vehicles, and has a 5.7 percent global market share. Its operating profit margin of 8.5 to 9.5 percent over the last several years is higher than that of most of its major competitors.

The Hyundai Motor Group has nine manufacturing plants, including seven outside Korea (in Brazil, China, Czech Republic, India, Russia, Turkey, and the United States), all using an extensive amount of automation such as robots in its assembly plants. It operates the world's largest, integrated automobile manufacturing facility in Ulsan, Korea, with an annual production capacity of 1.87 million vehicles. It is perhaps the most vertically integrated automotive manufacturing operation in the world; Hyundai even makes its own steel in an $8 billion plant southwest of Seoul.[3]

Once regarded as a manufacturer of cheap, low-quality cars, a perception Hyundai continues to work hard to reverse, the company has been winning numerous awards in the U.S. and its other major markets. In 2014 alone, Hyundai won the following awards in the U.S.: Ward's 10 Best Engines Award, Residual Value Award, top rank in APEAL, Top Safety Pick, and Family Car of the Year. As a result, Hyundai has improved its brand value, achieving the 40th rank among the top 100 global brands in the Interbrand ranking for 2014, compared to the 65th rank in 2010. In the U.S., its third largest foreign market (after China and India), Hyundai offers "America's Best Warranty" on its cars, comprising

210

a 10-year/100,000 mile powertrain warranty, 5-year/60,000 mile bumper-to-bumper coverage, and roadside assistance for five years with unlimited mileage. According to Joe Philippi, president of AutoTrends Consulting LLC of New Jersey, U.S.A., "There's an acknowledgment by many designers right now that Hyundai has the hottest design in the industry."[4]

In a highly competitive, long-established global industry, Hyundai, a company from what was once a developing country, has achieved great success in less than five decades. There are a number of factors behind this success, such as government support, leadership, a culture of creativity and innovation, world-class capabilities, and up-to-the-minute control systems, among others.

Role of the Government and Top Company Leadership

While Hyundai has been learning and building capabilities since the 1960s, mostly through alliances with other companies (as discussed below), two factors were critical to the company's initial growth and success. The first was significant government support for Korea's automotive industry (especially from the 1970s to the 1990s), which was considered a growth engine for the nation's economy. Then, when government support ended in the early 2000s, that itself became a catalyst for the company to develop in-house expertise in design, quality, and innovation to survive in a highly competitive global environment.

Another factor in Hyundai's growth, as for most organizations, was the role played by its top leadership. Chung Mong-Koo, the eldest son of one of the founders, became the Chairman and CEO of Hyundai Motor Group in 1999. Chung Mong-Koo had previously worked at the company in various divisions and functions for many years and knew the company inside and out. Since taking over as chairman, he has been a prime mover in Hyundai's learning, capability-building, and quality-improvement journeys. According to Ed Kim, vice president of industry analysis at AutoPacific Inc. of Tustin, California, "The chairman decreed, 'Within this period of time, we will have the same quality as Toyota.'" And, whatever the chairman decreed, "the company mobilized and made it happen with breakneck speed."[5] Much of that was accomplished with the efforts of senior and top-level executives responsible for design, quality, operations, and other key functions. These executives included, among others, Chung Eui-Sun, Chung Mong-Koo's son, who previously headed Kia Motors and became Hyundai Motor Group's vice chairman in 2009, and Peter Schreyer, formerly a chief designer for Audi and VW, who had worked for Kia since 2006, appointed as vice president and Hyundai's first chief design officer in 2012.

Learning from Others

With no automotive-industry capabilities of its own in the 1960s, Hyundai's learning and capability-building journey began with an alliance with the Ford Motor Co. to assemble the Ford Cortina in Korea. Hyundai sent its engineers to Ford's

Detroit headquarters to learn and acquire the technology for making parts and components for the Cortina and later constructed its own assembly line. The first Cortinas came off the production line in November 1968. In the 1970s, Hyundai entered into an alliance with the Mitsubishi Motor Corporation of Japan to jointly develop powertrains and chassis. In another collaboration, Hyundai sent five engineers to Italdesign Giugiaro of Italy for a year to learn car styling, design, and product development. The Hyundai Motor Company set up its first design center in its Ulsan factory in 1974 and introduced its first independently designed and mass-produced car, the Pony, in 1975. The Pony became popular in Korea and was later successfully exported to countries in the Middle East, Africa, and Latin America.[6] Hyundai also adopted the best practices of some of its competitors through reverse engineering and hired top design talent from Germany, Italy, and the United States.

Learning from Own Experience

By the early 1990s, Hyundai's learning focus had shifted from technological dependence on Mitsubishi and others to developing its own capabilities through experimentation with different technologies and risk taking. Some of the key capabilities Hyundai developed included design, product development, manufacturing, and marketing.

The engine being the heart of an automobile, Hyundai independently developed a number of engines during the 1990s and 2000s for its vehicles (Table 8.2), some of which have gone on to win international recognition.

In 2003, the company created a 125-person research group to develop engines for its larger, premium car models, such as Hyundai Genesis, Kia Mohave, and Hyundai Equus. A Global Engine Manufacturing Alliance between Mitsubishi, Chrysler, and Hyundai Motor Co. selected the Theta as the foundation for a line of shared engines to be developed from it, resulting in licensing fees of $57 million for Hyundai. The 4.6L Tau V8 Engine was named one of Wards 10 Best Engines in 2009, 2010, and 2011.

Table 8.2 Timeline of Engines Developed by Hyundai Motor Group

Year	Engine	Size
1991	Alpha	1.6L
1995	Beta	1.6L, 1.8L, and 2.02L
1997	Epsilon	0.8L
1998	Delta	2.5L (V6)
1998	Sigma	3.0L (V6)
2005	Theta	2.0L, 2.4L
2007	Tau	4.6L, 5.0L (V8)

Source: Kyung-Won Chung, Yu-Jin Kim, and Sue Bencuya, "Hyundai Motor Company: Design Takes the Driver's Seat," Design Management Institute, Boston, 2014.

In addition to engines, other design innovations included an electric version of the Hyundai Sonata car model (1991), a solar powered version (1994), and the world's first mass-produced hydrogen fuel cell car, the Tucson ix in 2013.

Over the years, the Hyundai Motor Group has established a number of R&D and design centers in its major markets, each typically responsible for designing cars suitable for the markets or regions where the center is located (Table 8.3). In addition, the company has an Environmental Technology Center in Seoul responsible for developing hydrogen fuel and other environment-friendly vehicles, as well as clean manufacturing technologies, while the Korea Central Research Institute in Uiwang City focuses on developing frontier engine technologies.

For each new vehicle model to be developed, Hyundai selects a design center based on its target market. Often, the company encourages internal competition, which can sometimes get quite intense, between two or more design centers for a specific new model being developed. The final decision concerning the design to be selected rests with the Namyang Technology Research Center and marketing, reflecting the ongoing collaboration among design, engineering, and marketing.

Table 8.3 Hyundai Motor Group R&D and Design Centers

Year	Design Center	Location	Specialization
1982	Namyang Technology Research Center	Namyang, Korea	A comprehensive R&D center with 11,000 researchers
1990	America Technical Center	Ann Arbor, Michigan, and Irvine, California	R&D center in Ann Arbor, Michigan, which also operates the California Design & Technical Center
1995	Europe Technical Center	Frankfurt, Germany	Automobiles and engines that meet European environmental standards
1995	Japan Technical Center	Yokohama, Japan	Advanced technologies, including electronics and hybrid technologies
2007	China Hyundai-Kia Design Division	Beijing, China	The China Tech Center in Yantai (est. 2013) develops vehicles tailored to the Chinese market
2009	India Technical Center	Hyderabad, India	Designs vehicles for the Indian market and supports back-end operations

Source: Kyung-Won Chung, Yu-Jin Kim, and Sue Bencuya, "Hyundai Motor Company: Design Takes the Driver's Seat," Design Management Institute, Boston, 2014.

Control Systems

As highlighted in the previous chapter, having an effective control system is essential for strategy execution and achieving superior performance, which is also true for the Hyundai success story. Chairman Mong-Koo established a Quality Management Division in the company with a 24-hour "quality situation room" that had the ability to deal with quality issues as and when needed in any of the 150 countries where the company has operations.

The Hyundai Global Command and Control Center in Korea monitors every production line in its 27 plants worldwide, 24 hours a day, 365 days a year, with corrective action taken as needed. Plant managers can see assembly-line and other performance data on their smartphones. The company even developed a new metric, "qualitivity," which incorporates measures for quality, productivity, and customer satisfaction, to measure and control what happens in its manufacturing plants.

Knowledge and Learning

Organizations are repositories of knowledge—knowledge embedded in routines (standard operating procedures), stored in memory (e.g., paper and computer files), and carried by organization members inside their heads. The problem, however, is that sometimes it is hard for organization members to know what knowledge the organization has, where it resides, and how to access it. As Lew Platt of Hewlett-Packard once remarked, "I wish we knew what we know at HP," or Jerry Junkins, former Chairman and CEO of Texas Instruments, "If TI only knew what it knows." The larger, the more established, and the more product or geographically diversified an organization, the greater its repository of knowledge, and the more difficult it is for organization members to know what knowledge the organization has, where it resides, and how to access it.[7]

The good news is that knowledge does not deplete with use; it cannot be used up, though people can sometimes forget what they know, and knowledge can become obsolete. According to the principle of network externalities (or Metcalfe's Law), the value of information and knowledge to their owners and users increases exponentially as more people use them (Chapter 1). With developments in IT and the field of "knowledge management" over the past two decades or so, many companies have been becoming more knowledge-savvy in their ability to capture, store, retrieve, and utilize knowledge. Furthermore, with the current developments in data analytics, many scholars and practitioners believe that "big data" will transform business, government, and other aspects of the connected economy in major ways.

An example will help highlight the value of big data in decision making. Retail stores like Target have been collecting transaction data for a long time, including daily sales, sales by stores, products, and product categories. Nowadays, Target collects scanner data on who is buying what, where, at what price, the exact time of purchase, and so on, and links all such data to individual purchase histories, inventory levels, etc. For instance, Target can identify from an individual's purchase

214

history whether she is pregnant, and, if so, can send ads to her smartphone show-casing products she might need as she walks into a Target store. Sellers on the Internet can go much further. They can not only obtain the data that Target collects from its physical stores, but also data on customers' search queries, items viewed but discarded, time spent on reading buyer reviews, and much else. Once such data are linked to demographics, individual customers can be targeted with per-sonalized ads on their smart devices. A December 16, 2015, front-page headline in the *Washington Post* read, "Cruz's success aided by big data: 'Psychographic targeting' helps send him to top tier." Ted Cruz, one of the contenders for the U.S. Presidential Republican nomination for the fall 2016 election, has statisticians and behavioral psychologists working at his Houston headquarters to develop psycho-graphic profiles of potential supporters, which his staff uses to reach out to them. Using "psychographic targeting," his staff can classify a prospective supporter into one of several categories, such as a "temperamental conservative," a "stoic traditionalist," a "true believer," and so on. Depending on an individual's psycho-graphic profile, the campaign staff is instructed to talk to the prospect in language that would appeal to him/her. For instance, if a prospective supporter is a stoic tradi-tionalist, defined by the campaign as "a conservative whose top concerns included President Obama's use of executive orders on immigration," the campaign staff is "instructed to talk to her in a tone that was 'confident and warm and straight to the point' and ask her about her concerns regarding the Obama administration's positions on immigration, guns and other topics." Cruz's campaign believes that this approach is the reason for his rise in polls during November-December 2015 in many states. His staff aggressively collects personal information from public sources, social media, and other places. Ironically, though, Cruz himself has been a critic of excessive government data collection.[8]

Organizations acquire knowledge through learning, among other means. As indicated earlier, the global connected economy offers MNEs the opportunity to not only leverage their knowledge in foreign markets, but also to enhance it through learning from multiple geographies and multiple sources.

Learning

Learning involves thinking or mental processes such as perception, judgment, rea-soning, and memory, most of which are the domain of the individual rather than of the organization. Thus, all learning is individual learning, and an organization learns only through its individual members, i.e., by the learning of its members or by acquiring new members who have certain knowledge the organization lacks.[9] Organization members learn from education, training and development, appren-ticeships, mentors, practicing new skills, and imitation, among other approaches. Learning at the organizational level occurs through shared insights and shared knowledge and builds on the past knowledge and experiences of organization members. (See also the Bill Gates quote at the start of the chapter.) Subsequently, it may spread to others in the organization, indeed to other organizations through spill-over, competitive intelligence, or other means. As the Hyundai case study above showed, organizations learn from their own experience and history, as well as from the experiences and best practices of others. Organizations *learn from their own experience* through experimentation, research and development, internal benchmarking, problem solving, employee suggestion schemes, brainstorming, greenfield investment, and so on. They *learn from the experiences of others* through means such as training and development, external benchmarking, consultants, participation in global value chains, plant visits, chambers of commerce, trade shows, magazines and journals, M&As and alliances, competitive intelligence, and through imitation, euphemistically called reverse engineering.[10]

> What sets GE apart is a culture that uses diversity as a limitless source of learning opportunities, a storehouse of ideas whose breadth and richness is unmatched in world business. At the heart of this culture is an understanding that an organization's ability to learn, and translate that learning into action rapidly, is the ultimate competitive business advantage.
> —Jack Welch, former CEO, General Electric

Organizations seek knowledge and learning not for their own sake, but to build resources and capabilities that can be a source of superior performance and competitive advantage.

Resources, Capabilities, and Capability Building

While scholars have often debated the distinction between resources and capabilities, it should suffice here to suggest that resources can be thought of as nouns, the things a firm possesses, and capabilities as verbs, the things a firm does. A firm's resources can be *tangible* (e.g., plants and machinery, buildings, raw materials, financial capital, inventory, patents, and workforce) and *intangible* (e.g., brand names, marketplace relationships, goodwill, reputation, talent, knowledge, and corporate culture). Capabilities include the expertise, such as strategic planning, lean manufacturing, technology development, raising capital, inventory management, recruitment and selection, marketing, and order fulfilment, that firms develop with their tangible and intangible resources. For a firm to achieve competitive advantage, its capabilities, which are intangible by definition, and its intangible resources are generally more valuable than its tangible resources.

Not all capabilities are, of course, equally important in a firm's performance. Our interest here is in the capabilities that can provide a firm competitive advantage. For example, P&G is famous for its expertise in brand management and marketing of fast-moving consumer goods, Toyota for lean manufacturing, and Amazon.com for order fulfilment. Each of these MNEs has outperformed its rivals, at least partly based on its ability to build and leverage its resources and capabilities.

216

Firms, even within the same industry and country, have their own unique stocks of resources and capabilities, and there are no "identical twins" as far as resources and capabilities are concerned. This means that firms in an industry competing with the same strategy (e.g., a localization strategy) can indeed produce vastly different outcomes simply because they are competing with their unique sets of resources and capabilities. The key idea here is that the uniqueness of a firm, in terms of its resources, capabilities, and strategies, that can be the source of its superior performance and competitive advantage. For a resource or a capability to be a source of competitive advantage, it must satisfy at least two criteria—scarcity and immobility.

Scarcity

Resources and capabilities that are widely available cannot be a source of competitive advantage since anyone can have access to them. For a resource or a capability to be a source of competitive advantage, it must be scarce, i.e., not easily available to others. For instance, most airlines buy their aircraft from Boeing or Airbus, especially for long-haul flights. However, the aircraft in and of themselves, while essential for an airline to be in business and are very expensive, cannot be a source of competitive advantage in the highly competitive airline industry. An airline must have or develop certain capabilities to outperform its competition.

Immobility

For a firm to be able to leverage a certain capability or intangible resource, it must be immobile in the sense that others cannot have access to it without its permission. If someone can access such a capability or resource, with or without the firm's permission, then it is a mobile capability/resource and cannot be a source of its competitive advantage. For instance, a key source of Coca-Cola's success for so long has been its brand. In the 2015 Interbrand ranking, Coca-Cola came out as the world's third most valuable brand, after Apple and Google. Others can make a soft drink that looks and tastes like Coca-Cola, but, unless they can also use the Coca-Cola brand name, it will be a wasted effort.

Capabilities that are a source of competitive advantage typically require the expertise of several individuals working closely together within a firm and interacting with its internal and external environments. For example, Toyota's lean manufacturing system is well known, much has been written about it, and others can visit a Toyota plant to see it in action. However, few firms have been able to replicate Toyota's lean manufacturing capability in their own plants. A firm can potentially have the same plant and machinery, plant layout, and processes as Toyota, but will be hard pressed to recreate Toyota's corporate culture and the innumerable things that go on within a Toyota plant in their own operations.

MNEs do well by not only exploiting their existing resources and capabilities in foreign markets, but also by renewing capabilities and building new capabilities. As mentioned earlier, this presents an opportunity and a challenge for firms competing globally. According to Donald Lessard, Rafael Lucea, and Luis Vives, "The task of the global strategist is to build a platform of capabilities culled from the resources, experiences and innovations of units operating in multiple locations; to transplant those capabilities wherever appropriate; and then to systematically upgrade and renew them—ahead of the competition."[11]

Capability Building

Firms like Apple, Google, and Coca-Cola have unique sets of resources and capabilities that have made them hugely successful in their home markets, and which they have also successfully leveraged in many foreign markets. They continue to build capabilities through in-house R&D, mergers and acquisitions, and strategic alliances to remain at the forefront in their (product and geographic) markets. Google, in particular, has made over 180 acquisitions (and numerous alliances) during its lifetime to strengthen its resources, capabilities, and market position in fields as diverse as online advertising, search, security, robotics, and artificial intelligence. Dozens of the 180 acquisitions Google made were foreign acquisitions. Google, which derives over half its revenues from abroad, is not done yet. In May 2014, it told the U.S. Securities and Exchange Commission that it would spend up to $30 billion of its accumulated international profits to acquire foreign companies and technology rights.[12]

Netflix, Inc., which was first introduced in Chapter 4, is the Internet television network with over 70 million members in over 190 countries that access over 125 million hours of TV shows and movies each day, which accounts for about one-third of the Internet traffic in North America during peak hours. Of its many capabilities, the ones that touch the consumer directly are its DVD video rental service and video-on-demand online streaming service, both being keys to its competitive advantage. Its back-end control system is also an important capability that keeps the streaming service working almost flawlessly.

Companies build capabilities through their own efforts or acquire them through M&A and alliances. Sometimes, companies also acquire capabilities through imitation or by copying other companies' capabilities.

Building Capabilities Through Own Efforts

A capability consists of one or more organizational *routines*. A routine is a coordinated pattern of activities involving a sequence of actions undertaken by certain individuals within an organization.[13] Thus, a routine is essentially a standard operating procedure (SOP). For instance, brand building, lean manufacturing, customer service, and post-merger integration (PMI) are all capabilities, each requiring several routines, or several SOPs. Organizations develop

218

capabilities through trial-and-error, experimentation, and research and development, and they refine and standardize their routines over time through practice or learning-by-doing. CEMEX of Mexico is well-known for its PMI capability, honed over decades of M&A experience. CEMEX's PMI capability includes routines such as training of the integration team through cultural awareness and team-building workshops, cost reduction in energy usage, inventory rationalization, operations streamlining, and implementation of its satellite communication system, CEMEXNet, at the acquired companies.

The Hyundai case study highlighted several product innovations the company made, such as its first independently developed car, the Pony, in 1975, and its first engine, the Alpha, in 1991. Each of these innovations required specific sets of capabilities the company developed or purchased from other firms. For instance, to design the Pony, Hyundai built capabilities in auto styling and design, casting and forging, chassis design, tooling, and body production. For the design of its Alpha engine, Hyundai developed capabilities in hydrodynamics, thermodynamics, fuel engineering, emission control, lubrication, kinetics and vibration, ceramics, and electronic control systems.[14]

CAPABILITY BUILDING AT HBO

HBO (Home Box Office Inc.) is a U.S.-based pay-television network, owned by Time Warner Inc., and a direct competitor to Netflix, considering that they both operate in the same industry and with increasingly converging service offerings. Launched in 1972, HBO offers basic and premium television service available to about 127 million subscribers in some 150 countries worldwide, compared to Netflix's 70 million subscribers in over 190 countries. People subscribe to HBO through their television service provider for about $15 a month. HBO's 2014 revenue of $4.1 billion was eclipsed by its much younger competitor, Netflix, whose 2014 revenue was $4.7 billion, though HBO's adjusted operating income in 2014 was almost 10 times larger, $1.3 billion compared to Netflix's $164 million.

The subscription-television market is projected to be at $236 billion by 2018. This, along with the rapid rise of Netflix, encouraged HBO to offer a stand-alone, video-on-demand streaming service of its own that did not require a subscription to the HBO channels. In particular, HBO was interested in reaching out to the 70 million U.S. households that had cable service but no HBO subscription. In April 2015, HBO began offering "HBO Now," a video-streaming service similar to Netflix's.

HBO's preparation for offering its streaming service meant developing streaming capability, which it decided to develop on its own. In 2011, HBO hired Otto Berkes from Microsoft to develop the streaming technology, to be called HBO Now. Berkes, a long-time Microsoft employee and industry legend, had been responsible for co-creating the Xbox and had developed a tablet prototype long before the iPad appeared on the market. Berkes's goal was to develop and deliver the streaming technology by late 2016 by upgrading "HBO Go" service, a forerunner to HBO Now. This was a highly complex assignment and was to take a very long time to develop. According to an HBO insider, "With 2 million lines of code, you can't edit it like a book." In early 2014, however, HBO leadership decided to announce the HBO Now app during the forthcoming Time Warner investor conference in October 2014, a deadline that Berkes said he could not meet. It was then that HBO leadership decided to outsource streaming-capability development to the technology arm of Major League Baseball, MLB Advanced Media. MLB Advanced Media successfully streams baseball games live to its millions of subscribers throughout the U.S. and also has other media clients, including Sony, ESPN, and World Wrestling Entertainment. HBO Now was officially unveiled at Apple's "Spring Forward" event in San Francisco on March 9, 2015, and launched on April 7, 2015, with a $14.99 per month subscription.[15] (Berkes resigned his position at HBO shortly after the outsourcing arrangement was announced.)

Acquiring Capabilities Through M&As and Alliances

HBO, in the example discussed above, acquired streaming-technology capability through an outsourcing alliance when its in-house efforts were taking a great deal of time. As discussed in Chapter 6, companies make mergers, acquisitions, and alliances when they are seeking resources and capabilities they lack (and for other reasons, such as quicker access to the market, to broaden their product line, etc.) One of the examples discussed in the chapter was AMEC Foster Wheeler PLC, an engineering services and project management company from Britain. AMEC has made several acquisitions over the last three decades to expand its engineering capabilities and geographic footprint. In November, for instance, AMEC acquired Foster Wheeler of Switzerland for $3.2 billion, which turned out to be a "transformational" acquisition for the company. It provided AMEC with capabilities and capacity downstream in both oil and petrochemical industries, complementing its upstream capabilities, as well as the potential of achieving double-digit growth in earnings. Unlike AMEC, the Hyundai Motor Group acquired capabilities through alliances with major automakers, such as the Ford Motor Company and the Mitsubishi Motor Corporation, and later developed its own offerings to compete with them. This is a typical challenge MNEs face when they enter into an alliance with a current or potential competitor or with a firm that could become a competitor based on the learning and capabilities they acquire through the alliance. This is more likely to happen when the alliance is between an MNE from a developed country and a firm from a lesser developed country, though this is always a risk in alliances.

CAPABILITY BUILDING AT SUZLON ENERGY

Suzlon Energy Limited of India designs, manufactures, installs, and maintains wind turbines and was the world's fifth-largest turbine supplier as of 2013.

Headquartered in Pune, India, Suzlon has 14 manufacturing facilities in India, China (a joint venture), and the United States, as well as R&D centers in India, Denmark, Germany, and the Netherlands. Its international sales and marketing are handled out of Aarhus, Denmark. The company is vertically integrated for downstream operations, providing services and products ranging from feasibility studies, engineering design, manufacturing of wind turbines and components and the construction, installation and commissioning of wind farms, as well as their long-term operation and maintenance. Its global footprint (installed presence) now spans 19 countries in Asia, Australia, the Americas, Europe, the Middle East, and North Africa.[16]

Suzlon had little by way of expertise in the wind power industry, which it entered in 1995. In less than two decades, it has developed a great deal of expertise in the industry, much of it from its technologically superior foreign subsidiaries and alliance partners. While Suzlon now has an active R&D program, it built its capabilities largely through alliances and mergers and acquisitions. Similar to the Hyundai Motor Group's achievements, it is quite incredible that a company from an emerging market with no expertise in a high-tech industry was able to develop its resources and capabilities in less than two decades and compete with the dominant American, European, and Japanese MNEs, such as GE, Vestas, Siemens, and Mitsubishi, on a nearly equal footing.

Prior to founding Suzlon Energy, its chairman, Tulsi Tanti, ran his family's textile business. As electricity availability was unreliable in India, and a major cost component in a textile factory, Tanti looked for ways to cut down the electricity expense. He imported two wind turbines from Südwind of Germany, which helped reduce his electricity costs in an environmentally friendly way. Sensing an opportunity, Tanti signed a contract with Südwind to sell, install, and maintain its turbines in India. This is how Suzlon Energy got its start in 1995. In 1996, Tanti entered into a technology licensing agreement with Südwind, which agreed to license its wind turbine technology to Suzlon in return for royalty payments on the sale of Suzlon-made turbines for the next five years. This was the beginning of capability building in the wind turbine industry for Suzlon. When Südwind declared bankruptcy in 1997, Suzlon hired Südwind engineers and was now fully committed to the wind power business in a major way.

Suzlon's early acquisitions and alliances focused on developing its manufacturing capabilities, which allowed it to compete in the global wind power industry at the low- to mid-tech end of the industry value chain. These acquisitions were also a quicker means for revenue generation than developing and leveraging Suzlon's own R&D capabilities. Its later acquisitions were strategically designed to fill any gaps in its technology and to develop capabilities for performing higher value-added activities. For instance, to strengthen its expertise in rotor-blade design, Suzlon acquired AE-Rotor Techniek BV of the Netherlands in 2000 and entered into a licensing deal with another Dutch firm, Aerpac BV, in 2001. In that same year, Suzlon also obtained state-of-the-art rotor-blade manufacturing capabilities through an alliance with yet another Dutch firm, Enron

Wind Rotor Production BV. All of this led Suzlon to establish a rotor-blade R&D subsidiary in the Netherlands. In 2002, Suzlon established an R&D subsidiary in Germany, Suzlon Energy GmbH, to develop and design wind turbine generators by acquiring AX 215 Verwaltungsgesellschaft mbH.

From a technology standpoint, Suzlon made two of its most important acquisitions during 2006 and 2007—Hansen Transmissions of Belgium, the world's second largest gear manufacturer, and REpower Systems AG of Germany, a technology leader and manufacturer of the largest offshore wind turbines. These acquisitions gave Suzlon the targets' cutting-edge technologies as well as their manufacturing plants and customer base. Table 8.4 shows the timeline of Suzlon's alliances and acquisitions as well as the capabilities it acquired through them. (Suzlon sold off its stakes in Hansen and REpower in November 2011 and January 2015, respectively, to reduce its debt caused by the 1.3 billion euros it had paid for REpower and the financial global crisis of 2008–2010. However, it signed a long-term contract with Hansen for continued parts supply and a licensing deal with REpower for continued use of its technology.) Suzlon established its foreign subsidiaries in locations close to its major markets (e.g., Suzlon Energy GmbH in Germany, close to its key Northern European markets) and in the wind-energy strategic clusters (e.g., its international sales and marketing subsidiary in the Danish wind-energy cluster in Aarhus) where it could access industry-specific talent, technology, and value-chain partners.

Table 8.4 Timeline of Suzlon's Foreign Acquisitions and Alliances Through 2010

Year	Company	Country	Relationship	Expertise
1996	Sündwind	Germany	Technology licensing	Wind turbine technology
2000	AE-Rotor Techniek BV	Netherlands	Acquisition	Rotor-blade design
2001	Aerpac BV	Netherlands	Technology licensing	Rotor-blade design
2001	Enron Wind Rotor Production BV	Netherlands	Manufacturing and marketing rights (license)	Molds, production line, and technical support
2002	AX 215 Verwaltungs GmbH	Germany	Acquisition	R&D
2004	Elin Motoren GmbH	Germany	Joint venture	Generator manufacturing
2006	Hansen Transmissions	Belgium	Acquisition	Gearbox technology and manufacturing
2007	REpower	Germany	Acquisition	Large-capacity offshore turbines technology and manufacturing

Source: Snehal Awate, Ram Mudambi, and Arohini Narain, "Balancing the Power Equation: Suzlon Energy Limited," Indian School of Business Case Study No. ISB 049, January 27, 2015, p. 13.

The EMC Corporation (EMC[2]) provides another useful example of capability building. It was mostly a hardware and break-fix service provider until about the year 2000. It added implementation services during 2001–2006 and consulting services during 2005–2010 to its portfolio through acquisitions and alliances. EMC now offers data storage, information security, virtualization, analytics, and cloud computing products and services to help businesses store, manage, protect, and analyze data. For instance, it added open, platform-independent storage consulting services to its portfolio through a partnership agreement with Accenture in July 2002 and Intel-based virtual computing software solutions through the acquisition of VMware in January 2004.

Acquiring Capabilities Through Imitation

The Hyundai Motor Group and the Suzlon Energy Limited mini case studies above showed how these companies learned from foreign firms utilizing a variety of approaches, such as OEM production (Hyundai for Ford and Suzlon for Südwind) and technology licensing, to catch up and later compete with them on an equal footing. This has been true for the development of products and firm-level capabilities in a number of countries, including China, India, Japan, Korea, Malaysia, Taiwan, and many others.[17] Linsu Kim studied the case of Korean companies in the automotive, electronics, and semiconductor industries at depth and attributed their capability building to the imitation of foreign firms' products and technological capabilities, as well as to government policies (see Table 8.5), among other factors.[18] For instance, government policy allowed for the import of machinery, which could then be reverse-engineered by local firms.

Further, according to Rajneesh Narula: "The case of Korea… illustrates the evolution of the ability to assimilate R&D spillovers during the catching-up process. Korea relied on technology licensing and imports of capital goods from developed countries in acquiring external knowledge till the 1980s, but this enabled it only to access second-best practice technologies. Korea is now almost at the technology frontier in many sectors… There is now an increasing emphasis on technological capability building and on reverse technology transfer, that is, through outward FDI by Korean MNEs. …"[19]

In 2015, for example, Samsung received more U.S. utility patents than IBM for the first time; the top spot was held by IBM for 22 years.

Imitating the products and capabilities of other firms is not restricted to developing-country firms. In fact, product and capability imitation has long been the rule, rather than the exception, in countries both developing and developed— actually, more so in developed countries where much of the innovation happens in the first place. Steven Schnaars documented the case studies of 28 innovative products, practically all of which were developed and then imitated by developed-country firms, and where the imitators surpassed the innovators over time (Box 8.1).[20] According to Theodore Levitt, writing in 1966, "… [I]mitation is not only more abundant than innovation, but actually a much more prevalent

Table 8.5 Korea's Industrial and Science & Technology Policy Framework, 1960s–1990s

Policies	1960s and 1970s	1980s and 1990s
Industrial policy	Deliberate promotion of big businesses as an engine of technological learning Export orientation Promotion of technologically advanced heavy and chemical industries Repression of labor to maintain industrial peace	Promotion of SMEs Export orientation Antitrust and fair trade Trade liberalization Intellectual property rights protection Shifting emphasis on R&D and manpower development
Science and technology policy	Restrictions on FDI and foreign licenses Promotion of capital goods import Promotion of Government Research Institutes (GRIs) in lieu of university research	Promotion of FDI and foreign licenses Extensive diffusion networks Promotion of university research Promotion of corporate R&D activities Promotion of national R&D projects

Source: Adapted from Linsu Kim, *Imitation to Innovation: The Dynamics of Korea's Technological Learning* (Boston: Harvard Business School Press, 1997).

road to business growth and profits... Imitation is not just something which even the biggest, best managed, most resourceful company will, by force of competitive circumstances, have to be involved in; it is something it will have to practice as a carefully developed strategy."[21] The fact that Microsoft copied the early versions of its personal computer operating system, Windows, and its application software, Word, from other companies that had also been working on the same technologies is legendary. According to a 1991 *New York Times* article, competitors "have long complained that the rest of the industry has served as Microsoft's R&D lab."[22]

Hyundai, Suzlon, Microsoft, and most of the examples included in Box 8.1 highlight the fact that even though they initially imitated the products and capabilities of other firms, they eventually succeeded by building their own capabilities in R&D, marketing, distribution, and financial management. The following case studies (CAT Scanner and Computerized Ticketing Service) from Schnaars show how the imitators surpassed the innovators.

CAT SCANNERS (COMPUTED AXIAL TOMOGRAPHY)

The CAT scanner technology was developed in 1967 by Godfrey Hounsfield, a scientist working for the British music and entertainment company, EMI Ltd. His innovation was to integrate three pre-existing technologies (x-ray, data

Box 8.1 The List of the 28 Products for Which the Imitators Surpassed the Pioneers

Product	Pioneers/First Movers	Imitator/Later Entrants
35 mm Cameras	Leica (1925) Contax (1932) Exacta (1936)	Canon (1934) Nikon (1946) Nikon SLR (1959)
Automated Teller Machines (ATMs)	De La Rue of Britain (1967) Docutel (1969)	Diebold (1971) IBM (1973) NCR (1974)
Ballpoint Pens	Reynolds (1945) Eversharp (1946)	Parker "Jotter" (1954) Bic (1960)
Caffeine-Free Soft Drinks	Canada Dry's "Sport" (1967) Royal Crown's RC100	Pepsi Free (1982) Caffeine-Free Coke
CAT Scanners (Computed Axial Tomography)	EMI (1972)	Pfizer (1974) Technicare (1975) General Electric (1976) Johnson & Johnson (1978)
Commercial Jet Aircraft	De Havilland Comet 1 (1952)	Boeing 707 (1958) Douglas DC-8
Computerized Ticketing Service	Ticketron (1968)	Ticketmaster (1982)
Credit/Charge Cards	Diners Club (1950)	American Express (1958) Visa/MasterCard (1966)
Diet Soft Drinks	Kirsch's No-Cal (1952) Royal Crown's Diet Rite Cola (1962)	Pepsi's Patio Cola (1962) Coke's Tab (1963) Diet Pepsi (1964) Diet Coke (1982)
Dry Beers	Asahi (1987)	Japan's Kirin, Sapporo, and Suntory (1988) Michelob Dry (1988) Bud Dry (1989)
Food Processors	Cuisinart (1973)	Black & Decker (late 1970s) Sunbeam "Oskar" (1984)
Light Beers	Rheingold's Gablinger's (1966) Meister Brau Lite (1967)	Miller Lite (1973) Natural Light (1977) Coors Light (1978) Bud Light (1982)
Mainframe Computers	Atanasoff's ABC Computer (1939) Eckert-Mauchly's ENIAC/UNIVAC (1946)	IBM (1953)

Microwave Ovens	Raytheon Radarange for the Commercial Market (1946) Tappan (1955) Amana (1968) Litton (1971)	Panasonic (early 1970s) Sharp (mid-1970s) Samsung (1980)
Money Market Mutual Funds	Reserve Fund of New York (1973)	Dreyfus Liquid Assets (1974) Fidelity Income Trust (1974) Merrill Lynch Ready Assets (1975)
MRI (Magnetic Resonance Imaging)	Fonar (1978)	Johnson & Johnson's Technicare (1981) General Electric (1982)
Nonalcoholic Beers	G. Heileman's Kingsbuy (early 1980s) Moussy of Switzerland (1983)	Miller's Sharp's (1989) Anheuser-Busch's O'Doul's (1989) Coor's Cutter (1991)
Operating System for Personal Computers	CP/M (1974)	MS-DOS by Microsoft (1981) Microsoft Windows (1985)
Paperback Books	Penguin (1935 in England, 1939 in the U.S.) Modern Age Books (1937) Pocket Books (1939)	Avon (1941) Popular Library (1942) Dell (1943) Bantam (1946)
Personal Computers	MITS Altair 8800 (1975) Apple II (1971) Radio Shack (1977)	IBM PC (1981) Compaq (1982) Dell (1984)
Pocket Calculators	Bowmar (1971)	Texas Instruments (1972)
Projection Television	Advent (1973) Sony's Industrial Model (1973) Kloss Video (1977)	Panasonic (1978) Mitsubishi (1980)
Spreadsheet Software	VisiCalc (1979)	Lotus 1–2–3 (1983)
Telephone Answering Machines	Code-A-Phone (1958)	Panasonic (mid-1970s) AT&T (1983)
Video Cassette Recorders	Ampex (1956) CBS-EVR (1970) Sony U-Matic (1971) Cartrivision (1972) Sony Betamax (1975)	JVC HHS (1976) RCA Selectra Vision by Matsushita (1977)
Videogames	Magnavix Odyssey (1972), the first home video game Atari's Pong (1972), the first coin-operated arcade game	Nintendo Home Entertainment System (1985) Sega "Genesis" (1989) NEC "TurboGrafx" (1989)

Warehouse Clubs	Price Club (1972)	Sam's Club, Costco, Pace, and BJ's Wholesale Club (all entered in 1983)
Word Processing Software	Wordstar (1979)	WordPerfect (1982) Microsoft Word (1983)

Source: Adapted from Steven P. Schnaars, *Managing Imitation Strategies: How Late Entrants Seize Markets from Pioneers* (New York: Free Press, 1994).

processing, and cathode ray tube display) in a complex and precise manner to create 3-dimensional (3D) images of the brain for medical diagnostics. His invention came to be known as the CAT scanner. EMI took a patent on the CAT scanner in 1969 and developed and successfully tested early prototypes in both England and the United States in the early 1970s. The technology turned out to be a breakthrough innovation that allowed doctors to examine someone's brain via 3D images without risking surgery. Sensing a great business opportunity, EMI decided to manufacture and market the world's first CAT scanners in 1972. As the market for the CAT scanner exploded by 1973, EMI ramped up production, developed after-sales service and customer-support capabilities, and practically ruled the industry for the next three years. However, EMI's expertise was in record labels and promoting rock groups, not in medical diagnostics technologies, an industry dominated by major U.S. and European firms such as GE, Philips, and Siemens. EMI's success brought several competitors to the market, some of which developed CAT scanners with even more features, such as the ability to perform a full-body scan, not just the brain scan, and do so in less time. GE, which already marketed x-ray equipment and was an industry insider, entered the CAT scanner market in 1976 and became the market leader by 1978, overtaking not just EMI, but also Technicare's Ohio Nuclear, Pfizer, and other companies that had entered the CAT scanner market. As EMI's performance continued to decline, its CAT scanner business was acquired by GE in 1980. In addition to its long history in medical diagnostics and related products, GE had extensive service capability, reputation, and market power. (Godfrey Hounslow, the EMI scientist who developed the CAT scanner technology, was a co-winner of the Nobel Prize for medicine in 1979.)[23]

COMPUTERIZED TICKETING SERVICE

Ticketron, a subsidiary of the (erstwhile) Control Data Corporation of the United States, developed and began offering computerized ticketing services in 1968 to sell tickets for a major Los Angeles event. Even though a few small, regional players entered the computerized ticketing market, Ticketron became the undisputed market leader with reach throughout the United States and remained so for the next 12 years. Ticketmaster, which entered the market in 1976 as a regional player, overtook the industry leader and eventually acquired it in June 1991.[24]

Ticketmaster, now owned by Live Nation Entertainment, the largest concert pro-moter in the U.S., is the world's largest online ticketing platform, selling event tickets over the phone, online, and through retail partners.

How did Ticketmaster overtake Ticketron and become the industry leader? The first factor was its business model, which was diametrically opposite that of Ticketron. Ticketron received a commission from event organizers for every ticket it sold. Ticketmaster, on the other hand, offered a business proposition to event organizers they could not refuse. Instead of the event organizers paying the ticket seller (e.g., Ticketron) to sell their tickets, Ticketmaster told them that, in exchange for an exclusive contract to sell their tickets, it would pay them a portion of the service fees it collected from consumers. Second, Ticketmaster, being an online business, benefits from strong network effects. As the number of event venues that sold tickets through Ticketmaster increased, the value of the platform to the consumers increased, and, as more consumers purchased their tickets through Ticketmaster, it attracted even more events to its platform. It is the classic winner-take-all outcome of network effects. Third, Ticketmas-ter's merger with Live Nation in January 2010 significantly expanded its market power. Live Nation is not only the largest concert promoter in the U.S., it also owns a large number of amphitheaters and promotes or produces over 22,000 events per year globally. Finally, the operational expertise and technological capabilities Ticketmaster has developed over the years have placed it ahead of the pack. Some of the other capabilities Ticketmaster developed included its ability to sense the needs of its customers (event organizers) and offer them solutions more conveniently, more quickly, and at lesser cost than the competi-tion, an ability to raise capital as needed, and continuous product improvement through R&D.

First Mover Advantages and Disadvantages

A first mover in an industry has many advantages. It has the opportunity to reduce its per-unit cost by riding down the learning curve ahead of late movers and by developing economies of scale through large-scale production, sometimes even ahead of demand. It can pre-empt market segments and valuable resources from being accessed by late movers and also build buyer switching costs. It can edu-cate customers for its new product category and thus build reputation and brand equity. It can continue to improve its product offerings through R&D and stay a step ahead of the competition. For online products, it can benefit from network effects. For a product for which multiple early movers are attempting to get their products to become the industry standards, a first mover has the potential to get its product to become the industry standard.

First movers also face some disadvantages (Chapter 4). The first mover must incur pioneering costs, e.g., the cost of ongoing R&D, educating customers, and building a distribution system for entirely new products. The first movers also face a greater risk of failure since they may not understand the "rules of the game" in a new market, risk piracy of their intellectual property, and risk the latecomers taking a free ride on their pioneering investments. If the market does not develop as expected, or if the first mover is not able to successfully leverage the opportunity, it may also suffer from a "lock-in/ lock-out" effect. Since foreign market investments are often major investments that are difficult, if not impossible, to reverse without much cost, the first mover may be locked into a foreign market and get locked out of other potential opportunities that may arise later. The same is also true for being locked into an inferior technology due to early investment and getting locked out of superior technologies as the industry reaches the growth phase in its life cycle. (See Box 8.2 for a brief discussion of a typical "industry life cycle.")

Box 8.2 Industry Life Cycle

The Industry Life Cycle (ILC) represents how industries are born, grow, become mature, decline, and eventually die, just like biological organisms do. This is a typical pattern, though not all industries follow it. Some industries die before they become mature, or even before they start growing, while some like the carbonated soda industry continue to live in maturity for decades. Also, different firms in an industry can be at different stages of the industry life cycle. Further, an industry can be at a growth or shakeout stage in one country and still in the introductory stage in another. Figure 8.1 shows a typical ILC pattern. The ILC is an important concept in strategy because its different stages represent different competitive dynamics and hence the need for different strategies.

The **introductory (embryonic) stage** of an industry represents its birth and slow evolution, characterized initially by one/two innovators or first movers. The typical challenges the industry faces at this stage are technology development, the need for capital to continue technology development, and educating prospective customers about the innovation. As other firms begin to enter the industry, the competitive challenge is in technology

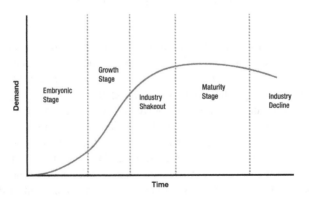

Figure 8.1 A Typical Industry Life Cycle

---

development rather than gaining markets or customers. An example, as of late 2015 in the U.S., is the autonomous vehicles (e.g., self-driving cars) industry that is still in the embryonic stage, but likely to jump to the growth stage within the near term since most of the major automotive companies have announced plans to introduce autonomous vehicles.

The **growth stage** is characterized by fast growth as more and more customers and competitors enter the market. The industry is growing at an increasing rate of change, and the challenge for companies is to keep growing. There is a high need for working capital as companies must quicken the pace of technology development, manufacturing, marketing, and so on. This is the stage when one/two dominant designs emerge. Some examples of industries in the growth stage are personal drones and smart watches.

During the **shakeout stage**, the industry is still growing quickly but at a decreasing rate of change. As some companies are not able to keep pace with the faster-growing competitors, they exit the market or become acquisition targets for the dominant firms or late movers. Barriers to entry start to increase by the shakeout stage.

Industries in the **maturity stage** face stable demand and, thus, a more or less flat growth curve. A mature industry is often an oligopoly with a few dominant players and high barriers to entry as the incumbents try to safeguard their market shares. Most industries in advanced countries today happen to be in their maturity phase, including industries such as GPS (global positioning system) and refrigerators. Companies often continue upgrading their products through innovation or find new uses or new markets for them and thus continue their life cycle.

Industries in the **decline stage** face reduced demand due to new innovations, availability of substitute products, or changing customer needs and tastes and hence negative growth rates. Some examples of industries in the decline stage are the cigarette industry and the VCR (video cassette recorder) industry. Industries in the decline stage have relatively few players, and some of them can indeed be quite profitable.

The disadvantages of the first mover are the advantages of imitators, fast seconds, and late movers. Since the highest rate of product failures occurs during the introductory stage of the industry life cycle, a prospective late mover can avoid investing in a product that has no market potential. It is also almost always cheaper to imitate than to innovate, due to the lower cost of R&D, educating customers, and the opportunity to leverage an existing distribution system rather than setting up a new one. If the technology is changing rapidly, the imitator or late mover has an advantage over the first mover because it can improve upon the first mover's technology. Finally, since first movers are often small, entrepreneurial firms, an imitator or a late entrant with market power can sometimes control the market even if it lacked enough R&D expertise at the time of entry into the market.

The pharmaceutical industry provides a good example of the value of being a first or early mover for novel prescription drugs. Myoung Cha and Flora Yu of McKinsey & Company analyzed 492 drug launches in 131 classes over a 27-year period (1986–2002). The sample included drugs that generated at least $100 million in annual sales and had one or more direct competitors during their patented life. They analyzed the order-of-entry effect by market share for each entrant in the tenth year after the launch of the first drug.

Table 8.6 presents their findings. Unsurprisingly, the first-to-enter companies for a particular drug achieved a greater-than-fair market share, defined as 100 percent market share divided by the number of entrants. They had an average market share of 40 percent, compared to 33 percent for the second-to-enter companies, 19 percent for the third-to-enter companies, and so on. The third column in Table 8.6 shows the advantage or disadvantage due to a company's order of entry into the market for a specific drug. Cha and Yu also found a more pronounced first-mover advantage in specialty areas with small numbers of patients and prescribers and also for injectable drugs over oral preparations. In cases where there were only two players, the first mover had a much greater advantage. When the first mover was a large pharmaceutical company, it had a significant advantage over late movers; however, when the first mover was not a large company, it achieved less than its fair market share. They also found that companies with prior experience in a therapeutic area had almost twice the first-to-market advantage over companies with little experience in the area. Finally, lead time provided a substantial advantage to the first movers, especially if they had a lead of at least three years before other entrants appeared in the market.

However, the authors also offer a note of caution: "Despite these circumstances, it is important to note that late movers win in 50 percent of the drug classes we evaluated. And we find that the odds are greatly improved for late entrants when they are second entrants to the market, fast followers (launched within the same year or one year after the first entrant), and marketed by a large pharma company."[25]

Table 8.6 Average Market Share 10 Years after First Launch in Class

Order of Entry	Average Market Share	Average Market Share Advantage/Disadvantage	Number of Drugs
1st to Market	40%	6%	131
2nd to Market	33%	−1%	131
3rd to Market	19%	−3%	84
4th to Market	13%	−2%	52
5th to Market	8%	−1%	31
6th to Market and Beyond	2%	−9%	63

Source: Myoung Cha and Flora Yu, "Pharma's First-to-Market Advantage," McKinsey & Company, September 2014.

The pharmaceutical industry is a highly specialized industry where different companies can offer different medications for the same condition without impinging on each other's patents. For instance, high cholesterol can be treated by drugs from different classes, such as a statin (e.g., Lipitor), a cholesterol absorption inhibitor (e.g., Zetia), a prescription niacin (e.g., Niaspan), and so on.

Imitation Strategies

The imitators and late movers in Schannar's 28 case studies leapfrogged over the first movers technologically through their own R&D or used their market power to overtake them. This included the use of legal and regulatory challenges, such as safety and antitrust, to slow down their progress. In some cases, the first movers were so confident of their success that they did not take the imitators seriously. In others, the imitators benefited from economies of scope by adding another product line to their existing lines of business, such as GE, which expanded its business by adding the CAT scanner to its x-ray business. In the absence of a patent, e.g., when an innovation was made by a small, entrepreneurial firm that did not patent its innovation, the imitator simply copied the product or used reverse engineering to come up with an alternative design to accomplish the same task. Often, the imitators were able to offer the same or a similar product at a much lower price. In practically every case, though, the imitators developed resources and capabilities they needed to compete with, and eventually overtake, the first movers.

The timing of imitation is critical to success. An imitator can potentially overtake the first mover if it enters the market early, e.g., during the introductory phase when there are opportunities to leapfrog the innovator technologically and competition is still not intense, or during the shake-out phase when the weaker competitors exit the market or become potential targets for the first or late movers. An imitator who tries to enter the market during its maturity phase will find intense entry barriers and also risk retaliation from incumbents.

In his 1966 *Harvard Business Review* article referred to earlier, Theodore Levitt concluded that "Having an affirmative policy of supporting a strategy of imitation in some organized fashion would have the virtue not only of getting necessary imitative activities into motion early, but of communicating to the entire organization that while innovators are valued, so are the creative imitators. It would legitimize systematic imitative thinking as much as the more glamorous innovative thinking."[26]

This is not to say that imitators always win over the first movers or innovators. There are indeed thousands of cases where the innovators succeeded in achieving and sustaining a dominant market position. For instance, ASML of the Netherlands, the world's largest supplier of photolithography systems for the semiconductor industry, has an 80 percent global market share. It has relentlessly attempted to be the first to market with each new generation of integrated circuits. This has enabled its customers, like Intel and Samsung, to be leaders in their own markets.[27]

232

Concluding Remarks

As indicated at the very start of the chapter, learning, capability building, and innovation provide the foundation for strategy implementation and superior performance. The chapter presented the case studies of several companies, e.g., Hyundai Motors, Suzlon Energy, and HBO, that achieved market leadership positions in their respective industries by building capabilities systematically through their own experience and through the experiences of others, such as through M&As and alliances. The discussion on first-mover advantages showed that first movers have the opportunity to become dominant players in their evolving industries, but only if they are able to build the resources and capabilities needed to stay ahead of imitators and late movers. The McKinsey & Company study of the pharmaceutical industry by Cha and Yu provided validation of the value of being a first mover. The chapter also presented examples of late movers who became industry leaders through imitation and reverse engineering, though this almost always required market power, leapfrogging the first movers technologically, or competitive default by the first movers. The other component of the learning-capability building-performance equation is innovation, which is taken up in the next chapter.

Notes

1 Richard Benson-Armer, Silke-Susann Otto, and Gina Webster, "Building Capabilities for Performance," *McKinsey Quarterly*, January 2015.
2 Susan Adams, "Survey Suggests Executives Are in Over Their Heads," *Forbes*, June 6, 2013.
3 Much of the information for this mini case study was taken from company websites and Hyundai Motor Company Investor Presentation, February 2015. Any other sources used are cited separately.
4 William J. Holstein, "Hyundai's Capabilities Play," *Strategy+Business*, Spring 2013.
5 Holstein, 2013.
6 Kyung-Won Chung, Yu-Jin Kim, and Sue Bencuya, "Hyundai Motor Company: Design Takes the Driver's Seat," Design Management Institute, Boston, 2014.
7 A part of this chapter is based on Vinod K. Jain, "Managing Knowledge in the Extended Enterprise." In *Borderless Business: Managing the Far-Flung Enterprise*, edited by Clarence J. Mann and Klaus Götz (Westport, CT: Praeger, 2006).
8 Tom Hamburger, "Cruz's Success Aided by Big Data," *The Washington Post*, December 16, 2015: A1.
9 Herbert A. Simon, "Bounded Rationality and Organizational Learning," *Organization Science*, 2, 1991: 125–34.
10 Edwin A. Locke and Vinod K. Jain, "Organizational Learning and Continuous Improvement," *International Journal of Organizational Analysis*, 3 (1995): pp. 45–68.
11 Donald Lessard, Rafael Lucea, and Luis Vives, "Building Your Company's Capabilities through Global Expansion," *Sloan Management Review*, 54(2), Winter 2013.
12 Vinod Jain, "Google's Unprecedented Shopping Spree," Letters to the Editor, *The Washington Post*, August 16, 2015.
13 Richard R. Nelson and Sidney G. Winter, *An Evolutionary Theory of Economic Change* (Cambridge, MA: Belknap Press, 1982).

14 Linsu Kim, "Crisis Construction and Organizational Learning: Capability Building and Catching Up at Hyundai Motor," *Organizational Science*, 9 (1998): pp. 506–21.
15 Various sources including company website (www.hbo.com); Nicole LaPorte, "HBO to Netflix: Bring It on," *Fast Company*, May 2015; and Liam Boluk, "The State and Future of Netflix v. HBO in 2015," REDEF Original, March 5, 2015, accessed from http://redef.com/original/the-state-and-future-of-netflix-v-hbo-in-2015.
16 Much of the information in this mini case study was taken from the company website (www.suzlon.com) and especially from Snehal Awate, Ram Mudambi, and Arohini Narain, "Balancing the Power Equation: Suzlon Energy Limited," Indian School of Business Case Study No. ISB 049, January 27, 2015.
17 See, for example, M.K. Bolton, "Imitation versus Innovation: Lessons to be Learned from the Japanese," *Organizational Dynamics*, Winter 1993: pp. 30–45; Rajneesh Narula, *Globalization and Technology: Interdependence, Innovation Systems, and Industrial Policy* (Cambridge, UK: Polity Press, 2003); and Shaker A. Zahra, Harry J. Sapienza, and Per Davidsson, "Entrepreneurial and Dynamic Capabilities: A Review, Model and Research Agenda," *Journal of Management Studies*, 43 (2006): pp. 917–55.
18 Linsu Kim, *Imitation to Innovation: The Dynamics of Korea's Technological Learning* (Boston: Harvard Business School Press, 1997).
19 Rajneesh Narula, *Globalization and Technology: Interdependence, Innovation Systems, and Industrial Policy.* (Cambridge, UK: Polity Press, 2003), p. 208.
20 Steven P. Schnaars, *Managing Imitation Strategies: How Late Entrants Seize Markets from Pioneers* (New York: Free Press, 1994).
21 Theodore Levitt, "Innovative Imitation," *Harvard Business Review*, September 1966.
22 Andrew Pollack, "One Day, Junior Got Too Big," *The New York Times*, August 4, 1991.
23 For more information, refer to Schnaars, 1994, pp. 63–68, and Christopher A. Bartlett, "EMI and the CT Scanner (A)," Harvard Business School Publishing Case Study No. 9-383-194, November 8, 2001.
24 For more information, refer to Schnaars, 1994, pp. 75–81.
25 Myoung Cha and Flora Yu, "Pharma's First-to-Market Advantage," McKinsey & Company, September 2014.
26 Levitt, 1966.
27 Marc de Jong, Nathan Marston, Erik Roth, and Peet van Bijon, "The Eight Essentials of Innovation Performance," McKinsey & Company, December 2013.

9

INNOVATION AND THE MNE

Innovation distinguishes between a leader and a follower.
                                                    —Steve Jobs

Innovation involves creating something significantly new, better, and of value.[1] The "something significantly new" can be a product, service, process, design, business concept, business model, or even a new feature in an existing product or service. Innovation is often incremental but can also be disruptive, breakthrough, or transformational for an organization. It can arise from anywhere inside an organization, from its innovation ecosystem that extends to individuals and entities outside the organization, and, increasingly, from sources beyond its ecosystem.

Why Do It

Innovation helps create new products, new industries, and better-paying jobs in nations. According to Michael Porter, innovation leads to productivity growth, firms' and nations' international competitiveness, GDP growth, and prosperity for a nation's citizens.[2] Innovation has also helped solve some of the most critical challenges facing society.

The Policy Perspective

Innovation has for decades been dominated by the advanced nations. Now, however, with new global players, new playing fields, and new rules of the game, competition in the connected economy of the 21st century is an entirely new ball game (Chapter 1). This has given cause for many countries to reconsider their innovation priorities and policies. In the United States, for example, the Congress, concerned about the nation's global standing in science and technology, tasked the pre-eminent National Academies in 2005 to respond to the following questions:

What are the top 10 actions, in priority order, that federal policymakers could take to enhance the science and technology enterprise so that the

United States can successfully compete, prosper, and be secure in the global community of the 21st century? What strategy, with several concrete steps, could be used to implement each of those actions?

The National Academies' 2005 report, *Rising above the Gathering Storm: Energizing and Employing America for a Better Economic Future* offered many recommendations and concluded:

> This nation must prepare with great urgency to preserve its strategic and economic security. Because other nations have, and probably will continue to have, the competitive advantage of a low wage structure, the United States must compete by optimizing its knowledge-based resources, particularly in science and technology, and by sustaining the most fertile environment for new and revitalized industries and the well-paying jobs they bring. We have already seen that capital, factories, and laboratories readily move wherever they are thought to have the greatest promise of return to investors.[3]

The 2005 *Rising above the Gathering Storm* report was updated in 2010 by the same committee that prepared the 2005 report. In the update, the committee reviewed the progress made by the nation since the earlier report was published and commented:

> The unanimous view of the committee members participating in the preparation of this [2010] report is that our nation's outlook has worsened ... many other nations have been markedly progressing, thereby affecting America's relative ability to compete effectively for new factories, research laboratories, administrative centers—and jobs. While this progress by other nations is to be encouraged and welcomed, so too is the notion that Americans wish to continue to be among those people who do prosper. ... The only promising avenue for achieving this latter outcome, in the view of the *Gathering Storm* committee and many others, is through innovation.[4]

Within the developed world, such concerns are not restricted to the United States alone. James Wilsdon, Head of Science and Innovation, DEMOS, The Atlas of Ideas (U.K.), commented in 2007:

> The case we are making very strongly is that there are a lot of opportunities out there. If the UK can get the right mix of policy and incentives to encourage our best scientists to collaborate with these countries [China, India, and South Korea], that would be for the greater good of everyone. Britain needs to act now to ready itself for a world where innovation was not dominated by Europe and US—or face being left behind.[5]

The Business Perspective

A 2010 McKinsey & Company survey of global executives found that most companies understand the importance of innovation to their success and growth but fall short when it comes to execution. Eighty-four percent of the global executives surveyed claimed that innovation was very or extremely important for their growth strategies; however, 94 percent of the executives were unsatisfied with their innovation performance.[6] Most companies' annual reports to shareholders highlight what they have done regarding innovation. Innovation is also a key theme in many business publications—newspapers, magazines, professional journals, books, blogs, etc. During the last 10 to 15 years, business schools have increasingly added courses on entrepreneurship and innovation to their curricula, and innovation is a growing practice at major strategy consulting firms (as some of the citations in this chapter testify).

Innovation Trends

Multinationals from developed countries have lately been investing in R&D and innovation in emerging markets. PricewaterhouseCoopers' (PwC's) strategy consulting arm, Strategy&, has been conducting the *Global Innovation 1000* study of the top 1000 public corporations worldwide that spend the most on R&D for several years. The 2015 study found that the geographic footprint of innovation has expanded dramatically in the years since 2008 (Table 9.1). The table shows in-country spending on R&D by Global Innovation 1000 companies, including both domestic and imported R&D, i.e., R&D investments by foreign companies in the country. These changes reflect major regional shifts, as more and more MNEs locate their R&D and innovation efforts abroad in search of talent and high-growth markets.[7]

Table 9.1 Global Shifts in R&D Spending, 2007–2015

Country	In-country R&D Spending (US$ Billion)		
	2007	*2015*	*% Change*
United States	109	145	33%
Japan	40	50	25
Germany	28	32	14
China	25	55	120
U.K.	23	22	− 4
France	20	16	− 20
India	13	28	115
Canada	9	10	11
Italy	8	11	38
South Korea	7	13	86
Israel	7	11	57

Source: 2015 Global Innovation 1000 Study, p. 5.

According to the study's authors, "An overwhelming 94 percent of the world's largest innovators now conduct elements of their R&D programs abroad. ... These companies are shifting their innovation investment to countries in which their sales and manufacturing are growing fastest, and where they can access the right technical talent. Not surprisingly, innovation spending has boomed in China and India since our 2008 study.... Collectively, in fact, more R&D is now conducted in Asia than in North America or Europe." Further, companies that disperse their R&D globally perform as well as, or better than, companies with a focused R&D footprint.[8]

Table 9.2 shows the 20 companies that spend the most on R&D. The top 5 sectors with the most R&D spending in the 2015 study were: Computing and Electronics (24.5 percent of total R&D expenditure by the 1000 companies); Healthcare (21.3 percent); Automotive (16.1 percent); Software and Internet (11.2 percent); and Industrials (11.1 percent). From a regional perspective, companies headquartered in North America, Europe, and Japan dominate the Global Innovation 1000. As a percent of annual revenue, healthcare companies spend the most on R&D, and automotive companies the least.

The study also identified the 10 most innovative companies based on the study participants' responses (Table 9.3). Apple, Google, Samsung, 3M, GE, Microsoft, and IBM have shown up on the list of the 10 most innovative companies every year since 2008. Toyota rejoined the Top 10 list in 2015 after a two-year hiatus. For the sixth year running, no pharmaceutical company made the list of the top 10 innovative companies, even though they generally spend the most as a percent of their annual revenues on R&D. (The ranking is based on survey responses.) It is interesting to note that the top R&D spenders are not necessarily the most innovative companies, a result PwC has consistently found every year since 2008. Furthermore, the 10 most innovative companies outperformed the 10 biggest R&D spenders on revenue growth, in terms of EBITDA as a percentage of revenue, and market-cap growth.

The Globalization of R&D and Innovation

As more and more MNEs locate their R&D away from their corporate headquarters, what is behind this phenomenon? A number of factors and trends underlie the globalization of R&D and innovation.[9]

- Decentralization of "big science," such as the Genome Project, and the increasing complexity and cross-disciplinary nature of frontier science and technology.
- Spread of science and technology around the world through cross-border M&A, technology alliances, and increased mobility of scientists and inventors across institutional and national boundaries.
- Advances in information and communication technologies and significant reductions in transportation, communication, and logistics costs.

Table 9.2 The Top 20 R&D Spenders, 2015

2015 Rank	2014 Rank	Company	2015 R&D Spend ($Bn)	% of Revenue	Headquarters	Industry
1	1	**Volkswagen**	15.3	5.7	Europe	Automotive
2	2	**Samsung**	14.1	7.2	South Korea	Computing and Electronics
3	3	Intel	11.5	20.6	United States	Computing and Electronics
4	4	**Microsoft**	11.4	13.1	United States	Software and Internet
5	5	**Roche**	10.8	20.8	Europe	Healthcare
6	9	Google	9.8	14.9	United States	Software and Internet
7	14	Amazon	9.3	10.4	United States	Software and Internet
8	7	**Toyota**	9.2	3.7	Japan	Automotive
9	6	**Novartis**	9.1	17.3	Europe	Healthcare
10	8	**Johnson & Johnson**	8.5	11.4	United States	Healthcare
11	13	**Pfizer**	8.4	16.9	United States	Healthcare
12	12	Daimler	7.6	4.4	Europe	Automotive
13	11	General Motors	7.4	4.7	United States	Automotive
14	10	Merck	7.2	17.0	United States	Healthcare
15	15	Ford	6.9	4.8	United States	Automotive
16	16	**Sanofi**	6.4	14.1	Europe	Healthcare
17	20	Cisco Systems	6.3	13.4	United States	Computing and Electronics
18	32	Apple	6.0	3.3	United States	Computing and Electronics
19	19	**GlaxoSmithKline**	5.7	15.0	Europe	Healthcare
20	28	AstraZeneca	5.6	21.4	Europe	Healthcare
		Average 20 Total	8.1	8.4		

Source: Adapted from the 2015 Global Innovation 1000 Study, p. 6.
Note: Companies shown in **bold** have been among the top 20 R&D spenders every year since 2005.

Table 9.3 The 10 Most Innovative Companies

2015 Rank	2014 Rank	Company	Geography	Industry	R&D Spend ($Bn)
1	1	**Apple**	United States	Computing and Electronics	6.0
2	2	**Google**	United States	Software and Internet	9.8
3	5	Tesla Motors	United States	Automotive	0.5
4	4	**Samsung**	South Korea	Computing and Electronics	14.1
5	3	Amazon	United States	Software and Internet	9.3
6	6	**3M**	United States	Industrials	1.8
7	7	**General Electric**	United States	Industrials	4.2
8	8	**Microsoft**	United States	Software and Internet	11.4
9	9	**IBM**	United States	Computing and Electronics	5.4
10	N/A	Toyota	Japan	Automotive	9.2

Source: Adapted from the 2015 Global Innovation 1000 Study, p. 9.
Note: Companies in **bold** have been among the 10 most innovative companies every year since 2010.

- Changes in trade and investment regimes (GATT and WTO) over the last 70 years and the signing of the WTO's Trade Related Intellectual Property Rights (TRIPS) Agreement that encouraged companies to locate their R&D operations in emerging markets
- Increasing harmonization of technical and regulatory standards, leading to internationally accepted product specifications and business process protocols
- High wage differentials between developed and developing countries for scientific and technical personnel, shortage of such personnel in developed countries, and their increasing availability in developing countries
- Growing capabilities of emerging market firms for taking on higher and higher level innovation and R&D work in many fields
- Need for MNEs to be close to their customers so that they can offer customized products and services to them

How to Innovate

The Build|Buy|Ally framework of how firms grow in foreign markets (Chapter 6) also applies to how MNEs might approach innovation: through internal development (Build), through M&A (Buy), and through partnerships (Ally). Irrespective of the method used, having an effective innovation system requires an organizational structure that supports innovation, shows an absence of the NIH ("Not Invented Here") syndrome, and has an appropriate benchmarking and control system. Additionally, according to a 2012 McKinsey & Company global survey, for a company to be successful at innovation, it is vitally important that it has an innovation strategy that is well integrated with its corporate strategy.[10] The Build|Buy|Ally framework for creating innovation is presented below, followed by seven rules for achieving innovation results. The two case studies toward the end of the chapter and several examples below present how different MNEs approach innovation.

Innovation Through Internal Development (Build)

MNEs have employed some of the following structural approaches for creating innovation through their own efforts: R&D or innovation corporate functions, new-business development functions, global innovation centers, emerging-business-opportunity groups, emerging-technology business groups, advanced-technology institutes, and in-house incubators and accelerators. Such efforts are good for innovation but can also lead to dispersed teams of researchers, unconnected with each other—unless effective integration and control mechanisms are in place.

Wolters Kluwer, a Netherlands-based multi-billion dollar publishing and information services company that operates in over 150 countries and has grown largely through M&A, runs an internal R&D program called Innovation Labs. It helps the company experiment with new ideas and refine them before investing in the process of full product development and launch.[11]

Axalta Coating Systems of Philadelphia, United States, announced in September 2015 that it is setting up a global innovation center (GIC) at the Navy Yard in Philadelphia. The 175,000 square foot GIC facility, which will be fully operational by early 2018, will house the company's global research, product development, and technology initiatives and partner with its other technology centers in the Americas, Europe, and Asia Pacific. A 150-year-old, $4.4 billion company, Axalta has 35 manufacturing plants and 7 R&D centers worldwide and has business in 130 countries. It develops, manufactures, and sells coatings for automobiles, white goods, and hundreds of other products exposed to the elements.[12]

Mars Petcare, owned by the U.S.-based and privately held Mars, Incorporated is the world's largest pet foods company, with five billion-dollar brands (PEDIGREE®, WHISKAS®, ROYAL CANIN®, BANFIELD®, and IAMS®). It has had global innovation centers in Germany and France for many years for creating pet food innovations. In October 2014, it set up its first GIC in the U.S. at Thompson's Station, Tennessee.[13]

Some companies set up their own incubators or accelerators, in addition to R&D units, to innovate from within. An in-house incubator allows highly creative and motivated employees to work on specific projects in which they or the company might be interested. Many companies, including Microsoft and Google, have in-house incubators. For instance, "the Garage" at Microsoft serves as an in-house incubator for employees to work on projects about which they are passionate. It is an "an internal community of engineers, designers, hardware tinkerers and others from all different parts of the company who work on their own or with others on pet projects, some of which could potentially benefit the company." Under Microsoft's new CEO, Satya Nadella, the Garage is being extended to include customers who can provide quick feedback on lightweight, single-scenario apps developed for them. (Such incubators are to be distinguished from company-owned incubators/accelerators that provide venture-capital funding to seasoned entrepreneurs and founders from outside the company. An example is the Samsung Accelerator, with locations in San Francisco, California, and New York City.[14])

Acquiring Innovation Through M&A (Buy)

Acquiring innovations through M&A, rather than doing innovation organically, is a common method used by MNEs. Sometimes such acquisitions are opportunistic, but often an MNE waits for someone else to innovate and build a business around the innovation and then attempts to acquire the whole company. Building innovation capability through M&A is undertaken by companies entering a new market, as well as by companies wanting to strengthen their existing products and innovation capabilities. For instance, Apple introduced iTunes in 2001, which was based on the SoftJam MP technology developed by Casady & Greene, a company Apple had acquired the previous year; SoftJam MP was an early Mac operating system-compatible MP3 player. Apple's iTunes, and its iPod introduced in 2003, eventually disrupted the digital music industry. IBM made several acquisitions to support its new Information on Demand business-intelligence service launched in February 2006. As part of this initiative, IBM acquired Cognos from Canada in 2007, as well as many other companies to support this new line of business.[15] Other examples of companies entering new lines of business through the acquisition of companies and innovation capabilities include Facebook's acquisition of Instagram and WhatsApp and Google's acquisition of Android.

Large pharmaceutical companies routinely acquire or invest in smaller biotechnology companies working on or with new and novel drugs (see also "corporate venture capital" below). For instance, the Bristol-Myers Squibb Company of the U.S. paid $105 million to ZymoGenetics Inc., also of the U.S., in January 2009 for its Phase I drug for Hepatitis C. In June 2010, Bayer AG of Germany paid $40 million to OncoMed Pharmaceuticals Inc. of the U.S. for access to its experimental anti-cancer drug, which had yet to enter Phase I human trials at the time of the investment. Both deals provide for further investments by the pharmaceutical companies if the drugs are successful in subsequent testing and development, as well as royalties on eventual sales.[16]

The Walt Disney Company acquired Pixar, an animation studio, headed by Steve Jobs, in May 2006 to strengthen its animation-innovation capabilities. Disney had been the distributor for all of Pixar's movies in the past, but its contract was slated to end by summer and there had been disagreements between the two companies on profit sharing and movie rights. The acquisition brought Disney's animated characters, such as Mickey Mouse and Donald Duck, together with Pixar's blockbuster animated movies like *Toy Story* and *The Incredibles*. In 2009, Disney acquired Marvel Entertainment, which makes movies based on Marvel's comic book characters such as Spider-Man, Iron Man, and Captain America. Both acquisitions have been very successful for Disney in terms of strengthening its entertainment-innovation capabilities and producing high levels of profits for the company.

Major companies are also increasingly acquiring other technology-focused companies in new and evolving domains such as social, mobile, analytics, and cloud (SMAC) technologies, driving business innovation. Table 9.4 offers some well-known (and some not so well-known) examples of these and other innovation-inspired acquisitions. The examples show that the acquirers are not only from IT, telecom, or pharmaceutical industries, but also from non-technology companies whose competitive advantage derives from the use of technology in their operations.

Innovation requires not just smart engineers and scientists, but also engineers and scientists who are entrepreneurs. This is a difficult combination to have among researchers, partly because of their education and training and partly because of organizational dynamics, e.g., organizational structure, decision making, bureaucracy, the existence of the NIH (not invented here) syndrome, and so on. According to LinkedIn co-founder Reid Hoffman:

> What sets innovators apart is that they envision a future that defies conventional wisdom, then assemble (and reassemble) the plans and resources needed to make it a reality.
>
> In Silicon Valley, we have overcome these issues by using acquisitions to bring in innovative, entrepreneurial talent. … At LinkedIn, we used acquisitions to fuel innovation when we acquired Pulse and Newsle. Both had built killer products. But we also wanted to transplant their entrepreneurs (and the future innovations they would create) into LinkedIn— Ankit Gupta and Akshay Kothari at Pulse, and Axel Hansen and Jonah Varon at Newsle.[17]

Table 9.4 Examples of Innovation- and Technology-Inspired Acquisitions

Acquirer	Target	Industry	Technology
Verizon	Terremark	Telecommunications	Cloud Computing
Google	Boston Dynamics	Internet	Robotics
VMware	Nicira	IT	Mobility/Cloud
Apple	Siri	IT	Mobility/Cloud
Home Depot	Black Locus	Retail	Cloud Computing
Walmart	OneOps	Retail	Cloud Computing
Monsanto	Climate Corp	Agriculture	Big Data Analytics
Novo Nordisk	Xellia	Pharmaceuticals	Drug Discovery
Intuit	Check	Financial Services	Mobility
Siemens	eMeter	Energy	Smart Grid
Nokia	Desti	Mobility Services	Mobile Applications
Avis	Zipcar	Transportation	Sharing Economy

Source: Evangelos Simoudis, "Re-Imagining Corporate Innovation with a Silicon Valley Perspective," The Corporate Innovation Blog, July 7, 2014. Adapted from http://corporate-innovation.co/2014/07/07/acquiring-innovation/

Acquiring Innovation Through Alliances (Ally)

An increasingly popular approach, innovation through alliances, can take many forms, such as innovation through joint ventures, licensing, technology alliances, leveraging the firm's innovation ecosystem consisting of individuals and groups outside the organization, setting up a corporate venture capital (CVC) unit, and open innovation. Alliances can be a source of innovations that a firm is unable to achieve on its own or unable to acquire through M&A. Many innovations, especially those involving frontier science and technology, require collaboration among multiple partners with complementary capabilities because none of them is able to undertake such a project on their own. Partnering with others on an R&D project enables a firm to expand its innovation capabilities and outcomes, while sharing the cost and risk of getting into new technologies and new markets. However, as in any relationship, conflicts may arise when the alliance partners' values and objectives are not aligned to their common end goals, or due to contractual issues. (See Chapter 6 for more on challenges faced by alliances and suggestions for improving alliance performance.) Successful innovations via alliances, and especially via open innovation, are possible in companies that do not suffer from the NIH syndrome.

In Chapter 8, we discussed examples of companies like Hyundai Motors, Suzlon Energy, EMC², and others, that acquired innovations and innovation capabilities through M&A, as well as through licensing and other alliances. A few other examples of innovation alliances follow.

INNOVATION ECOSYSTEMS

Some large firms, like Google and Cisco Systems, have created innovation ecosystems, which are platforms to encourage collaboration between individuals from within the firm and individuals from their extended enterprise. The Google Innovation Ecosystem (Figure 9.1), for example, is an "innovation hub where third parties can share access and create new applications that incorporate elements of Google functionality. These outsiders can easily test and launch applications and have them hosted in the Google world, where there is an enormous target audience—132 million customers globally—and a practically unlimited capacity for customer interactions." This benefits both Google and its ecosystem-alliance partners, though Google, since it owns the platform, gets its products adopted widely and is able to extract a greater share of the value created.[18] The Cisco innovation ecosystem, called the Cisco Innovation Engine, is discussed in the Cisco Systems case study toward the end of the chapter.

CORPORATE VENTURE CAPITAL

Corporate venture capital, a subset of the traditional venture capital (VC) industry, involves major companies investing in nascent startups developing new or complementary technologies in which they are interested. This is a way for them to test ideas at a relatively low cost and acquire the innovations if the startups are successful. Most of the major MNEs have active CVC funds to invest in startups with promising innovations. Google Ventures, the world's largest CVC investor, is reported to have invested in over 300 startups in search of future blockbuster innovations. Some of the other prominent CVCs are Intel Capital, Salesforce Ventures, Qualcomm Ventures, Comcast Ventures, Novartis Venture Funds, Samsung Ventures, Siemens Venture Capital, Fidelity Biosciences, and so on. Corporate venture capital investing is quite prevalent and is increasing in the computer and IT, biotechnology, and energy sectors, but not so much in consumer goods industries. In 2014, CVC investing accounted for "18.6% of total venture investment in the computer and peripherals sector, 13.7% in biotech and more than 10% in five other industries."[19]

Corporate venture capital investing is also popular in Japan. For instance, Softbank is the fastest-growing mobile carrier, largest broadband network, and most popular search engine and e-commerce site in Japan. With its innovation ecosystem comprising some 5,000 companies, Softbank is the preferred partner for others due to its quick decision making, willingness to pay high prices, and commitment to fully support and fund joint ventures. In addition to its numerous

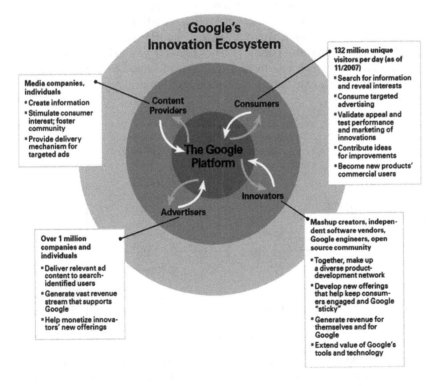

Figure 9.1 Google's Innovation Ecosystem

Source: Bala Iyer and Thomas H. Davenport, "Reverse Engineering Google's Innovation Machine," *Harvard Business Review*, April 2008. Reprinted with permission.

245

joint ventures and partnerships, Softbank has made minority investments in 27 high-potential startups worldwide.[20]

OUTSOURCING INNOVATION

MNEs from developed countries have been outsourcing corporate functions such as manufacturing for decades, to developing and middle-income countries that offer skilled workers at low cost. In the 2000s, they began to offshore even core innovation and R&D functions to their captive centers and third-party vendors abroad. While MNEs have been performing R&D in foreign countries for a long time, what is relatively new is that they also now perform (and outsource) R&D in emerging markets.[21] They do so because of the availability of low-cost talent in many emerging markets and the availability of third-party innovation providers with the requisite expertise, as well as to be close to their major markets. (See also the Global Innovation 1000 study discussed above, Tables 9.1–9.3.)

Figure 9.2 shows the basic models (Build|Buy|Ally) for acquiring innovation. When a firm offshores innovation, it can do so by setting up a wholly owned R&D subsidiary abroad, called a "captive center" or a "global in-house center," or by outsourcing (offshoring) innovation to a third-party vendor in the foreign market. For example, dozens of major MNEs, including Cisco Systems, Computer Sciences Corporation, General Electric, and IBM have captive R&D centers in India, and they also outsource innovation projects to local vendors such as Tata Consultancy Services, Infosys, and Wipro Technologies. (See also the IT Services Offshoring case study toward the end of the chapter.)

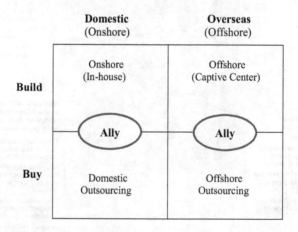

Figure 9.2 A Basic Model for Acquiring Innovations and Innovation Capabilities

Source: Vinod K. Jain and S. Raghunath, "Strengthening America's International Competitiveness through Innovation and Global Value Chains." In Ben L. Kedia and Subhash C. Jain, eds., *Restoring America's Global Competitiveness through Innovation*, Cheltenham, U.K.: Edward Elgar, 2013, p. 257. Reprinted with permission.

When the collaborators in an innovation alliance are from different industries, this is referred to as crossover collaboration or crossover innovation. For instance, several industry clusters in Northern Netherlands (e.g., Healthy Aging Network Northern Netherlands, Water Alliance, Sensor Universe, and Energy Valley) support innovation not only within their own industries, but also through crossover collaboration.[22]

Open Innovation

The concept of open innovation, or innovation through crowdsourcing or "open source," was popularized by Henry Chesbrough in his 2003 bestseller, *Open Innovation: The New Imperative for Creating and Profiting from Technology* (Harvard Business Review Press, 2003). He distinguished between closed innovation, where R&D is performed in-house with little external inputs, and open innovation, where an organization also leverages external partners through crowdsourcing or other means to achieve innovation. He highlighted the need for companies to shift from a closed model of innovation to an open model to leverage the knowledge and ingenuity that exists outside the company. Though the idea of open innovation had existed and been used by companies like IBM much earlier than Chesbrough's publication, his main contribution was to democratize the idea to such an extent that hundreds of business, government, and nonprofit organizations now swear by it. The key ideas of open innovation he proposed are:

- Not all of the world's smartest people work for us, so we must find ways to access the knowledge and creativity of people outside the organization;
- We do not have to originate innovation to benefit from it;
- Sometimes, the best solution to a problem comes from outside the industry that was seeking the solution;
- Making the best use of both internal and external ideas is the winning proposition; and
- We should buy others' IP if it advances our business and should profit from others using our IP.

Open innovation thus involves accessing the knowledge and intellectual property of others (outside-in), as well as profiting by allowing others to use our knowledge and IP (inside-out).

Inside-Out

As indicated earlier, biotechnology firms routinely license or sell their technologies to large pharmaceutical firms. Licensing one's technology is common in many other industries as well. However, companies like IBM, Xerox, and

Samsung have thousands of patents that they do not use for various reasons. Chesbrough has suggested that firms with intellectual property should profit by letting others use their IP through licensing, for example. About a decade ago, IBM and some other IT companies allowed free use of hundreds of their patents, creating something like an IP-free zone, pledging not to enforce their IP rights if the patents were used only for open-source applications. This came about with the publication of a 2004 report that showed that the open-source operating system Linux had (inadvertently) infringed upon more than 250 patents of other companies. This led to further growth of open-source software, unhindered by legal challenges, and IBM substantially increased its global share of Linux-based software.[23] Another example of inside-out is the innovation ecosystem of companies like Google, Cisco Systems, and Softbank.

Outside-In

The outside-in approach to innovation includes collaborating with individuals and entities outside the organization though crowdsourcing and other means. Some examples of the outside-in approach were presented above, such as incubators/accelerators and corporate venture capital. One of the most powerful open-innovation ideas is prize-based innovation, i.e., innovation challenges backed by prizes offered by organizations seeking solutions to their problems through crowdsourcing. There are several innovation platforms that serve as intermediaries connecting organizations seeking solutions to specific problems and potential "solvers" from throughout the world, such as InnoCentive, Nine-Sigma, and IdeaConnection. Many large organizations, including P&G, Unilever, IBM, Henkel, and Staples, have their own corporate open-innovation platforms serving their specific needs. The Unilever platform (Ideas4Unilever), for instance, invites suppliers, start-ups, academics, designers, and individual inventors—in fact, anyone with a practical innovation that can help the company meet its challenges—to submit their solutions to the company through its platform. Some of the challenges posted on Ideas4Unilver as of the end of 2015 included safe drinking water, better packaging, cleaning up fat from fabrics, and so on.

While the practice of offering a prize for a solution to a problem is an age-old idea, InnoCentive was the first company to develop a systematic approach and a platform for connecting organizations and potential solvers. InnoCentive got its start in the year 2000 as an incubator for Eli Lilly, a large U.S.-based pharmaceutical company, to try and crowdsource solutions to its technology-related problems. As the platform became well-known, other companies wanted to use it, Eli Lilly spun it off as an independent company in 2005. InnoCentive links organizations (seekers) with specific problems (challenges) to people all over the world (solvers) who can win a prize for solving the problem. InnoCentive gets a "posting fee," plus, if the problem is solved, a percentage of the prize as a "finder's fee." InnoCentive ensures IP confidentiality for both the seeker and the solver and helps transfer IP rights from the solver to the seeker.

One of the early successes InnoCentive had was a challenge posted on inno-centive.com by the Oil Recovery Institute of Cordova, Alaska, to keep oil in storage tanks from freezing, with a prize of $20,000 for a solution acceptable to the Institute. A chemist from the construction industry, John Davis, won the prize by suggesting that they could keep oil from freezing by using a device sim-ilar to the one used in the construction industry to keep concrete from solidifying during delivery to a customer site by keeping it in a vibrating tanker. This was a simple solution that took John Davis just a few minutes to figure out, and he was not even from the oil industry. This is a key rationale for opening up innovation to anyone and everyone.

As of late 2015, over 365,000 people from 200 countries were registered as solvers at innocentive.com, with a reach to over 13 million potential solvers through its strategic partners, such as Nature Publishing and Scientific American. Prizes range from $5,000 to over $1 million, depending on the challenge, with over $40 million in prizes given out so far. Over 50 percent of the registered solvers come from China, India, and Russia. As of late 2015, there are dozens of challenges posted on innocentive.com, with prizes ranging up to $700,000 for the "Conquer Paralysis Now Challenge" Stage 1 awards.

Similar prize-based challenges are announced by hundreds of organizations each year on intermediary platforms, like innocentive.com and ninesigma.com, as well as on their own corporate platforms. Governments have also gotten into the action. In December 2015, for example, the U.S. Department of Transpor-tation announced a $40 million challenge for a midsize city to come up with the best plan to develop their city into a smart city. The winning city will cre-ate a "fully integrated city that uses data, technology and creativity to shape how people and goods move in the future." A former mayor of Charlotte, North Carolina, said, "The question I would be asking myself if I were still a mayor is, 'What do I want my community to look like 30, 40, 50 years from now and what kinds of things should I be doing now to prepare the community for that?'" Vulcan, a company founded by Microsoft co-founder Paul G. Allen, will add another $10 million to the prize to further its philanthropic objective of reducing greenhouse gases.[24]

The Five Rules of Effective Innovation

In addition to learning, capability building, and an innovation strategy aligned with the company's corporate strategy, here are five additional lessons derived from successful MNEs that are effective at innovation.

1. Design an Organization that Supports Innovation

An organization focused on innovation requires an organizational architecture and culture that support experimentation, patience, and risk taking. W.L. Gore & Associates, a company that makes electronics, fabrics, and industrial and medical products, encourages hands-on employee experimentation and prototyping of new product concepts. Employees also have the right to question the leaders' decisions and the rationale behind them. The company believes that their organizational model has helped it to refine ideas and increase decision-making quality.[25]

Intuit is an 8,000-person software company that develops and sells financial and tax preparation software and related services for individuals, accountants, and small businesses. Intuit is ranked Number 2 on Fortune's 2015 list of the most admired software companies, and of its two blockbuster products, QuickBooks and TurboTax, each has a 90 percent market share in its respective market. Intuit Labs is where the company makes innovation happen. It uses unstructured time, "innovation catalyst mentors," brainstorming, and innovation awards to create a culture of innovation in the company. According to Scott Cook, its co-founder and chairman:

> ...we put in a series of systems and a culture where the expectation is that if there's an idea that someone's passionate about, we put in a system to make it easy and fast and cheap for them to run an experiment. ... And a culture of experimentation can only work when it's put in place by leaders. Intuit also changed how it made decisions, from decisions by bureaucracy, decision by PowerPoint, persuasion, position, power, to decision by experiment.[26]

In a 2012 global survey of organizational structures that facilitate innovation, McKinsey & Company found that companies used different organizational structures to execute innovation. However, nearly half of the executives surveyed said that innovation was a separate function at their companies, located at the company headquarters, and reported directly to the CEO. Furthermore, 56 percent of the respondents identified C-level support as a key driver of their innovation success.[27] Offering rewards and recognition for successful innovations was also a common practice among companies.

2. Remember—What You Measure is What You Get

Organizational structure and control systems are critical for achieving superior organizational performance, as highlighted in Chapter 7. This is true for achieving superior innovation performance as well. While MNEs often have well-designed control mechanisms in their organizations, unfortunately, not all have an equally well-designed system for measuring innovation effectiveness. A 2008 McKinsey & Company global survey of 1,075 executives on "assessing innovation metrics" found that companies that get the highest returns from innovation make better and more comprehensive use of innovation metrics than others. They measure innovation across the entire innovation process—eight metrics on average—including both input and output metrics.[28]

Table 9.5 lists the innovation metrics used by the organizations represented by the executives surveyed, along with the percentage of executives who reported using a specific metric ranked as Number 1 in terms of its importance to their organizations. For instance, 16 percent of the respondents said that their companies ranked "Revenue growth due to new products or services" as Number 1 in their portfolio of metrics in terms of its importance. No doubt, they use many other innovation metrics as well.

Fifty-four percent of the respondents said that their companies formally assess product innovation, 37 percent assess service innovation, another 37 percent assess process innovation, and 28 percent assess business model innovation. Fifty-five percent of the survey respondents said that their companies track the relationship between innovation spending and shareholder value. For these companies, the three most important metrics are revenue growth, customer satisfaction, and the percentage of sales from new products or services. For companies where innovation is the most important strategic priority, the top three metrics include an output metric (customer satisfaction) and two input metrics (number of ideas in the pipeline and R&D spending as a percentage of sales).

While companies would like to also benchmark their performance relative to their peers, few are able to do so because of the difficulty of obtaining peer data on the innovation metrics used.

Table 9.5 Innovation Metrics Ranked Number 1 in Terms of Importance

Output Metrics	*% of Respondents*	*Input Metrics*	*% of Respondents*
Revenue growth due to new products or services	16	Number of ideas or concepts in the pipeline	10
Customer satisfaction with new products or services	13	R&D spending as a percentage of sales	8
Percentage of sales from new products/services in a given time period	8	Number of R&D projects	6
Number of new products or services launched	8	Number of people actively devoted to innovation	4
Return on investment (ROI) in new products or services	6		
Profit growth due to new products or services	4		
Potential of the entire new product/service portfolio to meet growth targets	3		
Changes in market share resulting from new products/services	3		
Net present value (NPV) of the entire new product/service portfolio	2		

Source: Vanessa Chan, Chris Musso, and Venkatesh Shanker, "McKinsey Global Survey Results: Assessing Innovation Metrics," McKinsey & Company, 2008.

3. Have a Strong Pipeline of Innovative Ideas

Successful innovation involves a number of steps, such as generating breakthrough ideas, selecting the right ideas through experimentation, proof of concept, prototyping, developing a business case, product launch, and scaling up. Having a strong pipeline of creative ideas is a pre-requisite to future steps in the innovation process. Companies have used different approaches for generating innovative ideas. Google, 3M, and some other companies budget free time for employees to hatch new ideas of their own. Google allows 20 percent paid free time to its tech employees to work on projects of their own, with the remaining 80 percent of time devoted to the company's core business of search and advertising. Even managers devote 10 percent of their time to entirely new businesses and projects. According to company sources, over half of Google's new products and new features (e.g., AdSence, Gmail, and Google News) came from the 20 percent time investment.

3M, which sells over 50,000 products, started offering 15 percent paid free time to every employee in 1948, since no one knows where the next innovation will come from. Employees use the "15 percent time" to pursue ideas of their own or to work on things they discovered during their regular work hours but did not have the time to work on. 3M is famous for its innovative culture and innovations, and its P/E ratio has outperformed the S&P 500 every year since 2001. 3M's core technologies are films, adhesives, and coatings, using which it continually invents new products. Its Post-It Notes product was created by a 3M scientist, Art Fry, during his "15 percent time."

Royal Dutch Shell installed a company-wide, intranet-based GameChanger process for idea submission and seed funding. All submitted ideas, whether from a corporate vice president or an hourly employee, get the same review. The Whirlpool Corporation has the "innovation e-space" where any employee, even those not involved in innovation, can post an idea on the bulletin board or find tools necessary to get his/her idea funded. At General Electric, high-potential executives are asked to submit at least three "Imagination Breakthrough" proposals each year—ideas that expand GE's business into a new category, new geography, or a new customer segment. Over the years, the company has funded more than 120 such projects that generate over $3 billion in annual revenues.

4. Cannibalize Yourself, Before Someone Else Does

Joseph Schumpeter, writing in 1934, powerfully suggested that capitalism or the free market is an evolutionary process of innovation, entrepreneurial activity, and "creative destruction." Industries contain the seeds of their own destruction through incursions by both new and established firms using innovative products and strategies to destroy the incumbents' advantage.[29] According to Thomas K. McCaw, who wrote Schumpeter's biography:

> The main takeaway is the absolute relentlessness of creative destruction and entrepreneurship. In a free economy, they never stop—never. Schumpeter

wrote that all firms must try, all the time, 'to keep on their feet, on ground that is slipping away from under them.' So, no serious businessperson can ever completely relax. Someone, somewhere, is always trying to think of a way to do the job better, at every point along the value chain. Whatever has been built is going to be destroyed by a better product or a better method or a better organization or a better strategy.[30]

Schumpeter's seminal insight about competition is more true today than ever before. Kodak (Eastman Kodak Co.) is a classic case of Schumpeterian creative destruction. A 135-year-old U.S. company, Kodak was once a household name for its film business and had 145,000 employees and $19 billion in sales, as of 1990. Kodak's film business got disrupted as new competitors and new technologies emerged. With the advent of digital photography, invented by a Kodak engineer in 1975, the company, hesitant to cannibalize its cash-cow film business, moved into digital cameras in the late 1990s. Kodak's performance has since been on a downward spiral. It filed for bankruptcy in January 2012, then emerged from it in September 2013, serving only niche markets and selling nothing to consumers. Today, it has only 8,000 employees and $2 billion in sales.

Many industries, especially those with rapidly evolving technologies, are subject to Schumpeterian creative destruction. Companies in such industries should themselves cannibalize their products and innovations before others do it for them. (In fact, companies in all industries should attempt to do so.) As we observed earlier, Apple's iPod, along with iTunes, disrupted the music business when it was introduced in 2003. iPod itself was disrupted when Steve Jobs decided to introduce the iPhone in 2007, which incorporated a fully functional MP3 player. The iPod was a $5 billion business for Apple, which Jobs cannibalized despite internal objections to the idea, and went on to create even more value for the company. Even firms in industries with slowly evolving technologies can avoid being cannibalized by others by doing it themselves. For example, Gillette (now part of P&G) cannibalized its highly successful Sensor Excel shaving system by introducing in January 2014 a higher-priced Mach 3 Power shaving system, the world's first 3-blade shaving system. Mach 3 became the Number 1 global men's shaving brand within a few months of its introduction. However, shortly after Mach 3's introduction, Gillette's 100-year-old rival Schick introduced a four-blade shaver, called the Quattro.

5. Leverage the Connected Economy

The connected economy consists of firms and other actors from the old economy, the digital economy, and the age of the smart machines (Chapter 1). Irrespective of which part of the connected economy a firm comes from, it has the opportunity to learn, innovate, and imitate based on what others have done. The connected economy, a storehouse of incredible resources and capabilities, enables their sharing in ways that could not have been imagined even five or ten years ago. Refer to the next chapter for ideas on how to leverage the connected economy.

Mini Case Study: Innovation at Cisco Systems

Founded in 1994, Cisco Systems, Inc. is one of the first companies in the world to sell routers that supported multiprotocol networks. Currently, the company sells networking equipment and services in over 165 countries. Its internationalization was driven by private and public investments in Internet infrastructure worldwide starting in the early-1990s. As of 2015, it had over 71,500 employees, 70,000 channel partners, and annual revenue of $49 billion, including both products ($38 billion) and services ($11 billion). It is positioned as Number 1 or Number 2 in most of the markets it serves (Table 9.6). It is a classic example of a connected enterprise in the global connected economy.[31]

Cisco outsources over 90 percent of its manufacturing to component suppliers and contract manufacturers, and over 90 percent of its sales and service to its channel partners and logistics providers. Over the years, Cisco has received numerous awards, including the 2015 J.D. Powers & Associates award for outstanding customer service, the 2015 Technology Services Industry Association's STAR Award for Best Practices in Knowledge Management, and recognition from Frost & Sullivan in 2015 for having one of the largest partner ecosystems in the world.

Cisco Systems spent 13.4 percent of its 2014 revenues on R&D, though it was not among the Top 10 R&D spenders or the Top 10 most innovative companies in the 2015 PwC study of the world's largest R&D spenders (Tables 9.2 and 9.3). However, such stellar performance could not have been achieved without equally stellar innovation performance, a result of the company's innovation strategy that is integrated with its corporate strategy.

Cisco's innovation strategy has gone beyond the Build|Buy|Ally framework presented earlier in the chapter. Its innovation strategy, announced on October 6, 2015, consists of five pillars: Build|Buy|Partner|Invest|Co-Develop (Figure 9.3). Figure 9.3 shows how major companies typically approach innovation; Cisco simply articulated the approach in an infographic.

Table 9.6 Cisco System's Market Share and Market Position

Market	Market Share	Market Position
Routing	51%	1
TelePresence	46%	1
Wireless LAN	50%	1
Switching	67%	1
Voice	39%	1
Web Conferencing	50%	1
x86 Blade Servers	34%	2
Storage Area Networks	45%	2
Security	31%	1

Source: Cisco Company Overview Presentation, June 15, 2015.

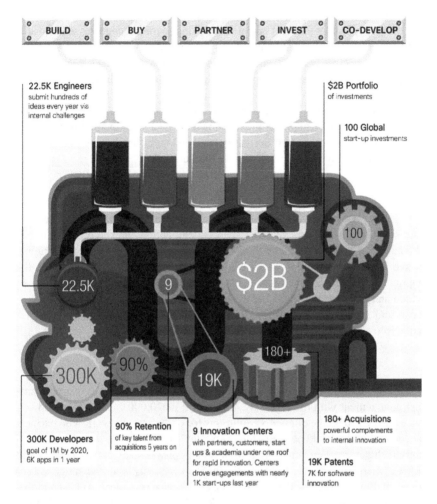

Figure 9.3 Cisco's Innovation Engine, 2015

Source: Reprinted with permission. Courtesy of Cisco Systems, Inc. Unauthorized use not permitted. Accessed on February 12, 2016 from http://newsroom.cisco.com/feature-content?articleId=1720841.

Build

About 35 percent of Cisco employees worldwide are engineers, and its 380 global sites include 170 labs and 9 global innovation centers. It has over 19,000 patents, of which some 12,000 came from its labs in the United States. Innovation is part of Cisco's DNA and corporate culture. Cisco engineers submit hundreds of ideas each year through internal challenges. Its company culture fosters innovation, with employees working in smaller, agile teams on innovation projects. For example, the Cisco "Alpha" projects are designed to facilitate disruptive innovation. The Cisco Idea Zone (I-Zone), a Web-based innovation portal where employees can submit new ideas, has played an important role in fostering an innovation culture within the company. The Digital and Social Champion program recognizes and rewards subject matter experts engaging in meaningful conversations on social media channels as well as those who lead adoption of social media within the company.

Since new ideas can come from anywhere, Cisco also relies on innovations created in its lower-cost, emerging-market locations. Some of the products Cisco engineers developed in emerging markets for local use are then adopted for use in developed-country markets; this is known as reverse innovation (Chapter 2). An example is the ASR 900 Series router developed for emerging markets by Cisco India but now also sold in mature markets.

Buy

Since 1993, Cisco has made some 180 acquisitions to strengthen its products and services, innovation capabilities, and talent, and to enter into new markets. Acquisitions are treated as an extension of the company's innovation engine. Cisco has a structured post-merger integration (PMI) process that involves the input of several cross-functional teams. The PMI process makes extensive use of video and collaboration tools before and during the acquisition to reduce travel costs and expedite the acquisition process. Video and collaboration technologies cut Cisco's travel costs by a billion dollars through 2012.

Partner

The Cisco innovation engine is a highly scalable ecosystem used to support partner engagement with the company. It relies on its 70,000+ technology and service partners to create innovative solutions for customers. Its work with partners accounts for almost 90 percent of the company's revenue. The list of Cisco partners includes: (a) large enterprise-solution companies such as Accenture, IBM, EMC, Microsoft, Oracle, Fujitsu, Hitachi Data Systems, and Samsung; and (b) over 70,000 channel resellers, engineers, and service providers. At Cisco global innovation centers, Cisco engineers work with partners, customers, academics, and startups under one roof for rapid innovation. In 2014, the nine Internet of Everything Innovation Centers drove engagements with almost 1,000 startups.

Open innovation at Cisco extends beyond its innovation ecosystem (Figure 9.3). For instance, the Cisco I-Prize program is a global contest for new product ideas that involves the global community for innovation through grassroots efforts. Anyone over the age of 18 can participate.

Its nine Innovation Centers, located in innovation hotspots such as London (two centers), Berlin, Barcelona, Rio de Janeiro, Sydney, Tokyo, and Toronto, serve as a hub to:

- Showcase what is possible with the Internet of Everything (IoE);
- Build solutions with partners and startups, and engage in rapid prototyping; and
- Invest and partner with startups, accelerators, and universities.

At an IoE Innovation Center, companies can try out the newest products and technologies and collaborate with the right people to solve their business challenges.

Since 2014, the company has run the Cisco Innovation Grand Challenge, a worldwide open competition designed to engage and support startups, entrepreneurs, and developers around the world and intended to create industry-disrupting solutions. For its 2015 Innovation Grand Challenge, Cisco received 3,000 entries from over 100 countries, of which the "super six" entries were invited to present at the Cisco Internet of Things World Forum in Dubai on December 6–8, 2015. The six finalists presented their ideas before a live audience and a panel of judges, who selected three winners. The first, second, and third winners received cash awards of $150,000, $75,000, and $25,000, respectively, and were given access to Cisco's Internet of Everything (IoE) Innovation Centers and labs across the world. The first-place winner of the 2014 Grand Challenge, Relayr of Germany, recently closed on an $11 million Series-A financing round from Cisco Investments, Kleiner Perkins Caulfield & Byers, and Munich Venture Partners.[32]

Invest

Cisco has a technology innovation fund of over $2 billion that has so far invested in over 100 startups and 40 limited partnerships in 25 countries. In addition to receiving funding, the startups are given access to the company's engineering talent and network of channel partners, as well as customer events such as Cisco Live! While Cisco is continuing its 20-year history of investing strategically in its core business areas, it recently launched "thematic" investing to support companies with innovative ideas that will shape the networking ecosystem of the future. In June 2014, for instance, Cisco Investments, the company's corporate venture capital arm, announced an additional $40 million to be invested under the "India Innovation Theme." The investment will fund products and technologies unique and relevant to India and other emerging markets, including big data and analytics, the Internet of Things (IoT), connected mobility, storage, and content technology systems. One of the first investments under the connected mobility theme was an investment in MobStac, a Bangalore-based startup.

Co-Develop

Cisco participates in co-development projects with its 300,000 developer partners and others. An example is the Entrepreneur-in-Residence program, a startup incubator, where entrepreneurs and startups can stay for six months until graduation. The program has a footprint in five cities and is designed to encourage the development of disruptive technologies. Some of these developments lead to a long-term relationship with the company, while some others get acquired by the company (27 so far).

Case Study: Capability Building and Innovation in India's Offshore IT Services Industry

Multinational enterprises from the developed world have been offshoring IT services to emerging markets since the early 2000s. What is relatively new is that, during the last 5 to 10 years, they have also been offshoring their core innovation and R&D functions to emerging markets, to their captive centers and third-party vendors there. (See Figure 9.2 for the basic sourcing models used by MNEs.) Over the last decade, India has emerged as the world's largest offshoring hub for IT and business process outsourcing (BPO) services, with about 55 percent of total global offshoring going to India as of 2015. India has also been gaining global share in the offshoring of engineering, R&D, and product development services, with its 2015 global share estimated at 22 percent (ranked Number 2 among all R&D offshoring hubs).[33]

The question of *how* IT services providers in India became so dominant in the offshore IT services industry remains largely unanswered. This case study provides evidence of how India's IT services firms, especially the major players, became dominant by systematically and continually acquiring the learning, knowledge, and capabilities needed by their foreign clients. The information presented here is based on in-depth personal interviews with over 20 senior and top-level executives of leading IT services firms in India and some of their foreign clients. The list of companies interviewed is included in the methodology section toward the end of the case study.

The Global IT Industry

The research firm, Gartner, classifies the global IT industry into five segments: data center systems, enterprise software, devices, IT services, and communication (telecom) services. Table 9.7 presents Gartner's worldwide IT spending forecasts for 2015–2019 in current U.S. dollars as well as the compounded annual growth rate (CAGR) for 2014–2019. The global IT industry in 2014 was a $3.77 trillion industry, of which the share of enterprise software and IT services was $1.27 trillion. Of all industry segments, software and IT services are expected to grow at the fastest rates during 2014–2019, while the others have nominal or negative growth rates.

The Top 10 IT services firms in 2014, according to Gartner, were IBM, HP, Accenture, Deloitte, Fujitsu, Tata Consultancy Services, Capgemini, PwC, NTT Data, and Oracle. Tata Consultancy Services (TCS) became the first Indian IT services firm to join the ranks of the world's Top 10 IT services firms. The global IT services industry consists of three types of enterprises: product companies, service companies, and business process outsourcing (BPO) companies. However, the boundary between products and services is getting blurred all the time. The top IT product companies, such as Microsoft, typically have net global revenue per employee in the range of $0.5 million to $1.0 million, though there

258

are exceptions such as Apple. There are no major IT product companies head-quartered in India. IT services companies, such as IBM, Accenture, and TCS have much less net global revenue per employee compared to product companies. Product companies also provide services, but typically only to support their own products and customers. Finally, BPO companies that provide services like accounting and call centers have even smaller net revenue per employee. Most IT services companies also offer lower value-added BPO services.

India's IT Services Industry

According to NASSCOM, India's premier IT software and services association, India's IT services industry's (including BPO and engineering and R&D) estimated 2015 revenue was $146 billion. Of this, $98 billion was in exports (i.e., foreign MNEs' offshoring to India) and $48 billion in domestic sales. India's IT services industry[34] grew at 13 percent from 2014 to 2015, compared to a growth rate of −5.5 percent for the global IT industry and −3 percent for the global software and IT services industry. Table 9.8 lists the top 10 IT and BPO services firms in India.

The Evolution of India's IT Services Industry

The IT services industry in India began in the early 1980s, and by the mid-1980s, a few companies such as TCS and Infosys did considerable business

Table 9.7 Worldwide IT Spending and Forecasts for 2013–2019 (Current US$ Billion)

Industry Segment	2013 Spending	2014 Spending	2015 Forecast	2016 Forecast	2017 Forecast	2018 Forecast	2019 Forecast	CAGR 2014–2019
Data Center Systems	164	168	169	172	174	176	177	1.05%
Enterprise Software	297	314	312	332	353	375	400	4.96
Devices	677	694	658	659	665	673	681	−0.38
IT Services	937	955	919	955	996	1,039	1,087	2.62
Communication Services	1,605	1,606	1,495	1,499	1,527	1,551	1,572	−0.43
Overall IT	3,680	3,767	3,555	3,616	3,714	3,815	3,917	0.78
Software & IT Services	1,234	1,269	1,231	1,287	1,349	1,414	1,487	3.22

Source: Gartner, October 2, 2015 Gartner's Definitions of IT Industry Segments: **Data Center Systems**: Servers, external controller-based storage, enterprise network equipment, and enterprise communications applications. **Enterprise Software**: Applications and infrastructure software. **Devices**: PCs, tablets, mobile phones, and printers. **IT Services**: Business IT services and IT product support services. **Communication Services**: Mobile voice and data, and fixed voice and data services for both consumers and enterprises.

Table 9.8 The Top 10 IT and BPM Services Firms in India, 2013–2014

Rank	Top IT Services Firms	Top BPM Services Firms
1	Tata Consultancy Services Ltd.	Genpact Ltd.
2	Infosys Ltd.	Tata Consultancy Services Ltd.
3	Wipro Ltd.	Serco Global Services Ltd.
4	HCL Technologies Ltd.	Wipro BPO
5	Tech Mahindra Ltd.	Infosys BPO
6	L&T Infotech	WNS Global Services (P) Ltd.
7	Syntel Ltd.	Firstsource Solutions Ltd.
8	Mphasis Ltd.	Aegis Ltd.
9	Genpact India Ltd.	Hinduja Global Solutions Ltd.
10	iGate	EXL

Source: NASSCOM, IT-BPM Sector in India: Strategic Review, February 2015.

supplying tech manpower to clients overseas, especially in the U.S., a practice that came to be known as body-shopping (now known by its more respectable term, *staff augmentation*). Indian IT services firms became first movers in the offshore segment of the industry in the 1990s. The dawn of the new millennium was the tipping point for India's IT services industry when literally thousands of companies needed programmers to rid their computers of the Y2K bug. With much of the Y2K manpower supplied by Indian IT services firms and by pure-play *body shops*, the corporate world finally woke up to India's potential in information technology services. The 1990s also saw the birth of the BPO (or business process management, BPM) industry, when many Western firms began to offshore call-center and other back-office work to India. At the same time, many Indian IT services firms started to take up "complete jobs," such as ERP implementation, rather than just supplying manpower to their clients abroad.

By the 2000s, having thus proven themselves, Indian IT services firms were leading in several technology domains and client industry verticals, taking on more and more high value-added work for their foreign clients. Foreign MNEs also began to set up their captive centers (global in-house centers) in India during the 2000s. Foreign companies offshore to India to benefit from labor cost arbitrage and Indian professionals' English language skills, but soon find other reasons to be in India, such as a growing domestic market and a large and high quality pool of multi-skilled engineers with a breadth of knowledge and expertise and the ability to quickly understand clients' IT challenges and help resolve them. They also find that India's major IT services firms have deep knowledge of multiple verticals and technology domains, state-of-the-art processes, project management skills, and highly developed HR practices.

By now, large Indian companies have the scale and the slack resources to be able to ramp up the needed resources for a client quickly and cost effectively. And, with delivery centers and operations in dozens of countries and locations, they are able to service the needs of their clients offshore, onshore, or near-shore as needed by the client. They have the highest industry certifications, such as CMMI Level 5,[35] and have successfully handled some very large projects for their clients. For instance, Mastek, ranked Number 20 among India's top IT services firms, created the IT backbone for one of the largest public health services in the world, the National Health Service of Britain, and helped reduce traffic congestion in London by 20 percent.[36] One of TCS China's key projects is the iCity (intelligent city) project involving a host of cloud-based IT solutions to provide integrated urban management services to promote economic, social, and sustainable growth in China.[37]

The Indian IT services companies have been in business for a long time and by now have the maturity, expertise, client relationships, and scale needed for large and complex projects for their overseas clients. For many of the major players, the core senior management teams have stayed together for five, ten, or more years and have not only acquired deep domain knowledge and knowledge of the verticals they serve, but have also developed and nurtured long-standing relationships with their clients. Their clients, typically chief information officers, tend to be risk-averse and to stick for quite some time with providers with whom they have had good experiences. The IT-BPO industry now contributes almost 10 percent to India's GDP and is the largest private-sector employer in the country.

Challenges Faced by Indian IT Services Companies

Indian IT companies face high employee attrition rates and rising wages and benefits; the annual attrition rate can be as high as 30 or 40 percent. This places a huge burden on employee recruitment, selection, training, placement, and retention. Research by McKinsey & Company refers to this as "the war for talent,"[38] which of course is prevalent in many industries and not just in India.

To deal with high attrition rates and to continue to meet staffing needs due to industry growth, companies typically have aggressive recruitment, selection, and training programs. Other retention approaches include employee stock ownership programs (e.g., Infosys), opportunities to live and work in other countries (e.g., TCS), employee training and development (used by most of the major companies), and the promotion of employees relatively early in their careers. As the market for IT talent continues to heat up in Tier-1 cities such as Bangalore and Hyderabad (and even in some Tier-2 city like Pune and Gurgaon), companies are beginning to move to Tier-2 cities where competition for talent and wages is not so high and the talent supply plentiful.

Given challenges such as these faced by Indian IT services firms, it is a bit of a surprise that they became so successful and dominant in the offshore IT services industry. While there are many possible explanations, one explanation is the efforts made by industry players to develop and continually upgrade their capabilities to be able to serve their global clients. Another is the innovation approaches adopted by them to remain at the forefront of their industry.

Capability Building in the Offshore IT Services Industry in India

According to a survey by the Conference Board, human capital is the second most critical challenge facing CEOs worldwide, and in India (and China) it is the most critical challenge they face.[39] A 2005 report by the McKinsey Global Institute on the demand for talent in services found that of all the engineering graduates coming out of colleges in India, only about 25 percent are suitable for employment by multinational corporations.[40] It is therefore not surprising that many Indian IT services firms have well-developed training and competency development programs for new (as well as continuing) employees.

Capability-Building Approaches

Most of the major and mid-sized IT services firms in India interviewed for this project have good to extensive capability-building programs. Due to space limitations, the discussion below focuses mostly on the human capital angle in capability building at some of the companies interviewed. Competency development at TCS starts with the identification of competency needs at the company and regular surveys of employees' proficiency levels. This leads to recruitment, selection, and training and development plans to have employees with the requisite knowledge and skills. Recruitment and selection include both campus and lateral hiring.

RECRUITMENT AND SELECTION

Since employee attrition is a major concern, companies typically have aggressive recruitment, selection, and training and development programs. Capability building begins with a firm's recruitment and selection policies and practices. Major IT services companies in India have huge recruitment and selection programs. The largest private sector employer in India, TCS, for instance, hired about 70,000 new employees worldwide each year from 2010–2011 to 2012–2013 (Table 9.9). They were hired through both campus and lateral recruitment programs in India and overseas, especially in the United States, Canada, China, Uruguay, and Hungary. In 2012–2013, the company had employees from 118 nationalities spread across almost 60 countries. The attrition rate at TCS was about the lowest in the IT services industry in India, ranging between 11 and 14 percent during these three years. The Infosys Group hired an average of 42,000 new employees each year during the three years, with the attrition rate ranging between 15 and 17 percent annually.

With an employee base and growth like this, it is not hard to visualize the recruitment and selection policies and processes that major IT services companies in India must have to function effectively and remain at the forefront of their industry. During 2012–2013, for instance, TCS visited 371 college campuses in India and made 24,531 job offers to students to join the company after graduation. This is in addition to their regular recruitment program worldwide.

Table 9.9 Number of Employees, New Hires, and Attrition Rate for TCS and Infosys

Year	Tata Consultancy Services			Infosys Group		
	Total No. of Employees*	No. of New Hires	Attrition Rate	Total No. of Employees*	No. of New Hires	Attrition Rate
2012–13	276,196	69,728	10.6%	156,686	37,036	16.3%
2011–12	238,583	70,400	12.2%	149,994	45,605	14.7%
2010–11	198,618	69,685	14.4%	130,820	43,120	17.0%

* As of end of Fiscal Year (March 31).

Source: Company annual reports.

The highly competitive TCS campus recruitment process includes (1) an online aptitude test of quantitative, critical reasoning, analytical reasoning, and reading comprehension skills, and (2) a personal interview with technical and managerial employees. Infosys has a somewhat similar recruitment and selection process, with some of its recruitment tests being tougher than the GMAT and GRE tests. Of almost 3.8 million applications received in 2012–2013, Infosys selected only about one percent of the applicants (37,036) for jobs at the company.

INTERNAL TRAINING AND DEVELOPMENT

Even with such highly selective recruitment and selection processes, major IT services companies put new recruits through intensive classroom and on-the-job training. For instance, at TCS, all campus hires begin their careers with an Initial Learning Program (ILP), a training program designed to provide them with the knowledge and skills necessary to succeed at TCS and in client engagements. Software engineers attend the ILP for six weeks, and all other entry-level associates for one week, receiving additional post-ILP training on the job and at client sites as needed. They have access to numerous web-based training courses in multiple disciplines and can also earn technical and professional certifications while at TCS. Employees are put through job rotation, not just within a function, but also between functions such as delivery and sales. All employees get exposure to different verticals and geographies, especially people identified for middle management positions. Each TCS employee receives at least 14 days of training per year, and there are tailored programs for leadership development. The company spends about 6 percent of its earnings on staff training and development each year. TCS invested 12,789 person years of effort in employee training and development during 2012–2013.[41]

At Infosys, continuous learning opportunities are offered to employees along four dimensions—technology, client business domains, processes, and behavioral skills. The company's four in-house educational institutions and programs are Education & Research (E&R), the Infosys Leadership Institute (ILI), InStep—Infosys Global Internship Program, and Campus Connect. The

E&R group has state-of-the art technology and offers training to about 30,000 new recruits each year, as well as just-in-time courses delivered to employees based on unforeseen client needs and other educational programs via e-learning. Employees have the opportunity to not only improve their competencies but to also obtain recognized certifications to further their careers. The Infosys Leadership Institute (ILI) is an in-house global business school offering leadership and management development programs intended for the top 600 or so employees in the company. Infosys spends about 2 percent of its annual revenues on employee training and competency development, making continuing education available to all employees at all levels. During 2012–2013, Infosys provided employee training to the tune of 1.4 million person days, in addition to the external training and certifications received by employees.[42]

EXTERNAL TRAINING

Since the traditional colleges and universities do not produce enough students to meet the increasing demand for IT professionals, a number of private sector training institutions have been filling the gap in India. The most prominent of these is NIIT (formerly, National Institute of Information Technology), established in 1981. With hundreds of training centers in Asia, Europe, North America, and Oceania, NIIT is one of the top five training companies in the world. In 2004, the company was reorganized into two units: NIIT Limited, the training company, and NIIT Technologies Limited, which offers IT services.

The Government of India has established several Indian Institutes of Information Technology (IIITs) with a view to meeting the demand for IT professionals with the requisite knowledge and skills for the IT industry. Twenty more IIITs are planned to be set up in the country as public-private partnerships, with plans to have an IIIT in each major state.

CORPORATE UNIVERSITIES

Many companies have set up their own "corporate universities" to not only have the workforce they need but to also improve employee retention rates. Zoho Corporation, with operations in United States, India, China, and other countries, has established the Zoho University in Chennai, India, which pays high school graduates in India and the U.S. to learn to code. Over 60,000 high school graduates compete for some 60 places at Zoho University each year—an acceptance rate of 0.1 percent. Graduates of its 18-month program now make up about 15 percent of programmers employed by the company.

The most prominent corporate university in India is the "Infosys University," formally known as the Global Education Center (GEC), in Mysore. Spread across 337 acres with 200 classrooms and 500 instructors, the GEC is the largest corporate education center in the world, with capacity to accommodate up to 5,000 students at a time. The GEC runs the Infosys Foundation Program for fresh engineering graduates as well as programs for other employees. Given its educational, residential, and recreational facilities, *Fortune* magazine has dubbed it as "an odd combination of Disney World, Club Med, and a modern American university." The Infosys corporate university model has been copied by other companies, with training campuses proliferating in India's office parks and electronic cities and not just in the IT industry.[43]

Innovation in the IT Services Industry in India

Digital economy companies survive and grow on innovations and new product introductions. Apple, Microsoft, Adobe Acrobat, and other IT product companies come up with new, upgraded versions of their digital products every few years. Companies selling smart phones, tablets, etc., and try to come up with new, upgraded products every year, if not more often. For IT services companies, however, innovation is almost entirely customer driven. IT services firms engage in innovation to also improve processes and quality, lower costs, and to enter new technology domains and new industry verticals.

Innovation Through Own Efforts

Some of the larger IT services firms in India have a strategic focus on innovation, with activities such as R&D labs, technology innovation centers, centers of excellence, in-house research and education groups, and other formal initiatives to encourage innovation within the company. TCS, for instance, has had a long history of innovation and established its first innovation lab in 1981—the first ever and the largest software R&D center in India. In addition to working on client-specific innovation projects, a key purpose of such initiatives is to create reusable assets based on the company's own IP and to develop IP-based products and business platforms. For example, Infosys has a portfolio of some 20 IP-based products and business platforms, called the Infosys Edge™, which it uses to offer services with an outcome-based pricing model. The research and innovation group at iGate has developed over 300 reusable assets in cloud computing, social analytics, big data, enterprise mobility, and high-performance computing. A summary of some of the innovation and R&D initiatives taken up by IT services firms in India is presented below, much of which pertains to large IT services firms.

INNOVATION LABS

TCS has a network of 19 global Innovation Labs located in India, the U.S., and the U.K. focused on technologies such as Web 2.0 and software engineering and verticals such as insurance and telecom. The Infosys Software Engineering and Technology Labs (SETLabs), established in 2000, are designed to identify technology drivers to help the company stay at the technology frontier. The Labs enable Infosys' 500 researchers to work with standards bodies on future technologies, share best practices, and maintain relationships with academic bodies, industry forums, conferences, and journals. The Technology Innovation Center at NIIT Technologies has a somewhat similar focus and works on both current and future technologies.

RESEARCH AND INNOVATION GROUPS

Many of the major IT services firms in India also have research and innovation groups, often involved in long-term, futuristic projects intended to sustain their competitive advantage. For instance, the Research & Education (R&E) Group at Infosys has dozens of Ph.D. scientists working on "totally futuristic" and long-term projects, and researching ideas "beyond IT" with potentially big impact. The Research and Innovation Group at iGate focuses on delivery innovation, technology incubation, business analysis, and industry thought leadership.

INNOVATION PORTALS

Some companies have established innovation portals within their organizations to help employees exchange ideas among themselves and to encourage grass-roots innovation. For instance, the Value Portal at HCL Technologies is an ideas exchange platform for employees and is the largest company-based ideas platform in the world. As of June 2012, over 10,000 employees had been involved in idea generation, generating some 12,600 ideas, of which 2,242 had been implemented and 629 were under implementation.

Open and Collaborative Innovation

Genpact's *SolutionXchange* is an open-innovation platform in which industry experts help generate solutions to business challenges posted by company employees and clients; significant financial rewards are offered to those submitting the most innovative solutions. Several of the companies interviewed for this project use collaborative innovation approaches whereby a company collaborates with clients and universities to develop technologies and applications. These typically include annual innovation forums held in different parts of the world in collaboration with clients and others (e.g., TCS), innovation workshops held jointly with clients (e.g., TCS's client innovation days and NIIT Technologies' innovation workshops for its largest 8–10 clients once/twice a year), innovation co-creation jointly with clients and partners (e.g., TCS and Infosys), ongoing partnerships with major universities (e.g., TCS and Infosys), and running R&D centers for clients using the offshore development center model.

An example of innovation co-creation is the Infosys Oracle Innovation Center housed in a state-of-the-art facility at Oracle headquarters in Redwood Shores, California, and at Infosys's offshore development center in Shanghai and involved in joint research, joint IP licensing, and joint product development. TCS's

Collaborative Innovation Network (COIN™), anchored at TCS Innovation Labs, connects players in the technology space, both large and small, to source innovations from multiple sources, including academic institutions, start-up companies, venture funds, multi-lateral organizations, and key clients, to develop innovative solutions for clients. Most recently, TCS announced in August 2015 a $35 million gift to the Carnegie Mellon University of the U.S. to fund a new facility, a technology center, student scholarships, and education and cutting-edge research by faculty. This was the largest corporate gift ever received by CMU.

The Future of the Offshore IT Services Industry in India

The global IT services and enterprise software industry, valued at $1.2 trillion in 2015, is estimated to grow at 3.2 percent a year through 2019. From the demand side, this implies potential *new* business worth over $60 billion a year, representing a significant new business opportunity for IT services firms from India (and from other geographies in this space). This is in addition to their existing, long-term business contracts with over $100 billion worth of renewals coming up in the next 2–3 years.[44]

From the supply side, India will more than double the pool of engineers over the next 4 to 5 years, and the advantages of labor cost arbitrage will not disappear any time soon. Dozens of companies, especially companies from India, have built deep expertise in their respective domains, achieving process maturity and scale, and have slack resources as well as long-standing, *sticky* relationships with customers. The immediate future for IT services companies from India, therefore, looks promising, though they are not likely to be growing at 10 to 15 percent a year for much longer.

Not every company will benefit from the projected market growth, however. Only companies that continually upgrade their capabilities in line with emerging technologies and market imperatives, build deep domain expertise, extend the scope of the verticals they serve, nurture client relationships, are innovative, and use the right business models can hope to survive and even prosper in this hypercompetitive business environment.

Companies looking for competitive advantages other than cost must look at their approaches for capability building and innovation as well as the quality of their client relationships. For capability building, they should explore avenues other than just training and development, such as overseas joint ventures, M&As, and licensing and technology collaborations. Innovation today is the lifeblood of industry and commerce and is not (nor should be) restricted to only the larger players or to structured innovation within the company. Open and collaborative innovation has opened up numerous avenues for companies to source ideas and innovations from outside the company, often with great results and significant cost effectiveness. And, as they continue to move up the value chain, offering end-to-end business solutions, they also will need to develop deep relationships inside the C-suite, not just with the CIOs.

Research Methodology

Findings in this study are based on in-depth, personal interviews with about 20 senior and top-level executives of 15 leading Indian IT services firms and their foreign clients, conducted mostly in spring 2013. (The study was funded by Ernst & Young through the Institute for Emerging Market Studies.) Interviewees were asked questions related to their business models, core strengths and weaknesses, and specific approaches used for developing and upgrading knowledge, skills, and capabilities, as well as their views on the IT services industry in India. Each of the interviews lasted one-and-a-half to two hours or more and was conducted onsite at the companies' premises in India, China, and the United States. Some of the interviews were followed up with phone calls to get more information from the companies. This information was supplemented with information obtained from secondary sources such as company websites, industry publications, and published research reports. After the analysis of the interview data, the findings were presented back to some of the research participants for discussion and validation.

List of Companies Interviewed

IT Industry Association (India)
NASSCOM
Indian IT Services Companies
Genpact, Gurgaon
HCL Technologies, Noida
iGate, Mumbai and Bangalore
iknowvate Technologies, Mumbai
Infosys Limited, Bangalore
Mastek, Mumbai
MindTree, Bangalore
NIIT Technologies, Noida and Bangalore
Quatrro Global Services, Gurgaon
Tata Consultancy Services, Beijing
American IT Companies
Cisco (India)
Computer Sciences Corporation (U.S.A. and India)
Google India, Bangalore*
IBM, Bangalore*
indicates interview in December 2010

Notes

1 Cisco's New Innovation Engine accessed from http://newsroom.cisco.com/feature-content?articleId=1720841.
2 Michael E. Porter, *Clusters of Innovation Initiative: Regional Foundations of U.S. Competitiveness* (Boston, MA: Monitor Group and Council on Competitiveness, 2001).

268

3 National Academies, *Rising above the Gathering Storm: Energizing and Employing America for a Better Economic Future* (Washington DC: The National Academies Press, 2005), p. 4.

4 National Academies, *Rising above the Gathering Storm, Revisited: Rapidly Approaching Category 5* (Washington, DC: The National Academies Press, 2010), pp. 4–5.

5 BBC News, "Asia 'may sideline UK scientists,'" January 17, 2007. Accessed from http://news.bbc.co.uk/2/hi/science/nature/6267285.stm.

6 Marla M. Capozzi, Brian Gregg, and Amy Howe, "McKinsey Global Survey Results: Innovation and Commercialization 2010," McKinsey & Company, 2010.

7 Barry Jaruzelski, Kevin Schwartz, and Volker Staack, "The 2015 Global Innovation 1000: Innovation's New World Order," *Strategy+Business*, Winter 2015.

8 Jaruzelski et al., 2015, p. 2.

9 Vinod K. Jain and S. Raghunath, "Strengthening America's International Competitiveness through Innovation and Global Value Chains." In *Restoring America's Global Competitiveness through Innovation*, edited by Ben L. Kedia and Subhash C. Jain (Cheltenham, U.K.: Edward Elgar, 2013).

10 Marla M. Capozzi, Ari Kellen, and Rebecca Somers, "Making Innovation Structures Work: McKinsey Global Survey Results," McKinsey & Company, September 2012.

11 Marielle Segarra, "Innovation: A Make-or-Buy Decision," CFO, September 18, 2013. Accessed from http://ww2.cfo.com/innovation/2013/09/innovation-a-make-or-buy-decision/.

12 The Yard Blog, "Axalta Coating Systems Will Locate New Global Innovation Center at The Navy Yard in Philadelphia," September 9, 2015. Accessed from http://www.navyyard.org/theyardblog/2015/09/09/axalta-coating-systems-will-locate-new-global-innovation-center-at-the-navy-yard-in-philadelphia/.

13 Company Press Release, "Mars Petcare Opens First Innovation Center In the United States," October 1, 2014. Accessed from http://www.mars.com/global/press-center/press-list/news-releases.aspx?SiteId=94&Id=6145.

14 Source: www.samsungaccelerator.com.

15 IBM's Press Release, "IBM to Acquire Cognos to Accelerate Information on Demand Initiative," November 12, 2007. Accessed from http://www-03.ibm.com/press/us/en/pressrelease/22572.wss.

16 Jason Douglas, "Big Pharma Won't Wait in Rush for Biotech Drugs," *The Wall Street Journal*, August 4, 2010.

17 Reid Hoffman, "Acquiring Proven Entrepreneurs Is a Smart Way to Innovate," *Financial Times*, May 26, 2015.

18 Bala Iyer and Thomas H. Davenport, "Reverse Engineering Google's Innovation Machine," *Harvard Business Review*, April 2008.

19 Ryan Caldbeck, "The Rise of Corporate Venture Capital: As It Booms in Tech, Consumer Giants Should Follow," *Forbes*, September 11, 2015.

20 Marc de Jong, Nathan Marston, Erik Roth, and Peet van Bijon, "The Eight Essentials of Innovation Performance," McKinsey & Company, December 2013.

21 Jain and Raghunath, 2013.

22 Water Alliance, The Netherlands, "Crossover: Innovation through Collaboration." Accessed from http://wateralliance.nl/en/.

23 Oliver Alexy and Markus Reitzig, "Managing the Business Risks of Open Innovation," *McKinsey Quarterly*, January 2012.

24 Ashley Halsey III, "$40 Million Prize to City with Best Smart Plan," *The Washington Post*, December 9, 2015.

25 Marc de Jong et al., 2013.

26 Michael Chui, "How Big Companies Can Innovate," McKinsey & Company Insights, February 2015. http://www.mckinsey.com/insights/innovation/how_big_companies_can_innovate.

27 Capozzi et al., 2012.

28 Vanessa Chan, Chris Musso, and Venkatesh Shanker, "McKinsey Global Survey Results: Assessing Innovation Metrics," McKinsey & Company, 2008.

29 Joseph A. Schumpeter, *The Theory of Economic Development* (Cambridge, MA: Harvard University Press, 1934).

30 Sean Silverthorne's interview of Thomas K. McCaw, "Rediscovering Schumpeter: The Power of Capitalism," Harvard Business School Working Knowledge, May 7, 2007.

31 The case study is based on information taken from the company website and published sources, including Patrick Moorhead, "Demystifying Cisco's Five Pillar Innovation Strategy," *Forbes*, December 18, 2015, and Jawahar Sivasankaran, "Transforming Innovation and New Business Models," Cisco IT Article, July 2012.

32 Stephanie Chan, "And the Innovation Grand Challenge Winner Is...," The Network, Cisco's Technology News Site, December 8, 2015. Accessed from http://newsroom.cisco.com/feature-content?type=webcontent&articleId=1732501.

33 The source for all data related to India is India's premier IT services association, NASSCOM (www.nasscom.in). Information about specific companies is based mostly on personal interviews and company websites.

34 For the rest of the chapter, the term "IT services" is used to represent IT services, BPM services, and engineering and R&D services.

35 Carnegie Mellon University's Capability Maturity Model Integration (CMMI) is a process improvement appraisal system, especially for software development, with CMMI Level 5 being the highest certification level a company can achieve.

36 Source: www.mastek.com.

37 Source: http://www.tata.com/article/inside/bc4sLh1NIyI=/TLYVr3YPkMU=

38 Steven Hankin of McKinsey & Co. coined the term, "the war for talent" in 1997, later popularized by the 2001 Harvard Business School Press book with the same title and authored by Ed Michaels, Helen Handfield-Jones, and Beth Axelrod. The "war" continues to this day, according to research by McKinsey Global Institute's Richard Dobbs, Susan Lund, and Anu Madgavkar. In a CEO briefing in November 2012, "Talent Tensions Ahead," they concluded that there could be a shortage of 18 million workers in the high-skill, college-educated category in advanced economies by 2020. With China included, the shortage could exceed 35 million high-skill workers by 2020.

39 Charles Mitchell, Rebecca L. Ray, and Bart van Ark, *The Conference Board CEO Challenge 2012: Risky Business–Focusing on Innovation and Talent in a Volatile World.* The Conference Board Research Report 1491, March 2012.

40 Diana Farrell, Martha Laboissiére, Robert Pascal, Jaeson Rosenfeld, Charles de Segundo, and Sascha Stürze, "The Emerging Global Labor Market: The Demand for Offshore Talent in Services," McKinsey Global Institute, June 2005.

41 Tata Consultancy Services Limited Annual Report, 2012–2013.

42 Infosys Annual Report, 2012–2013.

43 The Economist, "A Special Report on Innovation in Emerging Markets," *The Economist*, April 17, 2010.

44 Interview with Mr. Ashank Desai, Founder, Mastek Limited.

10

LEVERAGING OPPORTUNITIES IN THE CONNECTED ECONOMY

The diffusion of power among countries will have a dramatic impact by 2030. Asia will have surpassed North America and Europe combined in terms of global power, based upon GDP, population size, military spending, and technological investment.... The shift in national power may be overshadowed by an even more fundamental shift in the nature of power. Enabled by communications technologies, power will shift toward multifaceted and amorphous networks that will form to influence state and global actions.
—*Global Trends 2030: Alternative Worlds*, National Intelligence Council, 2012

In this final chapter, we return to some of the evolving trends in the connected economy from the first chapter, and how firms could leverage them to their benefit. The connected economy of the 2010s comprises the old economy, the digital economy, and the age of the smart machines. It consists of markets, firms, consumers, governments, and other actors that are more connected to each other than at any time in the past. And, with new players emerging on the global scene, with new playing fields, and with new rules of the game, competition is an entirely new ball game now. However, this is nothing compared to what MNEs might face in the coming one/two decades (see the quote above).

The key features of the connected economy, as presented in Chapter 1, are:

- Global—encompassing both developed and developing nations.
- Goods—range from physical goods, digital goods, and smart machines, i.e., goods with digital characteristics (hardware, software, and sensors) embedded into them and connected to the Internet.
- Services—range from simple location-bound services to services that can be performed anywhere and everywhere, not necessarily close to the customer.
- Connectivity—provided by multilateral institutions, governments, multinational corporations, competition, and digital technologies and networks.
- Speed—business and economic phenomena operate in real time, 24/7, and at increasing speeds.

This chapter explores how to leverage opportunities in the connected economy for both developed-economy firms and emerging-economy firms. While a great deal of business takes place within the developed world, our focus here is developed-economy firms doing business in emerging economies and emerging-economy firms doing business in developed economies.

The World in 2016 and Beyond

Since the end of the recession of 2008–2010, emerging economies have provided a large component of the global growth, and the trends until recently looked quite favorable for the developing and emerging world. However, for now (late 2015 and early 2016), there is reason to be less sanguine about emerging economies. Given their current and recent performance, the *Economist* even referred to them as "submerging" economies. The BRICs have not been doing well lately. The Brazilian and Russian economies both plunged in 2015 and are not likely to do very much better in 2016. China, facing very high debt, high loan-default rates, and other challenges, twice shut down trading on the Shanghai Stock Exchange as it plunged by seven percent on Monday (January 4) and again on Thursday (January 7) during the early days of 2016. Of the four BRIC nations, India's outlook seems the most promising with 2016 GDP growth expected to be about 7 percent, though still less than what India achieved during 2005 to 2010. It is the developed economies that have been contributing the most to global growth since 2014 and are likely to continue doing so in the near future.[1]

These are, however, short-term difficulties being faced by emerging economies. In the medium to long term, their prospects look quite bright, and, not just India, China, and Brazil. Countries such as Colombia, Indonesia, Nigeria, South Africa, Turkey, and many other emerging economies are becoming important sources of global growth. A competing scenario for the global economy for the medium term depends on China and its ability to weather its current and recent crises. If not, the world will be in the throes of another recession, this time "made in China."[2]

The Four Game Changers

The current emerging-economy difficulties notwithstanding, this book has highlighted some game-changing opportunities and challenges facing the MNE, mostly developments of the last two to three decades.

Game Changer 1: Billions of Consumers

The fall of the Berlin Wall in 1989 opened up new markets—markets that had been behind the Iron Curtain for over 50 years. The arrival of the emerging and developing economies on the global arena, especially since the

2000s, has created a much larger market for companies from everywhere. This newly opened market comprises some four billion consumers, people at all socio-economic levels but especially those at the bottom-of-the-pyramid—micro-consumers who collectively represent a huge buying power.[3] As a result, more and more global issues are now being discussed by the leaders of the G20 nations, a group of 19 nations and the European Union, rather than by the leaders of the erstwhile G7 nations that had become increasingly unrepresentative of the rich and growing world economy.[4] The G20 is now the global forum for discussing global economic, social, environmental, and other major issues, legitimized by former U.S. President George W. Bush when he invited the G20 leaders to a summit in Washington D.C. in 2008. The G20 represents two-thirds of the world's population, 80 percent of world trade, and 90 percent of the global economy.

Game Changer 2: Billions of Entrepreneurs

Along with billions of consumers, the world now also has billions of entrepreneurs—not in the narrow sense of people starting and running businesses, but people doing things in new and innovative ways to change their lives. The theme for this game changer derives from Harvard Business School professor Tarun Khanna's immensely readable book comparing China and India, *Billions of Entrepreneurs: How China and India Are Reshaping Their Futures and Yours* (Harvard Business School Press, 2007), though our focus extends to a much larger world—to both developed and emerging economies. The G20 is a good proxy for the focus of this book. New entrepreneurs and newly established companies from emerging markets are giving incumbents in most nations a run for their money. Speaking of emerging markets at the height of their power in 2010, the *Economist* said, "… many of the developing world's champions have risen from zero to hero in just a couple of decades. In 1990 Mittal was an unknown producer making steel in Indonesia. Today, as ArcelorMittal, it is the world's largest steel company, bigger than the next three combined… There is a buccaneering spirit abroad that is rare in the West, born from a mixture of optimism and arrogance."[5]

Game Changer 3: Technology on Steroids

Over the last two decades or so, technology has advanced at an increasing rate of change in multiple fields—information technology, manufacturing and automation, life sciences, genetic engineering, renewable energy, materials, automotive, services, processes, and more. Computers and IT, in particular, which form the backbone of an increasing number of new products and services that simply did not exist 5 to 10 years ago, have grown the fastest. Digital technologies are behind most of the innovations we see today in practically all fields of human endeavor, and their progress has been *exponential* due especially to network effects. Innovations from multiple sources get connected and enhanced through networks and open innovation to create entirely new products and services. Even within the IT domain, the fastest growth is being experienced by smart machines or products with embedded software and sensors that are connected to the Internet.

Game Changer 4: A Changed Competition Paradigm

As competition becomes incessantly more global, incorporating new players, new playing fields, and new rules of the game, it is already an entirely new ballgame—not just competition for markets, but also competition for talent and resources and capabilities. The *new players* joining the global arena are the Fortune Global 500 or the Forbes Global 2000 companies from emerging economies as well as tens of thousands of small and medium-sized enterprises new to international competition from both developed and emerging economies. They all want a share of the global pie. The *new playing fields* are truly global, not just the 200 countries that companies like Netflix want to be in, but also the online marketplaces populated by the Amazons and the Alibabas of the world. And, the *new rules of the game* in the connected economy include the enduring "scale and scope" *law* of the old economy[6] as well as the "information rules" of the information age and Metcalfe's Law of network externalities in the digital economy. (See Chapter 1 for more details.)

Opportunities in the Connected Economy

Some of the opportunities in the connected economy were highlighted in the discussion of the four Game Changers above, such as the emergence of huge mega markets and the opportunity to leverage technology to reach those markets. The connected economy also offers MNEs and aspiring firms the opportunity to significantly cut costs, leverage their core competencies in foreign markets, and learn from multiple geographies, multiple industries, and multiple players.

Challenges in the Connected Economy

Opportunities always come with challenges and risks. Two of the challenges were included among the four Game Changers, namely, the emergence of new competitors ("billions of entrepreneurs") and the changed paradigm of global competition. During the 1970s and 1980s, new global competitors came from Japan, during the 1990s and 2000s from the newly industrialized countries (NICs) such as South Korea, and, now in the 2000s and 2010s, they are coming from emerging markets like China, India, and Brazil. While the Japanese competitors grew mostly organically, the Korean competitors grew both organically and through M&A; the new global competitors from China and India seem to be in a great hurry to make their mark and have grown largely through M&A.

Chinese global players, which include a large number of state-owned enterprises (SOEs), have benefited greatly from the support of their government in their internationalization journey. For instance, of the 98 Fortune Global 500 (FG500) companies in China in 2015, 76 were SOEs. Firms competing globally face intense competition from incumbents, other MNEs, SOEs, the "new players" (e.g., FG500 from emerging markets), and from "billions of entrepreneurs."

Firms doing business abroad face "liability of foreignness," especially if they go to countries that are very different from their own—economically, socially, culturally, and politically. Liability of foreignness implies that foreign firms in a market face certain disadvantages relative to domestic firms there, which imposes additional costs on them. Firms from both developed and emerging economies face liability of foreignness to a lesser or a greater extent depending on their familiarity with and experience in the foreign market of interest.

Challenges Faced by Developed-Country Firms in Developing Countries

Some of the more common challenges faced by developed-country firms in developing countries include entrenched competition, a lack of understanding of business practices and government regulations, a lack of cross-cultural understanding and sensitivity, inadequate infrastructure and under-developed institutions (institutional voids), under-developed distribution channels, economic and political instability, the difficulty of building relationships (e.g., *guanxi* in China), and diversity of markets, especially in large countries. See also the mini case study on the challenges faced by American companies in China (Chapter 3).

As an example of the diversity of markets, P&G sells its laundry detergent powder Tide in India in almost a dozen different packages and fragrances to meet the needs of different market segments—ranging from a 20 gm single-use sachet priced at about three cents (U.S.) to a 1-kilogram package of Tide Plus Jasmine and Rose priced at about $1.50. P&G's flagship brand Ariel comes in even more varieties and is priced much higher than Tide. Ariel powder 1-kilogram package costs about $3, Ariel Matic powder 1-kilogram package about $4, and Ariel liquid laundry detergent 1.2-liter package about $20 (or about $16 per kilogram). Figures 10.1 to 10.4 represent market diversity in China, where a particular warehouse store sells hair care products aimed at four different market segments—Super Premium, Premium, Middle Tier, and Welfare Recommendation.[7] These examples go to show that, in large countries like India and China, there is a good deal of diversity based on factors like per capita income and socio-economic status. Other factors impacting diversity in such markets are language, culture, and religion and politics (in India).

Challenges Faced by Developing-Country Firms in Developed Countries

Some of the challenges discussed above, such as entrenched competition, a lack of understanding of business practices and government regulations, and a lack

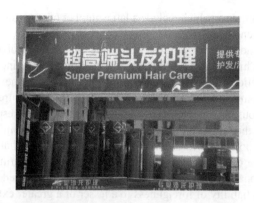

Figure 10.1 Super Premium Hair Care Products
Source: A warehouse store in Ningbo, China.

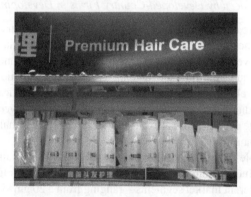

Figure 10.2 Premium Hair Care Products
Source: A warehouse store in Ningbo, China.

Figure 10.3 Medium-priced Hair Care Products
Source: A warehouse store in Ningbo, China.

Figure 10.4 Lowest-priced Hair Care Products
Source: A warehouse store in Ningbo, China.

of cross-cultural understanding and sensitivity are also likely to be faced by developing-country firms doing business in developed-country markets. The additional challenges they may face include the difficulty of accessing distribution channels, the lack of brand image and reputation, a lack of the needed resources such as capital and technology, and high cost of operating in a developed country.

Leveraging Opportunities in the Connected Economy

With an understanding of the Game Changers and the opportunities and challenges faced by firms doing business abroad, we can now offer some suggestions on how to leverage opportunities in the connected economy. The frameworks and strategies presented previously for entering, competing in, and growing in foreign markets (Chapters 4–6) and for designing organizational architecture to compete internationally (Chapter 7) do not need repeating.

Some basic premises to bear in mind as you go exploring the world: (a) Markets, irrespective of size, are never homogeneous; even a poor country has super rich people, and a rich country has very poor people; so a consistent strategy for an entire market rarely works. (b) Take every opportunity to learn; achieving success in foreign markets is a race to learn; there's no shame in copying others' good ideas (so long as it is legal!) (c) Success in any nation comes from leveraging the comparative advantages of the nation along with your own competitive advantages.

Have at Least a Medium-Term Plan and a Business Model for the Market You Are Entering

Success in foreign markets takes longer than doing business at home. Have at least a medium-term strategy for the foreign market(s) of interest, and be patient. Decide if it is going to be a toehold entry as you test the waters in a new market

277

or a foothold entry with a longer-term commitment of resources for the market. A toehold entry allows the firm to learn about a new foreign market, without opening itself up to significant risks, and can also set the stage for it to increase its commitment to the market in the future. However, a foothold entry is typically reserved for major companies with the resources and capabilities (e.g., managerial and capital and a global mindset) to invest in new foreign markets. As noted in Chapter 4, DuPont of the U.S. announced in the early 1990s that it would be making investments worth a billion dollars in Spain over the next 10 years. This was a long-term commitment on DuPont's part into a country that had joined the European Union (then called the European Economic Community) just five years earlier and was still a lower-cost country compared to most other EU member states at the time. The investment in Spain opened up the EU market for DuPont.

Regarding your business model for foreign markets, don't be bogged down by the local-global dilemma. Companies with a localization strategy can indeed derive economies of scale and scope in large host markets. Groupe Danone of France customizes most of its food products to suit the tastes, habits, and nutritional needs of consumers in most of its foreign markets. However, given the large size of the U.S. market, it is able to derive economies of scale and scope even though it sells six varieties of its probiotic yogurt product Activia there. And companies with a global strategy can benefit from customizing some of their products in large markets. For example, most fast food companies adapt their menus to the needs of customers in large markets like India and Japan. Ikea, the quintessential global firm selling Scandinavian furniture and furnishings worldwide, customizes its marketing mix for the U.S. market.

Overcome Liability of Foreignness

As indicated earlier, liability of foreignness imposes additional costs for MNEs in host markets compared to their domestic counterparts. Some suggestions for overcoming the liability of foreignness are given below.

The real estate industry has the cliché, location, location, location. A similar cliché can be helpful for MNEs in foreign markets, localization, localization, localization. The more localized a foreign MNE is in a market, the less its exposure to liability of foreignness. This does not mean that it has to follow a complete localization (multidomestic) strategy for the market. It can adopt practices such as hiring local staff and executives; utilizing local supply chains; involvement in local civic activities; joining a local chamber of commerce, a bilateral chamber of commerce, a local trade association; supporting local causes; and giving greater autonomy to foreign subsidiaries. The author once worked for the Indian subsidiary of a British machine tool company that held an annual "eye camp" where hundreds of people with eye problems received treatment, even cataract removal, each year.

Be a partner in the progress of the host nation.[8] Positioning the MNE as a partner in the progress of the host market can be very helpful in signaling to the market your good intentions. This is how India-based NIIT Limited positioned itself in China. Established in 1981, the company has grown to be amongst world's leading talent development companies offering learning solutions for individuals, enterprises, and institutions across 40 countries. NIIT began its globalization journey in 1996 with an education center in Hong Kong and then entered mainland China in 1998. From the very beginning, it endeavored to embed the NIIT curriculum and training methodologies into China's higher education institutions. As of November 2013, NIIT China had 4,000 employees, of which only 42 were from India. They are in 66 cities, offering IT courses through 129 universities and colleges. Being an early mover into IT training and education in China gave the company a head start and the opportunity to build its brand and gain "the mindshare of the student community, the Chinese IT industry, and [most importantly] the government," according to Prakash Menon, President of NIIT China, who has lived in China since 1997. China is a difficult market for many foreign companies, even more so in the mid-1990s when NIIT entered the country. What helped NIIT was that it positioned the company as a partner in developing China's IT manpower, thus gaining the support and respect of the IT industry and the government.[9]

Benefit From What the Host Market Has To Offer

Most countries offer incentives to foreign companies to attract FDI into the country. In the U.S., for instance, incentives are typically offered by state and local jurisdictions, and, depending on the investment involved, can be worth millions of dollars to the foreign enterprise. For companies from Sub-Saharan Africa (SSA) specially, the United States offers the most liberal access to its market available to any country with which it does not have a free trade agreement. These benefits are offered to 34 SSA countries under the African Growth and Opportunity Act (AGOA) passed by the U.S. Congress in 2000, which has since been renewed to 2025. AGOA benefits for SSA countries range from credit and technical assistance to duty-free imports for specific products. For instance, SSA countries with per capita GNP under $1,500 in 1998 can export to the U.S. duty-free/quota-free apparel made there from fabric originating anywhere in the world.

Another good example is the Japan External Trade Organization (JETRO) which was established in 1958 to promote Japanese exports. However, JETRO's focus in the 21st century shifted to promoting FDI into Japan and helping small to medium-sized Japanese firms maximize their export potential. JETRO currently has a network of 121 offices, located in more than 55 countries worldwide, that offer complimentary services such as comprehensive business support, market intelligence, regulation and legal policy updates, and business seminars to firms interested in doing business in Japan. For instance, JETRO's six offices in the U.S. offer complimentary information and support to American businesses seeking to successfully enter and expand into the Japanese market. What is less well known is that even exporters to Japan can seek assistance from JETRO to further their business interests.[10]

Countries often have special economic zones, foreign trade zones, and industry clusters that can be utilized by foreign companies to their advantage. General Motors, for instance, set up its auto assembly plant in the Katowice Special Economic Zone, Poland, during the 1990s (Chapter 6, Box 6.3). Suzlon Energy of India established its international sales and marketing subsidiary in the wind-energy industry cluster in Aarhus, Denmark, where it could easily access industry-specific talent, technology, and value-chain partners (Chapter 8).

Another often overlooked resource is made up of the major universities in host markets. Many have incubators that can be utilized by foreign startups and other companies as a means of entering the market at low cost and low risk. For instance, the University of Maryland International Incubator in College Park, MD, offers foreign companies the opportunity to not only have physical space in the incubator, but also an array of services, including access to the university's faculty, students, and research facilities; hands-on mentoring and training; and networking opportunities with potential partners and investors.

An association with a university can provide many other advantages, as well such as access to professors and researchers, their research output, student assistants, and the opportunity to work with professors on joint projects. In July 2011, Canon U.S. Life Sciences, Inc. (the R&D subsidiary of Canon U.S.A., Inc.) entered into a new research collaboration with the University of Maryland to develop a highly automated system to provide the rapid diagnosis of infectious diseases. According to Takayoshi Hanagata, president, Canon U.S. Life Sciences, Inc., "The combination of Canon U.S. Life Sciences core technologies and the University's leading-edge research capabilities, will allow us to create new diagnostic applications designed to offer enhanced flexibility as well as reduced costs and biomedical waste."[11] Canon U.S. Life Sciences had previously graduated from the University of Maryland Incubator, where it had resided for several years.

Samsung of Korea has established a Digital Health Innovation Lab jointly with the University of California, San Francisco, to validate their new digital health sensor technologies and algorithms.

Learn From Emerging Markets

Doing business in foreign markets is a race to learn. MNEs can learn a great deal from emerging markets, such as frugal innovation, innovative marketing approaches, and the ability to serve the bottom-of-pyramid consumers, among other skills.

Frugal innovation is an approach to innovate and design products and services using minimal (financial, material, institutional) resources and at the lowest possible cost. The frugal-innovation approach was born in India, which has a huge population but suffers from shortages of all kinds. Individuals and companies improvise, using ingenuity and whatever resources they can find, to do what needs to be done. Necessity is truly the mother of invention. Big multinationals, like GE and Siemens, have also caught the frugal-innovation bug and are using the approach to develop products and services for emerging markets, which they sometimes sell in developed markets as well (known as reverse innovation). One well-known example of frugal innovation is the heart surgeries performed by Dr. Devi Shetty in Bangalore, each costing about $2,000 to $5,000, compared to heart surgeries performed in the U.S. that cost 10 to 20 times as much. Despite performing 60 free surgeries a week for poor patients, his hospital has a higher profit margin than the average U.S. hospital. Frugal innovation is based on *jugaad*, a Hindi term meaning creative improvisation to develop workable solutions with limited resources. Other examples include a battery-operated, ultra-low-cost refrigerator and a flour mill powered by a scooter to deal with the power shortages that are endemic throughout India.

Many emerging-market firms are succeeding in foreign markets with creative marketing approaches. Mahindra & Mahindra of India sells small, less than 100-HP tractors in the U.S. and other countries. In the U.S. it targets hobby farmers and landscaping companies in just two Southern states and has been quite successful in taking market share from long-established incumbents such as John Deere. Wipro Technologies, also of India, which has a minuscule marketing budget compared to, say, IBM, targets CEOs of Fortune 1000 companies at lounges at the Narita, Kennedy, and Heathrow airports.

Learn From Developed-Country Markets

Just like developed-country MNEs can learn from emerging markets, MNEs from emerging markets can learn from developed markets. In Chapter 8, we discussed cases of companies like Hyundai Motor Company and Suzlon Energy that learned systematically from the best companies in their industry through licensing, joint ventures, and M&A. Emerging-market companies starting on their internationalization journey can learn a great deal from their counterparts and institutions in advanced countries, things such as business and management practices, brand building, dealing with media, accessing capital, and much else.

Deal With and Leverage Institutional Voids in Emerging Markets

Emerging markets often face institutional voids, such as inadequate legal protections, under-developed capital markets, lack of intermediaries such as certification agencies, and so on (Chapter 4). An advantage that emerging-market firms have over firms from developed countries that do not typically have to contend with such issues at home is that they have learned to deal with institutional voids. For example, Studio Moderna developed its own call centers in the 1990s, when such intermediaries were not yet available in the newly independent Central and Eastern Europe region (Chapter 5). Institutional voids can be a source of advantage for both domestic and foreign companies if they have or can develop local knowledge and capabilities to substitute for the missing institutions. For instance, if a market lacks a certain intermediary, an entrepreneur could create value by creating an intermediary to fill the gap. Obtaining such knowledge and capabilities can help the MNE in not only the country where it obtained the knowledge and capabilities but in other emerging markets as well.[12]

Be a Good Corporate Citizen

Much has been written about corporate citizenship and what it means to be a good corporate citizen. Suffice to say that a business must be socially responsible and meet its legal, economic, and ethical responsibilities toward not just its shareholders, but toward its broader group of stakeholders. Businesses should aim to create higher standards of living and better quality of life in the communities where they operate.[13] Companies strive to achieve such objectives through initiatives such as corporate governance and corporate social responsibility and increasingly through corporate philanthropy. For obvious reasons, giving back to the society is especially important for firms operating in foreign countries, developing or developed.

As discussed earlier, DuPont of the U.S. made a commitment to invest a billion dollars in Spain starting in the 1990s. Its first investment was in Asturias, Northern Spain. The investment reinvigorated a formerly declining region through employment creation, tax revenues, and even environmental sustainability. For instance, the company was responsible for planting some 160,000 trees and shrubs to restore the region's original habitat. During the mid-1990s, DuPont made record profits after several years of declining, and the company's stock price surged from a low of $15 in 1990 to a high of almost $50 by 1996. According to the company website, much of the success was attributable to DuPont's community relations efforts in Spain and other host markets.[14]

Corporate philanthropy is based on the idea that successful businesses must recognize their *noblesse oblige* to give back to the societies that made them successful. *Noblesse oblige*, a French phrase, implies that people of noble (high) birth have the responsibility to act with generosity toward those less privileged. Corporate philanthropy can take many forms, including cash contributions, grants, salary-sacrifice programs, and donations of products and services to the local communities.

MNEs can also benefit by funding research institutes, endowed chairs, and student scholarships at universities in the countries where they operate. For instance, the Tata Consultancy Services (TCS) of India gave a $35 million gift to the Carnegie Mellon University of the U.S. to fund a new facility, a technology center, student scholarships, and education and cutting-edge research by faculty. There are hundreds of other examples of corporate gifts to universities by MNEs based in the U.S. and abroad.

Notes

1 Leo Abruzzese, "Submerging World," *The World in 2016* (annual feature), *The Economist*, 2015.
2 Ruchir Sharma, "A Global Recession May Be Brewing in China," *The Wall Street Journal*, August 15, 2015.
3 C.K. Prahalad, *The Fortune at the Bottom-of-the-Pyramid: Eradicating Poverty Through Profits* (Philadelphia: Wharton School Publishing, 2006).
4 The G20 nations are Argentina, Australia, Brazil, Canada, the People's Republic of China, France, Germany, India, Indonesia, Italy, Japan, Mexico, Republic of Korea, Russia, Saudi Arabia, South Africa, Turkey, United Kingdom, the United States of America, and the European Union.
5 The Economist, "What Makes Emerging-market Companies Run," *The Economist*, April 15, 2010.
6 Alfred D. Chandler, Jr., *Scale and Scope: The Dynamics of Industrial Capitalism* (Cambridge, MA: Belknap Press, 1994).
7 The photographs were taken by the author in Ningbo, China, in spring 2013.
8 Tarun Khanna and Krishna G. Palepu, *Winning in Emerging Markets: A Road Map for Strategy and Execution* (Cambridge, MA: Harvard Business School Press, 2010).
9 Based on the author's in-person, on-site interview with Mr. Praksah Menon, President, NIIT China on November 23, 2013.
10 The author utilized JETRO office facilities and services in Yokohama during a two-week business visit to Japan in 2001 on behalf of the Toledo Area International Trade Association which he headed at the time.
11 News Release, "Canon U.S. Life Sciences and the University of Maryland Launch New Collaboration," A. James Clark School of Engineering, University of Maryland, July 19, 2011. Accessed from http://bioe.umd.edu/news/news_story.php?id=5876.
12 See also Khanna and Palepu, 2010, Chapters 2–3.
13 Adapted from Investopedia.
14 See also Chapter 4.

INDEX

285